Sabine Nunius

Coping with Difference

D1703338

Acknowledgements

I would like to thank my supervisor Prof. Dr. Doris Feldmann and all of my colleagues at the University of Erlangen-Nürnberg who offered comments and pieces of advice during the writing process of my dissertation. Special thanks are due to my co-supervisor Prof. Dr. Ria Blaicher, who sacrificed hours of her own spare time when accepting my thesis after her retirement from official university life. Moreover, I am grateful for her constant encouragement and support in times of doubts and difficulties.

In view of their almost superhuman patience, their invariable support, as well as their unshakable belief in my work, I would like to dedicate this study to my mother and personal reader Birgit and to my father Werner.

Erlanger Studien zur Anglistik und Amerikanistik

herausgegeben von

Rudolf Freiburg und Heike Paul

Band 11

LIT

Sabine Nunius

Coping with Difference

New Approaches in the
Contemporary British Novel
(2000 – 2006)

LIT

Dissertation an der Friedrich-Alexander-Universität Erlangen-Nürnberg
2009 (D29)
(Tag der mündlichen Prüfung: 27. 05. 2009)

Umschlagbild: Werner Kropf

Gedruckt auf alterungsbeständigem Werkdruckpapier entsprechend
ANSI Z3948   DIN ISO 9706

Bibliographic information published by the Deutsche Nationalbibliothek
The Deutsche Nationalbibliothek lists this publication in the Deutsche
Nationalbibliografie; detailed bibliographic data are available in the Internet at
http://dnb.d-nb.de.

ISBN 978-3-643-10159-4
Zugl.: Erlangen-Nürnberg, Univ., Diss., 2009

A catalogue record for this book is available from the British Library

©LIT VERLAG Dr. W. Hopf Berlin 2009
Fresnostr. 2   D-48159 Münster
Tel. +49 (0) 2 51-620 32 22   Fax +49 (0) 2 51-922 60 99
e-Mail: lit@lit-verlag.de   http://www.lit-verlag.de

Distribution:
In Germany: LIT Verlag Fresnostr. 2, D-48159 Münster
Tel. +49 (0) 2 51-620 32 22, Fax +49 (0) 2 51-922 60 99, e-Mail: vertrieb@lit-verlag.de

In Austria: Medienlogistik Pichler-ÖBZ GmbH & Co KG
IZ-NÖ, Süd, Straße 1, Objekt 34, A-2355 Wiener Neudorf
Tel. +43 (0) 22 36-63 53 52 90, Fax +43 (0) 22 36-63 53 52 43, e-Mail: mlo@medien-logistik.at

In Switzerland: B + M Buch- und Medienvertriebs AG
Hochstr. 357, CH-8200 Schaffhausen
Tel. +41 (0) 52-643 54 30, Fax +41 (0) 52-643 54 35, e-Mail: order@buch-medien.ch

In the UK by: Global Book Marketing, 99B Wallis Rd, London, E9 5LN
Phone: +44 (0) 20 8533 5800 – Fax: +44 (0) 1600 775 663
http://www.centralbooks.co.uk/html

In North America by:

Transaction Publishers
New Brunswick (U.S.A.) and London (U.K.)

Transaction Publishers
Rutgers University
35 Berrue Circle
Piscataway, NJ 08854

Phone: +1 (732) 445 - 2280
Fax: + 1 (732) 445 - 3138
for orders (U. S. only):
toll free (888) 999 - 6778
e-mail: orders@transactionpub.com

Table of Contents

Affiliation, Belonging, and 'Sameness' - New Tendencies in Dealing with Difference in the Contemporary British Novel

Over the last decades, 'difference' has established itself as one of the concepts with the most lasting impact on theoretical discourses in the humanities. Accordingly, references and discussions may be found in disciplines as varied as philosophy, postcolonial studies, and sociology, to name but a few. Yet, despite its seeming ubiquitousness in theoretical discourse, definitions of difference are far from homogenous with the term being employed in all but jarring fashions in the respective subdisciplines.[1] As far as literary and cultural studies are concerned, though, we observe the persistence of certain core categories around which examinations usually revolve and which recur especially in debates about the connection between difference and identity. Special significance is usually attributed to the 'holy trinity'[2] of race/ethnicity, class and sex, which, in more recent analyses, is increasingly coupled with a discussion of age as a crucial factor. Notably, despite their great heterogeneity in terms of style and subject-matter, the texts which deal with the problem of difference and its counter-part sameness almost invariably address at least one of the core categories listed above.

Nevertheless, while there is undoubtedly a continuity in terms of the reference to a limited set of differential categories, we may at present witness a novel development with regard to the engagement with difference as such in the field of contemporary British literature. It is the explicit aim of the present study to analyse and illustrate this new tendency and to attempt a classification of that growing body of literary texts with regard to generic issues as well as a possible periodisation. As pertains to the latter aspect, there is no denying the fact that

---

[1] In view of this lack of consensus on the ultimate definition of difference, it does not come as a surprise that publications on the topic abound. With respect to the general significance of the concept as well as the different approaches towards its theorisation, see Plotnitsky's entry on "difference", which offers an elucidating overview (Plotnitsky, Arkady. „Difference." *Glossalalia – An Alphabet of Critical Keywords*. Ed. Julian Wolfreys. Edinburgh: Edinburgh UP, 2003). As far as a comparison of the specific uses in single subdisciplines is concerned, the issue is complicated even further because of the, at times, highly specialised employment of the oppositional pair 'difference' and 'sameness' in, for instance, mathematics and philosophy, especially as far as Heidegger's writings are concerned. Despite this complexity, I have nevertheless chosen to operate with both terms and attempted to circumvent the problem of terminological inaccuracy by indicating my specific usage in the respective cases.

[2] Feldmann, Doris. „Beyond Difference? Recent Developments in Postcolonial and Gender Studies." *English Studies Today. Recent Developments and New Directions*. Eds. Ansgar Nünning and Jürgen Schlaeger. Trier: WVT, 2007. 117-37. 118. This assumption is likewise maintained by Martín Alcoff who lists race, class, nationality, and sexuality as the four most prominent basic elements of identity (Martín Alcoff, Linda. „Introduction. Identities: Modern and Postmodern." *Identities. Race, Class, Gender, and Nationality*. Eds. Linda Martín Alcoff and Eduardo Mendieta. Malden, MA *et al.*: Blackwell, 2003. 1-8. 5).

periodisations and the demarcation of literary eras constitute a highly controversial issue since all labels and characterisations of the resulting periods are by necessity encumbered with a certain reductiveness. It is precisely for this reason that I will avoid the use of catch-all categories and attempt to proceed primarily in a descriptive fashion. Apparently, a limited number of references to established notions and currents proved inevitable all the same. This necessity arises mainly from the fact that the newly emergent strategies in dealing with difference may be considered to clash with characteristically 'postmodern' approaches, at least if postmodernism is understood to denote a specific attitude which includes the subversion of values as well as the breaking up of dichotomies and binary oppositions.[3] Therefore, one of the major research interests of this study consists in the characteristic features of a currently evolving line in contemporary British fiction which seems to offer an alternative to 'postmodern' ways of dealing with difference. While postmodern and poststructuralist theories emphasise, on the one hand, the divisive and fragmentarising aspects of difference and the ensuing destabilisation of both personal and collective identities, or highlight, on the other hand, the deferral of difference in the sense of différance, we presently may witness the emergence of a third tendency which diverges from these approaches. By way of illustration for this new trend, six novels have been chosen for closer scrutiny in the following chapters. They all distinguish themselves from 'postmodern' narratives inasmuch as they focus on strategies in dealing with difference which allow for the construction of identities that are perceived as stable by the protagonists themselves[4] or shed a new

---

[3] This — undoubtedly somewhat simplistic — view of postmodernism is first and foremostly promoted in introductions and overviews directed at students. These publications usually aim at providing neat, easily understandable definitions and are therefore especially prone to use a large number of catchy labels. For this procedure, Jones's entry on postmodernism may be considered prototypical: According to Jones, the nexus between Postmodernism, Poststructuralism and Deconstruction may be explained as follows: "Post-structuralism and deconstruction can be seen as the theoretical formulations of the post-modern condition. Modernity, which began intellectually with the Enlightenment, attempted to describe the world in rational, empirical and objective terms. It assumed that there was a truth to be uncovered, a way of obtaining answers to the question posed by the human condition. Post-modernism does not exhibit this confidence, gone are the underlying certainties that reason promised. Reason itself is now seen as a particular historical form, as parochial in its own way as the ancient explanations of the universe in terms of Gods. The postmodern subject has no rational way to evaluate a preference in relation to judgements of truth, morality, aesthetic experience or objectivity. As the old hierarchies of thought are torn down, a new clearing is formed on the frontiers of understanding: quite what hybrids of thought will metamorphose, interbreed and grow is this clearing is for the future to decide" (Jones, Roger. "Postmodernism." 14.06.2009. <<http://www.philosopher.org.uk/index.htm>>). Even though the heuristic value of this type of characterisation is questionable, the practice as such undoubtedly has a certain appeal as it seems to provide quick and accessible information despite the fact that these highly condensed overviews might lead to a skewed perspective on the literary developments within a specific period of time.

light on the perception of difference, for instance, by (re)introducing further dimensions such as social obligations or (cultural) memory.

As already mentioned above, 'postmodernism' constitutes a controversial concept with a vast range of definitions focussing on a variety of aspects that cannot be integrated into a homogeneous description. As a result of this lack of consensus on the characteristic features of the period (provided one chooses to consider it as a period rather than a style) individual definitions of 'postmodernism'[5] frequently contradict each other or at any rate set different priorities. In a retrospective account of his own engagement with the phenomenon of postmodern literature, Bertens, for instance, lists "the by now usual suspects: Barthelme, Coover, Gass, Sontag, Brautigan, Hawkes, Sukenick, Barth, Pynchon, Gaddis, Nabokov (*Pale Fire*, *Ada*) and so on. Curiously – at least with hindsight – we also included James Purdy, Stanley Elkin, Kurt Vonnegut, Thomas Berger, and

---

[4] At this point, we frequently need to differentitate between character perspective and narrator perspective. Even though the general plot structure, which does not unfold in its entirety to the limited perspective of the protagonists, or comments by an extradiegetic-heterodiegetic narrator may indicate that, ultimately, the characters are merely succumbing to the illusion of stability or 'sameness' – a concept I will define in greater detail below – this illusion remains functional on the figural level. The resulting identities which are based on unifying aspects serve as a foundation for the consolidation of groups and communities, even though they are easily recognisable as social constructs. Moreover, despite their social constructedness, they prove satisfactory on a subjective level and are presented as valuable inasmuch as they cater to an individual's need for stability and belonging.

[5] Among many others, Welsch comments on the difficulties to accurately define the expression 'Postmoderne' which arises from the at times incompatible forms of usages of the term as well as from clashing associations with the concepts of postmodernism and postmodernity. In order to outline the contradictory stances, he distinguishes between two types of postmodernism, a diffuse and a precise one: "Der diffuse ist der grassierende. Seine Spielarten reichen von wissenschaftlichen Universal-Mixturen in Lacan-Derrida-Tunke bis zu aufgedrehten Beliebigkeits-Szenarien chicer Kulturmode. Das Credo dieses diffusen Postmodernismus scheint zu sein, dass alles, was den Standards der Rationalität nicht genügt oder Bekanntes allenfalls verdreht wiedergibt, damit auch schon gut, ja gar gelungen sei, daß man den Cocktail nur ordentlich mixen und mit reichlich Exotischem versetzen müsse. […] Ihm gegenüber gilt es dem präzisen Postmodernismus Raum zu schaffen. Dieser ist der veritable und effiziente Postmodernismus. Er frönt nicht dem Rummel des Potpourri und folgt nicht einer läppisch-beliebigen Verwirrungslizenz, sondern tritt für wirkliche Pluralität ein und wahrt und entwickelt diese, indem er einem Unterscheidungsgebot folgt" (Welsch, Wolfgang. *Unsere postmoderne Moderne*. Weinheim: VCH, Acta Humaniora, 1987. 2-3. For a detailed discussion of the origins and different uses of the term 'Postmoderne', see Chapter 1). As Welsch's study in particular demonstrates, the distinction between postmodernism and postmodernity is made with much less precision in the German context than is the case in publications in the English language such as Best's and Kellner's *Postmodern Theory*: "[T]o avoid conceptual confusion, in this book, we shall use the term 'postmodernity' to describe the supposed epoch that follows modernity, and 'postmodernism' to describe movements and artifacts in the cultural field that can be distinguished from modernist movements, texts, and practices" (Best, Steven and Douglas Kellner. *Postmodern Theory. Critical Interrogations*. Houndmills, Basingstoke and London: Macmillan, 1991. 5). A similar differentiation is offered by Zima (Zima, Peter V. „Why the Postmodern Age Will Last." *Beyond Postmodernism. Reassessments in Literature, Theory, and Culture*. Ed. Klaus Stierstorfer. Berlin and New York: de Gruyter, 2003. 13-27).

even Ken Kesey"[6]. Due to these terminological imprecisions, I will use the terms 'postmodernism' and 'postmodern' in the sense of a literary strategy or technique which highlights the pluralising, deferred nature of difference and orchestrates the instability of identities, values, and meanings.[7]

In general, one may argue that the instability to be currently registered with regard to both personal and collective identities is, at least partly, provoked by the loss of established markers of reference in the wake of developments such as internationalisation and globalisation.[8] This hypothesis chimes in with McHale's suggestion that postmodernism represents a discursive formation rather than a material cultural artefact: "[P]ostmodernism exists discursively, in the discourses we produce *about* it and *using* it."[9] In order to allow for a differ-

---

[6] Bertens, Hans. „The Fiction and the Theory: A Personal Retrospective." *Teaching Postmodernism – Postmodern Teaching*. Eds. Klaus Stierstorfer and Laurenz Volkmann. Tübingen: Stauffenburg, 2004. 27-34. 27.

[7] Especially with respect to deconstruction, the term 'strategy' proves highly problematic since Derrida himself states explicitly that "deconstruction is neither an *analysis* nor a *critique* and its translation would have to take that into consideration. […] I would say the same about *method*. Deconstruction is not a method and cannot be transformed into one" (Derrida, Jacques. „Letter to a Japanese Friend." *Deconstruction. Critical Concepts in Literary and Cultural Studies*. Vol. I. Ed. Jonathan Culler. London and New York: Routledge, 2003. 23-7. 25, orig. emphases). Bennington puts forth a similar point when claiming that "[d]econstruction is not a form of hermeneutics, however supposedly radical, for just this reason: hermeneutics always proposes a convergent movement towards a unitary meaning (however much it may wish to respect ambiguity on the way), the word of God; deconstruction discerns a dispersive perspective in which there is no (one) meaning" (Bennington, Geoffrey. „Jacques Derrida." *Deconstruction. Critical Concepts in Literary and Cultural Studies*. Vol. I. Ed. Jonathan Culler. London and New York: Routledge, 2003. 41-51. 45). Nevertheless, I would like to argue that, by now, a 'deconstructive convention' has been established which aims at the demonstration of the infixibility of meaning as well as its permanent deferral. It is this approach towards the interpretation of texts that I refer to when using expressions such as 'poststructural technique' or 'deconstructionist approach'. On the gradual privileging of the term deconstruction and its foundation in the work of German philosopher Martin Heidegger, see Newmark, Kevin. „Deconstruction. See elsewhere, *la différence*, *la dissemination*, for example." *Deconstruction. Critical Concepts in Literary and Cultural Studies*. Vol. I. Ed. Jonathan Culler. London and New York: Routledge, 2003. 28-40.

[8] In her account of postmodern identity politics, Mercer dismissively comments on the exploitation of specific keywords in contemporary political discourse: "Like 'identity', difference, diversity and fragmentation are keywords in the postmodern vocabulary where they are saturated with groovy connotations. But it should be clear that there is nothing particularly groovy about the postmodern condition at all. As a bestseller ideology in artistic and intellectual circles the postmodern paradigm has been and gone, but as a pervasive sensibility in everyday life its smelly ideological effect lingers on. Postmodernism means many different things to many different people, but the key motifs of displacement, decentring and disenchantment have a specific resonance and relevance for the Left and new social movements after the demoralising decade of Thatcherism" (Mercer, Kobena. „Welcome to the Jungle: Identity and Diversity in Postmodern Politics." *Identity. Community, Culture, Difference*. Ed. Jonathan Rutherford. London: Lawrence & Wishart, 1990. 43-71. 49). Moreover, Mercer expounds on the loss of traditional sources of authority and identity as well as the ensuing insecurity and perceived lack of stable affiliations.

[9] McHale, Brian. *Constructing Postmodernism*. London and New York: Routledge, 1992. 1, orig. emphasis.

entiation between the set of new strategies in dealing with difference diagnosed in this study and potentially 'postmodern' ways of engagement I follow Hassan's catalogue of central features of 'postmodern' literature and styles, which he characterises as "fragments, hybridity, relativism, play, parody, pastiche, an ironic, sophistical stance, an ethos bordering on kitsch and camp"[10]. These aspects figure particularly prominently in the context of identity formation and the discussion of the various influences involved in the process of subject-constitution. Moreover, the large number of academic publications on the topic of identity[11] – likened by Hall to a "discursive explosion" – suggests the emergence of an increasing longing for a re-definition of previous conceptualisations in order to re-render them compatible with an individual's daily experiences in globalised societies.[12] Hall, who treats identity basically as a discursive construction, therefore comes up with the following definition:

> I use 'identity' to refer to the meeting point, the point of *suture*, between on the one hand the discourses and practices which attempt to 'interpellate', speak to us or hail us into place as the social subjects of particular discourses, and on the other hand, the processes which produce subjectivities, which construct us as subjects which can be 'spoken'.[13]

In fact, this assertion seems to reflect a widely held conviction within present cultural studies. Although I do not wish to challenge its general validity, I would nevertheless like to argue that, in the range of texts illustrated in the fol-

---

[10] Hassan, Ihab. „Beyond Postmodernism: Toward an Aesthetic of Trust." *Beyond Postmodernism. Reassessments in Literature, Theory, and Culture*. Ed. Klaus Stierstorfer. Berlin and New York: de Gruyter, 2003. 199-212. 200.

[11] For an overview of recent tendencies and theories in the field, see Hall's essay "Who Needs 'Identity'?" (Hall, Stuart. „Introduction: Who Needs 'Identity'?" *Questions of Cultural Identity*. Eds. Stuart Hall and Paul du Gay. London *et al.*: Sage, 1996. 1-17). On identity in cultural studies, likewise consult Grossberg, Lawrence. "Identity and Cultural Studies: Is That All There Is?" *Questions of Cultural Identity*. Eds. Stuart Hall and Paul du Gay. London *et al.*: Sage, 1996. 87-107.

[12] Mercer, among many others, discusses the effects of recent social transformations on identity formation: "In sociological terms, this means a recognition of the fragmentation of traditional sources of authority and identity, the displacement of collective sources of membership and belonging such as 'class' and 'community' that help to construct political loyalties, affinities and identifications. [...] While certain structures associated with the highly centralised logic of mass production and mass consumption give way to more flexible transnational arrangements that undermine the boundaries of the sovereign nation-state, other boundaries become more rigid, such as those that exclude the late modern underclass from participation in free-market choices" (Mercer, 1990, 50). Apart from those more recent accounts, Andersons's seminal publication *Imagined Communities* still constitutes one of the most influential studies on the topic.

[13] Hall, 1996, 5-6.

lowing analyses, one may detect a divergent perception of identity.[14] As will be demonstrated below, belonging and affiliation – as well as the collective identities resulting from various types of bonding – are apparently not experienced as mere discursive constructs. Instead, the identities derived from sources such as shared origins or a similar ethnical background are depicted as integral parts of an individual's self-image and are treated as lasting features of their personality. We may therefore detect a renewed emphasis on persistent, graspable elements informing processes of identity formation.

The approach as such, i.e. a general endeavour to underscore the significance of materiality or even a biological component in the construction of (personal) identities, does by no means represent a tendency characteristic of post-2000 engagements with the topic. To the contrary, the idea has already been brought forward in previous decades and has, for example, been promoted with particular verve by exponents of Materialist Feminism. With respect to the materiality of the body and its impact on gender identity Ramazanoglu, to pick just one sample, observes:

> The boundaries between male and female are *simultaneously* both those of variable elements of bodily existence and also of variable cultural categories through which sameness and difference are specified. These boundaries cannot always be clearly drawn for each individual, and each culture has to deal with anatomical ambiguity (for example, through flexible or multiple categories, or by the rigid imposition of two categories in which a person must be declared either male or female). *But the fact that bodily boundaries cannot be specified independently of cultural categories does not mean that they are not there.*[15]

While this perspective has been embedded in the framework of Gender Studies for several years, the emphasis on the material basis of identities as well as literary renditions of the topic seem to constitute a comparatively recent development, at least in this pronounced form. What is more, I would like to claim that an intersection between sociological and literary discourses is discernible since

---

[14] In this context, I would like to draw attention to another feature of postmodern conceptualisations of identity which is underlined by Musschenga who argues that "[m]uch of post-modern literature on identity is not on personal identity in the sense of what makes an individual into the person he is, but deals with the issue of the 'subjectivity' of an individual, of whether he is a truly autonomous subject" (Musschenga, Albert W. „Introduction." *Personal and Moral Identity*. Ed. Albert W. Musschenga *et al.* Dordrecht: Kluwer, 2002. 3-22. 10).

[15] Ramazanoglu, Caroline. „Back to Basics: Heterosexuality, Biology and Why Men Stay on Top." *(Hetero)sexual Politics*. Eds. Mary Maynard and June Purvis. Oxon: Taylor & Francis, 1995. 27-41. 35, second emphasis mine.

the novels under discussion here seem to mirror a desire experienced by 'real life' individuals.[16] One may thus conceivably argue that a purely discursive conception of identity does, in a number of cases, not conform to individual experiences and self-images. A further important aspect in this context consists in the fact that new conceptualisations seem to require approaches in both dealing with difference and integrating it into the framework of personal and collective identities other than those currently available. In my readings of the selected narrative texts, this impression is backed especially by repeated comments on the issue of corporeality uttered by single characters as well as by the significance they attribute to aspects such as skin colour, weight, shaping one's body, dress, and hairstyle. What is more, besides this turn to materiality, the protagonists seek lasting affiliations on which to ground their self-images and personal identities. The phenomenon of an increasingly discernible longing for stability, unity, and coherence – or at least reliability – is likewise described by Korte and Müller:

> In postmodernism, notions of stable and homogeneous identities, whether personal or cultural, have been abandoned in favour of ones that allow for discontinuity and internal differences. Nevertheless, relative identities and unities are still being sought. A need for unities, for identities – even unstable, fluid ones – and for the orientation provided by values has increasingly emerged in the 1990s, along with critical assessment of radical postmodernist positions and their abyss of the 'anything goes'.[17]

Although I would like to proceed even one step further by arguing that fluid, unstable identities are precisely not what is being sought for, I agree with the general thrust of Korte's and Müller's account inasmuch as the search for new points of reference and orientation is concerned. Moreover, they acknowledge a general desire for unity, which I consider one of the main features of the novels discussed here. In fact, precisely this aspect provides a connecting thread between the growing body of texts which may potentially supply a basis for the formation of a 'second', late modern or even 'non-postmodern' strand in British fiction. Curiously enough, these texts display a certain 'intentional' proximity to postmodernism in its initial conception since both formations seem to cater to

---

[16] Of course, as far as attitudes in 'reality' are concerned, one must by necessity rely on the detour of sociological studies as well as empirical analyses in the realm of cultural studies. Nevertheless, the indications offered by these sources seem strong enough to suggest a parallel development in present British society and engagements with the topic of identity formations in contemporary literature.

[17] Korte, Barbara and Klaus Peter Müller. „Unity in Diversity Revisited: Complex Paradoxes Beyond Post-/Modernism." *Unity in Diversity Revisited? British Literature and Culture in the 1990s*. Tübingen: Narr, 1998. 9-33. 14.

needs and sensitivities in (Western) late modern societies, where belonging and affiliations have obviously come to adopt an incrementally important role and represent a recurrent concern. Geisen subsumes this phenomenon under the expression "Paradox der modernen Gesellschaften", in which communities are constructed on the basis of difference: "Gemeinsamkeit entsteht hier über Getrenntheit, über die Konstruktion und Aufrechterhaltung von Differenzen."[18] For the reasons outlined above, one of the main foci of the study thus consists in an examination of strategies in the depiction of both personal and collective identities; moreover, particular attention will be paid to the function ascribed to specific differential categories in the process of identity formation.

Whereas the discrepancy between the approach adopted by the texts covered here and other strategies in the negotiation of difference shows most clearly when contrasted with 'postmodern' fiction, it must, at the same time, not be forgotten that postmodernism does by no means constitute the sole literary style discernible in the last decades. Even though overviews over contemporary British literature tend to highlight postmodernist tendencies and often classify the period following Modernism as "Postmodernism"[19], a closer examination of the literary production over the last decades reveals that the creative output has been far more varied and is by no means reducible to postmodern writing. Undoubtedly, 'postmodern' fiction – provided that a homogeneous body of texts to be labelled in this way exists at all – certainly exerted a considerable influence

---

[18] Geisen, Thomas. „Kultur und Identität – Zum Problem der Thematisierung von Gleichheit und Differenz in modernen Gesellschaften." *Kulturelle Differenzen begreifen. Das Konzept der Transdifferenz aus interdisziplinärer Sicht.* Hg. Britta Kalscheuer und Lars Allolio-Näcke. Frankfurt und New York: Campus, 2008. 167-87. 176.

[19] Interestingly enough, the *Introduction to the Study of English and American Literature* in the Klett Uni-Wissen series – a publication intended especially for students of English literature – uses the expression "Post-war era" to cover the entire period from 1945 to 2004 in British fiction without even mentioning the term postmodernism. With regard to American literary history, though, the self-same era is labelled "Postmodernism to present day" (Nünning, Ansgar and Vera. *An Introduction to the Study of English and American Literature.* Tr. Jane Dewhurst. Klett: Stuttgart *et al.*: 2004. 163-5). Gelfert's *Kleine Literaturgeschichte*, an overview likewise primarily intended for the use by students, follows this approach in designating the last period under discussion as "Nachkriegszeit und Postmoderne" (Gelfert, Hans-Dieter. *Kleine Geschichte der englischen Literatur.* München: Beck, ²2005). A further example of this stance may be found in Löffler *et al.* who, in their timeline offered at the end of their study, posit the succession of "Modernism (1910-1940)" by "Postmodernism (1955-)" (Löffler, Arno *et al. Einführung in das Studium der englischen Literatur.* Tübingen und Basel: Francke, ⁶2001). Despite the high lucidity and great perspicacity of her account, which acknowledges the existence of 'non-postmodern' tendencies in the late 20th century, Schabert likewise titles her last chapter "Postmoderne (1970-2000)" (Schabert, Ina. *Englische Literaturgeschichte des 20. Jahrhunderts. Eine neue Darstellung aus Sicht der Geschlechterforschung.* Stuttgart: Kröner, 2006). Since this list could be supplemented by several more examples, on first sight, the impression easily imposes itself that, at least since the after-war period with its kitchen sink dramas and angry young men, British literature has been dominated by 'postmodern' writers. On more thorough study, though, this assumption turns out to be untenable in such a crude form.

on the development of British literature and offered stylistic patterns adopted by many writers. At the same time, however, decidedly 'non-postmodern' texts were published as well. By way of example one might, in this context, cite 'canonical' writers such as David Lodge and Jonathan Coe alongside many other novelists producing 'popular fiction' like Tim Lott, Helen Fielding, and Nick Hornby.[20] Therefore, apart from highlighting the distinctions to 'postmodern' engagements with the topic of difference, this study will pay special attention to the reflection of whether a certain continuity of modern(ist) strategies is visible and whether those are currently becoming more pronounced again. Seeing that the narratives chosen for interpretation frequently rely on 'conventional' textual strategies and quote long-established genres such as the bildungsroman and (traditional) autobiographical writing, I aim to demonstrate in which way a recourse to previous modes is performed and how the texts connect to the body of narratives that have continuously been produced alongside 'postmodern' novels.

What appears to be of utmost importance with regard to the subject-matter dealt with in the respective texts is their engagement with the complex of community building, social affiliations, and bonding. It its precisely at this point that we encounter an intersection between discourses in sociology or cultural studies and the discursive formations in the literary field since a number of fictional texts produced in the last decade are obviously informed by a longing for unity and coherence, a tendency which has likewise been diagnosed in sociological accounts of the present social situation[21]. The resulting desire for stability seems

---

[20] These writers have only been chosen by way of illustration; indubitably, the list could be prolonged almost ad infinitum.

[21] With respect to globalisation and internationalisation, the re-establishment of 'locality', i.e. the turn to units on a much smaller scale than, for instance, the nation state has by now been acknowledged and described under the label of glocalisation (Appadurai offers a detailed discussion of the concept of locality in Chapter 9 of *Modernity at Large*. See Appadurai, Arjun. *Modernity at Large. Cultural Dimensions of Globalization*. Minneapolis MN and London: Minnesota UP, 1996). Wagner describes the process as follows: "Die immer weitere Ausbreitung westlicher Konsumgüter und Kulturmuster geht mit einer verstärkten Rückbesinnung auf lokale kulturelle Traditionen und ihre Wiederentdeckung einher. [...] Kulturelle Identitätssuche in lokalen, regionalen und nationalen Bezügen zur Selbstvergewisserung bildet nicht nur bei Migranten, nationalen Minderheiten und in Ländern des Südens die andere Seite der kulturellen Nationalisierung. Lokal- und Nationalkulturen als Ausdruck kultureller Traditionen sollen dabei ein Zusammengehörigkeitsgefühl vermitteln und dadurch den Menschen in den kulturellen Globalisierungsprozessen einen Orientierungspunkt und Identitätsanker bieten. [...] Inzwischen ist unstrittig, dass Globalisierung immer auch mit »Lokalisierung« und »Regionalisierung« einhergeht und es gerade in Anbetracht von Globalisierung und Globalität zu einer neuen Betonung des Lokalen kommt" (Wagner, Bernd. „Kulturelle Globalisierung: Weltkultur, Glokalität und Hybridisierung. Einleitung" *Kulturelle Globalisierung – Zwischen Weltkultur und kultureller Fragmentierung*. Hg. Bernd Wagner. Essen: Klartext, 2001. 9-38. 15). Beck comes to a similar conclusion when he states that "Globalisierung heißt gerade nicht automatisch und einseitig, eindimensional Globalisierung [...]. Vielmehr kommt es unter der Regierung des »g-words« im Gegenteil überall zu einer *neuen Betonung des Lokalen*" (Beck, Ulrich. *Was ist Globalisierung? Irrtümer des Globa-*

to have necessitated a turn towards forms of writing which put a stronger emphasis on community and coherency and which engage actively in the process of creating and strengthening affiliations:

> Dekonstruktivistisches Erzählen [...], das Handlungszusammenhänge auflöst und personale Identität in Frage stellt, kann eine solche gemeinschaftsstiftende, konsolidierende oder revisionistische Leistung kaum erbringen. [...] Doch bereits seit Mitte der 1980er Jahre wendet sich das Erzählen wieder von der Dekonstruktion ab oder stellt sie dar als eine Position unter mehreren in einer pluralistischen Welt.[22]

In addition to that, as Schabert likewise states, the process of narration (re)assumes the function of generating meaning and of producing a feeling of communality and cohesion.[23] While one may well object that this intention to produce meaning by way of narrative texts does by no means constitute a novel development, I would like to argue that a crucial aspect consists in the (re-newed) perception of literature as a potential source for meaning and insights which are in some way transferable to a reader's life reality.

Besides their highlighting aspects of community building and affiliation, the novels presented in the following chapters abandon an exclusive concentration on the potentially divisive effects of difference. Thus, instead of treating difference as a factor distinguishing individuals from each other, the narratives draw upon differential categories for the establishment of unity and coherency. Seeing that this conceptualisation differs from previous takes on the topic, I deem it necessary to reflect on possibilities for an adequate theoretical description and explanation. Since existing concepts do not seem to grasp the specificities of this new way of coping with difference in its entirety, I suggest the introduction of a notion that is intended to adequately express the characteristic features of this novel approach; as a designation for this conceptualisation I have chosen the term 'sameness'. In order to set off 'sameness' as a concept from the every-

---

lismus – Antworten auf Globalisierung. Frankfurt a. M.: Suhrkamp, 1997. 86, orig. emphasis). A detailed account of the impact of globalisation on processes of identity formation (especially with respect to cultural identity) may be found in Featherstone, Mike. „Localism, Globalism and Cultural Identity." *Identities. Race, Class, Gender, and Nationality*. Eds. Linda Martín Alcoff and Eduardo Mendieata. Malden MA *et al.*: Blackwell, 2003. 342-59. On the phenomenon of globalisation as such and the various processes involved, see Held, David and Anthony McGrew. „The Great Globalization Debate: An Introduction." *The Global Transformations Reader. An Introduction to the Globalization Debate*. Eds. David Held and Anthony McGrew. Cambridge: Polity, [2]2003. 1-50, as well as Drechsel, Paul *et al. Kultur im Zeitalter der Globalisierung. Von Identität zu Differenzen*. Frankfurt a. M.: IKO, 2000.
[22] Schabert, 2006, 431.
[23] Schabert, 2006, 436.

day meaning of the term, i.e. its use as an expression of likeness or similarity, I will, throughout this study, refer to the concept as Sameness – capital S – whereas I will stick to the regular spelling (no capitalisation) when referring to common connotations of the term[24]. As regards the coinage as such, I want to emphasise that my aim does not consist in the addition of yet another category to the (already extensive) list of both established and more recent formulations of strategies in coping with difference. Instead, Sameness is intended as a purely analytic tool. This status likewise differentiates this category from other conceptualisations. Nevertheless, I deem the definition of a new method necessary since the literary development which I describe in the following chapters can, at least to my assessment, not be projected sufficiently by established notions as, for instance, multiculturalism, transculturalism, hybridity, and transdifference.[25]

Yet, despite the potential benefits of the concept, there are, undoubtedly, a number of objections towards the introduction of another category into the already quite saturated field. The possibly most controversial aspects of Sameness consist in its a) bearing various connotations not necessarily included in my concept[26] and b) the employment of the term in everyday discourse as well as in other academic disciplines. A further difficulty arises from the fact that Sameness cannot be conceived without difference – and vice versa:

> What could be more straightforward than the idea of difference? It is the opposite of sameness. [...] By relating the word 'difference' to its oppo-

---

[24] Gilroy uses the same term in *Against Race*; he, however, does not offer a definition of the concept but rather employs sameness as a synonym for great similarity or a large number of shared features. Gilroy, Paul. *Against Race. Imagining Political Culture beyond the Color Line.* Cambridge, MA.: Belknap, 2000.

[25] With regard to the introduction of Sameness in this study, I am highly grateful to a comment by Ria Blaicher, who suggested that the processes described by my concept might also be expressed by the notion of social bonding. Even though I likewise consider the two ideas highly similar, I nevertheless believe that social bonding describes a wider phenomenon and that Sameness should thus possibly be treated as a subcategory. I will return to this proposition in the respective chapters in order to highlight proximities as well as potentially divergent points.

[26] In academic discourse, it is first and foremostly in philosophical writings that the term 'sameness' is employed. In this context, it serves, for example, as a counter-concept to difference as in Weinsheimer's essay "Skinner and Gadamer: The Hermeneutics of Sameness and Difference" (Weinsheimer, Joel. „Skinner and Gadamer: The Hermeneutics of Sameness and Difference." *Mitteilungen des Verbandes Deutscher Anglisten* 4:2 (1993): 42-57). Likewise, in English translations of Heidegger's *Identität und Differenz*, 'sameness' (for the German term 'Selbigkeit') is used in a very specific way to signify "the relation of "with", that is, a mediation, a connection, a synthesis: the unification into a unity" (Heidegger, Martin. *Identity and Difference.* Tr. Joan Stammbaugh. New York, Evanston and London: Harper & Row, 1969. 25). Even though this usage of the term comes close to my definition of Sameness, the two concepts must not be confused. Therefore, as indicated above, I chose to indicate my formulation of Sameness by capitalisation of the first letter.

site, the dictionary and I have gone some way to explaining its meaning, but we have also introduced the way that the word 'difference' might act as a principle for explaining how words get their meaning in general. I have explained 'difference' through the concept of difference, in that I pointed to the difference between it and another word. [...] In fact if I tried to explain the meaning of 'sameness', I would find it very difficult to do it without reference to the concept of difference, so that its solidity as a foundation is compromised and my definition becomes rather circular. My definition of difference has nowhere to rest, and I find myself rebounding between one word and the other indefinitely.[27]

This impasse has been repeatedly acknowledged and the last years have seen the development of a number of strategies which attempted to grasp the 'merging' of differential categories and to offer theories transcending essentialising dualisms and binary oppositions. These approaches range from concepts firmly established in critical discourse such as hybridity but also cover more recent ones as, for instance, transculturality and transdifference. What these strategies appear to have in common is that they, ultimately, all rely on the (albeit covered) retention of a binary opposition which serves as a foundation or basis. As Feldmann and Habermann state with respect to transdifference,

> [n]euere Ansätze in den Kulturstudien haben sich bemüht, das damit einhergehende Denken in binären Oppositionen zu überwinden und Orte des 'Dritten' auszumachen, oft in Verbindung mit dem Postulat einer intrinsischen Subversivität des Hybriden. Transdifferenz betont demgegenüber die Unvermeidbarkeit des Denkens von Differenz bei gleichzeitigem Bewußtsein für die vielfältigen Überlagerungen, Mehrfachzugehörigkeiten und Zwischenbefindlichkeiten, welche die Komplexität der Lebenswelt ausmachen.[28]

---

[27] Currie, Mark. *Difference*. London and New York: Routledge, 2004. 1-2. Young specifies this problem further by applying it to the process of identity formation: "In the postcolonial period, for those outside the West, and for those minorities within it, the opposition of sameness and difference, and its relation to identity, has been fundamental. Since Derrida, identity has come to mean not sameness, but difference. [...] Yet, if identity is sameness it is also specified by being different – paradoxically it can only be defined by difference from others. As a concept, identity has thus the unusual characteristic of necessarily immediately summoning up its opposite, difference" (Young, Robert J. C. „Deconstruction and the Postcolonial." *Deconstructions. A User's Guide.* Ed. Nicholas Royle. Houndmills, Basingstoke and New York: Palgrave, 2000. 187-210. 199).
[28] Feldmann, Doris und Ina Habermann: „Das Graduiertenkolleg "Kulturhermeneutik im Zeichen von Differenz und Transdifferenz" an der Friedrich-Alexander-Universität Erlangen-Nürnberg." *Anglistik* 14:2 (2003): 105-12. 105-6.

In principle, I agree with the assumption that unity/commonality is inextricably linked to difference and that even in concepts such as hybridity, which aim, as it were, at the 'fusion' of two different poles, difference continues to play a role. Nevertheless, I would like to argue that, in the field of contemporary British fiction, we may detect first signs of a perception of difference which is not covered by the available concepts.[29] According to my definition, Sameness denotes a state in which one differential category is temporarily privileged while all other differential categories likewise present at this specific moment in time are simultaneously suppressed. As a result, an actively sought for feeling of unity, belonging, and possibly even harmony ensues.[30] The element chosen as the basis of Sameness hereby serves as the main point of reference on which the illusion of total commonality is grounded and which relegates all other markers of affiliation to second place. Unless actively suppressed, these additional features inevitably provoke ruptures or breaks in the temporary feeling of 'absolute' belonging and unity. Sameness may therefore be described both as a process of selection and of hierarchisation: First, one criterion is chosen which, in a specific context, is presented as particularly significant. Secondly, a momentary erasure of one 'side' of a binary opposition is performed and, in addition to that, all further elements, which might potentially cause ruptures of the constructed homogeneity, are suppressed. Although these constructions fulfil their purpose for the time being, they, be default, cannot be maintained once the suppressed elements become too prominent to be kept at bay any longer. For this reason, the state of Sameness never achieves a permanent quality but only occurs in form of temporarily limited instances.

In order to illustrate these processes in greater detail, I have, by way of example, selected blackness as a category which may serve as a basis for the creation of Sameness. In this case, we are thus dealing with Sameness grounded on the differential category of race. Accordingly, a group of black people is presented as bound together by a strong feeling of belonging which erases potentially divisive elements such as age, class, sex, religion or education. As a result, the

---

[29] Gilroy describes a comparable process in black British communities: „Religious and political movements have emerged which regiment and synchronize the bodies of their black affiliates with uniforms and mass rituals. Unlike the Garvey movement which preceded them, these groups are trying to create and harness a sense of sameness that does not exist prior to their attempts to manufacture it. Their increasingly popular activities are a response to a situation where neither the effects of white supremacy nor the historic momentum of subaltern racial identities marked by slavery and colonialism can be relied upon to establish the feelings of connectedness that have been identified as a precondition for racial survival" (Gilroy, Paul. *Small Acts. Thoughts on the politics of black cultures*. London and New York: Serpent's Tail, 1993. 2).

[30] One might argue that this feature, i.e. the pre-condition of commonality being actively sought for provides a possible starting point for a distinction between social bonding and Sameness since social bonding might likewise take place on a sub- or semi-conscious level. Moreover, the instances of Sameness described in the ensuing chapters are restricted to a limited period of time, which is not necessarily the case with regard to social bonding.

group experiences a feeling of complete homogeneity for a restricted period of time. This desire for belonging and unity is also expressed by single characters with regard to their personal identities. In fact, this 'extreme' form of an entirely homogeneous collective identity allows them to give a firm grounding to their respective self-images. When compared to other forms of theorising difference with respect to its impact on identity formations, the main discrepancy between those concepts and the notion of Sameness consists in the fact that, in the latter case, we are dealing with a temporary effect as the disruptive elements have to be constantly kept at bay so as not to dispel the state of unity. Sooner or later, however, these suppressed elements regain their strength and dismantle the idea of a seamless community since they reveal it as an illusion and highlight its constructed quality. Nevertheless, on the level of the protagonists, this does not mean that the respective 'imagined communities' (pun intended) are completely futile. To the contrary, passages presented from the perspective of a focalizer as well as comments by autodiegetic narrators imply that the characters themselves perceive those realised moments of Sameness as an important source of support and rate them as a significant aid in the creation of their self-images.

One may therefore conclude that the strategy in the construction of personal identities described above runs counter to theories on identity formation which emphasise aspects such as fragmentarisation, instability, and heterogeneity[31] or consider identity as being generated by difference. In the latter case, especially as far as a poststructuralist perspective is concerned, those differences are not assumed to lead to dialectical structures in the Hegelian sense. Rather, "[i]dentities depend on traces of other identities: but the trace 'itself', now the logically prior term, is not answerable, to any metaphysical characterisation (it is, for example, neither present nor absent, and, as the condition of identity in general, is not itself *identifiable*)"[32]. The depiction of identities as unstable (and to some extent even ungraspable) constructs impacts considerably on subject-conceptions and may potentially even provoke concerns for persons in 'real life', a fact likewise acknowledged in sociological studies on the topic. As Melucci states, we may observe two core strategies in solving the predicament of the conception of the subject in a globalised society:

> One frequent way out of the impasse is to dissolve the self and elimi-
> nate the social actor. Thus identity becomes merely a presentation of
> self, a game of masks, a play acted out on the public stage which dis-

---

[31] Apparently, these features are often associated with so-called 'postmodern' theories on identity formation. Bertens even goes so far as to proclaim that postmodernism wages a 'war' on sameness. (Bertens, Hans. „The Debate on Postmodernism." *International Postmodernism. Theory and Literary Practice*. Eds. Hans Bertens and Douwe Fokkema. Amsterdam and Philadelphia. Benjamins, 1997. 3-14).

[32] Bennington, 2003, 46, orig. emphasis.

guises a void. Or we must once again attach ourselves to a stable nu-
cleus in a desperate attempt to reconstitute an essence – for example, by
reviving primary bonds of belonging, like kinship or local and geographical ties. *This reawakening of primary identities, this need to an-
chor oneself to something essential which is permanent and has visible
confines, lies at the basis of many contemporary collective phenomena.
Ethnic or geographical identification, the attachment to traditional culture, express the attempt to resist the dissolution of identity as an essence and the difficulty of accepting it in the form of a relation.*[33]

Apart from its concentration on (seemingly) palpable, material bonds, Sameness
can furthermore be set off from other concepts by the fact that the two poles of
an oppositional pair are no longer born in mind and are therefore not implicitly
present as is, for instance, the case with transdifference. By contrast, one element is completely edited out for the moment and superseded by its opposite
pole so that a hierarchical structure ensues, in which one differential category is
temporarily raised above all others.[34] Seeing that Sameness constitutes only one
possible strategy among others, though, it will not figure in all of the following
analyses but will be limited to a selected number of cases.

Difference and/in the Contemporary British Novel

Despite their heterogeneity in terms of style and generic features, the texts under discussion here rely on a comparatively small set of differential categories
around which discussions on identity formation and community building revolve. With regard to the analysis of strategies in dealing with those categories,
special emphasis will be placed on the following aspects: To begin with, I intend to demonstrate which differential categories are foregrounded and how
they are presented, i.e. how the characters themselves are shown to perceive
them. This step also includes reflections on how the reader's reactions might be

---

[33] Melucci, Alberto. „Identity and Difference in a Globalized World." *Debating Cultural Hybridity. Multi-Cultural Identities and the Politics of Anti-Racism.* Eds. Pnina Werbner and Tariq Modood. London and New Jersey: Zed, 1997. 58-69. 65, my emphasis.
[34] Baumann describes a similar process with respect to the formation of collective identities,
which he considers as dual discursive constructs. His concept provides an explanation of how
individuals deal with the problem of multiple affiliations, i.e. their belonging to different groups,
which do not necessarily share the same features (Baumann, Gerd. „Collective Identity as a Dual
Discursive Construction. Dominant v. Demotic Discourses of Culture and the Negotiation of
Historical Memory." *Identities. Time, Difference, and Boundaries.* Ed. Heidrun Friese. New York
and Oxford: Berghahn, 2002. 189-200. 190). A possible application of Baumann's concept will be
demonstrated in the analysis of Smith's *On Beauty.*

guided by, for instance, comments of an extradiegetic-heterodiegetic narrator.[35] At the same time, attention will be paid to the issue of how specific types of difference are dealt with and how they are employed as a potential basis for the formation of communities and the construction of collective identities. Hereby, I follow the observation brought forward by Schabert that, in the current literary production, we witness a tendency to assume that the act of narration may be instrumentalised for the purpose of community building: "Als Gestaltungs-, Kommunikations- und Verstehensprozess wirkt es [= das Erzählen] sich, wie alle Literatur, kohärenzstiftend und gemeinschaftsfördernd aus."[36] In view of the long tradition of prose writing intended to create coherency and affiliations, it proves hard to ultimately assess the novelty of this development; likewise, this fact renders the feature as such insufficient as defining characteristic of a 'new' strand in British literature. Nevertheless, one may undoubtedly state that the importance attributed to this potential function of literary texts and the stress placed on it in the writings themselves seem to be increasing irrespective of whether one chooses to diagnose this phenomenon as indicative of the beginnings of a new period or whether one classifies it as a re-strengthening of tendencies already observable in previous eras. What appears to be equally important is the concomitant consolidation of the position of the subject and its presentation as a capable agent. While I wish to avoid over-generalising ascriptions of catch-all labels, the contrast of these strategies proves most blatant when compared with so-called postmodern texts. It is for this reason that I will occasionally point out potential differences and divergences. At the same time, as briefly indicated above, though, modern(ist) modes of presentation seem to have re-gained a certain prominence. Thus, I will likewise highlight elements which may be considered heralds of a re-connection to these allegedly pre-postmodern structures.

In view of the subject-matter of the single narratives, the issue of ethics and/in the novel all but imposes itself. Of course, there can be no denying the fact that recent years have seen a discursive explosion with an abundant number of studies covering a vast range of ethically-inspired topics. By now, this phenomenon is generally referred to as the 'ethical turn'[37]. Even though the outlook as such,

---

[35] For the analysis of narratological structures, I draw upon the terminological system established by Genette.

[36] Schabert, 2006, 436.

[37] At present, usage of the term 'ethical turn' abounds and we are currently being confronted with a welter of studies brandishing the term 'ethics' in their title. These publications deal with subject-matters as diverse as *Academic Ethics*, *A Casebook of Medical Ethics*, *Belief's own Ethics*, *Aesthetics and Ethics*, *Ethics of Coercion and Authority*, and *The Ethics of Deconstruction*, to name but a few. As far as the ethical turn in cultural studies is concerned, many accounts posit a relationship or interconnectedness between a postmodern lack of orientation and the turn to ethics as a reaction in order to compensate for that perceived desideratum. Thus, Gras, for instance, claims that "the recent ethical turn in literary studies seems more a centripetal product of post-

i.e. the attempt to read a text against the background of ethical consideration, certainly constitutes a valid endeavour and may provide intriguing insights, 'ethical criticism' at present still appears to be fraught with certain methodological problems. First of all, studies focussing on the storyline of a narrative often concentrate on aspects such as a character's motivation or the approvability of their conduct and thus fail to make the crucial distinction between ethics and morals[38]. Even though, in everyday discourse, the two terms are sometimes used interchangeably, there is a decisive difference, which should be born in mind in academic usage of the terms. Fischer outlines this distinction as follows:

> Betrachten wir die Etymologie der Wörter Ethik und Moral [...], dann fällt auf, daß sich zwei unterschiedliche Ansprüche mit ihnen verbinden. Der eine Teil der Verwendungsweisen bezieht sich darauf, daß sich das Leben und Zusammenleben der Menschen immer in bestimmten Üblichkeiten und Gewohnheiten vollzieht: Jeder einzelne wird in bestehende sittliche Verhältnisse hineingeboren und dann entsprechend sozialisiert. Trotz mancher biographischer Unterschiede lernt im gewissen Maße ein jeder, was entweder als anständig oder unanständig gilt, wird ein jeder in bestimmte Bräuche eingeweiht, erfährt, welche Lebenspläne die Menschen seiner Sozietät verfolgen. Wer vom Üblichen abweicht,

---

modernism, responding to a need to provide guidance in an era bereft of foundations and facing confusing options, incommensurable values, and a mindless relativism" (Gras, Vernon W. „The Recent Ethical Turn in Literary Studies." *Mitteilungen des Verbandes Deutscher Anglisten*. 4: 2 (Sep. 1993): 30-41. 30). Even though I would like to argue against postmodernism's advocating a 'mindless relativism', I agree to the observation that many literary texts attempt to (re-)establish systems of values or at least ask the question of which values and points of reference and orientation are still reliable. For a more balanced and perspicacious account of the re-discovery of ethics in the field of literary and cultural criticism, see Feldmann's "Beyond Difference? Recent Developments in Postcolonial and Gender Studies". Feldmann likewise points out that a paradigm change is taking place as "[a]uthors and theorists now tend to invite us to bring words like empathy, love, nostalgia and the sacred back into a discourse which has discredited or even pathologized dreams of coherence and wholeness" (Feldmann, 2007, 131). For an account of the firm philosophical grounding of the 'ethical turn' as well as some of its major exponents, see Parker, David. „Introduction: The Turn to Ethics in the 1990s." *Renegotiating Ethics in Literature, Philosophy and Theory*. Eds. Jane Adamson *et al*. Cambridge: Cambridge UP, 1998. 1-17. On the interplay between literary and ethical theory, i.e. the connection between literary criticism and the philosophical discourse, see, in particular, Chapter 6 of Nussbaum's *Love's Knowledge* (Nussbaum, Martha C. *Love's Knowledge. Essays on Philosophy and Literature*. New York and Oxford: Oxford UP, 1990). In *Experiments and Ethics*, Appiah offers a detailed account of the practical application of ethics in real life and, in addition to that, performs several readings of canonical literary texts, in which he traces the significance of ethics, morality, and virtue (Appiah, Kwame Antony. *Experiments in Ethics*. Cambridge, M.A. and London: Harvard UP, 2008).

[38] Goldberg aptly subtitles his study *Agents and Lives* with the formulation "moral thinking in literature" and thus indicates that, as far as the plot level is concerned, we are in the majority of cases dealing with morals rather than ethics (Goldberg, S. L. *Agents and Lives. Moral Thinking in Literature*. Cambridge: Cambridge UP, 1993).

gilt oft als unmoralisch oder unsittlich. [...] Die gelebten Sitten werden zum Gegenstand der Reflexion, um als Sittlichkeit entweder gerechtfertigt oder verworfen oder doch wenigstens verändert zu werden. Hinausgehend über die Frage, wie wir leben oder «schon immer» gelebt haben, geht es jetzt darum, wie wir besser oder richtig leben sollen. Und damit haben wir eine erste Bestimmung dessen, worum es in der Ethik geht, gewonnen [...]. Wir können sagen: In der Ethik geht es um die Reflexion unserer Lebens- und Verhaltensweisen. Es geht darum, diese zu prüfen, um eine begründete Antwort auf die Fragen geben zu können: Wie sollen wir leben? Was sollen wir tun? Wie handeln wir richtig?[39]

What is more, even in cases when considerations conforming to this definition of ethics do form the analytic focus of an analysis, the very type of the ethics in question is frequently not specified.[40] Here, a critical issue arises from the fact that studies often fail to consider the precise location of the 'ethical' quality of a text, which in fact can be situated on at least three different levels. Accordingly, one may choose to scrutinise actions and motivations on the level of the protagonists, i.e. focus on the realm of the diegesis. A second approach consists in an analysis of the 'ethical' potential of aesthetics. Lastly, one can range ethics on a meta-level and argue that reading is to be understood as an ethical act performed by the reader.[41] Within the present study, considerations of 'ethical' implications will only play a role inasmuch as the presentation of alterity is

---

[39] Fischer, Peter. *Einführung in die Ethik*. München: Fink, 2003. 11-13.

[40] Apart from these methodological objections, the approach as such has been criticised in caustic terms by French philosopher Alain Badiou who describes his motivation for writing *Ethics. An Essay on the Understanding of Evil* as follows: "On the one hand, I was driven by a genuine fury. The world was deeply plunged in 'ethical' delirium. Everyone was busily confusing politics with the hypocrisy of a mindless catechism. The intellectual counter-revolution, in the form of moral terrorism, was imposing the infamies of Western capitalism as the new universal model. The presumed 'rights of man' were serving at every point to annihilate any attempt to invent forms of free thought" (Badiou, Alain. *Ethics. An Essay on the Understanding of Evil*. Tr. Peter Hallward. London and New York: Verso, 2001. liiv).

[41] Davis and Womack propose similar forms of 'ethical' engagement with a text by suggesting that "the ethical consideration of a given work of literature ranges from the close reading of the text itself – particularly in terms of the dilemmas and conundrums presented in the lives of the characters that we encounter there – to the ethical questions that the story raises in the reader's own life beyond the margins of the text. Ethical criticism, at other times, focuses upon the life of the author and how his or her own ethical or moral commitments have shaped the construction, production, and performance of narrative" (Davis, Todd. F. and Kenneth Womack. „Preface. Reading Literature and the Ethics of Criticism." *Mapping the Ethical Turn. A Reader in Ethics, Culture, and Literary Theory*. Eds. Todd F. Davis and Kenneth Womack. Charlottesville and London: Virginia UP, 2001. ix-xiv. x). Predating the 'ethical turn', Frye offers yet another form of 'ethical criticism' in his second essay "Ethical Criticism: Theory of Symbols" (Frye, Northrop. *Anatomy of Criticism. Four Essays*. Princeton NJ: Princeton UP, 1971). Moving away from the question of ethics as such, however, Frye's study quickly turns to a consideration of the various usages of basic literary terms such as symbol, mythos, and allegory.

concerned. I will thus exclusively centre on the aspect of ethicality when such reflections seem to be necessitated by the subject-matter of the texts in question, especially when it comes to the construction of hierarchies and the postulation of binary oppositions in which one side is ascribed an inferior position. Further deliberations on, for instance, a potential ethical obligation on the part of the reader had to be left out since they would have transcended the scope of this study.

For these reasons, I will mainly concentrate on the alleged return of the subject as one major topic in my analyses since this feature proved of crucial signifi-cance with regard to the assessment of the single narratives and their treatment of difference, especially with regard to the role ascribed to the subject in proc-esses of identity formation. As will be demonstrated below, there are presently strong indications of a re-valuation of subjectivity, subjective experience, and individual agency. Accordingly, we find an increasing number of (at least seem-ingly) 'authentic' and 'trustworthy' autodiegetic narrators as well as a growing concern with topics such as individuality, subjectivity, and consciousness. Ad-mittedly, the themes as such do not represent new areas of inquiry but rather result from a long philosophical tradition dating back to early modern philoso-phers such as Descartes and Spinoza.[42] Before turning to different forms of engagement with this theme, I would like to draw attention to an essential ter-minological issue arising in this context: the distinction between the key catego-ries subject, individual, and person. Similarly, we likewise need to differentiate between subjectivity, which Frank defines as "ein Allgemeines, eine Eigen-schaft, die allen selbstbewußten Wesen gemein ist"[43] and individuality, "der Seinsweise eines *einzelnen* Subjekts"[44]. These preliminary reflections lead Frank to the following definitions of the three core concepts: ">Subjekt< (und >ich<) meinen ein Allgemeines, >Person< ein Besonderes, >Individuum< ein

---

[42] As Hübener points out, the category of the subject and its conception have been the topic of philosophical reflections since antique times. Present notions of the subject, however, did only emerge in early modern times, with, for instance, the acknowledgement of the faculty of reason and the capacity of introspection: "Der Subjektbegriff der aristotelischen Onto-Logik eignet sich denkbar schlecht für eine Verbindung mit ihm im heutigen Verständnis an die Seite gestellten Grundbegriffen. So verbinden sich der Sachausdruck »Person« und der Reflexionsausdruck »In-dividuum« zwar schon in der Spätantike miteinander, aber auch in der Prämoderne noch nicht mit dem Reflexionsausdruck »Subjekt«" (Hübener, Wolfgang. „Der dreifache Tod des modernen Subjekts." *Die Frage nach dem Subjekt*. Hg. Manfred Frank *et al*. Frankfurt a. M.: Suhrkamp, 1988. 101-27. 109). For an insightful discussion of the concept of the (social) self, see Bakhurst, David and Christine Sypnowich (eds.). *The Social Self*. London *et al*.: Sage, 1995.
[43] Frank, Manfred. „Subjekt, Person, Individuum." *Individualität*. Hg. Manfred Frank und Anselm Haverkamp. München: Fink, 1988. 3-20. 4.
[44] Frank, 1988, 11, orig. emphasis.

Einzelnes".[45] At the same time, however, the notion of the subject as such proves controversial. In his discussion of the alleged death of the subject, Wetz offers two different conceptions, which he terms the transcendental I and the empirical I.

> Unter ersterem versteht man gewöhnlich ein nicht zur Natur gehörendes Absolutes, das angeblich von sich aus die Welt setzt. Dabei wird das transzendentale Ich einmal vernunftmetaphysisch, einmal geltungslogisch oder konstitutionstheoretisch verstanden, mit absoluter Vernunft oder reinem Denken gleichgesetzt. […] Je nach philosophischem Ansatz gelten wir Menschen entweder als Selbstbewußtsein dieses absoluten Subjekts oder als dieses selbst. […] Von diesem äußerst starken Subjektbegriff, der insbesondere in der Philosophie des Deutschen Idealismus, Neukantianismus und der Phänomenologie entwickelt wurde, läßt sich ein schwächerer unterscheiden. Danach ist jeder Mensch zwar auch ein Subjekt, aber ein endliches, vergängliches, bedingtes, das, weit entfernt von jeglicher Absolutheit, ein von Natur und Geschichte abhängiges Wesen ist. Es wird grundsätzlich bestimmt von Momenten wie Körperlichkeit, Zeitlichkeit, Geschichtlichkeit, Sprachlichkeit.[46]

In the present study, I follow the latter definition since the engagements with the topic of subject-constitution under consideration here tend to emphasise precisely those qualities outlined by Wetz. Accordingly, we, for instance, detect a clear focus on aspects such as corporeality and materiality. Even though the selected novels do not outrightly deny the social and discursive constructedness of the subject, the subject is nevertheless presented as a complete and coherent unity or is at least perceived by the protagonists in this way. Obviously, this perception has considerable repercussions on the construction of identity, which clashes with what Frank terms the postmodern or deconstructivist claim of the death of the subject.[47]

With respect to the literary reaction to these recent transformations and shifts, Schabert posits a connection between the renewed interest in the subject and the re-emergence of humanistic approaches:

---

[45] Frank, Manfred. *Die Unhintergehbarkeit von Individualität. Reflexionen über Subjekt, Person und Individuum aus Anlaß ihrer >postmodernen< Toterklärung*. Frankfurt a. M.: Suhrkamp, 1986. 25.
[46] Wetz, Franz Josef. „Wie das Subjekt sein Ende überlebt: Die Rückkehr des Individuums in Foucaults und Rortys Spätwerk." *Geschichte und Vorgeschichte der modernen Subjektivität*. Bd. 2. Hg. Reto Luzius Fetz *et al*. Berlin und New York: de Gruyter, 1998. 1277-90. 1278.
[47] Frank, 1986, 7.

> Mit der Umorientierung schließt die Literatur an eine lange Tradition
> des Engagements an. Sie trifft wieder zusammen mit einer feministi-
> schen Ethik, die die 1970er Jahre überlebt hat (MATILAND, BARKER,
> CHURCHILL, DANKIELS und andere), macht gemeinsame Sache mit
> der Immigrantenliteratur, die ihrerseits Gesellschaftskritik übt und Mo-
> delle positiver Gemeinsamkeit entwirft [...]. Doch Nach-Postmoderne
> ist nicht gleich Vor-Postmoderne. Im Unterschied zum alten *liberal hu-*
> *manism* fühlt sich der neue Humanismus zur theoretischen Rechtferti-
> gung verpflichtet. Man weiß, dass die eigene Position nur eine Setzung
> ist, die gegenüber anderen Positionen begründet werden sollte.[48]

Even though I basically agree with Schabert's statement on a theoretical foundation which distinguishes the old liberal humanism from the new humanism, I
will refrain from using the term new or New Humanism as, denoting a very
specific type of humanism, it might easily prove misleading since it carries associations which do not apply in the present context[49].

As my interpretations aim to demonstrate, the novelty in the treatment of difference lies especially in the individual orchestrations of subject-formation. At this
point, we may likewise detect one of the most prominent deviations from what
may be termed the 'postmodern' pattern: By contrast to the latter narratives, the
texts covered here promote the possibility of a stable, coherent identity. Nevertheless, they, at the same time, do not subscribe to essentialising notions of

---

[48] Schabert, 2006, 415, orig. emphasis.
[49] Lüking describes the "New Humanism" as a particular 'brand' of (American) Humanism, the
heyday of which can be dated to the period from 1890 to 1940. For the characteristic features of
this movement, see Lüking, Bernd. *Der amerikanische «New Humanism» Eine Darstellung seiner
Theorie und Geschichte*. Bern *et al.*: Lang, 1975. By contrast, Puledda does not define the New
Humanism as confined to a specific period in the history of ideas of a specific cultural formation
but rather considers it a possible future development or project. Writing before the turn of the
millennium he states, "it may be that we are glimpsing the outlines of the first planetary civiliza-
tion. If that does turn out to be the case, then it is possible that New Humanism will indeed find
fertile ground for the growth and spread of its ideas. [...] And it will be then perhaps that we can
truly begin, both as a human organization, as a community, and in our own lives as individuals, to
ask ourselves profoundly about the destiny of humanity and the meaning of our own actions. New
Humanism is precisely an attempt to give answers to these questions" (Puledda, Salvatore. *On
Being Human. Interpretations of Humanism from The Renaissance to the Present*. Tr. Andrew
Hurley. San Diego: Latitude, 1997. 152). What is more, the term 'humanism' in itself proves
ambiguous as it cannot be considered a homogeneous, clearly defined approach or concept. On
the contrary, the term 'humanism' – frequently coupled with additional labels such as 'new',
'liberal', 'secular' or 'critical' – has been applied in a variety of different contexts and has therefore also been associated with opposing tenets and aims. It is for this reason that Halliwell and
Mousley suggest that, rather than assuming the existence of one unified concept of humanism, we
need to acknowledge the fact that we are dealing with humanisms in the plural (Halliwell, Martin
and Andy Mousley. *Critical Humanisms. Humanist/Anti-Humanist Dialogues*. Edinburgh: Edinburgh UP, 2003. 1-2).

identity. Instead of foregrounding the fluid, temporary, and constructed quality of any identity formation, they acknowledge the desire for a modicum of stability and continuity and try to cater to that need. Most importantly, while the single narratives do not deny that, in the realm of identity formation, we are dealing with social constructs, they still may be understood to suggest that this aspect proves primarily of theoretical interest since individual subjects (or, to be more precise, their literary counterparts) are shown to strive for lasting identities and apparently search for an 'eternal quality' or 'inner core' so as to endow their self-images with a certain continuity. This phenomenon mirrors Tew's finding that "[r]ecent negotiations of any 'core identity' perversely encourage both a sense of dislocation and loss, *and* a nostalgia for the illusory lost centre evoked."[50] Accordingly, we are not merely presented with a naïve return to essentialist positions on identity construction but are rather confronted with a possible reaction to the partial inapplicability of theorisations of identity to the lived reality of concrete persons. In fact, there seems to be increasing support for the conviction that most human beings search for an identity or self-image based on a stable core, i.e. that they need at least the illusion that identities are ultimately grounded on some kind of unchanging, lasting quality inherent in every human being, which, so to speak, constitutes their 'true self'.[51] Even though this assumption carries a certain metaphysical element as it is faintly reminiscent of religious ideas such as the (eternal) soul, one may nevertheless argue that this search for stability is likewise closely connected to a tendency to bring the materiality of human existence back to the fore. Rather than considering 'reality' exclusively as the product of specific discursive formations, a growing body of recent theorising has begun to take the tangible, material aspects of life into account as well. My diagnosis therefore chimes in with the recent turn to categories and entities such as the body, presence, and reality to be observed in philosophical discourses and cultural studies.[52]

---

[50] Tew, Philip. *The Contemporary British Novel*. London and New York: Continuum, 2004. 151, orig. emphasis.

[51] Maalouf discussed the "need to belong" and the significance of affiliations in a globalised world already a decade ago. Despite some lucid insights into the varying prominence of specific markers of identity such as 'Muslim' (mainly brought about by changes in political constellations), his study leads him to the rather shallow conclusion that "every individual should be able to identify, at least to some degree, both with the country he lives in and with our present-day world. [...] Each of us should be encouraged to accept his own diversity, to see his identity as the sum of all his various affiliations, instead of as only one of them raised to the status of the most important, made into an instrument of exclusion and sometimes into a weapon of war" (Maalouf, Amin. *In the Name of Identity. Violence and the Need to Belong*. Tr. Barbara Bray. London: Penguin, 2003. 159).

[52] This seems to be implied by an increasing number of conferences and panels focussing on this topic, as, for instance, the International Graduate Conference in Philosophy at the FU Berlin on the topic "Beyond Signification – Nach den Zeichen" (07./08.12.2007; for individual talks, see „Beyond Signification – Nach den Zeichen. Internationale Graduiertenkonferenz." *Institut für Philosophie. Freie Universität Berlin*. 17.02.08. <http://userpage.fu-berlin.de/~jgs/english.html>) or the conference "Das Andere der Trans/Differenz?" organised by the Graduiertenkolleg Kultur-

The current academic interest in categories such as presence and materiality and their re-valuation in literary and cultural studies have similarly been confirmed by the propositions brought forward in a special edition of the periodical *Merkur*. In their introductory note, the authors state: „Richtig jedoch ist die Beobachtung, daß seit geraumer Zeit ein größeres Interesse für die konkrete Erscheinung, für Präsenz, Substanzialität, das Phänomenale aufgekommen ist."[53] This tendency towards a return to the 'real' and a growing concern about materiality is mirrored by the increasing willingness to engage in interdisciplinary studies in order to find new ways of theorising the 'matter' of things. In the introduction to his aptly titled study *Material Cultures. Why some things matter*, Miller highlights the change of perspective currently emerging in the examination of things:

> The development of material culture studies may then be seen as a two-stage process. The first phase came in the insistence that things matter and that to focus upon material worlds does not fetishize them since they are not some separate superstructure to social worlds. [...] This book represents a second stage in the development of material culture studies inasmuch as the point that things matter can now be argued to have been made. [...] The volume demonstrates what is to be gained by focussing upon the diversity of material worlds which become each other's contexts rather than reducing them either to models of the social world or to specific subdisciplinary concerns such as the study of textiles or architecture.[54]

Whereas the studies collected in Miller's volume centre on the sheer materiality of things and are thus not directly related to the analysis of texts, the aspect of a connection between objects and specific meanings or symbolic functions also bears a certain relevancy for the topics under discussion here. Among the aspects stressed in the novels, one concern, for instance, consists in the signifi-

---

hermeneutik at Friedrich-Alexander-Universität Erlangen-Nürnberg in November 2008, which focused on the following aspect: „Wenn Transdifferenz dabei Sinnformen bezeichnet, in denen semiotische Differenzen durchkreuzt aber nicht aufgelöst werden, die also durch Ungewissheit und Unschärfe gekennzeichnet sind, liegt das Andere der Transdifferenz in jenem Bereich der Sinnkonstitution, in dem Sinn (scheinbar) ohne semiotische Vermittlung generiert wird: als Gegebenheit, Evidenz, Präsenz oder Unmittelbarkeit" („Das Andere der Trans/Differenz?" *Graduiertenkolleg Kulturhermneutik, Friedrich-Alexander-Universität Erlangen-Nürnberg*. 17.02.08. <http://www.kulturhermeneutik.uni-erlangen.de/konferenz2008/Konferenz%20-%20Das%20Andere%20der%20Trans-Differenz.pdf>).

[53] Bohrer, Karl Heinz und Kurt Scheel (Hg.). *Merkur. Deutsche Zeitschrift für europäisches Denken*. 9, 10 (2005): n.p.

[54] Miller, Daniel. „Why some Things Matter." *Material Cultures. Why some Things Matter*. Ed. Daniel Miller. Chicago: U of Chicago P, 1998. 3-21. 3.

cance of material objects and goods in processes of identity construction, especially as far as collective identities are concerned. It is primarily in the novels covered in the first set of analyses that the protagonists frequently refer to brand names, film titles, and celebrities in order to express certain affiliations and to create specific personae for themselves. Seeing the particularly prominent function of brand names, aspects of material culture have to be taken into account in order to grasp the symbolic value of specific objects. Hereby, another topic worthy of deeper investigation results from the representation of certain modes of behaviour as 'authentic'. Interestingly enough, what the protagonists promote as authentic forms of behaviour often prove, on closer examination, to consist of an amalgam of various 'cultural' influences, which, due to the way they are staged, assume the status of representing the only 'truthful' or 'real' type of conduct. Invariably, these reflections on authentic and therefore 'correct' or sanctioned modes of behaviour are linked to considerations of ethnic identity and the significance of a person's cultural background.

As far as the collective identities resulting from the adoption of, for instance, 'authentic' black or desi behaviour are concerned, I would like to draw attention to some crucial features of the concept of collective identity as such. As Wren states,

> the seemingly obvious distinction between personal and group identity is much more complex than first appears, as is the subdivision of the latter into social identity and cultural identity. Part of the complexity is the fact that each of these terms has a subjective sense as well as an objective one.[55]

In my interpretations, I follow Wren's usage of the terms 'group identity' and 'cultural identity' "to denote [...] the subjective fact that a person perceives himself or herself as participating in a certain web of human relationship"[56]. Yet, seeing that I rely on fictional texts as source material, I will focus primarily on the literary and rhetorical structures by which a sense of affiliation is expressed; simultaneously, it will be demonstrated which motives and symbols are used in order to convey ideas such as commonality and belonging.

A further link between literary texts and concepts of identity construction emerges from the fact that both personal and collective identities may be con-

---

[55] Wren, Thomas. „Cultural and Personal Identity. Philosophical Reflections on the Identity Discourse of Social Psychology." *Personal and Moral Identity*. Ed. Albert W. Musschenga *et al.* Dordrecht: Kluwer, 2002. 231-58. 233.
[56] Wren, 2002, 234.

sidered to contain a narrative component. For this reason, Appiah assumes a close connection between specific narrative forms and their application in 'daily reality'. Moreover, he treats collective identities as a kind of template which may serve as a model for individual types of identity constructions:

> Collective identities, in short, provide what we might call scripts: narratives that people can use in shaping their projects and in telling their life stories. [...] So we should acknowledge how much our personal histories, the stories we tell of where we have been and where we are going, are constructed, like novels and movies, short stories and folktales, within narrative conventions. Indeed, one of the things that popular narratives (whether filmed or televised, spoken or written) do for us is to provide models for telling our lives. At the same time, part of the function of our collective identities – of the whole repertory of them that a society makes available to its members – is to structure possible narratives of the individual self.[57]

Therefore, my reading of the chosen texts will first of all be guided by the question of how the act of narration is employed to generate meaning. This aspect is closely connected to the following considerations: Are narratives employed to create meaning as well as to establish a feeling of community and belonging? Are the resulting constructions confined to a particular circle? To whose needs do they cater? And, finally, how is the notion of authenticity conveyed in this context and in which way are 'authentic' (collective) identities created via narrative means? Undoubtedly, the relevancy of these issues is not confined to the intratextual level but likewise pertains to the perception of narrative texts as such as they impact on the assessment of their potential for the generation of meaning in real-life contexts.

Text Selection and Analytic Approach

In order to study recent developments with regard to changes in the presentation of difference, texts that may be ranged under the generic label of the 'contemporary British novel' novel appear particularly well suited for the provision of source material. In my case, the ascription 'contemporary' refers to narratives which were published in the years 2000 to 2006, i.e. a period of time which

---

[57] Appiah, Kwame Anthony. *The Ethics of Identity*. Princeton and Oxford: Princeton UP, 2005. 22.

roughly coincides with the era of the Blair government.[58] Although both the term 'contemporary' and the term 'British' – probably even the concept of 'fiction' as such – prove controversial[59], I chose those labels to indicate my concern with prose writings which, on the one hand, deal with topics particularly relevant in the late 1990s and at the beginning of the new millennium and which, on the other hand, were produced in the 'cultural climate' of this time.

The choice of this thematic outlook was provoked by a variety of reasons which arise from the specific propensities of the genre of the novel, its status in the current literary production, and its reception by the literary market. In view of the fact that one of the intentions of this study consists in outlining possible points of intersection between fiction and social reality, the choice of prose texts stood to reason since the novel is traditionally perceived as the genre closest to life and therefore assumed to mirror 'real life' most adequately.[60] This supposi-

---

[58] Bentley discusses the definition of the term 'contemporary' fiction in greater detail in the Introduction to his study *Contemporary British Fiction*. In this context, he states that „[i]n one sense the very idea of the contemporary in literature is problematic in that the term in common usage refers to the immediate present, and once a book is published it inevitably becomes part of a literary history.[…] Until fairly recently, literature of the second half of the twentieth century tended to be called post-war literature, referring to the Second World War as the starting point fort his literary-historical category. There are a number of problems with that nomenclature […]. Contemporary fiction, then, tends to be defined as the period from the mid-1970s to the present" (Bentley, Nick. *Contemporary British Fiction*. Edinburgh: Edinburgh UP, 2008. 1-2). Even though I, personally, would no longer employ the term 'contemporary' with respect to texts from the 1970s, the quote clearly shows that – as is the case with any periodisation – the category of 'contemporary' remains by necessity somewhat arbitrary. What is more, theorists can only take dates of publication as a point of reference for their classification since the actual starting point or duration of the process of writing cannot ultimately be assessed with precision. Nevertheless, I would like to argue that the publication date in many cases may be treated as an indication on the period in which work on the text was undertaken; moreover, in my examples, the subject-matter frequently suggests that the writing of a novel was to some extent provoked by topical events and social problems characteristic of the late 20th and early 21st century.

[59] For an extended discussion of terminological issues, see Tew, Philip and Mark Addis. „Final Report: Survey on Teaching Contemporary British Fiction." *English Subject Centre* (2007). 03.10.08. <http://www.english.heacademy.ac.uk/explore/projects/archive/contemp/contemp1.php>. For further problems related to the study and teaching of 'contemporary' literature such as canonization or the role of academia in 'privileging' certain writers, see Tönnies, Merle and Steven Barfield (eds.). *Teaching Contemporary Fiction: Anglistik & Englischunterricht*. Special Issue 69 (2007).

[60] With respect to early attempts to define the novel and to set it off against other genres such as romance, the assumption of the novel mirroring 'real life' has been raised over and over again and has been emphasised in particular with respect to the realist novel (see, for instance, Walder, Dennis (ed.). *The Realist Novel*. London and New York: Routledge, 1995). Moreover, Watt's study on "Realism and the Novel Form" may still be considered one of the seminal writings on the topic. With regard to the realisation of realism in a novelistic text, Watt makes an important point by stating that "the 'realism' of the novels of Defoe, Richardson and Fielding is closely associated with the fact that Moll Flanders is a thief, Pamela a hypocrite, and Tom Jones a fornicator. This use of 'realism', however, has the grave defect of obscuring what is probably the most original feature of the novel form. If the novel were realistic merely because it saw life from the

tion is shared, among others, by Head, who grounds his study on British fiction from 1950 to 2000 on the conjecture that "the novel in Britain from 1950-2000 yields a special insight into the most important areas of social and cultural history"[61]. Seeing that the titles selected for discussion here deal primarily with the life realities of different strata of British society, I would like to claim the same for the period covered, i.e. the years 2000 to 2006.

Especially as far as the contemporary literary production in Great Britain is concerned, the novel undoubtedly constitutes the form with the highest output and the largest number of readers. In view of the recent ascent of so-called 'Black British'[62] writers and the hype created around authors such as Monica Ali and Zadie Smith, who have been turned into literary superstars and are deliberately marketed as hyphenated Britons (thereby being promoted as spokes-

---

seamy side, it would only be an inverted romance; but in fact it surely attempts to portray all the varieties of human experience, and not merely those suited to one particular literary perspective: *the novel's realism does not reside in the kind of life it presents, but in the way it presents it*" (Watt, Ian. *The Rise of the Novel. Studies in Defoe, Richardson and Fielding*. Berkely and Los Angeles: California UP, 1960. 11, my emphasis). On the problem of the function of the novel as well as its representational qualities, see Zerweck, Bruno. *Die Synthese aus Realismus und Experiment: Der englische Roman der 1980er und 1990er Jahre aus erzähltheoretischer und kulturwissenschaftlicher Sicht*. Trier: WVT, 2001.

[61] Head, Dominic. *The Cambridge Introduction to Modern British Fiction, 1950-2000*. Cambridge: Cambridge UP, 2002. 1.

[62] I am well aware of the fact that this label is highly controversial and frequently rejected by the writers to whom it is attributed. Nevertheless, I will occasionally use the term 'Black British fiction', in particular when referring to the specific marketing strategies employed to boost sales figures in this genre and when trying to draw attention to the discursive context in which those texts enter the literary market. On the concept of Black British fiction as well as its exploitation as a marketing asset see Nowak, Helge. „Black British Literature – Unity or Diversity?" *Unity in Diversity Revisited? British Literature and Culture in the 1990s*. Eds. Barbara Korte and Klaus Peter Müller. Tübingen: Narr, 1998. 71-87. As English points out, despite the low heuristic value of the expression 'Black British fiction', it has to some extent been established as a hold-all category to encompass a variety of works by formerly 'unclassifiable' authors: "The term "Black British" emerged originally for reasons of political strategy, to unite various minority constituencies into a "counter-hegemonic bloc" (to use the language of those years), but it was taken up in literary and other cultural spheres partly for reasons of commercial and curricular convenience, as a rough and ready way of situating a diverse and as yet uncatalogued array of writers, artists, and works. A third- or fourth-generation Londoner of African descent; an Irish-identified native of Belfast whose father had emigrated from Pakistan; a recent illegal immigrant from Jamaica doing casual labor in Glasgow; or the daughter of a wealthy Parsi businessman, educated in Mumbai and Geneva but now a resident of Holland Park – subjects as differently positioned as these could, if they entered the literary field, be shelved and taught together under the sign of "Black British" writing" (English, James F. „Introduction: British Fiction in a Global Frame." *A Concise Companion to Contemporary British Fiction*. Ed. James F. English. Malden, MA *et al*.: Blackwell, 2006. 1-15. 4). For the problematic of reducing black writers to the role of representatives of a specific experience or community, see likewise Procter, James. „New Ethnicities, the Novel, and the Burdens of Representation." *A Concise Companion to Contemporary British Fiction*. Ed. James F. English. Malden *et al*.: Blackwell, 2006. 101-20.

persons for the 'second generation'), novelistic texts offer a large pool of material on which to draw in a study on strategies in dealing with (internal) difference.[63] Yet, although I believe that a connection or interrelation between 'fact' and 'fiction' exists, I do not wish to suggest a simplistic correspondence between the momentary social situation in Britain and the (re)-negotiation of Britishness in narrative texts, i.e. a one-to-one relationship between 'fact' and 'fiction'. By contrast, I consider literature a particular discursive formation, with the potential to interact in a specific way with 'reality':

> So verstanden bietet die Literatur also nicht lediglich ein Abbild der Realität, das es uns in Analogie zur Subjekt-Objekt-Relation einer naturwissenschaftlichen Theorie ermöglicht, 'die Realität' besser zu verstehen, sondern sie ist als integraler Bestandteil in das kulturelle Apriori verwoben, im Rahmen dessen allein Realität spezifische (perspektivisch gebrochene und raum-zeitlich relative) Formen annehmen kann. Die Literatur bietet aber nicht nur die Möglichkeit, das kulturelle Relationierungspotential in Bewegung zu halten, sondern sie ermöglicht zugleich den reflexiven Blick auf eben dieses Geschehen [...]. Dies resultiert nicht zuletzt aus dem Umstand, daß die Literatur zwar einerseits als Spezialdiskurs neben anderen anzusehen ist, andererseits aber zutiefst *interdiskursiv* geprägt ist.[64]

Moreover, I follow Iser's presuppositions on the interaction between 'fact' and 'fiction':

> A piece of fiction devoid of any connection with known reality would be incomprehensible, consequently, if we are to attempt a description of what is fictional in fiction, there seems to be little point in our clinging

---

[63] Although the increasing power of publishing houses with respect to the selection of texts accepted for publication – and the ensuing marketing campaigns for individual titles – must certainly be taken into account, I am still convinced that the production of literary texts, and novels in particular, can at the same time be strongly influenced by social changes and the general cultural climate at a certain point in time. Although it is undoubtedly possible to list several counter-examples, I would nevertheless like to argue that a considerable body of texts does engage with 'reality' and that literature constitutes one possible way of presenting and discussing social problems – albeit on a different discursive level than, for instance, politics or sociology. For the influence of the literary market on the creation of certain 'fashion trends' within the literary production, see Todd, Richard. „Literary Fiction and the Book Trade." *A Concise Companion to Contemporary British Fiction*. Ed. James F. English. Malden, MA *et al.*: Blackwell, 2006. 19-38.
[64] Glomb, Stefan. „Jenseits von Einheit und Vielheit, Autonomie und Heteronomie – Die fiktionale Erkundung 'dritter Wege' der Repräsentation und Reflexion von Modernisierungsprozessen." *Beyond Extremes. Repräsentation und Reflexion von Modernisierungsprozessen im zeitgenössischen britischen Roman.* Hg. Stefan Glomb und Stefan Horlacher. Tübingen: Narr, 2004. 9-52. 49, orig. emphasis.

> to the old fiction vs. reality concept as a frame of reference; the literary text is a mixture of reality and fiction, and as such it brings about an interaction between the given and the imagined. This interaction produces far more than just a contrast between the two, so that I suggest we discard the opposition of fiction and reality altogether and replace this duality by a triad: the real, the fictional and what I shall term the imaginary. It is out of this triad that I see the text as arising: it cannot be confined to its real elements; nor can it be pinned down to its fictional features, for these in turn do not constitute an end in themselves but are the medium for the appearance of the imaginary.[65]

Thus, while the study is, to some extent, informed by New Historicist principles, it does not represent a purely New Historicist examination, since I do, for instance, not subscribe to the assumption that "there is no division between text and context, or between literature and politics"[66]; I rather intend to treat literature as a discourse holding a special status and, at the same time, being an interdiscursive formation in the sense quoted above. Nevertheless, my analysis is still in tune with several of the basic tenets of New Historicism such as the conviction that the social and the aesthetic discourse exert a reciprocal influence on each other. Consequently, in Greenblatt's words,

> [w]e need to develop terms to describe the ways in which material – here official documents, private papers, newspaper clippings, and so forth – is transferred from one discursive sphere to another and becomes aesthetic property. It would, I think, be a mistake to regard this process as uni-directional – from social discourse to aesthetic discourse – not only because the aesthetic discourse in this case is so entirely bound up with capitalist venture but because social discourse is already charged with aesthetic energies.[67]

Against the background of these considerations, I have chosen the following six novels that can be divided into two subgroups: Section I, which comprises Smith's *On Beauty* (2005), Malkani's *Londonstani* (2006), and Singh Dhali-

---

[65] Iser, Wolfgang. „Fictionalising Acts." *American Studies* 31 (1986): 5-15. 5-6. For a more detailed analysis of the interplay between 'fact' and 'fiction' as well as the processes involved in the act of fictionalisation, see also Iser, Wolfgang. *Das Fiktive und das Imaginäre. Perspektiven literarischer Anthropologie.* Frankfurt: Suhrkamp, 1991. On the problem of fiction and fictionality with respect to Realism, consult Fluck, Winfried. „Fiction and Fictionality in American Realism." *American Studies* 31 (1986): 101-12.

[66] Brannigan, John. *New Historicism and Cultural Materialism.* Houndmills, Basingstoke and London: Macmillan, 1998. 21.

[67] Greenblatt, Stephen. „Towards a Poetics of Culture." *The New Historicism.* Ed. H. Aram Veeser. New York and London: Routledge, 1989. 1-14. 11.

wal's *Tourism* (2006), contains examples of 'Black-British fiction' that deal primarily with ethnic difference. In this part of the study, I will demonstrate how communities are forged on the basis of ethnicity and which further differential categories come into play. Moreover, special attention will be paid to both the rhetoric make-up of the texts and the images and metaphors used to convey ideas such as commonality, community, and belonging.

Section II, covering Evaristo's *Soul Tourists* (2005), McEwan's *Saturday* (2005), and Doughty's *Stone Cradle* (2006), sheds light on the construction of Britishness in particular with respect to strategies of coping with 'the other/Other within'. This second set of texts differs from the first one inasmuch as it focuses on aspects of established differential categories which are often neglected or less frequently discussed than the currently rather topical debate on 'visible alterity' within Britain, i.e. in particular the status of second-generation immigrants who can be singled out merely on the grounds of their skin colour and outer appearance. This thematic outlook with its focus on potentially competing definitions and re-definitions of Englishness[68] and/or Britishness mirrors some of the social tensions and problems which figured dominantly in the political discourse during the years in which the novels were produced and published. Even though I am aware of the fact that the work on a novelistic text does not completely coincide with its date of publication – and that it is only in rare cases such as McEwan's *Saturday* that one specific event may be singled out as the trigger for the creation of a narrative – the chosen novels may nevertheless be roughly dated to the years 2000 to 2006 and thus stem from the second half of the Blair government. Accordingly, they issue from a period in which the appeal of the Cool Britannia campaign had already abated:

> "Challenge", "change", "modernise", "reform", "nation" – by now most of these key words sound very familiar if not worn-out. They have become empty phrases and can be used quite differently, according to the needs of both Labour and Conservatives, as Britain's post-war history testifies. Thus, the spell of New Labour lost much of its previous glamour; no wonder that after 2001 Blair refrained from using the 'New Labour' magic formula officially without giving up his claim that he would create a New Britain and modernise and reform the country.[69]

---

[68] For an extensive discussion of the concept of Englishness as well as individual approaches towards the (re-)definition of the concept, see Habermann's introductory chapter to her study on Englishness in early 20th Century film and literature. Habermann, Ina. *Englishness as a Symbolic Form - Identity, Myth and Memory in 1930s and 1940s English Literature and Film* (Manuscript: 2007).
[69] Kamm, Jürgen and Bernd Lenz. „New Britain: Into the Third Millennium." *New Britain. Politics and Culture*. Ed. Bernd Lenz. Passau: Stutz, 2006. 7-23. 13.

A further increasingly pressing social problem in this decade arose from the blatant lack of integration of a large number of second-generation immigrants, who, even though British citizens by passport, obviously did and still do not identify with England or Great Britain as 'their' nation. Gilroy addresses this problem in *After Empire. Melancholia or Convivial Culture?*, where he comments sarcastically on the status of immigrants and refugees in British society and highlights their changed status after the 9/11 attacks:

> Politically, the detainees' perverse tenure of British citizenship becomes nothing more than a retroactive indictment of the United Kingdom's overly lax immigration control and nationality legislation in the past. A good many of them can, if it becomes politically expedient, be retrospectively stripped of the citizenship they have wrongfully acquired. They have been among us, but they were never actually of us. [...] The real source of their treacherous choices is likely to remain a private, spiritual matter disconnected from the patterns of everyday life inside Britain. [...] They are traitors because immigrants are doomed in perpetuity to be outsiders. [...] Irrespective of where they are born, even their children and grandchildren will never really belong.[70]

This exclusion of certain strata of the population from established society constitutes one of the prime subject-matters addressed in the six novels. As the following analyses will demonstrate, the suggested solutions and the reactions to the growing suspicion towards 'foreign-looking' citizens cover a broad variety of strategies ranging from a retreat to 'one's own' community to an unearthing of allegedly suppressed 'black' elements in European history which finally allow for a reconciliation with one's personal past.

Despite the great heterogeneity of the individual texts in terms of style and thematic outlook, they all share two important features: Each of them tries to develop new strategies in coping with difference that go beyond a mere pluralisation. In addition to that, they aim at the establishment of communities and affiliations and thus, ultimately, attempt to create a feeling of belonging. What is more, all novels centre on one individual or a small group of individuals linked within a family-like structure either on the grounds of 'true' family relationships in terms of bloodline or on the grounds of an ideational relationship. Although the scope of this study does not allow for the consideration of this aspect in greater detail, it nevertheless proves worthwhile to reflect on the following question raised by Freeman:

---

[70] Gilroy, Paul. *After Empire. Melancholia or convivial culture?* Abingdon: Routledge, 2006. 134.

> Is there some dimension of narrativity involved in human life as such? Acknowledging, in other words, the vast differences in conceptions of identity, selfhood, and life itself that have obtained across the course of history, and acknowledging as well the relatively recent emergence of autobiographical narrative (at least in its "post-confessional" phase, where the individual ego takes center stage rather than God), are there any features of the relationship between narrative and identity that are *trans*-historical, that is, universal?[71]

If so, the present thesis may be considered a first point of connection between literary criticism and philosophical as well as sociological discourse.

---

[71] Freeman, Mark. „From Substance to Story. Narrative, Identity, and the Reconstruction of the Self." *Narrative and Identity. Studies in Autobiography, Self and Culture*. Eds. Jens Brockmeier and Donal Carbaugh. Amsterdam and Philadelphia: John Benjamins, 2001. 283-98. 285, orig. emphasis.

Section I – Ethnic Other- and Sameness

This first set of analyses comprises texts which all foreground ethnicity or race[72] as a central differential category. It is from this particular perspective that the novels explore the interplay between individual and collective identity. Despite the fact that ethnicity is generally considered a primarily 'cultural' category based on elements such as traditions, rituals, and habits which are perceived as characteristic of a particular group (usually in a social minority), the narratives nonetheless highlight specific (bodily) features such as skin colour as well as specific dress codes and show that they play an important role with respect to the creation of ethnic affiliations and individual self-images.[73] In addition to that, a striking feature displayed by the novels in Section I consists in the fact that the idea of shared experiences which establish a spiritual bond between people from entirely different strata of society figures much more prominently than in the second set of texts ranged under Section II. Once again, 'bodily' markers – skin colour in particular – are perceived as prime indicators of potentially common experiences. While, in these contexts, aspects such as religious bonds likewise impact on the construction of ethnic identities, they nevertheless appear to be intricately bound up with more 'visible' features. Therefore, the distinction between race and ethnicity – especially if race is likewise considered

---

[72] Over the last years, both of the concepts, i.e. race as well as ethnicity, have been challenged as exclusionist and essentialising. While, at first, only race had been recognised as a potentially problematic category – especially because of its exploitation as a means to naturalise hierarchical binary oppositions and to inferiorise certain social groups – it is only quite recently that concerns about ethnicity as an analytic category have been voiced as well. Accordingly, in 2000, Ashcroft *et al.* still claimed that "[r]ace in the time of neo-colonialism is just as vague and just as resilient as it was at the beginning of the history of European imperialism. It is perhaps up to the concept of *ethnicity* to change the direction of the debate" (Ashcroft, Bill *et al.* „Race." *Post-Colonial Studies. The Key Concepts*. London and New York: Routledge, 2000, orig. emphasis). I would like to argue that this perception has undergone a decisive change with ethnicity now likewise being seen as a less neutral category. In view of the use of the term ethnicity, in particular as the adjective 'ethnic', we come to realise that, in everyday discourse, it is frequently employed as a strategy to set off the 'exotic' or 'foreign' from the (white) norm. It is for this reason that I regard the definition offered by Ashcroft *et al.* as not entirely applicable to the present situation in Britain as their theorisation of ethnicity as being "usually deployed as an expression of a positive self-perception that offers certain advantages to its members" (Ashcroft, Bill *et al.* „Ethnicity." *Post-Colonial Studies. The Key Concepts*. London and New York: Routledge, 2000) neglects to take into account that ethnicity frequently does not constitute a self-chosen label but rather represents a strategic categorisation for the implicit affirmation of a white (so to speak 'non-ethnic') norm. For a highly insightful discussion of the categories of 'race' and 'ethnicity' including a section on instances when the two labels can actually be seen to overlap, consult Cornell, Stephen and Douglas Hartmann. *Ethnicity and Race. Making Identity in a Changing World*. Thousand Oaks, London and New Delhi: Pine Forge Press, 1998.

[73] Interestingly enough, these texts all stem from writers who hail from a so-called 'ethnic' background and who have therefore frequently been classified as Black British writers. As already stated above, this label persists despite its controversial quality and its use could therefore not be entirely avoided here.

a cultural construct which is not founded on 'biological' or genetic facts – proves virtually untenable and the apparently clear-cut boundaries between the two concepts begin to blur.

Seeing that, at the moment, there seems to be a rather broad consensus on the preferability of ethnicity over race, I would like to elaborate on this problem by considering the status of the concept of 'ethnicity' in greater detail before turning to the examination of the selected texts. In view of the historical abuses of race as a category – starting with theorists such as de Gobineau and culminating in the atrocities of the Nazi regime – race as a criterion for scientific analysis has been largely abandoned in academic discourse. Especially in the disciplines of sociology and cultural studies, the category is today deemed dated[74] with 'ethnicity' being in general favoured in discussions of the issue. Hereby, one may observe that sociologists often privilege the term 'ethnicity' over the term 'race' because it is considered to take into account the social constructedness of any seemingly 'natural' analytic category and therefore does (apparently) not fall prey to essentialising notions. Nevertheless, on closer examination, 'ethnicity' does not prove as unproblematic as it appears on first sight. One controversial aspect consists in the fact that the term is frequently employed in a much less reflected fashion than 'race.' Accordingly, in the majority of cases, the term 'race' is used with great caution and, in general, a high awareness of possibly discriminating associations exists. Especially in a German context, there is hardly any usage of the term without the use of scare quotes to indicate the writer's distancing him- or herself from Third Reich ideology. By contrast, the potentially exclusive elements inherent in the notion of ethnicity are, on the grounds of it allegedly being a purely 'cultural' category, less obvious and therefore frequently disregarded. As a result, we witness a broad consensus that 'ethnic groups' are not formed on the basis of shared biological or genetic features but rather emerge because of shared customs, traditions, and habits. Despite the general agreement on the lack of any biological 'foundation', the usages of the concept of ethnicity often fail to take into account the fact that notions of 'ethnicity' are likewise subject to change and that the composition of 'ethnic' groups is far from being stable. The process of labelling individuals as members of a particular ethnic group may therefore nonetheless involve an essentialising act since individuals are reduced to specific (bodily) features – frequently highly 'visible' markers such as complexion or hair texture – according to which they are classified and put into pidgeonholes. Even though the features deemed characteristic of the respective groups are, at least in theory, considered purely social, it is not uncommon that biology, or to be more precise, racial

---

[74] Giddens, Anthony. *Sociology*. Cambridge and Malden, M.A.: polity, [5]2006. 486. For a discussion of the lasting significance of race and ethnicity as crucial markers of both individual and collective identities as well as an account of the interplay between the two categories, see Song, Miri. *Choosing Ethnic Identity*. Cambridge: Polity, 2003.

ideology enters the equation again. This phenomenon shows best when we examine the status of those social groups which are generally referred to as 'ethnic'. As has been pointed out above, the term 'ethnic' is often employed to demarcate 'visibly different' groups from the 'white norm'. Thus, in the last instance, essentialist notions on biologically or genetically defined characteristic traits are veiled by the employment of the allegedly more neutral and reflexive term 'ethnicity'. The same holds true for so-called 'ethnic' commodities, practices, and traditions. Here, we may also observe the implicit establishment of a non-ethnic norm – covering the known and familiar – as opposed to what is 'ethnic', i.e. foreign to the 'indigenous' culture. Therefore, the label 'ethnic' may serve to erect boundaries between the 'true' locals, i.e. fully-fledged citizens, and the 'newcomers' who, to some extent, still remain outsiders to their 'host' society. Giddens confirms this finding in his discussion of the concept of 'ethnicity':

> [R]eferences to ethnicity and ethnic differences can be problematic, especially if they suggest contrast with a 'non-ethnic' norm. In Britain, for example, ethnicity is commonly used to refer to cultural practices and traditions that differ from 'indigenous' British practices. The term 'ethnic' is applied to realms as diverse as cuisine, clothing, music and neighbourhoods to designate practices that are 'non-British'. Using ethnic labels in this collective manner risks producing divisions between 'us' and 'them', where certain parts of the population are seen as 'ethnic' and others not.[75]

In the socio-political context, ethnicity likewise plays a decisive role. When we contemplate ascriptions such as 'Black-British'[76] or 'Asian-British', it becomes

---

[75] Giddens, 2006, 488.

[76] In fact, the category 'Black British' comprises two controversial elements. First of all, notions of Britishness constitute a persistent bone of contention in both the sociological and the cultural studies discourse. Moreover, 'black' as an umbrella term proves, on closer examination, a very vague, only fluidly defined concept. Nowak draws attention to the divisive features of the groups of people covered by the 'Black British' label. In doing so, he emphasises that we are by no means dealing with a homogeneous group of people, as they "do not share a common heritage, but rather belong to several groups of diverse ethnic and cultural origins", they hail from different geographical regions, both as far as their family background and their actual place of living is concerned, they do not share the same social positions in terms of education, profession and family situations, and "finally, while inter-ethnic marriages between black (Caribbean or African) and white partners are becoming more and more common, inter-ethnic marriages between people of Asian descent and either black or white partners continue to be comparatively rare" (Nowak, 1998, 73-4). Despite this heterogeneity of 'Black British' citizens as a group, the construction of a potential bond due to shared experiences and allegedly common 'roots' proves functional in a number of situations as will be demonstrated below. Thus, 'Black Britishness' as a discursive construction may apparently nevertheless offer a foundation for bonding, which Britishness or Englishness on their own do not seem to provide.

obvious to which degree our perception of ethnicity is guided by the 'white norm'. Apparently, Britishness – as long as it is not prefixed by a specifying adjective such as black or Asian – is still taken to imply whiteness.[77] This fact raises a particularly pressing problem for so-called second-generation immigrants who, legally, represent British citizens but are, in everyday life, nevertheless singled out as 'alien' to established society. As a consequence, for this group of mainly young people, any type of collective identity is all but forcibly connected with ethnicity, whereas their white peers are usually not confronted with being reduced to their skin colour.[78] It is only quite recently that the idea of an 'English' ethnicity has been suggested. In his study of the same title, Young traces the development of this concept and demonstrates the differences in terms of orchestration and intended effect in the construction of an English ethnicity (as opposed to the marginalising depiction of 'ethnic' groups usually to be witnessed in everyday discourses):

> Englishness was never really about England, its cultural essence or national character, at all. The concept of Englishness in the nineteenth century was not so much developed as a self-definition of the English themselves, as a way of characterizing the essence of their national identity – after all, being English already, they hardly needed it. It was rather elaborated as a variety of what Benedict Anderson has called 'long-distance nationalism', though of a distinct kind. Rather than being the creation of the far-off diasporic community, as Anderson describes,

---

[77] Interestingly enough, in the material compiled for the participants of a conference on the future of multi-ethnic Britain held at the University of Reading in 1994, the Runnymede Trust refrained from referring to Black people as an ethnic minority and rather chose the expression "Black and ethnic minority", arguing that "virtually all Black people, and also some South Asian people, define themselves and each other as Black rather than as belonging to an ethnic minority" (The Runnymede Trust. „The Report of the Commission on the Future of Multi-Ethnic Britain. 25.11.08. <http://www.runnymedetrust.org/publications/29/74.html> 12). An extended version of the document was published in 2000 as the so-called Parekh Report (Parekh, Bhikhu C. *The Future of Multi-Ethnic Britain. The Report of the Commission on the Future of Multiethnic Britain*. Profile: London, 2000).The minute distinctions and the high level of reflexion displayed by these publications, however, seems to constitute an exception rather than the norm with respect to the general perception of members of 'ethnic groups' in Britain.

[78] This phenomenon is wittily exploited in *Londonstani*, the second novel under discussion in this section. I would like to argue that the production of narrative texts which acknowledge the lasting significance of race/ethnicity and recognise its impact on young people's lives but nevertheless deal with it in creative ways indicates that new strategies are being developed to cope especially with ethnicity/race as a differential category. These novels, for instance, topple established stereotypical notions on ethnicity and thereby disclose the degree to which they have become naturalised. What is likewise striking here is the light, humoristic note many of the narratives adopt. Thus, instead of succumbing to moralistic identity politics, the texts attempt to offer a new perspective on ethnicity without trying to, as it were, educate the reader.

Englishness was created for the diaspora – an ethnic identity designed for those who were not English, but rather of English descent.[79]

With respect to second-generation immigrants, we encounter a similar phenomenon albeit with a reverse effect. In their case, the label 'ethnic' is applied to a diasporic community. While, for the parent generation, this diasporic grounding resulted from their having migrated to a foreign country, the second generation rather lives in a 'felt diaspora': Although, from a legal point of view, they represent British citizens, many youths with an 'ethnic' background apparently still consider themselves as members of a diaspora rather than British subjects. Even though the situation has undergone considerable changes since the late 1960s – with Powell's infamous Rivers of Blood speech as a sad culmination – the implicit confusion of race with ethnicity still continues today. Moreover, even though open discrimination against black people may have abated, the perception of Black-British communities as an element 'foreign' to established British society has not been dispelled. Strikingly, Alexander's explicit aim in her study on black youth culture in Britain is "to show that black youths are concerned with *the construction of new cultural alternatives*, in which identity is created and re-created as part of an ongoing and dynamic process"[80]. As this brief quote reveals, what is sought for are *not* possible ways of assimilation but rather the development of alternatives to the existing system.

A further problem which afflicts members of the second generation consists in finding possible bases for collective identities and forms of identification with other subjects sharing the same experiences so as to build up group affiliations. Having immigrated to Britain as their new – and projected *temporary* home country – the parental generation could still identify with their peers from the 'old home country' and consciously locate their roots on, for instance, the Indian subcontinent. This possibility, however, is closed off to the second-generation who, apparently, often feel marginalised in white British society and do not consider themselves as fully accepted members of the English nation with the same status as their white counterparts.[81] At the same time, the assumption of their being rooted in a different cultural context assumes an all but mythological quality. While members of the second generation have been born and raised in Britain and frequently have never even been to their alleged 'home

---

[79] Young, Robert J. C. *The Idea of English Ethnicity*. Malden MA *et al.*: Blackwell, 2008. 1.

[80] Alexander, Claire E. *The Art of Being Black. The Creation of Black British Youth Identities*. Oxford and New York: Oxford UP, 1996. 18, my emphasis.

[81] Especially after the London bombings, a heated discussion arose about the state of integration of second generation immigrants. Apparently, the shock of the attacks was increased considerably by the realisation that the bombings had not been perpetrated by foreign Islamists infiltrating British society but had rather been committed by youngsters who had been born and raised in the UK but obviously did not identify with Britain as 'their' country.

country', they still refer to their parents' place of origin when talking about their (spiritual) home.

Another difficulty arises from the fact that idea(l)s of individual vitae will, by necessity, have to undergo considerable transformations. While a great number of first-generation immigrants entertained hopes of ultimately leaving Great Britain in order to move back home – a phenomenon referred to as the 'return myth' – the second generation do no longer have this option of going back to the allegedly familiar and welcoming realm of the old 'home'.[82] It is for this reason that the frugal way of life adopted by many first-generation immigrants in order to save enough money for a speedy return will most probably not prove satisfactory to their offspring. This problem of clashing expectations towards one's personal goals in life is raised repeatedly in both literary and filmic renditions of the topic and constitutes a pressing concern which causes much intergenerational conflict. Due to those different preconditions, the younger generation is confronted with a lack of role models to provide guidelines for their future lives. It is not least due to this reason that the 'return myth' has by now come to be increasingly replaced by other myths which cater to the second generation's changed situation and offer the potential for bonding outside established British society. In this process, one of the most prominent developments is the creation of an 'imaginary homeland'. Especially for black people, Africa is rendered an all but mythological space which serves as a substitute for 'real' roots and thus acts as a supplement for the concrete homeland they, in contrast to their parents, lack.

> In some non-specific way, then, a new idea of African-ness conveniently dissociated from the politics of contemporary Africa operates transnationally and interculturally through the symbolic projection of 'race' as kinship. [...] Although contemporary nationalism draws creatively on the traces of romantic theories, of national belonging, and national identity derived from the ethnic metaphysics of eighteenth-century Europe, Afrocentric thinking attempts to construct a sense of

---

[82] In his study on the living conditions and ways of life of first generation immigrants, Dahya underlines an important difference between the first and the second generation. Even though the majority ultimately stayed in Britain, the 'return myth' provided a pivotal point of reference to those having immigrated to Britain in the hope of financial gain. As Dahya states, "the immigrants consider themselves to be transients and not settlers. However, this is not to imply that the immigrants, or any significant number of them, will in fact return home. None the less, this myth or ideology of return is an important factor that has consequences with regard to the immigrant community's social organization, the immigrants' willingness to endure hardship in work and living conditions, and their emphasis on savings which are remitted to their families in Pakistan" (Dahya, Badr. „The Nature of Pakistani Ethnicity in Industrial Cities in Britain." *Urban Ethnicity.* Ed. Abner Cohen. London *et al.*: Tavistock, 1974. 77-118. 83). This myth is obviously lost to the British-born generation, who frequently have not even been to their alleged 'home country'.

black particularity *outside* the notion of national identity. Its founding problem lies in the effort to figure sameness across national boundaries and between nation-states.[83]

Among the novels covered in Section I, it is especially Smith's *On Beauty* which deals with the fiction of shared African roots and the idea of a universal bond between all black people due to their shared ancestry.

Obviously, the increasing number of British citizens with a migratory background likewise necessitates a re-consideration of the definitions of Englishness and Britishness[84]. This topic is raised by the second and by the third novel included in this section, *Londonstani* and *Tourism*. Once again, the events related in the narratives mirror developments also accounted for in sociological studies describing the impact of globalisation and internationalisation on British society. With respect to the changes in concepts of identity resulting from these processes, it has repeatedly been underscored that former, allegedly reliable points of reference such as the nation state have broken away and that affiliations have become much less stable and self-explicatory. As Hall explains in his seminal essay "Old and New Identities, Old and New Ethnicities", the old logics of identity prove no longer applicable since the "great collective social identities which we thought of as large-scale, all-encompassing, homogeneous, as unified collective identities"[85] have been disclosed as social constructs and lost their former viability. Nevertheless,

> [t]hese great collective social identities have not disappeared. Their purchase and efficacy in the real world that we all occupy is ever present. But the fact is that none of them is, any longer, in either the social historical or epistemological place where they were in our conceptualizations of the world in the recent past. They cannot any longer be thought in the same homogeneous form. We are as attentive to their inner differences, their inner contradictions, their segmentations and their frag-

---

[83] Gilroy,1993, 195, orig. emphasis.

[84] In this respect, it is interesting to note that apparently the majority of hyphenated Britons do not identify with Englishness but rather prefer Britishness. Strikingly, the labels used for all types of hyphenated identities unvaryingly employ the adjective British as, for instance, in Black British (rather than Black English) even though the term British might, for instance, also be asscociated with the British Empire and the time of Colonialism. For a detailed discussion of 'Black Britishness' in fiction, see Stein, Mark. „The Black British Bildungsroman and the Transformation of Britain." *Unity in Diversity Revisited? British Literature and Culture in the 1990s*. Tübingen: Narr, 1998. 89-105.

[85] Hall, Stuart. „Old and New Identities, Old and New Ethnicities." *Culture, Globalization and the World-System. Contemporary Conditions for the Representation of Identity*. Ed. Anthony D. King. London: Macmillan, 1991. 41-68. 44.

mentations as we are to their already-completed homogeneity, their unity and so on.[86]

In all of the three novels discussed in Section I, ethnicity is foregrounded as the main component of the protagonists' personal identities and it is shown to play an important role in the construction of their self-images. With respect to the production of these self-images, we detect a clear interaction between personal and collective identities as the former rely heavily on elements such as group affiliations and the ideas of self-fashioning perpetuated within a specific circle. As a result, personal identities are strongly informed by the collective identities an individual choses for themselves (or is obliged to conform to). Consequently, the formation of identities and self-images must not be seen as an exclusively individual process limited to the decisions and aspirations of a single person but rather be treated as a process of negotiation between different sets of expectations, values, and ideals. Even though the paths chosen by the respective characters differ to a high degree, one may nevertheless, among all of them, detect a general longing for lasting affiliations and points of reference which provide a certain security and stability. Frequently, this desire results in attempts to establish oneself as a member of a group in which membership and non-membership is unambiguously defined. Thus, binary structures are being sought or deliberately introduced as they, despite their potentially essentialising effects, at least provide definite guidelines on who belongs and who is excluded, and thereby create the illusion that all members share certain features (among them 'ethnic' ones). This move allows for the perception of single groups as homogeneous entities. Apparently, what the protagonists are ultimately in search of is a clearly defined position within a confined circle in which strict rules on membership status exist so that the question of affiliations may be solved unambiguously.[87] In view of the loss of significance of larger entities such as the nation state, it does not come as a surprise that small-scale units, the family or a specific neighbourhood being prime examples in this context, seem to be increasingly taking over the function formerly fulfilled by 'official', i.e. politically implemented, networks. In all of the texts chosen for analysis, the protagonists have abandoned – or were, in a certain respect, forced to do so – the great social collective identities described by Hall in favour of lower-scale, locally grounded units.[88]

---

[86] Hall, 1991, 45.

[87] Of course, the situation is complicated as individuals are in general members of more than one group. This problem, however, is solved comparatively easily by the context-depending foregrounding of specific aspects: Accordingly, the strength of the feeling of connectivity to one group or another may vary as a figure moves between different social and cultural spheres.

[88] One might argue that this tendency to some extent reflects the phenomenon referred to as 'glocalization', i.e. the idea that, simultaneously to an increasing globalisation, the local re-gains increasing significance.

With regard to the respective groups which provide the context for the construction of collective identities, it is striking to note that the metaphor of the family is repeatedly drawn upon to characterise the relationship between individual members.[89] Hereby, two aspects prove remarkable: First, the family is perceived as a somewhat 'natural' entity even though, from a sociological standpoint (and in view of the variety of different types of family groupings presently existing or coming into existence), attempts to define the term 'family' by necessity remain very vague. Accordingly, Giddens describes it as "a group of persons directly linked by kin connections, the adult members of which assume responsibility for caring for children"[90]. Although ideas such as the obligation to support other (grown-up) members of the family or to show an unquestioned solidarity towards each other constitute widespread associations, they do by no means represent inherent characteristic features of the family from a sociological angle. It is furthermore remarkable that, especially in *On Beauty* and *Tourism*, the values attributed to the family are almost exclusively positive ones. Despite occasional rows and ruptures, the family, in these two texts, is perceived as a source of stability and support and seen as a framework for the establishment of close personal connections and bonds. As will be demonstrated below, this plot element may be considered a further potentially 'postpostmodern' feature as we observe a return to 'traditional' values with the restoration of the family being presented as a worthwhile goal.

---

[89] With respect to this metaphor, we observe the journey of a trope through numerous discursive systems: In history, the metaphor of the family has repeatedly been used to express the proximity between members of a group. Examples may be found in a variety of discourses ranging from religion, over politics to youth culture. Worsley explains this fact by the ubiquity of the family as a basic structure of life at least in Western society: "Thus because family relationships are so basic, familistic terms are often used in *non*-family circumstances to emphasize certain ideal types of relationships" (Worsley, Peter. *Introducing Sociology*. Penguin: Harmondsworth, 1970. 116, orig. emphasis).

[90] Giddens, 2006, 206.

Zadie Smith's *On Beauty* – The Creation of Sameness via the Metaphor of the Family

The following analysis of Zadie Smith's *On Beauty* traces the instrumentalisation of the metaphor of the family for the creation of Sameness. In view of the fact that the engagement with the 'role model' for the narrative – Forster's *Howards End* – as well as the narrative techniques applied in the text have been discussed elsewhere, I will, in my reading of the text, focus exclusively on the aspect of how a rhetorical structure serves to convey a specific idea, i.e. how, in this case, the metaphor of the family is employed as a means to express ideas such as ultimate belonging and unity.[91] Smith's novel *On Beauty* revolves around questions such as family affiliations, loyalty, and solidarity. Here, the focus of attention lies on the Belsey family, consisting of Howard, a white university lecturer, his black wife Kiki, who works as a nurse, and their teenage children Jerome, Levi, and Zora. Being set in Wellington, a fictive US-American university town on the East coast in the 21st century, the novel constitutes a modern-day re-writing of Forster's *Howards End*.[92] While individual roles are slightly altered (with the main protagonist's sex being changed from female to male), the basic plot elements from Forster's novel are still clearly discernible. As in the 'original' text, the action concentrates on the mishaps, errors, and confusions within the lives of two families who are staged as the foil to each other. In the context of the present discussion, however, I will limit my scrutiny to the Belsey family and its members. This real-life family – i.e. a group of people directly related by blood – does, however, by no means form the only family-like grouping discussed in the novel. By contrast, we come across a number of families in the metaphorical sense who derive their affiliations from criteria such as skin colour, membership of a specific social circle such as academia, or a shared work-place. In my following interpretation, I will discuss these groups individually and point out, in which way the metaphor of

---

[91] An initial version of this study has been published in the collection of essays reporting the outcomes of the Multi-Ethnic Britain 2000+ conference held in Freiburg in February 2007 (Nunius, Sabine. „'Sameness' in Contemporary British Fiction: (Metaporical) Families in Zadie Smith's *On Beauty* (2005)." *Multi-Ethnic Britain 2000+. New Perspectives in Literature, Film and the Arts*. Eds. Lars Eckstein *et al*. Amsterdam and New York: Rodopi, 2008. 109-22).

[92] As Tynan, amongst others, points out, we are, however, not dealing with what is frequently termed a 'postcolonial' re-writing of a canonical fictional work, i. e. the re-telling of a plot with a concomitant reversal of binary oppositions and the subversion of power structures implicitly posited in a text. While examples of this practice by now abound, Smith refrains from offering a critique of *Howards End* and does apparently not aim at rectifying any imbalances of her template. By contrast, she performs a modernisation of Forster's narrative with great fidelity to the plot structure of the 'original' text. For a positioning of *On Beauty* among other forms of re-writing, see Tynan, Maeve. „Only Connect": Intertextuality and Identity in Zadie Smith's *On Beauty*." *Zadie Smith. Critical Essays*. Ed. Tracey L. Walters. New York: Peter Lang, 2008. 73-89.

the family is employed for the construction of Sameness.[93] Hereby, special attention will be paid to the question of which differential categories are temporarily privileged and stressed. Moreover, I will highlight the potentially disruptive elements suppressed for the moment in order to create a feeling of belonging and discuss the point of their resurgence, an event which invariably leads to the interruption of the former state of complete homogeneity.

(Metaphorical) Families in *On Beauty*

In Smith's novel, we encounter several communities which either represent families in the traditional sense, that is a group of people related by blood, or are perceived as family-like structures by their members. In my reading of the text, I will focus on three types of families: the 'real' families embodied by the Belseys and the Kipps, the 'black family' promoted by Levi and Kiki, and, finally, the 'family' of workplace-colleagues. However, membership of these groups is not exclusive, a phenomenon which leads to various overlaps and cases of multiple affiliations. With respect to the construction and representation of Sameness, the following questions are of major interest: How do individual members perceive their 'family' and how do they relate to other members? How are 'outsiders' and 'traitors' dealt with? And, most importantly, which differential categories are temporarily privileged in order to suppress all other differences for the moment? Against the background of these questions, I will also inquire about the interplay between personal and collective identity.

A further aspect to be considered in this context consists in the specific stylistic and narratological strategies employed for the orchestration of each metaphorical family and for their instrumentalisation in the construction of Sameness. Due to the use of an extradiegetic-heterodiegetic narrator coupled with different focalizers, a tension arises between the assessment of specific situations by the characters themselves and the narrator's comments on them. These implicit judgements on the part of the extradiegetic narrator offer a second perspective and reveal the extent to which the protagonists sometimes succumb to illusions and ideals when constructing communities for themselves. Hereby, it is important to realise that the narrator's comments do not serve to ridicule individual

---

[93] Obviously, we may observe a proximity to the idea of social bonding here; however, I would like to argue that the pressing need to momentarily erase all differential categories but one constitutes an important aspect and allows for a distinction between Sameness and the concept of social bonding. Moreover, while Sameness always follows the same patterns, types of social bonding as well as the strategies involved may vary. As a solution to this predicament, I would like to suggest that Sameness may be understood as a specific form of social bonding in the sense of a subcategory with social bonding functioning as a generic term.

characters or to dismiss their ideals as futile.[94] To the contrary, they enable the reader to realise the 'ontological' status of Sameness. While there cannot be any doubt about the constructed quality of Sameness or about its representing a temporary state, the instances of bonding arising from those moments of Sameness are nevertheless perceived as 'authentic' and durable by the protagonists themselves. Moreover, the resulting communities and in-groups (offering starting points for the formation of collective identities) provide them with an important source of support in their search for stable self-images.

As I will illustrate below, one of the main functions of each (metaphorical) family consists in providing the characters with the necessary framework to construct firm, seemingly permanent identities. This obviously runs counter to the widely held 'postmodern' assumption that identities are always in a flux and cannot ultimately be traced back to a lasting, unchanging core.[95] At various points in the novel, the main figures are shown to be in search of precisely this sort of reliable identity, for instance when trying to achieve membership status in a group of people who allegedly share the same experiences and to thereby become endowed with a feeling of belonging. This form of behaviour may be interpreted as a first sign that at least the belief in an unalterable 'core identity' exists irrespective of all theorising to the contrary.[96]

Kinship on the Basis of Consanguinity

The first family the reader meets in the story are the Belseys: Howard Belsey, and, alongside him, his wife Kiki, and their three children. The second family,

---

[94] This aspect is in tune with Schabert's observation on the current use of irony in contemporary British fiction. As Schabert outlined in her presentation "Ironie als Signum des nach-postmodernen Erzählens" (Ethik in der Gegenwartsliteratur, 3 to 5 October 2008, Friedrich-Alexander-Universität Erlangen-Nürnberg), irony presently serves as a distancing mechanism for the author to, as it were, withdraw from the story. Thus, contrary to postmodern uses of irony which are frequently associated with an 'everything goes'-attitude, irony, in this context, is employed to underline the different levels of perception of, on the one hand, the protagonists, and, on the other hand, the narrator (or even the meta-level of author and/or reader).

[95] For a discussion of modern and postmodern aspects displayed by *On Beauty* as well as an assessment of the 'postmodern' quality of Smith's writing in general, see Paproth, Matthew. „The Flipping Coin: The Modernist and Postmodernist Zadie Smith." *Zadie Smith. Critical Essays*. Ed. Tracey L. Walters. New York: Lang, 2008. 9-29.

[96] The perceived need for stable identities as well as its possible connection to social transformations such as internationalisation and globalisation has already been discussed in the introductory chapter. What, once again, proves striking here is the turn away from larger units such as the nation state and its supplementation by considerably smaller communities such as 'brotherhoods' or families. One may conceivably argue that, in this case, the turn to the family constitutes a low-scale expression of the phenomenon of glocalisation as commonality is no longer sought for on a national level but rather within an individual's immediate environment.

represented by the Kippses, is, for the time being, introduced only indirectly via the accounts sent by the Belseys' eldest son, Jerome, who temporarily stays at the Kipps' place. At the outset of the narrative, the impression arises that these two families are the foil to each other. Accordingly, Jerome enthuses about the Kipps' family life:

> The rest of the family talk about sports and God and politics, and Carlene floats above it all like a kind of angel – and she's helping me with prayer. She really knows how to *pray* – and it's very cool to be able to pray without someone in your family coming into the room and (a) passing wind (b) shouting (c) analysing the 'phoney metaphysics' of prayer (d) singing loudly (e) laughing.[97]

It is for this reason that Jerome falls in love not only with their daughter Victoria but also with the rest of the family. Life at the Kipps' obviously offers a stark contrast to the situation in Wellington since, right at the beginning of the novel, Jerome's real family, the Belseys, find themselves in a state of disintegration. Due to a recently disclosed affair between Howard and – as turns out later on – his colleague Claire, the spouses are estranged and tensions run high. Nevertheless, each of the Belseys continues to believe in the importance of the family as an essential source of support. In view of the fact that all attempts to reconstruct the former state of harmony fail, the children perforce turn to substitute families in order to compensate for the loss of stability they experience at home. While Jerome, as briefly outlined above, takes refuge at the Kipps', Zora choses an 'intellectual family' and subsequently focuses on her university career, whereas Levi adopts a 'gangsta' image both in terms of speech and dresscode which he hopes will secure his position in the 'black family'.

Yet, despite the current crisis, the Belsey family has not lost all of its binding powers and, even though beset by tensions, it continues to unite partners with different (cultural) backgrounds and roots. This aspect constitutes a further contrast to the Kipps family whose members are without exception black.[98] The internal differences among the Belseys are most noticeable with respect to the spouses, Howard and Kiki. At first sight, they seem to belong to two entirely different realms, him being a white, highly educated male occupying the position of a university lecturer as opposed to his wife, a black woman, working as a

---

[97] Smith, Zadie. *On Beauty*. London: Penguin. 2005. 4. Hereafter quoted as On Beauty.
[98] Here, it is worthy of note that the family – a traditionally bourgeois concept or value – is unreflectedly presented as a value per se with the need to re-stabilise the family life hardly ever being questioned.

nurse.[99] While these differences in terms of race, class, and education are entirely overcome in specific situations – sex or 'the Hawaiian' (On Beauty 395)
hereby serving as the ultimate image of both corporeal and 'spiritual' union –
they regain prominence in other contexts. Especially in the company of Howard's friends and colleagues, Kiki feels acutely aware of her inability to participate in 'intellectual' discussions and suffers from her alleged inferiority:

> Meredith – if one were to remember two facts about each of one's
> guests in order to introduce them to other guests – was interested in
> Foucault and costume-wear. At various parties Kiki had listened care-
> fully and yet not understood what Meredith was saying while Meredith
> was dressed as an English punk, a *fin de siècle* dame in a drop-waisted
> Edwardian gown, a French movie star and, most memorably, a forties
> war bride, her hair set and curled like Bacall's, complete with stockings
> and stays and that compelling black line curving up the back of both her
> mighty calves. (On Beauty 100)

Despite the ironic tone displayed by this description of Meredith's self-
orchestration, there can be no doubt about Kiki's being intimidated by the considerably younger woman. This feeling of alienation and liminality is increased
by Kiki's skin colour: "Sometimes you get a flash of what you look like to other
people. This one was unpleasant: a black woman in a headwrap, approaching
with a bottle in one hand and a plate of food in the other, like a maid in an old
movie" (On Beauty 98). In general, skin colour is a subtle but nevertheless persistent topic in the Belseys' family life. Especially in moments of great tension,
clichés and essentialist notions are raised again as, for instance, when Howard
discusses his marital problems with his father (On Beauty 301). Even though
suppressed at most times, the differences in terms of colour create barriers
within the family as they set off white-skinned Howard against his children and
render them a likeness of their mother rather than an image of their father. In
fact, Levi's blackness causes experiences he cannot share with his father as is,

---

[99] In her analysis of female figures in Smith's fiction, Walters observes that, in *On Beauty*, *White
Teeth* and *The Autograph Man*, "Smith features black female characters that exemplify the
mammy, jezebel, and matriarch figures", with Kiki clearly embodying the mammy figure (Walters, Tracey L. „Still Mammies and Hos: Stereotypical Images of Black Women in Zadie Smith's
Novels." *Zadie Smith. Critical Essays*. Ed. Tracey L. Walters. New York: Peter Lang, 2008. 123-
39. 123). While I agree to Walter's designation of Kiki as the stereotypical image of the mammy,
I do not follow her reading of Kiki as an "asexual being" (130) since the couple's references to
earlier blissful moments doing 'the Hawaiian' undoubtedly suggest the opposite. Moreover, I do
not consider Kiki's personal development at the end of the novel so prominent as to erase the
previous image of stereotypical blackness. For a perspicacious analysis of the mammy figure as
such as well as the perception of black female bodies, see Shaw, Andrea. „The Other Side of the
Looking Glass: The Marginalization of Fatness and Blackness in the Construction of Gender
Identity." *Social Semiotics* 15 (2005): 143-52.

for instance, the case with his feeling of alienation when walking the streets of their bourgeois, all-white neighbourhood. Yet, in spite of the fundamental differences with respect to education and colour as well as the concomitant problems, all members of the Belsey family ultimately believe in the importance of the ties among them and try to prevent their family from disintegrating completely. Thus, the institution of the family is apparently perceived as a potential source of security and support, a kind of bulwark against the outside world. This assumption is backed by various passages, which employ one of the protagonists as a focalizing figure:

> Only Kiki supported it [Jerome's insistence on a family outing]. She believed she understood Jerome's motivation. […] Jerome must behave as if nothing had happened. They must *all* do that. *They must be united and strong.* (On Beauty 61, second emphasis mine)

For Kiki and Howard, the family finally even comes to assume all but existential qualities. After the disclosure of Howard's second affair and the subsequent split-up, Howard realises Kiki's significance for his life: 'You're for me – you *are* me" (On Beauty 398, orig. emphasis). What is more, despite Kiki's somewhat stereotypical intellectual 'inferiority' (conspicuously, it is once again the *woman*, who is less educated than her husband and falters on the academic stage), she is attributed a 'moral' or 'emotional' authority. Throughout the novel, attention is drawn to the tension between academic/scientific discourses and what may be termed the language of emotion and love. Strikingly, it is only Kiki who seems to master the latter: "Where Kiki had felt her way instinctively through her problem, Jerome had written his out, words and words and words. Not for the first time, Kiki felt grateful she was not an intellectual" (On Beauty 43). This association of women with emotions and irrational feelings (explicitly discussed by Carlene Kipps and Kiki at one point in the novel) clearly reflects the worn cliché of women being determined by their body or 'nature'. Nevertheless, at the same time, a turn away from a purely intellectual approach to life is promoted as the only possible way to happiness. Remarkably enough, emotions are not off-handedly dismissed as female whims but rather attributed a decisive function in human relationships. At least this seems to be implied by the ending of the novel when Howard fails to deliver his academic paper but may have succeeded in taking the first step towards a reconciliation with his wife. This emphasis on love and its uniting power is in tune with Schabert's observation that

> auch in literarischen Texten trotz aller theoriebelasteten Skepsis, allem intellektuellen Raffinement und aller kritischen Intelligenz ein ethischer Impuls, eine altruistische Art von Liebe als Gegenkraft zu den dominan-

ten gesellschaftsdestruktiven Kräften wiederentdeckt und als Ideal ge-
priesen wird.[100]

As can be derived from both the reaction of the Belsey children to the falling
apart of their family and from the possibility of a reunion between the spouses
alluded to in the end, love, coupled with the concept of the nuclear family, is
here presented as *the* constructive force which enables individuals to overcome
the divisive nature of difference. In this case, states of Sameness are therefore
erected on the basis of a (bourgeois) ideal. Moreover, the idea of Sameness is
closely connected to love, the power of which permits the temporary bridging of
differences such as sex/gender, race/colour, and education. Hereby, the repeated
shifts between moments of great intimacy and times of alienation illustrate that
separating elements still tend to return and that they have to be actively suppressed in order to retain the state of (alleged) homogeneity.

The 'Black Family'

A further 'family' in the novel is embodied by the black 'brother- or sisterhood'. Yet, before turning to actual representations of this group, I would like to
draw attention to the different ways in which individual characters in *On Beauty*
deal with their cultural heritage. Apparently, a fundamental difference may be
observed with respect to 'black' and 'white' approaches. In its entirety, the narrative provides ample information on individual family backgrounds – i.e. the
cultural 'roots' – of both spouses, to which each of them responds in a different
way. While Kiki derives satisfaction from her position within a continuous line
of 'strong' black women and is proud of her ancestors' (or, to be more precise,
her ancestresses') achievements, Howard is unable to cope with or even truly
accept his working-class background:

> It was an ancestry he referred to proudly at Marxist conferences and in
> print; it was a communion he occasionally felt on the streets of New
> York and in the urban outskirts of Paris. For the most part, however,
> Howard liked to keep his 'working-class roots' where they flourished
> best: in his imagination. (On Beauty 292)

---

[100] Schabert, 2006, 439. On love as a motive in literature in general as well as its treatment in related
discourses such as philosophy, see Cottom, Daniel. „Love." *Glossalalia – An Alphabet of Critical
Keywords*. Ed. Julian Wolfreys. Edinburgh: Edinburgh UP, 2003.

Not only does Kiki value her personal lineage, she also believes in a bond between all black people arising from their shared cultural roots. This conviction
constitutes the basis of her idea of an all-encompassing black community or
'family'.[101] In this context, it is striking to note which types of cultural references are drawn upon by the members of the black brother- or sisterhood and
which expressions are used to call up ideas of family and belonging. Interestingly enough clichéd, originally 'white' notions are adopted and, on the one
hand, internalised, but, on the other hand, also consciously exploited. This holds
particularly true for Kiki, whose self-image is to a high degree determined by
her body:

> The size [of her bosom] was sexual and at the same time more than sex-
> ual: sex was only one small element of its symbolic range. If she were
> white, maybe it would refer only to sex, but she was not. And so her
> chest gave off a mass of signals beyond her direct control: sassy, sis-
> terly, predatory, motherly, threatening, comforting – it was a mirror-
> world she had stepped into in her mid forties, a strange fabulation of the
> person she believed she was. […] Her body had directed her to a new
> personality. (On Beauty 47)

Apparently, Kiki unquestioningly accepts stereotypes such as the association of
blackness with a ferocious sexuality as well as other derogatory notions of
(black) femininity the majority of which originated in 19th century Imperialism.
What is more, she even incorporates them into her self-image. In contrast to this
unconscious internalisation of specific 'ethnic' features, Kiki, in other situations, is highly aware of the constructed nature of these stereotypes: "But then,
thought Kiki, they were brought up that way, these white American boys: I'm
the Aunt Jemima on the cookie boxes of their childhoods, the pair of thick an-
kles Tom and Jerry played around" (On Beauty 51). In some cases, Kiki even
deliberately meets (white) expectations by behaving in precisely the way she
knows to conform to 'white' clichés. It is against the background of this complex perception of blackness that the idea of the 'black family' evoked by Kiki
in her conversation with a street vendor must be considered:

---

[101] This stance chimes in with Alexander's findings in her field study on Black Britishness and the
significance of the idea of the 'black family'. In the sub-chapter "Family and 'Community'", she
describes the construction of families which transcend the bonds of kinship (Alexander, 1996. See
esp. pp. 64-70. On Africa as a symbol for shared roots and 'universal homeland', see "Home and
The World: Attitudes to Nationhood" (38-52). Even though the study focuses on a British context,
I believe that its statements are by and large applicable to *On Beauty* as well, especially as we are
only dealing with a fictional American context.).

'You're from Africa?' she asked sweetly, and picked up a charm brace-
let with tiny replicas of international totems hanging from it: the Eiffel
Tower, the Leaning Tower of Pisa, the Statue of Liberty. [...] 'Where
do you *think* I am from? You are African – no?'

'No, noooo, I'm from *here* – but of course...' said Kiki. She wiped
some sweat from her forehead with the back of her hand, waiting for
him to finish the sentence as she knew it would be finished.

'We are all from Africa,' said the man obligingly. He made a double
outward fan of his hands over the jewellery. 'All of this, from Africa.'
(On Beauty 48-9)

Ironically, neither Kiki nor the street vendor have ever been to their (spiritual)
home country, the so-called 'black continent'. They are therefore referring to
shared ethnic or cultural origins derived from an imaginary construct rather than
from a real genealogy. Moreover, the statement becomes slightly absurd with
respect to the vendor's merchandise allegedly likewise stemming from 'Africa'.
The items on display do by no means represent any symbols of Africa but rather
constitute landmarks of Western culture. At this moment, though, they are employed as signifiers of culture per se – stripped of their former connotations,
they come to serve as symbols of cultural authenticity.[102] This move leaves the
reader with the question of whether such icons continue to carry any symbolic
value anymore or whether they, in the wake of globalisation and its homogenis-
ing impact, have been rendered empty signs, available to be freely used as
markers of some non-specified form of culture/Culture. Yet, despite the lack of
'real' referents, the construction of an imaginary shared heritage does work on
the level of the characters and triggers a feeling of belonging in them.[103] The

---

[102] The instrumentalisation of cultural landmarks as signifiers of culture as such mirrors the establishment of a global system of reference: „Immer mehr Menschen beziehen sich heute auf eine
wachsende Anzahl universeller Kategorien, Konzepte und Standards sowie überall verfügbarer
Waren und Geschichten. Daraus ist ein *weltweites Referenzsystem entstanden, welches strukturel-
ler, aber nicht inhaltlicher Art ist*. [...] Immer mehr Menschen entwickeln ein kulturvergleichen-
des Bewusstsein, ziehen kulturfremde Konzepte heran und setzen sich zu anderen Gesellschaften
in Bezug" (Zukrigl, Ina. „Kulturelle Vielfalt und Identität in einer globalisierten Welt." *Kulturelle
Globalisierung – Zwischen Weltkultur und kultureller Fragmentierung*. Hg. Bernd Wagner. Essen: Klartext Verlag, 2001. 50-61. 58, my emphasis). Baudrillard observes a similar phenomenon
with respect to the re-ascription of functionality and significance to specific 'bygone' objects
chosen for collection: "[T]he bygone object [...] is purely mythological in its reference to the
past. It no longer has any practical importance, but exists solely in order to signify. It is astruc-
tural, it denies structure, and it epitomises the disavowal of primary function. Yet it is not afunc-
tional, nor is it simply 'decorative'. It has a quite specific function within the framework of the
system: it signifies time" (Baudrillard, Jean. *Revenge of the Crystal. Selected writings on the
modern object and its destiny, 1968-1983*. Ed. and tr. Paul Foss and Julian Pefanis. London and
Concord, Mass.: Pluto, 1990. 35-6).
[103] Apparently, we are not merely dealing with a literary construct or invention here. In contrast,
Baumann observes the same phenomenon among the Afro-Caribbean community of Southall

'black family' is thus perceived as a comparatively homogeneous group, in which bonding between individuals takes place on the grounds of their shared experiences. In her study on Black British youths, Alexander describes the effects of this phenomenon:

> The potency of the idea of 'the black community', for both black people and wider society, depends on its perception as a unified and largely separate entity. From an external perspective this facilitates targeting and labelling processes [...], while internally it enables the individual to position himself in relation to these labels and serves as a focus for political and social mobilization. [...] On the whole, projections of 'community' have created the illusion of fixity and absolute identification, premised on the correlation of 'Community' with 'Race'.[104]

As the conversation between Kiki and the street vendour shows, boundaries of class and sex are overcome as blackness – i.e. race – takes priority over all other potentially dividing elements. This moment of bonding is interrupted by the arrival of Kiki's (white) friends Claire and Warren which re-establishes class boundaries again.

For Kiki, the black community gains its importance primarily because of the possibilities it offers for socialising; it therefore forms only part of her self-image. To her son Levi, however, the idea of a black brotherhood assumes a vital significance. He approaches the project of creating an 'authentic' black identity in a radical way and attempts to stylise himself into a 'gangsta' by fashioning a 'street' persona for himself. Seeing that he stems from an affluent, upper-middle-class background, his efforts to sound and look 'street' have a comic effect on the reader and are repeatedly mocked, sometimes also criticised, by other characters:

> 'Street, street,' bellowed Zora. 'It's like, ''being street'', knowing the street – in Levi's sad little world if you're a Negro you have some kind of mysterious holy communion with sidewalks and corners.' (On Beauty 63)

---

intent on re-defining their cultural identity: "Across these approaches, however, one could discern one crucial historical revalidation. It consisted in a new emphasis on the historical unity of all people of African descent. [...] Both Rastafarians and secular pan-Africanists saw themselves as 'Africans, whatever the country you come from' and Africa was apostrophised, in the words of many informants, as 'our spiritual home', 'our common cultural identity', and 'the country where our true culture lies.' This new African identity constructs, not only a global history, but a new and global cultural identity" (Baumann, 2002, 193).

[104] Alexander, 1996, 32.

Ridiculous as Levi's subsequent sudden involvement in the Haitian cause and his zeal in the struggle for disadvantaged black 'bro's' may seem, several passages in which he acts as a focalizer imply that he feels an earnest desire to belong to a community in which he is not distinguished by his skin colour. This longing is triggered by the fact that he is painfully aware that his features set him off from the vast majority of inhabitants in Wellington's residential area.[105] Levi obviously seeks a substitute family in order to compensate for the lack of security and stability in his 'real' family. His ideal of a group of people inseparably connected to each other is symbolised by his very own vision of the 'black brotherhood'. In order to find his 'authentic' black identity, Levi resorts to an exaggerated imitation of the 'bro's' on the street in the desperate hope to become one of them in this way.[106] Especially Levi's attempts to 'sound street' demonstrate the discursive constructedness of collective identities. As Ellis underlines, the respective codes used in ethnically defined sub-groups prove particularly rigid as they are crucial for the creation of a strong feeling of coherency and affiliation: "Tightly connected and close neighbourhoods are the most typical way that ethnic groups develop their ethnic sub-code homodynamically. These conditions promote a strong sense of group identity where many verbal, nonverbal and attitudinal characteristics are shared."[107] Due to his lack of knowledge of the specificities of the code used by the gang of hustlers, Levi may easily be singled out as a non-member. His position as a bystander rather than a fully fledged member is furthermore highlighted by his hopeless endeav-

---

[105] Once again, we detect a parallel to the sociological findings offered by Alexander. With respect to one of her interviewees, she states that "Ricky too, who arrived back in Britain at the start of the fourth year, felt drawn to these groups *through a desire to 'fit in'*, and be accepted within a community he recognized" (Alexander, 1996, 52, my emphasis).

[106] This phenomenon of the notion of the family being extended beyond bonds in terms of blood-relationship is likewise observed by Alexander who reports that "[t]he nuclear family itself was marked by a closeness and level of support which was a source of strength to both its members and those who came into contact with them; it also formed the core of a wider, more inclusive and more loosely defined notion of 'family'" (Alexander, 1996, 67).

[107] Ellis, Don. „A Discourse Theory of Ethnic Identity." *Discursive Constructions of Identity in European Politics*. Ed. Richard C. M. Mole. Houndmills, Basingstoke and New York: Palgrave Macmillan, 2007. 25-44. 28. Ellis cites a further example of a similar case, in which we encounter a clash between outer experience and actual social/cultural background: "Garfinkel's (1967) famous case of Agnes is the research example that best illustrates the consequences of codes acquired homodynamically versus heterodynamically. Agnes had undergone a sex change operation from male to female and was confronted with the task of 'living as a woman'. Agnes began to construct a female identity by reading and utilising public media sources with hints and observations about female language, behaviour and attitudes. But her attempts to 'pass' as a female were unsuccessful. [...] Only when Agnes immersed herself in communication with other females, only when she shared an interactional identity with other women and acquired her cognitive and linguistic representations and skills in mutual interaction (homodynamically) did she pass as a female" (ibid.).

our to disguise his social background which results in a, at times, highly comic over-compensation.

Generally speaking, the notion of the 'black family' and the ways Kiki and Levi react to it hint at the interplay between personal and collective identity. The novel leaves us in no doubt about the fact that a universal 'black' identity does not exist – at least not in the clear-cut form sought by Levi – and must remain an (illusionary) construct. Yet, despite its constructed nature, the idea of a bond linking all black people provides an important point of reference for the creation of the characters' self-images and thus constitutes a crucial part of their personal identities. This seemingly stable basis is shaken as soon as alleged members of the group start to behave in a way contradictory to the idea of the black family. This is in particular the case when Monty Kipps, an outspoken black university lecturer, pronouncedly turns against the idea of a bond between all black people. His son Michael even denies the existence of a black identity as such "[arguing] that being black was not an identity but an accidental matter of pigment" (On Beauty 44). The controversy assumes a political hue when Kipps publicly speaks out against affirmative action. His stance proves highly troublesome for the liberal supporters of affirmative action as Monty Kipps begins to play off their 'own' values, first and foremost the right to free speech, against them. Here, Kiki, following her gut feeling, is the only one able to incorporate controversial ideas into her system of beliefs and to thereby uphold the notion of a functional black family. 'Intellectual' Howard, by contrast, continues to slander Monty as a conservative fascist. Once again, emotions are promoted as the only possible strategy to cope with internal tensions and to keep potentially divisive differences at bay. Thus, as in the first example, the unions or communities constructed on the basis of Sameness prove fragile and are constantly threatened by the renewed importance attributed to differential categories such as class, or by the 'counter-productive' behaviour of alleged members.

Workplace Families

As a last example, I would like to discuss the metaphorical family of co-workers or colleagues. The text deals with several examples of this type of 'family', for instance the group of employees at the music store where Levi works a part-time job, or the gang of hustlers he joins subsequently. When Levi first starts his Saturday job, he feels proud to belong to the big corporate 'family' lauded by his employer:

> Our companies are part of a family rather than a hierarchy. They are
> empowered to run their own affairs, yet other companies help one an-
> other, and solutions to problems come from all kinds of sources. In a
> sense we are a community, with shared ideas, values, interests and
> goals. (On Beauty 180)

While most readers will immediately realise that this statement only forms part
of the company's marketing spiel, it nevertheless strikes a tune with Levi as it
caters directly to his desire to belong to a community of people who share the
same ideals and goals. In terms of narrative perspective, we witness a discrepancy between the protagonist's perception of the situation and its assessment by
the narrator's ironic comments, which disclose the rationale behind the company's self-marketing strategies. Therefore, the final realisation that his workplace family has only been an illusion hits Levi hard: Trying to organise a mo-
tion against the company's orders to work on Christmas Day, he finds his 'al-
lies' quick to desert and to conform to the manager's expectations. At this point,
class barriers resurge since Levi turns out to be the only one to find himself in a
position which allows him to risk losing his part-time job: Levi still has the
option of returning to the (financial) safety of his middle-class home, whereas
his colleagues depend on their jobs for a regular income. Moreover, Levi secretly has to admit that he is actually ignorant of his fellow workers' ways of
life:

> There was an alternative universe that Levi occasionally entered in his
> imagination, one in which he accepted LaShonda's invitations, and then
> later they made love standing up in the basement of the store. [...] But
> the truth was he wouldn't know what to do with a woman like
> LaShonda. [...] Levi's girls were typically the giggly Hispanic teenag-
> ers from the Catholic school next door to his prep, and those girls had
> simple tastes: happy with a movie and some heavy petting in one of
> Wellington's public parks. (On Beauty 184)

Nevertheless, the failure of this first workplace family does not spoil Levi's
belief in the bonds among co-workers. For this reason, he turns away from the
realm of 'official' corporate business and replaces his job at the music store
with a new 'job' as a hustler. Via this entrance into an all-black male group, an
overlap ensues with Levi's ideal of the black brotherhood, a notion which he
tries to impose on the group of young men selling fake designer goods in the
street. Similar to his music store experience, Levi's dogged attempts to belong
are doomed to failure. Yet, Levi *himself* does not realise this fact and is thrilled
by his apparently being accepted into the group, which provokes a strong feeling of empowerment and pride in him:

He was *in*. Being *in* was a weird feeling. These past few days, coming to meet the guys after school, hanging with them, had been an eye-opener for Levi. Try walking down the street with fifteen Haitians if you want to see people get uncomfortable. He felt a little like Jesus taking a stroll with the lepers. (On Beauty 243, orig. emphases)

Repeatedly, Levi's over-enthusiasm leads to comic incidents, especially when he starts to act as the ultimate authority on 'street' and black 'bro's', hereby even going as far as re-naming one of his fellow hustlers to make his name sound more authentic. The extradiegetic narrator's comments leave the reader in no doubt that the other young men, who have to make a living out of their 'job', only play along but do not really share Levi's idea of "[t]he Street, the global Street, lined with hustling brothers working corners from Roxbury to Casablanca, from South Central to Cape Town" (On Beauty 245-6). Although the passages on Levi's 'street' life are narrated in a markedly ironic tone, they do neither aim at ridiculing Levi's search for a 'family' in which he is no longer an outsider nor do they undermine the concept of the 'workplace family' as such (here more or less identical with the black brotherhood). If only temporarily, Levi does gain some satisfaction from his bonding with the newfound 'bro's', an experience which is vital in his coming to terms with his own blackness.

The academic community at Wellington University represents a further group which can be considered a 'workplace family'. Zora is the character most attracted to this circle. She is portrayed as being constantly busy outlining her academic career and, to this end, pestering members of staff. Strikingly, Zora, who ridicules her brother Levi for his deluded notions of a black brotherhood, falls herself prey to the lure of an imaginary 'family'. As in Levi's case, an overlap with the black community may be detected as Zora is intent on supporting disadvantaged black fellow students and attempts to enable them to enter the closed-off realm of academia. Her enthusiasm in this project is not dissimilar from Levi's zeal and she likewise misinterprets other people's true ambitions and hopes since she silently expects them to share her own goals. Realising this potential, Claire exploits Zora's ambitious stance by asking her to argue the case of several black students participating in her poetry class without the required formal qualifications:

Depressing as it is, the truth is these people won't respond to an appeal to their consciences in any language other than Wellington language. And you *know* Wellington language, Zora. You of all people. (On Beauty 263)

At this point, the university is presented as a walled-off community only to be entered by the privileged few. This impression is backed by Elisha, who has been given a job at Wellington but doubts that she will ever truly belong to this academic 'family': "'But people like you and me,' continued Elisha severely, 'we're not really a part of this community, are we?'" (On Beauty 374).

While Zora, who stems from an upper-middle class background, manages to overcome ethnic and gender differences, the situation proves more complex in Carl's case since he fails to bridge the gap arising from class differences. There-fore, he, ultimately, does not become a member of Wellington's exclusive circle and even actively sets himself off from it. Ironically, the scene which follows immediately afterwards depicts Zora's realisation that, despite her established position within the academic community, she is ignorant of some of the events most important to her personally. In the ensuing argument, class differences constitute a virtually insurmountable barrier when Carl accuses Zora of a lack of 'authentic' blackness:

> 'But that's a *joke* around here, man. People like me are just toys to peo-ple like you... I'm just some experiment for you to play with. You peo-ple aren't even black any more, man – I don't know *what* you are. You think you're too good for your own people. You got your college de-grees, but you don't even live right. You people are all the same,' said Carl, looking down, addressing his words to his own shoes,' I need to be with *my* people, man – I can't do this no more'. (On Beauty 418-9, orig. emphases)

Although wounded pride certainly plays a role in this heated exchange, the fre-quency with which comparable discussions occur suggests that the relationship between the members of the 'academic' family and the 'black brotherhood' is loaded with tensions and that the two conceptions are not entirely compatible despite certain overlaps. Strikingly, the notion of the black family seems to work best in lower-class as well as in non-academic contexts. It is also at this point that the dynamic quality of Sameness shows most clearly: While Same-ness allows for the momentary privileging of a specific differential category, thereby relegating all other, potentially divisive differences to second place, this privileging can only be upheld within a specific context and for a limited period of time. As soon as the constellation changes, formerly suppressed differences return and may now likewise adopt the position of the 'top criterion'. For this reason, Sameness requires permanent efforts and adaptations to new contexts.

On Beauty – Metaphors as a Vehicle for Sameness and a Revaluation of the Family

As the foregoing analysis of the three different types of 'family' in *On Beauty* demonstrates, the specific use of this metaphor represents one possible strategy to convey the idea of Sameness by way of rhetorical means. In this case, the metaphor of the family is drawn upon to construct a feeling of community, stability, and belonging. On this basis, the protagonists endeavour to create (seemingly) coherent identities and – with regard to the purely metaphorical families – to compensate for the lack they experience in the context of their nuclear families. Even though each 'family' in the novel is afflicted by flaws and weaknesses and can only be maintained due to constant efforts to suppress incongruent elements, each of them is nevertheless perceived as an important source of stability and support by the protagonists themselves. Moreover, one may witness a strong interplay between personal and collective identities: In their attempts to achieve satisfying personal identities, the characters heavily rely on their affiliations to specific groups and derive considerable strength from the collective identity they feel to correspond closest to their self-images. In order to analyse this phenomenon, in particular with respect to the two purely metaphorical families, it proves fruitful to draw upon Baumann's theory on cultural identities as dual discursive constructs. Baumann reports that, during his studies in Southall, he found that

> [t]he more one listened, the more voices one heard that identified different cultures within the same quasi-ethnic community, while recognising the same culture across different communities as well. The equation between ethnic identity and culture, dominant as it is in much public discourse about ethnic minorities, disintegrated the more I got to know local people. [...] The data thus showed two different discourses of identity being engaged by Southallians themselves.[108]

This definition of collective identity as a dual discursive construct that comprises a reificatory and a demotic discourse provides a possible solution to the problem that Sameness does never exist in an absolute, enduring form but is always implicitly interspersed with differences, which have to be actively suppressed in order to uphold the illusion of homogeneity. Furthermore, Baumann's conceptualisation demonstrates that the 'adoption' of one collective identity does not automatically rule out membership in other communities, a

---

[108] Baumann, 2002, 190.

fact which explains the widespread phenomenon of multiple affiliations and context-depending overlaps.

With respect to the viability of these constructed communities and the assessment of their functionality, we have to distinguish between two levels. In doing so, we realise that a tension arises from the juxtaposition of the perspective of individual characters (employed as focalizers) and the evaluation of a situation by the extradiegetic narrator. In several cases, the narrator's ironic comments suggest that the feeling of commonality and belonging experienced by the protagonists results first and foremostly from idealised constructs rather than from ties or communities based on factual similarities. Nevertheless, those constructs are by no means dismissed as valueless or futile on the grounds that they lack a 'factual' basis. Strikingly, in the presentation of the discrepancy between individual perception and 'actual' situation, irony constitutes an important tool. By contrast to its 'postmodern' usage, though, it does not serve to dismantle or 'deconstruct' the sheer possibility of continuous identities and lasting affiliations; rather, it highlights the constructed quality of each metaphorical family (or its narrative in case of the real-life family) without denying its legitimacy and importance as a crucial point of reference. This strategy illustrates that, ultimately, each family represents an idealised construct. While the idea of its binding and uniting power (based on some inherent commonality of all members) could comparatively easily be dissolved by, for instance, citing class differences, the notion of a 'spiritual' bond or kinship assumes a certain reality for the characters in their everyday lives and fulfils an important function in their search for satisfactory, 'authentic' identities. This feature demonstrates that, for the characters, empirical facts ultimately seem to matter less than the bonds arising from the 'felt' reality of the constructions described above.

In this context, it is likewise striking to note to which high degree the creation of each metaphorical family depends on narrative means. The act of narration as such is thus employed for the generation of meaning with affiliations being produced via purely rhetorical means.[109] In my estimation, Schabert's observation on the meaning-generating function of narratives may therefore be applied on two levels. First, it can be seen to operate on an extratextual level with regard to novels as textual artefacts since they may be understood to offer examples of community building that may potentially serve as a role model to be imitated by the reader. Secondly, on an intratextual level, the protagonists em-

---

[109] As mentioned in the introduction to the present thesis, this feature is characteristic of a specific strand in contemporary British literature which has been discussed in some detail by Schabert. Even though Schabert primarily refers to the genre of the novel in her statement that, despite the depiction of fragmentarised communities, the act of narration ultimately serves to generate meaning (Schabert, 2006, 436), the same phenomenon may be witnessed with regard to the activity of narration in general.

ploy narrative means for the production of group identities, which, in turn, inform their personal identities. This perception of fiction as a tool for the generation of meaning clearly deviates from 'postmodern' assumptions about the status of literature. Moreover, as has been outlined in the introductory chapter to this study, the specific depiction of identity constructions to be observed here differs markedly from 'postmodern' conceptualisations. While the latter posit that identities are, by default, never stable but rather permanently changing, the examples in *On Beauty* imply that the protagonists themselves are in search for precisely those lasting, seemingly essentialist forms of identity decried by 'postmodern' theories. Moreover, although they have to overcome frequent backlashes, the characters, at least to some extent, succeed in their endeavour to form lasting affiliations. Despite the occasional need for re-orientation, the constructions of Sameness analysed above serve temporarily as momentous sources of stability and support. A further striking feature in this context consists in the fact that, even after failures, the protagonists do not abandon their belief in the viability of the concept as such (in Smith's case exemplified by the family) but rather seek new forms of application by, for example, turning to a different social context or by trying to apply the idea to a different set of people. Thus, on an intradiegetic level, i.e. within the perception of the protagonists, a certain continuity unfolds. Undoubtedly, the thrust of each construction could easily be dismantled on an extradiegetic level by, for instance, highlighting suppressed differential categories such as class or age. Nevertheless, I would like to argue that this fact does not automatically render the constructs as such dysfunctional since they obviously work for individual characters and provide at least the illusion that lasting and stable identities could ultimately be achieved.[110]

With regard to the concrete strategies used for the construction of the respective communities and in-groups, it is remarkable to note that the concept of the family itself is subject to a decisive re-valuation: Despite repeated altercations and tensions, the potential benefits to be derived from the family are never questioned. The institution of the family is apparently not perceived as the core of the problem; rather, it is the behaviour of individual members which is subjected to closer scrutiny and found to be faulty. Interestingly enough, the notion of the family promoted here turns out to be comparatively conventional and, on closer examination, does not truly mirror current developments in either British or American society. While sociological studies demonstrate the increase in 'new' family types consisting of, say, one spouse and their offspring or two partners with children from previous relationships, the idea of the family in *On Beauty* displays a much greater proximity to the bourgeois concept of the nu-

---

[110] Due to the scope of this thesis, it is not possible to include an assessment of similar cases in 'real-life' situations – as, for instance, the notion of 'Africa' as a shared homeland. Nevertheless, the question of whether similar strategies are at work in this context is undoubtedly worthy of further investigation.

clear family. Moreover, values such as solidarity and mutual support are clearly endorsed. This return to a fixed system of values likewise constitutes a feature which distinguishes this approach from the strategies adopted by 'postmodern' texts. It may therefore be considered one of the decisive elements by which to set off the strand of literature discussed here from other developments likewise observable in British fiction at present.

Re-established Boundaries and 'Faked' Authenticity in Gautam Malkani's *Londonstani*

Despite being a novel professedly written for teenagers,[111] Gautam Malkani's debut *Londonstani* was eagerly awaited by the papers' literary critics, who, right from the start, received it as the follow-up to previous highly successful and best-selling pieces of 'second-generation' fiction. Immediately, comparisons to writers such as Monica Ali and Zadie Smith abounded. Due to the novel's subject-matter and its extensive treatment of black Asian culture in London, great importance was attributed to the fact that the author himself stems from an 'ethnic' background. Irrespective of his education at Cambridge University and his subsequent career with the Financial Times – two aspects which clearly set him off from the milieu he describes – parallels between himself and his protagonists were drawn almost at once. The search for similarities culminated in Malkani's being labelled the "Muslim Irvine Welsh"[112], which, seeing his non-Muslim creed, cannot but appear absurd. An equally far-fetched discussion arose about the 'authenticity' of the language used by the protagonists.[113] With regard to this feature, *Londonstani* was strangely enough both praised for cap-

---

[111] See Clayton Moore's review on the subject. Clayton, Moore, S. „Londonstani." *About.com: Contemporary Literature.* 28.11.08.
<http://contemporarylit.about.com/od/fiction/fr/londonstani.htm>. In an interview with Bhasi, Malkani likewise states "I did my dissertation in Cambridge on Asian rude boys. The objective was to finds [sic!] links between ethnicity and masculinity. From then on I always wanted to turn it into a piece of non-fiction. I wanted to write something that young people will read. My book is about boys trying to be men. My aim is to write for kids who don't read books" (Bhasi, Ishara. „I hate it when they talk about me and not the book." *DNA.* 20.05.2006. 28.11.08.<http://www.dnaindia.com/report.asp?NewsID=1030354>). The fact that the novel was initially intended for a teenage readership provoked McCrum's dismissive comment: "Hype aside, this spirited coming-of-age story, narrated by Jas, a Hounslow schoolboy, in a mish-mash of patois, rap, text messaging and west London street-talk, is a promising debut. If it had been published, as its author once intended, as a teen novel, it might have found a secure place as a contemporary classroom cult. Alas, everything about its short life has been a disaster. Once Fourth Estate, hungry to cash in on the White Teeth and Brick Lane market, had paid an advance in excess of of [sic!] £ 300,000, the die was cast. Thereafter, Londonstani had to be 'the literary novel of the year'. Like a Fiat Uno entered for Formula 1, after a squeal of brakes and a loud bang, Londonstani was reduced to a stain of grease, and some scraps of rubber and tin, on the race track of the 2006 spring publishing season" (McCrum, Robert. "Has the novel lost its way?" *guardian.co.uk. The Observer.* 28.06.06. 28.11.08.
<http://observer.guardian.co.uk/review/story/0,,1784465,00.html>). In view of the considerable critical attention given to the novel, though, it still remains to be seen whether *Londonstani* will in fact turn out to be as shortlived as McCrum claims.
[112] Sethi, Anita. „The curse of being labelled the 'new Zadie'. *guardian.co.uk.* 14.11.05. 28.11.08. <http://books.guardian.co.uk/comment/story/0,,1642095,00.html>.
[113] Manzoor points out the absurdity of requesting an 'authentic' knowledge of each subject a writer covers in their fiction and underlines that this request is first and foremostly brought forward when 'black' writers are concerned. Manzoor, Sarfraz. „Why do Asian writers have to be 'authentic' to succeed?" *guardian.co.uk. The Observer.* 30.04.06. 28.11.08. <http://observer.guardian.co.uk/review/story/0,,1764420,00.html>.

turing the diction of London youths with enormous precision and, at the same time, dismissed for its 'unnatural' and constructed style which, according to certain critics, bespeaks an ignorance of the real-life equivalent of the environment described in the novel. Even though I deem the discussion as such slightly absurd, I will briefly return to the matter in my analysis of the rhetorical structures of the text since the register proves a vital component in the consolidation of collective desi[114] identity.

Apart from this aspect, the following sections will explore the differential categories addressed by the narrative and will trace how those categories are reasserted and strengthened in order to render them functional as a basis for the construction of collective identities. In the process, it will be demonstrated in how far *Londonstani* presents a new approach towards the formation of ethnic identity; moreover, light will be shed on the notion of 'authenticity' upheld by the protagonists, especially with regard to the promotion of specific customs and a particular way of life as the only 'real' or 'true' one.

Narratological and Stylistic Structures – An 'Authentic' Perspective?

Due to the consistent use of an autodiegetic narrator, *Londonstani* conveys the impression that it is related from an entirely homogeneous perspective. At least as far as the narrative voice is concerned, we are exclusively presented with the point of view of protagonist Jas. What is more, the narrative voice is endowed with a prominent presence due to frequent direct addresses to the reader. Although this strategy may be seen as an attempt to establish a bond with the (potentially likewise young, male) reader, some of these direct turns to the audience appear like comparatively clumsy attempts to provide the necessary (cultural) background information to elucidate certain references, for example when the narrator states: "In case you don't know, a rakhi is a special thread your sister ties on your right wrist."[115] This holds particularly true when the narrator comments explicitly on statements he made earlier in the text and reveals the source of one of his allusions or explains it a couple of pages later on. Sometimes, the impression arises that, having inserted a witty pun, the narrator becomes anxious that his hints have been lost on the reader after all. This is, for instance, the case when Jas, after quoting Take That, remarks about his own musings that he

---

[114] 'Desi' is the term used by the protagonists as a self-characterisation. It does not only connote a specific ethnic background but likewise refers to a whole way of life which, amongst other things, includes a specific dress code, an eclectic style in music, a 'correct' way of speaking, and a complex set of rules defining 'adequate' behaviour.
[115] Malkani, Gautam. *Londonstani*. London *et al.*: Harper Perennial, 2007. 175. Hereafter quoted as Londonstani.

should "stop it [his mind] singin fuckin Take That songs in my ear from inside my fuckin ear" (Londonstani 294).

A further moot point with regard to the structural arrangement of the text consists in the temporal sequence of the events. While large stretches of the novel are presented in the form of dialogues between alternating characters – a feature to be discussed in greater detail below – the story is periodically interrupted by passages which offer Jas's thoughts on specific topics or situations. As they do not differ markedly from the rest of the text in terms of style or tone, they are exclusively set off from the main narrative by their content. These passages, which, at times, extend over several pages, provide insights into Jas's mental struggles, his attempts to entirely comprehend 'desi' culture, and his anxiety to secure his status as a member of the gang. The use of present tense in these reflections lends the narrative a fast-paced, agitated tone, which proves slightly reminiscent of the stream of consciousness technique (even though Malkani never exploits this strategy to its full extent but rather chooses to offer at least a modicum of information on the context instead of exclusively reproducing Jas's impressions in an 'unfiltered' way).

At the beginning of Part Two entitled "Sher", there is a break in the tone of the novel. Whereas, in the previous chapters, dialogues where either staged as 'real' conversations between individual characters or as addresses to the reader, Jas now starts an 'internal' conversation, addressing himself as "you" (Londonstani 137ff.). Starting with his preparations for the first date with Samira, Jas gives a double account of the events and permanently switches between the present and what turns out to be his vision of the future. Despite the fact that the evening out with Samira is yet to take place, Jas already starts to picture it in is mind:

> You don't need an ashtray, Ravi, the carpet's fireproof. Anyway, they lay a new one every month.
>
> * * *
>
> I tell this to Samira when I bring her here tomorrow. She laughs at me. – Fireeproof? What, in case all these posh Hooray Henrys get too fast with their dance moves? (Londonstani 206-7)

At first, transitions between the two time levels are marked by either linguistic means or by visual signs such as the asterisks in the example given above; in contrast, towards the end of the story, the switches gradually become more abrupt until the cuts between present and future take place between individual paragraphs. These permanent switches between two time levels create a breathless, hectic tone, probably intended to reflect the protagonist's growing agitation and unrest. Yet, especially as far as the funeral scene is concerned, the technique, to my assessment, fails since, due to the complete lack of any signal indicating a prolepsis of several weeks, the blending of the funeral of Reena's grandfather with that of her husband-to-be is likely to provoke initial confusion with the reader. Moreover, the stylistic change in Part Three adds to the impression of the narrative's growing increasingly inconsistent as the change in style is not discernibly motivated by the subject-matter.

As pointed out above, the novel comprises several samples of 'pure' dialogue, in which a scenic mode of presentation is employed. Here, the narrator recedes almost entirely into the background as conversations are reproduced without any intervention on his part and may, in Genette´s terms[116], thus be labelled instances of external focalization. These conversations at times stretch over several pages, giving a 'voice' to other characters without having them act as either narrators or focalizers. Those passages prove remarkable in terms of style as the novel attempts to reproduce the protagonists' accents both with regard to the spelling of individual words and as far as (incorrect) grammatical constructions allegedly typical of first and second generation speakers of English are concerned:

> - Theekh hai, darling. He's *your* son too.
>
> - Oh thanks, Dad, why don't you just give me up for adoption while you're at it.
>
> - You not talk to your papa like this. I told you: too Westrenised. They don't phone us enough and our son he just sits there like a lump.
>
> - To say what, Mum? What do you want them to call and say?
>
> [...]
>
> - Beita, stop being Westrenised difficult boy. All we are saying is she should call us. She can also tell us vot's happening in her life. How we can know vot is happening in her life when she can't pick up phone to call us?

---

[116] Despite certain ambiguities and shortcomings of Genette's theory of focalization, I have chosen to adopt his terminology for descriptive purposes. On some of the problems arising from Genette`s employment of the concept of focalization see, among others, Kablitz, Andreas. „Realism as a Poetics of Observation. The Function of Narrative Perspective in the Classic French Novel: Flaubert – Stendhal – Balzac." *Reallexikon der deutschen Literaturwissenschaft*. Hg. Harald Fricke *et al*. Berlin: de Gruyter, ²1997. 99-136. For a sharpening and refinement of Genette's approach likewise see Bal's seminal study on narratology (Bal, Mieke. *Narratology. Introduction to the Theory of Narrative*. Tr. Christine van Boheemen. Toronto *et al*.: Toronto UP, 1985).

> - But what's she going to say? Aunty, you've really got to hear the
> latest Destiny's Child album? If you want to chat to her so much then
> why don't you phone her? (Londonstani 242)

This strategy lends the novel a certain cinematic quality. The impression of a stylistic proximity to filmic modes of presentation is heightened by the use of techniques frequently employed in popular cinema such as quick cuts, freeze frames as final images of a scene, and fade-outs at the end of passages. Moreover, the leitmotific strategy of characterising figures by way of their accents can be traced throughout the novel which is entirely written in a mixture of London slang expressions blended with neologisms from the Indian-British subculture[117]. As mentioned briefly in the introduction to this chapter, Malkani has been heavily criticised for the alleged inauthenticity of these rhetorical structures and been blamed for the 'unnatural' register of the protagonists in *Londonstani*. Likewise, Malkani has been reproached for venturing or even intruding into a milieu which is deemed closed off to him due to his upbringing and his high level of education. I, personally, consider both objections futile on the grounds that they do not take into account the function attributed to linguistic features in the text. As a more detailed examination of these 'ungrammatical' or 'incorrect' structures and expressions reveals, they are first and foremostly intended to indicate a deviation from the (RP) norm and to set the group of youngsters off from what may be termed established society. Moreover, Malkani does by no means claim to be offering a linguistic study of the Hounslow area. Especially in Jas's case, the unusual – and, at least for most grown-up readers unfamiliar – register primarily serves to underline the transformation the protagonist has undergone recently; Jas's desperate attempts to speak in a way which will not immediately betray his middle-class background highlight

---

[117] With respect to the study of subcultures, Hebdige's *Subculture. The Meaning of Style* still constitutes one of the seminal texts on the subject. Even though his examination focuses on groups such as the Mods and the Teddy Boys who have, by now, been replaced by other subcultural formations, Hebdige nevertheless offers important insights into the structure of subcultures and their ideological instrumentalisation. Drawing on the theories of Roland Barthes, Hebdige outlines three main strategies in coming to terms with the alleged threat posed by subcultural groups: "First, the Other can be trivialized, naturalized, domesticated. Here, the difference is simply denied ('Otherness is reduced to sameness'). Alternatively, the Other can be transformed into meaningless exotica, a 'pure object, a spectacle, a clown' […]. In this case, the difference is consigned to a place beyond analysis. Spectacular subcultures are continually being defined in precisely these terms" (Hebdige, Dick. *Subculture. The Meaning of Style*. London and New York: Methuen, 1979. 97). For a more recent account of the study of subcultures including a survey of the history of the sub-disciplines as well as a re-assessment of previous positions see Jenks's *Subculture. The Fragmentation of the Social*. Jenks likewise addresses the problem of how to differentiate between subcultures and communities. Hereby, he points out that, ultimately, subcultures must be perceived as a social construct to which specific assumptions and expectations are ascribed by 'established society' (Jenks, Chris. *Subculture. The Fragmentation of the Social*. London *et al.*: Sage, 2005).

the importance language assumes as a marker of group membership. This phenomenon is clearly discernible with respect to the gang gathered around Hardjit: Being able to communicate in the right type of slang, a sort of self-constructed 'desi-speak' sets off the 'real rudeboys' from ponces, 'coconuts', and other vilified characters.[118] As Jas's status as a member of the gang is still tenuous, he is particularly anxious to 'get his language right' in order to blend in with the others and not to be ridiculed for his 'gay' way of talking. Occasional lapses into former habits, however, betray his comparatively protected, middle-class upbringing. These passages, apart from hinting at Jas's position at the margins of the in-group, contribute to the light, entertaining tone of the novel with the blatant clashes between Jas's former register and his newly-found rudeboy style creating a profoundly comic effect:

> Most bredren round Hounslow were jealous a his designer desiness, with his perfectly built body, his perfectly shaped facial hair an his perfectly groomed garms that made it look like he went shopping with P Diddy. Me, I was jealous a his front – what someone like Mr Ashwood'd call a person's *linguistic prowess* or his *debating dexterity* or someshit. Hardjit always knew exactly how to tell others that it just weren't right to describe all desi boys as Pakis. (Londonstani 4, my emphases)

Generally speaking, terminology as such proves a highly complex and contested issue. First of all, there are various terms for the designation of people with an Asian background. The application of these terms follows an intricate maze of rules, which is further complicated by the fact that single terms can be used both as an insult and as a way of expressing proximity or friendship.[119] Moreover, the degree to which sub-differentiations are made between individual groups depends on the respective context. When set off against its white counterpart,

---

[118] This establishment of strict codes of behaviour in order to define 'authentic' forms of conduct as well as to demarcate clear boundaries between members and non-members of a specific group represents a phenomenon which may likewise be observed among African Americans in Britain. In this context, the ostracism of allegedly over-assimilated blacks constitutes a particularly remarkable feature, which Song describes in her study on ethnic identities: "Crossing cultural boundaries and behaving in ways which are regarded as White – for instance, in terms of speech or educational excellence – can be threatening to minority identity and security, as well as to their solidarity […]. Therefore, by engaging in behavior which is deemed to be White, some African American individuals risk not only condemnation, but also ostracization by their coethnics" (Song, 2003, 52).

[119] The same occurrence may be observed with regard to the term 'nigger'. While, initially, the label exclusively represented a derogatory, demeaning appellation, 'nigger' or 'nigga' is now likewise employed among black people (frequently with a grounding in rap-culture) to single somebody out as a 'brotha' and to underline the feeling of proximity to this person. When used by a white person, though, the word still causes offence and is perceived as a racist insult.

the category 'desi' includes various religious backgrounds and ethnic groups; by contrast, distinctions become far more elaborate in an all Asian-British environment.[120] As the variety of terms in *Londonstani* demonstrates, terminological issues shift and formulations used both for self-designation and as labels applied from the outside are frequently substituted by new expressions. This may be read as an indication of the fact that, at least as far as Hardjit and his posse are concerned, none of these categories results from a firmly grounded identity or stable self-image but rather serves as a temporary means to create a distance to traditional British society and to highlight the status of the gang as a group apart from white Establishment:

> I still use the word rudeboy cos it's been round for longer. People're always tryin to stick a label on our scene. That's the problem with havin a fuckin scene. First we was rudeboys, then we be Indian niggas, then rajamuffins, then raggastanis, Britasians, fuckin Indobrits. These days we try an use our own word for homeboy an so we just call ourselves desis but I still remember when we were happy with the word rudeboy. Anyway, whatever the fuck we are, Ravi an the others are better at doing it than I am. I swear I've watched as much MTV Base an Juggy D videos as they have, but I still can't attain the right level a rudeboy authenticity. (Londonstani 5-6)

The last paragraph hints at Jas's great anxiety to become a fully fledged member of the gang. His fear of not being recognised as one of the group can be derived from the repeated use of the pronouns 'our' and 'we', by which he permanently tries to assert his status as a 'real' rudeboy.

Apart from the significance of these linguistic labels, the passage quoted above proves remarkable with respect to Jas's failure to achieve a similar level of 'authenticity' as the others. As will be discussed in greater detail below, the need to display an 'authentic' version of desiness constitutes a pressing concern for the protagonists. Interestingly enough, what is promoted as an authentic ethnic identity here, on closer examination turns out to be an amalgam of different influences with a variety of elements taken from both Western and 'Indian', in this case Punjabi, culture. Despite its heterogeneity, this hybrid construct is

---

[120] According to Lipsitz, the same aspect shows in constructions of Blackness: "But they [West Indian immigrants] also became "Black" in Britain, an identity that they generally do not have in their home countries, but which becomes salient to them in England as a consequence of racism directed at them from outside their communities as well as from its utility to them as a device for building unity within and across aggrieved populations" (Lipsitz, George. *Dangerous Crossroads. Popular Music, Postmodernism and the Poetics of Place*. London and New York: Verso, 1994. 126).

presented as an 'authentic' expression of identity. Possibly due to its lack of any firm grounding in a confined, comparatively homogeneous cultural context, the ultimate definition of 'desiness' becomes highly difficult, an aspect which is further complicated by the fact that the group itself entertains only a vague notion of what desiness actually designates. Nevertheless, they doggedly stick to their version as the only 'authentic' one. Accordingly, for the youths, desiness consists, most importantly, of a detached, aloof way of behaviour mimicking the stance displayed by rap stars and actors considered cool. On a linguistic level, it comprises a maximum number of swear words and insults. While desiness remains a very vague category when considered from the inside, it is nevertheless firmly set off against non-members with rigid boundaries being drawn between, on the one hand, rudeboys and 'coconuts' (peers who are brown on the outside but white on the inside) and, on the other hand, rudeboys and goras, i.e. 'white' people with white being less a marker of complexion but rather an indicator of an affiliation to established British society. Due to the gang's self-stylisation as both an exclusive circle and an arbiter on questions of desiness, a complex web of codes and rules of behaviour unfolds which Jas is especially intent on following so as not to forfeit his membership.[121] While the binary oppositions set up by the group prove untenable on closer examination, the protagonists themselves apparently choose to ignore the contradictions within their system of classification since their very own form of desiness with its impenetrable set of rules enables them to create a strong group identity. In this context, the notion of Sameness serves as an adequate tool of analysis as it allows for a reading which reveals the tensions inherent in the construction of a collective 'desi' identity and discloses strategies by which potentially disruptive elements are suppressed. At the same time, though, it recognises the vital function of the resulting self-images and personal identities for individual group members. In the following, my interpretation will therefore move between the level of the protagonists, i.e. consider their own assessment of the situation, and a metalevel which deals with the processes of identity formation on a more theoretical plane.

---

[121] A parallel to this stance may be found in hip hop and its appeal to 'keep it real'. As Basu outlines, "'Keeping it real' introduces a discursive terrain with various meanings and evaluations in operation. The phrase relates both to the basic tenents [sic!] of creativity and artisistry [sic!], as well as a sense of identity and experience. In relation to artisitic [sic!] endeavours, there appears to be a broad distinction between those who consider themseselves [sic!] 'hip hop heads' and those that self-referentially call themselves 'niggaz'" (Basu, Dipa. „What is Real about Keeping it Real?" *Postcolonial Studies* 1,3 (1998): 371-88. 373).

Differences in *Londonstani* – A Return to Established Categories?

With respect to the types of differences discussed in the novel, *Londonstani* does not offer any innovations. We rather observe a return to the established categories of sex/gender and ethnicity/race, which are treated in a fairly conventional way and presented as based on binary oppositions with unambiguous boundaries. Due to the various overlaps and intersections, it turns out to be almost impossible to discuss the two aspects separately since various factors simultaneously exert an influence on the protagonists' perception of both of them. This holds particularly true for gender[122], the first differential category to be analysed in this chapter. As far as gender roles are concerned, the notions of 'correct' male and female behaviour are strongly informed by, on the one hand, the protagonists' age, and, on the other hand, by their ethnicity or rather by the 'cultural' group the person in question belongs to. Particularly strict rules are applied with respect to 'intercultural' dating; these guidelines do not only pertain to mixed 'black' and 'white' relationships but, for instance, also forbid the mingling of Muslims and Sikhs. Because of the great differences with regard to the conduct considered suitable for 'desi' girls as opposed to regulations for 'goras', I will limit the present analysis to the perception of masculinity and femininity within the protagonists' environment.[123] Moreover, special attention will be paid to the generation gap which shows in repeated discussions on the value of customs and traditions. Another focus will be placed on the impact of age on expectations concerning 'adequate' and respectful (female) behaviour.

To begin with, I will analyse the general stance towards women brandished by the younger generation as well as the male figures' almost obsessive assertions of their masculinity in order to circumvent the risk of being classified as gay which bespeaks their enormous fear of being regarded as a 'ponce'. As pertains to the interaction between the sexes, a tension arises from the fact that the boys are, as it were, forced to act in a markedly virile way, which also includes flirting with girls. At the same time, however, a complex set of rules regulates the

---

[122] While earlier discussions of difference frequently picked up the issue of sex, it is gender rather than sex that we are dealing with here, i.e. a term to describe "soziokulturelle Funktionen von Männlichkeit und Weiblichkeit" (Wende, Waltraud. „Gender/Geschlecht." *Metzler Lexikon Gender Studies. Geschlechterforschung*. Hg. Renate Kroll. Stuttgart und Weimar: Metzler, 2002) and to set them off from biological markers of sex.

[123] This decision is also motivated by the fact that white girls figure in the novel only as minor characters. Although it can be inferred from occasional comments by the (male) protagonists that white girls are considered morally loose or at least less strict than 'proper' desi girls, there are hardly any real encounters with non-desi girls which confirm this assumption upheld by the members of the gang. Therefore, the impression arises that we are not dealing with an actual 'fact' but rather with a heterostereotype which serves to heighten the status of girls from the protagonists' own sphere.

encounters and relationships between girls and boys. First of all, 'white' girls must not even be considered as potential dating partners. Secondly, a differentiation is made between the various religious groups subsumed under the label 'desi', which stipulates that the gang "stick to our own kinds" (Londonstani 49), i.e. not go out with Muslim girls. What is more, even fantasies come to be restricted by a complex and yet arbitrary set of norms:

> Problem is, you in't allowed to fantasise bout Bollywood actresses cos he [Hardjit] reckons they're s'posed to be all pure an everything. You in't allowed to fantasise bout someone real in case Hardjit thinks you're being serious bout them an you in't allowed to fantasise bout someone famous cos chances are they're a Bollywood actress. You in't allowed to fantasise bout blatant sluts like porn stars *cos desi girls in't meant to be into that kind a thing.* An you in't allowed to fantasise outside your own race, like when Ravi goes on bout Page Three models, glamour girls an lap dancers. (Londonstani 53, my emphasis)

Despite the light, ironic tone of this passage, Jas's breach of this rule by going out with a Muslim girl leads to his exclusion from the group and finally even culminates in threats to his life. The various discussions on 'decent' female behaviour as well as repeated displays of masculinity demonstrate the rigidity of gender roles within the group of 'proper' desis. While for girls, the two main criteria are their 'fitness', i.e. their outer appearance, and, simultaneously (and to some extent contradictory to the former criterion) their renouncement to flirt openly, masculinity is largely confined to bodily criteria, especially a muscular physique and the 'right' facial hair. To achieve the status of a real rudeboy, this look must be coupled with a tough, straightforward stance and the ability to quickly retort with witty rejoinders. Likewise, the male protagonists are highly anxious not to show any forms of behaviour which might be interpreted as a sign of weakness or effeminacy. In addition to that, technical gadgets such as mobile phones and powerful cars constitute crucial symbols of masculinity and are regarded as essential indicators of social status.[124]

---

[124] Especially with respect to the latter status symbol, it is striking to note that the traditional association of large, powerful, and expensive cars with masculine prowess is revived here. Ironically, the 'Beemers' driven by the boys are, in the majority of cases, not their own but belong to their parents or were given to them as birthday presents. While this fact undoubtedly adds an ironic tinge to these scenes, it can likewise be seen as another indication of the constructed quality of the gang's ideal of masculinity. Moreover, it reveals its all but theatrical quality: Although displayed with great pride while outside the family home, the boys' tough stance quickly wears off when in the company of older (and therefore higher-standing) members of their ethnic group or on entering one of the family homes. 'Masculine' behaviour thus turns out to be a role adopted within specific contexts rather than a lasting character trait or persistent element of the protagonists' personalities.

The passage cited previously is interesting in linguistic terms as well: Even though the expressions 'slut' and 'bitch' both designate derogatory appellations for women when used in everyday discourse, the protagonists obviously make a clear distinction between the two. While, as the quotation indicates, sluts are considered 'loose' women who engage in 'inappropriate' activities, the term bitch is frequently used to refer to desi girls. In these cases, it does not denote an indecent or immoral woman but rather constitutes a comparatively neutral term for a female person (often even coupled with a certain admiration for a girl's beauty or her striking physique). This attitude parallels current tendencies in rap, where women are likewise denoted as 'bitch' or 'ho'[125]. In this context, it is also interesting to note that allegedly non-masculine behaviour is immediately dismissed as womanish or batty, i.e. gay. At an early point in the novel, Jas explicitly comments critically on this extreme aversion towards everything judged as gay; moreover, he seems to be the only one to be bothered by the careless use of sexist terms such as bitch:

> I wouldn't decide that the proper word for a deep and dickless poncey sap is a gay batty boy or that the proper word for women is bitches. That shit in't right. I know what other poncey words like homophobic an misogynist mean an I know that shit in't right. But what am I s'posed to do bout it? If I don't speak proply using the proper words then these guys'd say I was actin like a batty boy or a woman or a woman actin like a batty boy. (Londonstani 45-6)

Strikingly, worn clichés such as the association of femininity with weakness or the stereotypical connection between impotence and homosexuality are revived and endorsed. In the process, clear demarcation lines are drawn between, on the one hand, male and female gender roles and, on the other hand, the conduct of 'real' men as opposed to homosexuals. Remarkably, the latter term does not exclusively refer to a specific sexual orientation but is rather used as a derogatory term to denote slack, effeminate, and allegedly uncool behaviour.[126] The

---

[125] The discussion on adequate, i.e. non-sexist, terms to refer to female persons has been particularly heated in debates about rap texts. In this context, the question of whether the term 'bitch' has by now lost its negative connotations still proves highly controversial. Assuming that many expressions used in rap lyrics still represent sexist or racist terms, Russell Simons even requested a ban on those appellations. See „Call for end to racist rap lyrics." *BBC News*. 24.04.2007. 30.11.2009. <http://news.bbc.co.uk/2/hi/entertainment/6586787.stm> for his demand to ban the sexist and racist terms 'nigger', 'ho' and 'bitch' from lyrics.

[126] The shift in meaning or at least in the possible range of application of certain terms likewise shows in passages where the term "Nazi" is used as a general insult instead of an indicator of a particular political stance. This is, for example, the case when Jas accuses Arun's mother of being a Nazi because of her dictatorial, oppressive style of 'governing' the family (Londonstani 236). In

worldview promoted by the young men is thus strongly dominated by the notion of heteronormativity and provokes a firm belief in the hierarchical relationship between the sexes. In order to maintain these dichotomies, all attempts to break out of established patterns are instantly quelled by the other members of the group.

To some extent, the youngsters' ideal of gender roles and 'proper' behaviour represents a legacy of their parents' attitudes. Despite recurrent protests and lamentations about the older generation's concepts, the norms perpetuated by the young are by no means less rigid. Moreover, they likewise contain ideas such as the need for women to oblige to their partners' wishes and to behave in a modest and passive way. The topic of traditional rules on female behaviour as well as the question of whether these rather old regulations have still to be followed is raised repeatedly in arguments between the members of the gang and their parents. Simultaneously, it constitutes a persistent topic among the youths themselves. Here, it is striking to note that, despite their permanent assertions of the imbecility and futility of certain codes of behaviour, the children, even though having almost reached adulthood, continue to obey their parents and to conform to their wishes. It is only in very rare cases that any of them dares to contradict their elders, let alone act against their directions. Apparently, open disobedience all but equals an act of rebellion and entails grave repercussions. While most of the conversations about their parents' backward views and the frequent lamentations about their exaggerated requirements tend to be carried out in a light, joking tone, controversial stances on gender roles assume an existential significance when it comes to Arun's marriage. Ultimately, his mother's immoderate expectations in terms of 'correct' behaviour on the bride's side and the ensuing quarrels within the family even prompt him to commit suicide.

In view of the clashing standards and expectations the second generation find themselves confronted with by a) their parents and b) their social environment, the youngsters are frequently faced with a double bind since the two sets of values prove irreconcilable in the majority of cases. This discord between a Western way of life and the norms of the parental generation apparently mirrors a problem encountered by many youths in real life as well:

---

general, the perception of the Nazi period (at least by the young) is undoubtedly skewed. This impression results in particular from scenes such as the following one, in which Jas dreams about being a Nazi: "I'll daydream that I'm a Nazi. I know it sounds like I'm being a wanker cos they were scum like suicide bombers, killin all them people an that. But were they all wankers? At least they walked an talked proply. An even if you reckoned they walked or dressed stupid, at least nobody'd take the piss outta them" (Londonstani 32). Obviously, Jas does not reflect on the cruelties perpetrated by a totalitarian system; to the contrary, he seems to perceive the Nazis as dangerous and potentially evil but, at the same time, frightening, self-confident, and therefore respected personalities.

> South Asian children born in the UK today are often exposed to two
> very different cultures. At home, their parents expect or demand con-
> formity to the norms of cooperation, respect and family loyalty. At
> school, they are expected to pursue academic success in a competitive
> and individualistic social environment. [...] The Western tradition of
> marrying 'for love' frequently comes into conflict with the practice of
> arranged marriages within Asian communities.[127]

This observation is reflected by the scenes which deal with Arun's family life.
These passages make it abundantly clear that hierarchical structures in the relationship between the sexes still prevail and that the woman is considered inferior to her husband. Even though the case in question constitutes the exact reverse of the conventional situation, in which the woman is accepted into her
husband's family where she must be provided for – as a trained surgeon, Reena
even disposes of a higher income than her fiancé – Arun's mother nevertheless
insists on the observance of traditions and demands a substantial dowry irrespective of the fact that Reena hardly represents a financial burden to the family. Tellingly, in the discussions about the issue, the woman is commodified and
treated as an asset rather than a person in her own right:

> – After the wedding, the bride will come off her father's balance sheet
> and onto Arun's father's list of liabilities. She is an underperforming
> asset that brings in no income. The dowry offsets this transfer of
> liabilities. [...] You could say these represent a father's final contribu-
> tion to the bride's pension, perhaps a redundancy package. [...]
> – But, Uncle, I go – Arun's fiancée isn't redundant, she's a surgeon.
> – Ah, but that will change when she has children. (Londonstani 180-1)

Again, as in previous conversations, the older generation insists on the necessity
to conform to traditions and to uphold customs. In these situations, counter-
arguments are laconically dismissed by reminders that this simply is the 'way it
has always been done' – a move which quells all further debate. Interestingly
enough, though, established rules are followed in such a minutely fashion only
in specific situations whereas they are freely bent in others. As a result, a permanent strain ensues which leaves the younger generation caught in constant
shifts between rebellion against dated customs and the obligation to obey their
parents. Accordingly, while the protagonists stylise themselves as tough rudeboys on the street, play truant, and indulge in abusive behaviour, they are, in

---

[127] Giddens, 2006, 215.

other contexts, strictly governed by family rules and do, in fact, not dare break out of this rigid system of guidelines. The resulting tension between the constructed rude front brandished while out on the street as opposed to the very limited degree of freedom within the circle of the family is repeatedly exploited for comical purposes: At one point in the story, the group, for instance, have to delay their drive to a fight as one of them is bound to do some shopping for his mother. Likewise, on entering Hardjit's family home, the youths all diligently put off their shoes and eagerly promise not to spoil the bed-cover. Thus, as is the case in Smith's *On Beauty*, the topic of family life also figures prominently in *Londonstani*. Contrary to the depiction of the family as a source of support and stability in *On Beauty*, though, *Londonstani* presents the strict hierarchies and severe rules in the home as a burden. For this reason, the desperately sought feeling of belonging and affiliation is primarily found among the community of friends whereby the gang acts as a sort of substitute family. This turn to units other than the family also shows in the language adopted by the protagonists. While they, by contrast to Levi, do not stylise themselves as 'bro's', they likewise use specific terms to highlight their membership in an in-group. The varying labels for self-description – 'rudeboy' hereby being the latest innovation – once again fulfil the function of establishing bonds and serve to create a feeling of commonality.

Seeing the standard of living in the respective families as well as the parents' occupations and their social positions, there can be no doubt about the fact that we are not dealing with a circle of underprivileged immigrants but are rather presented with a community of well-to-do businessmen well settled in Hounslow. Yet, despite their financial achievements, they obviously do not feel part of British society. This fact may be derived from various dismissive comments on British institutions and the professed preference to rely on one's own individual potential rather than to depend on the state for the provision of resources. Accordingly, Ravi's father expresses a general unwillingness to pay any taxes because of the alleged incompetence of the government:

> Why to pay the government? For what? So they can dig up the roads and give me traffic jam? So they can pay dole money to lazy people who call my family Pakis when they come into my brother's shop to spend their dole money on beer and cigarettes? They get lung cancer and I pay for their hospital. Bhanchods. NHS? Hah! I work like dog for private health, Indian food is better there. Defence? Bloody fool Americans should pay for it. Education? Fat lump of good it is, our beitas keep failing the A-levels. (Londonstani 181)

Thus, what Malkami describes here can be interpreted as the emergence of a 'counter-culture'[128]. In this case, the counter-cultural formation mainly consists of a set of affluent families from an Asian[129] background as well as their off-

---

[128] In view of the many different uses and definitions of the term 'culture', it comes as no surprise that the notion of 'counter-culture' likewise carries various associations resulting in different concepts. At times, the employment of the term in individual studies is even contradictory. (Comparing articles on the subject, we observe that even the spelling of the term is inconsistent with variants including its being spelled as one word, in a hyphenated form, and in two words). Apart from these linguistic issues, the concept as such also provokes considerable controversy both with respect to its temporal and local positioning and as far as its general assessment is concerned. Accordingly, Roszak, in his insightful study *The Making of a Counter Culture*, defines counter-culture as a specific formation which emerged in the United States in the 1960s. Retrospectively he comments on this movement as follows: "What I have called "the counter culture" took shape between these two points in time as a protest that was grounded paradoxically not in the failure, but in the success of a high industrial economy. It arose not out of misery but out of plenty; its role was to explore a new range of issues raised by an unprecedented increase in the standard of living. For a period of some twenty years the world's most prosperous industrial society became an arena of raucous and challenging moral inquiry, the likes of which we may never see again – at least not if those whose wealth, power, and authority are at stake have anything to say about it" (Roszak, Theodore. *The Making of a Counter Culture. Reflections on the Technocratic Society and its Youthful Opposition*. Berkeley *et al*.: California UP, 1995. xii). Nelson dismisses Roszak's study on the grounds that it, in her opinion, offers at best "a description of the counter-culture which is, arguably, almost as bizarre as the counter-culture itself appeared to the more timorous outsiders" (Nelson, Elizabeth. *The British Counter-Culture, 1966-73. A Study of the Underground Press*. Houndmills, Basingstoke and London: Macmillan, 1989. 6). Nevertheless, I would like to suggest that it still offers an informative 'snapshot' reading of a cultural formation at a specific point in time. By contrast to Roszak, Watts, who likewise locates the counter-culture movement in the United States of the 1960s, ascribes an all but redemptive quality to the emergence of a counter-culture: "Within each counterculture lies the seeds of a new beginning. One might even look upon participants as the problem solvers who ultimately help the culture by introducing its next adaptive phase" (ix). Towards the end of the introduction to *The Culture of Counter-Culture*, he even emphasises the possible metaphysical experiences to be gained from counter-cultures: "One finds here a clear view of the primary aspect of counterculture: its basis in experience, particularly in the experience of the divine" (Watts, Alan. *The Culture of Counter-Culture. The Edited Transcripts*. Boston *et al*.: Tuttle, 1998. x). As the title of her study *The British Counter-Culture, 1966-73. A Study of the Underground Press* indicates, Nelson also limits the existence of the counter-cultural movement to a confined period of time. Focussing on the British context, she highlights especially the role of the underground press; with respect to the ultimate definition of counter-culture, though, she refrains from offering any fixed formulations and rather outlines various possible approaches to the subject. What most of these theorisations of counter-cultures listed by Nelson seem to have in common is the moment of conflict with or rebellion against established society. Despite the fact that a concise characterisation of dominant society – counter-culture's other – proves almost impossible and that all attempts of a definition must, by necessity, remain somewhat subjective, I would nevertheless like to argue that the cultural formation described in *Londonstani* may be considered as an example of a counter-culture since it is located outside of 'mainstream' culture (a position which, to a certain degree, is deliberately chosen and maintained). Moreover, the element of conflict or at least tension between these groups and 'white' society is likewise clearly discernible.

[129] As Bennett, amongst others, emphasises, the term 'Asian' carries little heuristic value as it is generally used to refer to a highly heterogeneous group which, apart from a certain geographical background, do not share any 'cultural' roots (Bennett, Andy. *Popular Music and Youth Culture.*

spring. In view of the social activities of the protagonists' parents, which comprise saathis (social gatherings at private homes), receptions, and visits to Bollywood films, the degree to which this circle isolates itself from established British society becomes obvious. Having formed a close network of friends with the same (migratory) background, members of this new upper-middle class continue practising 'their' culture, stick to specific customs ranging from rakhi (Londonstani 175) to the habit of arranged marriages, and maintain traditions such as the payment of substantial dowries. As a consequence, ethnic difference comes to the fore as a decisive factor; in this case, the notion of ethnicity is closely connected to a specific way of life which sets off 'Asians' from the 'goras' living in the same neighbourhood.[130] While this behaviour is probably to some extent plausible among the first generation, who arrived as 'strangers' in a foreign country, the same tendency might prove worrying with regard to their children. This insistence to distinguish themselves from 'British society' displayed by the second generation – despite their forming part of the British nation, as least as far as nationality is concerned – is addressed explicitly the following excerpt:

> - In fact, I read an interview with him [Trevor McDonald] once and he said quite clearly that if you don't want to integrate, why did you come here?
> - We *din't fuckin come here*, innit, goes Ravi, - we *was fuckin born here*.
> (Londonstani 127, my emphasis)

Apparently, the protagonists take great pride in 'their' Indian culture, and are intent on delimiting it from English or 'gora' ways. Seeing the long period of time most of them have spent in Britain, with the majority even having been born and raised in England, 'Indianness' – or, in the youngsters' terms 'desiness' – assumes a special quality as it becomes detached from its roots. Moreover, under the impact of 'Western' elements, a new form of Indian culture emerges which is not congruent with the Indian way of life as lived on the subcontinent (provided one assumes the existence of such an all-encompassing version of Indianness, a notion which, in view of the sheer size of the country, appears reductive at best). On closer examination, the type of Indianness constructed by the rudeboys mainly serves as a means to highlight their distance,

---

Music, Identity and Place. Houndmills, Basingstoke and London: Macmillan, 2000). I chose to use the term here nevertheless as it is, especially in identity politics, frequently employed as a marker of identity in order to draw a line between 'Westerners' and the Indian/Pakistani/Bangladeshi community with origins on the Indian subcontinent.

[130] With respect to the situation in larger cities, we may detect a tendency that whole districts beging to be inhabited exclusively by either 'whites' or people with a migratory background.

probably even aversion, to established English/British society. The same holds true for renditions of 'cultural authenticity'. While the protagonists constantly insist on the need to stick to their own lot and to retain their culture in its pure form, they do not realise that this seemingly 'real' or 'true' form of desiness, which they are promoting, represents a construct only loosely grounded in 'factual' Indian culture. Rather than offering a possibility to practice one's 'original' culture in a diasporic environment, their English version of desiness primarily serves to strengthen a collective identity which caters to the demands of the second generation and recognises their need for bonds and affiliations. Moreover, as outlined above, it provides the necessary categories for a minute differentiation between desis and goras.

The habit of constructing a personal form of an 'authentic' cultural heritage may likewise be found in Hardjit's family home, where 'Eastern' religious symbols are displayed and revered irrespective of the fact that they stem from a variety of different creeds:

> There weren't no bed in bedroom number one. It was where they kept their copy a the Guru Granth Sahib on a table. They'd hung their pictures a various Sikh Gurus on the landing walls outside. They'd even got a couple a pictures a Hindu Gods too. Usually you only get Hindus who'll blend their religion with Sikhism but Hardjit's mum an dad were one a the few Sikh families who blended back. (Londonstani 51)

The same blending takes place among the younger generation. Once again, despite their firm belief in the 'authenticity' and quintessential Indianness of their version of desi culture, the members of the group unconsciously create a construct which comprises both elements of a (Western view of) Indian popular culture and icons of Western popular or youth culture. This feature shows best with regard to the points of reference explicitly mentioned in the novel. These cover a wide range of celebrities, places, and items including luxury fashion brands such as Dolce & Gabbana (Londonstani 4), Calvin Klein, Reiss, DKNY and Prada (Londonstani 199), famous actors (a list juxtaposing Bollywood icons with Hollywood stars), and fashionable London night clubs. With respect to women, though, a certain preference for 'Bollywood babes' may be detected with Kareena Kapoor taking first rank:

> Matter a fact, I reckon they're better than posters a fit goris like Kate Moss or Caprice or fit kaalis like Beyoncé Knowles or Halle Berry. Indian women (I know I should say bitches stead a women to keep things proper but I'm still workin on it) are different. Bollywood babes are ob-

viously not black or white so in't bootylicious or waifs. They're somewhere in between. (Londonstani 57)

With the possible exception of Bollywood actors and actresses, these references
do not come as a surprise as they represent well-known exponents of Western
popular culture. By contrast, references to musical genres prove worthy of further analysis as it is here that we observe a blending of various different styles
and witness the integration of a variety of heterogeneous elements into what is
finally perceived as 'authentic' desi culture. Amongst the singers and groups
referred to, bands such as Take That and Prince are placed alongside Rishi Rich
and Punjabi MC. Moreover, special value is attributed to bhangra; accordingly,
the novel repeatedly depicts the protagonists preparing for or talking about
bhangra gigs, which are usually held in the afternoon.[131] These parts of the
novel may be seen as a reflection of the current cultural scene in large British
cities, especially London and Birmingham. In these metropolitan areas, a bhangra scene has evolved over the recent years, which is by now firmly established
with concerts taking place almost every week-end. The music played on these
occasions assumes a specific significance as it is received as an expression of a
specifically British-Indian or British-Asian identity and is frequently referred to
in the construction of (Asian) cultural identities.[132] According to Leante, first
indications of this phenomenon can be traced back to Southall in the 1980s:

> Here at the beginning of the 1980s, a new form of hybridised *bhangra*
> developed and came to constitute a means for the younger generations
> to express their identity as "Punjabis in the West." […] British *bhangra*
> soon went beyond the borders of the Punjabi Sikh communities and
> started to connote a wider diasporic group: while Punjabis still represent
> the dominant group – especially in the production of this music – other
> South Asians (mostly those from the Northern regions of India) have

---

[131] In 'real life', those so-called 'daytimers' form an integral part of the current bhangra culture
and are especially popular with teenagers since they allow girls from stricter backgrounds to
attend without having to gain permission to go out in the evening. See Leante's study for different
forms of gigs and the usual structure of such events (Leante, Laura. „Shaping Diasporic Sounds:
Identity as Meaning in Bhangra." *The World of Music* 46(1), 2004: 109-32).
[132] Regarding the instrumentalisation of popular music for the creation or assertion of group identities in general, Lipsitz states: "Popular music in Britain plays an important role in building
solidarity within and across immigrant communities, while at the same time serving as a site for
negotiation and contestation between groups. Music is a powerful but easily recognizable marker
of cultural identity. […] Although popular music can never be a "pure" or "authentic" expression
of an undifferentiated group identity, as a highly visible (and audible) commodity, it comes to
stand for the specificity of social experience in identifiable communities when it captures the
attention, engagement, and even allegiance of people from many different social locations" (Lipsitz, 1994, 126-7).

also adopted it to express a broader shared diasporic identity, cutting across religious as well as regional divisions.[133]

Interestingly enough, even though bhangra is drawn upon for the construction of an Asian identity, the specific version of bhangra music most often listened to – in this case a type widely known under the name bhangramuffin – constitutes a British 'invention'.[134] Despite borrowings from traditional bhangra[135] (for instance with respect to the instruments used), the songs played at bhangra gigs represent a fusion of reggae and dancehall with occasional tinges of Western pop music.[136] In fact, influential artists such as Apache Indian, a "British-born Punjabi"[137] first rose to fame in the UK and were only subsequently discovered and celebrated in India, the alleged home-country of their music, as well. Revealingly, Apache openly admits that his music is infused by a profoundly British quality and is, for this reason, rejected by many Asian listeners and fellow musicians.[138]

Apart from bhangra, further musical genres influence the youngsters' behaviour considerably. In terms of style and dress code, it is striking to note that the protagonists often try to imitate the cool and aloof style of popular rappers.

---

[133] Leante, 2002, 112. Bennett, however, points out the restrictions resulting from the geographical limitation of bhangra events to larger cities with a considerable Asian population. It is only there that bhangra events take place on a regular basis (Bennet, 2000).

[134] This fact is highlighted by a laconic comment in the *DJ magazine*: "If you think that Asian music is just Bhangra, or the stuff you hear at one o'clock in your local curry house, you're wrong. This is second generation music from a culture that is as British as it is Asian" (*DJ magazine 74*, March 1997. qtd. in Banerjea, Koushik. „Sounds of Whose Underground? The Fine Tuning of Diaspora in an Age of Mechanical Reproduction." *Theory, Culture & Society* 17(3), 2000: 64-79. 7).

[135] For a detailed account of bhangra in its original form as a "harvest ritual of the Punjab region in North India", see Roy, Anjali Gera. „ 'Different, Youthful, Subjectivities': Resisting Bhangra." *ARIEL* 32(4), Oct. 2001: 211-28. 226-7.

[136] By now, there are various examples of traditional bhangra elements being fused with other contemporary styles; as Leante states, "[i]n *bhangra* tracks, it is therefore possible to find excerpts of disco or rock songs, or various other kinds of music" (Leante, 2004, 121).

[137] Taylor, Timothy D. *Global Pop. World Music, World Markets*. New York and London: Routledge, 1997. 155.

[138] In general, the reception of bhangra in a British context differs markedly from its reception in India. As Roy observes, "Desibhangra is robbed of its subaltern resistivity by its largely middle-class constituency. Unlike Br-Asian youth who use Bhangra to mark ethnic difference, Indian middle-class youth turn to Bhangra as World Music to participate in the centre" (Roy, 2001, 221). For the early history of bhangra and its instrumentalisation in the search for Asian unity, "[where] the new styles of *bhangra* provided not only a symbol, but the focal point of a new youth culture, complete with its own venues and conventions, activities and interests, within which divisions of class and caste, religion and nationality were consciously denied significance", see also Baumann's seminal essay "The Re-Invention of Bhangra" (Baumann, Gerd. „The Re-Invention of Bhangra." *The World of Music* 32 (1990): 81-98. 91).

Thereby, a third 'culture' enters the equation since rap originated in the context of (lower-class) black US-American culture and the majority of its dominant figures such as Eminem, Snoop (Doggy) Dog, Tupac Shakur and 50 Cent still hail from (lower class) urban American backgrounds.[139] This environment likewise forms the context from which bling culture emerged, which constitutes yet another form of cultural expression adopted by the group of rudeboys and integrated into their version of 'authentic desiness'. For the reader less well versed in contemporary urban youth culture, the novel offers a definition of bling brought forward by Sanjay in his first conversation with the boys:

> The word bling has made it into the *Oxford English Dictionary* precisely because it isn't some passing phase, boys. This lifestyle, these material possessions, this is how you big yourself up, as they say. You will forever be judged and judge yourselves by your luxury consumerist aspirations, your nice stuff. [...] Believe me, I've thought a lot about this, I used to be Mr Ashwood's favourite dork, remember. But there's no Marxist alternative any more. The fall of communism, the rise of bling. (Londonstani 167-8)

It is here that we witness an intersection of the storyline with the everyday reality of at least part of the readership primarily targeted by the author. Even though the world of high-end London night life will be closed off to most of them, a great number of second-generation youths are undoubtedly familiar with TV channels such as MTV Base and probably have attended bhangra events themselves. Moreover, the novel caters directly to the habits and demands of the 'Web 2.0-generation' by offering a list of "Jas's favourite websites" at the very end of the book including blogs on myspace and sites on current music events in the UK.[140] In a certain respect, this move can be seen as a crossing over from 'fiction' into 'reality', which lends the novel an 'authentic' tinge as it implicitly claims to cite real-life sources. This impression is strengthened by the inclusion of photographs on the final pages of the book which dis-

---

[139] On the 'black origins' of rap and hip hop, see Perry, Imani. *Prophets of the Hood. Politics and Poetics in Hip Hop*. Durham and London: Duke UP, 2004. Even though the notion that "a musical composition, and musical forms in general, have identities rooted in community [...] [which] might be as small as an artistic collective or as vast as a continent" (9) is clearly contestable, there is no denying the fact that rap and hip hop at least partially originated in a black US-American context. As to the subsequent instrumentalisation (and financial exploitation) by the mainstream film industry as well as the commercialisation of hip hop and rap, see Donalson, Melvin. *Hip Hop in American Cinema*. New York *et al.*: Peter Lang, 2007 (esp. Chapter 6, "Beyond the Reel: Rappers, Bling, and Floss").

[140] In view of the fact that, at the time of writing of the present thesis, some of the pages have already gone off the web, it appears dubitable whether this 'gimmick' will have a lasting appeal. Surprisingly enough, the pictures as well as the website were only introduced for the paperback version of the book and cannot be found in the first hardback copy.

play elements from bling culture and confer a greater visual – and thereby
probably also more 'real' or 'factual' – quality to the status symbols cited in the
novel.

The phenomenon of blending different styles and 'traditions' may furthermore
be detected with regard to filmic references. Apart from the occasional mention
of Hollywood blockbusters such as *The Sixth Sense*, great emphasis is placed on
Bollywood film[141]. As Ganti points out, this genre carries a huge potential for
identification and appeals to a great number of spectators as, unlike other Indian
cinemas, it is not bound to a specific language or region:

> There was no one Hindi, as it varied according to region. Filmmakers
> finally settled on a type of spoken Hindi known as Hindustani – a mix-
> ture of Hindi and Urdu – a language associated with bazaars and trading
> that served as a lingua franca across northern and central India. This led
> to a peculiarity – Bombay became the only city where the language of
> the film industry was not congruent with the language of the region;
> Gujarati and Marathi being the dominant languages of the region. The
> fact that cinema in the Hindi language developed in multi-lingual Bom-
> bay, rather than in the Hindi-speaking north, disassociated Hindi films
> from any regional identification, imbuing it with a more "national"
> character.[142]

---

[141] Seeing the popularity of bhangra, it does not come as a surprise that Bollywood is likewise
referred to in the novel on several occasions. With regard to the connection between those two
forms of cultural expression Bennett states that "for many consumers of bhangra the music is now
associated with 'Bollywood' […] as with it is [sic!] with the Punjab" (Bennett, 2000, 121). The
connection is likewise pointed out by Leante (2004).

[142] Ganti, Tejaswini. *Bollywood. A Guidebook to Popular Hindi Cinema*. New York and London:
Routledge, 2004. 12. With respect to the potential Bollywood cinema offers for the formation of
collective identities, it is worthy of note that apparently a 'blending back' is currently taking
place, which portrays Indians living abroad as following a more 'authentic' way of life than Indians living on the subcontinent: "In fact since the mid-1990s, Hindi films have frequently represented Indians living abroad as more traditional and culturally authentic than their counterparts in
India. […] Thus an authentic "Indian" identity – represented by religious ritual, elaborate wed-
dings, large extended families, respect for parental authority, adherence to norms of female mod-
esty, injunctions against premarital sex, and intense pride and love for India – is mobile and not
tied to geography" (ibid. 42-3). In a certain respect, this holds also true for the depiction of 'Indian' life in *Londonstani*. Here, the first generation in particular is shown to adhere firmly to their
allegedly original customs and to anxiously follow rituals and traditions. The younger generation
likewise pride themselves on their 'cultural authenticity' and point out their connections to the
Indian subcontinent even though some of them have not even visited their 'home country', yet.
This stance intersects with a similar phenomenon among black British people who likewise refer
to 'Africa' as their home country, sometimes without ever having been there.

Interestingly enough, an analysis of the current production of films in England reveals the growing influence of Bollywood elements. Still, we are not dealing with a mere transfer of images and conventions but are rather presented with an adaptation of specific motives and strategies – for instance the integration of song and dance – and their being implemented into genres with which Western audiences are already familiar.[143] This development is presumably furthered by two aspects: First, numbers of audiences with a 'mixed' background have grown considerably; especially those Indians living in the diaspora or belonging to the second generation are likely to choose film productions which cite the cultural contexts in which they have grown up or which have been passed on to them via their parents. Secondly, interest in the ('palatable') exotic has been steadily increasing among Western audiences, a tendency which may likewise be perceived with respect to the growing popularity of Asian music. As to the films explicitly referred to in *Londonstani*, one title in particular is reflected on extensively. *Devdas*, the adaptation of a novel by Saratchandra Chatterjee, was first put into film in 1928 and has by now undergone various re-makes. The film offers an example of a plot-structure highly characteristic of Bollywood movies, which describes how the possibility of a successful love match is thwarted by class boundaries.[144] On his evening out with Samira, Jas comments dismissively on this recurrent storyline:

> Boy an Girl are always just bout to live happily ever after but then peo-
> ple in their families with nothin better to do with their time start buttin
> in an havin problems with it, gettin all hung up bout this shit an that
> shit. […] In *Devdas* all the izzat shit involves Shah Rukh Khan being a
> Brahmin an Aishwarya Rai not. Then some sister-in-law makes Shah
> Rukh Khan's mum insult Aishwarya Rai's mum or someshit an pretty
> soon the dude starts drinkin himself to death (sorry if I just ruined it for
> you). An that's how Bollywood films say all kinds a important shit bout
> how fucked up things can get if you get too hung up bout your pride an
> your izzat an shit. (*Londonstani* 250)

Despite Jas's derogatory summary of the plot, the film reflects a pressing prob-lem likewise covered in the novel: As Arun's case illustrates, the younger gen-

---

[143] *Bride and Prejudice*, the Bollywood adaption of Austen's classic *Pride and Prejudice*, defi-nitely represents one of the first commercially successful examples of such an adaptation.
[144] Remarkably, the subject-matter of Bollywood films seems to have undergone a transformation in recent years; in this process, the rebellion-plot has frequently been substituted with more con-servative storylines: "[S]ince the mid-1990s, the theme of compliant lovers willing to sacrifice their love for the sake of family honor and harmony has become dominant. The hero and hero-ine's passivity and obeisance to patriarchal norms of honor and notions of filial duty illustrate the essentially conservative outlook of many contemporary Hindi films, regardless of their cosmo-politan and MTV-inspired visual style" (Ganti, 2004, 40-1).

eration find themselves caught between, on the one hand, the obligation to show respect to their parents as well as to conform to their wishes and, on the other hand, their personal desire to lead an autonomous life and to make their own decisions. Tragically, Arun, after a prolonged period of tensions, cannot bear his mother's constant nagging any longer and finally commits suicide.

This suicide is closely linked to the second film discussed at length in *Londonstani*: the Wachowski Brothers' *The Matrix*. In his conversation with Arun, Jas tries to boost Arun's self-confidence by quoting Morpheus, one of the protagonists in *The Matrix*:

> There's a difference between expecting them to show *some* respect an *more* respect. The former is fair enough. The latter, on the other hand, is some fucked-up, lowlife, retarded Nazi bullshit. [...] That gets Samira lookin back at me now. Lookin, as if to say, OK, Jas, so tell me, where's all this coming from? I never had you figured as a revolutionary leader of men. *Ah, but that's because you can't see the base of my skull. The tiny porthole. Plugging me into the mainframe. Uploading the program, the knowledge, the truth into my mind. So that I, Morpheus, can free the minds of others.* (Londonstani 237-8, orig. emphases)

There is a certain tragic irony to the fact that Jas's advice taken from a Hollywood blockbuster provokes Arun to terminate his life in an almost Bollywood-like scene. Even though Jas refuses to be blamed and tries to present the events as the result of a fatal misunderstanding, the incident can still be taken to imply that the second-generation either has to break completely with family traditions or to accept them, a depiction which outrules the possibility of an independent life within the context of the nuclear family. Once again, ethnicity is thus re-established as a differential category which rigidly demarcates English-born members of the second generation from their non-hyphenated peers.

Nevertheless, at the very end of the novel, ethnicity as a basis for a stable group identity is revealed as a construct without any grounding in biological 'facts'. Despite occasional remarks on Jas's being different from the rest of the group, there is, for vast parts of the story, no reason to assume that he had initially not belonged to the gang because of his ethnic background. Even though instances can be found which, in hindsight, point to Jas's not being Asian, the passages in question always allow for a reading which traces certain oddities and exceptions back to the fact that his family is not Muslim (which does not necessarily imply their not being Hindu or Sikh either). Moreover, repeated comments on Jas's 'ponceyness' and his level of education which likewise set him off from the other members of the group lead the reader to explain away Jas's semi-outsider status by his lack of self-confidence and his frequently insecure, non-rudeboy-like behaviour. It is only on the last pages of the book that, in the final show-down between Jas and his parents, his factual ethnicity is disclosed:

> And while Harjit's father is always saying how his son abuses his Sikh religion, I've respected your ways, your youngster's version of Indian culture. And we both tried. Your mother and I. We tried for your sake to be friends with them, to be like them, to get to know them. […] Your mother here, she even tried to cook like their mothers. We tried. You're not like them, son. […] I don't even know why we agree to use this Jas nonsense nickname of yours anyway, I mean what kind a name is that, Jason? […] What nonsense is this you don't even respond to your own name? Jason Bartholomew-Cliveden, do you hear what I'm saying? […] It says your name here on your medical chart: Jason Bartholomew-Cliveden, aged nineteen, white, male. (Londonstani 340)

This revelation elucidates the motivation behind Jas's over-eagerness to assert his affiliation to the gang and his exaggerated use of pronouns such as 'we' and 'us' in order to emphasise that he, by now, belongs to the group, too. Similarly, his frantic attempts to adopt the other members' 'authentic' version of desiness are shown to result from an ardent wish to be accepted. For this reason, I would like to argue that Jas, in a certain respect, shares his Asian peers' diasporic or immigrant status as he, just like them, obviously does not feel 'at home' in the English middle-class context into which he was born. To the contrary, Jas seems desperate to forge new affiliations which will finally allow him to achieve a satisfying personal identity.

In order to analyse this phenomenon in greater detail, it proves fruitful to apply the concept of Sameness so as to grasp the instrumentalisation of ethnicity as a differential category. Similar to the portrayal of the situation in *On Beauty*, permanent efforts are required to uphold the notion of a closely-knit community and to maintain its functionality as the grounding of a collective identity. By contrast to the groups discussed in *On Beauty*, though, we are here not dealing with cases of multiple affiliations but rather with one single group, which is drawn upon as a basis for the formation of coherent self-images by its members. Within this group, the elements indicating affiliation stressed primarily are age, sex/gender, and ethnicity. The resulting self-image is that of a cool teenage Asian male with great sexual prowess and high virility, who is well-versed in the rules of street-life. Since this self-image is completely at odds with the ac-tual living conditions of the protagonists and their families, aspects which might contest this constructed form of desiness have to be suppressed, if possible even erased, immediately. In the last instance, though, these efforts are necessarily doomed to failure.

Despite this ultimate failure of desiness as a lasting basis of a British-Asian collective identity (at least as far as Jas is concerned), the novel does not end on an entirely gloomy note. The outcome of the story might rather be seen to suggest that successful inter-ethnic relations are possible after all and that they do not even require the pretence of an 'adopted' ethnicity. In tune with this assumption, the last scene allows for the interpretation that, even though Jas has been forced to shed his grounding in desi culture and to acknowledge his 'true' ethnicity, he succeeds in establishing a bond with the Punjabi nurse and thus bridges ethnic boundaries.

Londonstani – A Reversal of Established Boundaries and a Revaluation of Difference

As the foregoing examination of *Londonstani* demonstrates, the novel foregrounds race/ethnicity as the main differential category on the basis of which boundaries are erected, communities constructed, and, ultimately, identities forged. Moreover, all further differences which might likewise play a role are, to some extent, subsumed under this category or are at least evaluated according to the 'ethnic' norms defined by the protagonists, i.e. regulations on gender roles, for instance, are always simultaneously informed by a person's ethnic background. At this point, it is interesting to note that, in its general approach towards difference, the novel proves comparatively conventional: Apart from the race/ethnicity dichotomy, it draws almost exclusively upon established categories such as sex/gender and age. Strikingly, these features are all integrated into the project of strengthening a collective *desi* identity. The desire to create such identity arises from the assumption that a strict opposition between 'British', or rather established white, society and desi culture exists. This perception results in a classical 'us-vs.-them' scenario.

A closer analysis of the employment of ethnicity as a differential category reveals several significant characteristics which distinguish *Londonstani* from other narratives focussing on the same topic. First of all, 'inborn' visual features of affiliation play a less dominant role and are not central in the construction of desiness. By contrast, desiness is – as far as outer appearance is concerned – primarily defined via a specific dress code and particular ways of grooming. Secondly, 'authentic' desiness is not merely a matter of birth or ancestry but rather a question of adequate behaviour. Accordingly, Asianness does not automatically guarantee an individual's status as a desi. This decision rather depends on the subjective estimation of the 'in-group' who assess whether a new aspirant displays a sufficient distance to English establishment and whether he abstains from assimilating to 'indigenous' British culture, the second precondition to be met before being granted access to the group of rudeboys. Simultaneously, the recovery of 'Indian' habits and traditions is promoted and, for that matter, members are urged to adhere to their 'original' culture. In this context, the discussion between Ravi and his former teacher Mr Ashwood turns out to be highly informative:

> - [...] Anyway, dat man is jus anotha BBC ponce.
>
> - Trevor McDonald?
>
> - Yeh, man. Only Trevor I got time for is Trevor Nelson.
>
> - I sincerely hope you're just feigning your ignorance, Ravi. Trevor McDonald is on ITV, not the BBC. He's a national institution, for crying out loud.
>
> - ITV, BBC. How does dat make him any less poncey? Put him on MTV Base an I'll listen to him.
>
> - Correct me if I'm wrong, Ravi, but isn't this Trevor Nelson fellow a BBC man?
>
> - A'ight, wiseguy, so you know yo shit. So wat? There're loadsa Asians on da BBC but Trevor Nelson don't act like a BBC ponce. He ain't a sap. (Londonstani 127)

This passage aptly demonstrates the arbitrariness with which Indians in prominent positions are judged. While some are dismissed as 'ponces', others are highly estimated despite their being employed by institutions deemed backward and conservative such as the BBC. Even though Ravi's eclectic hierarchisation of TV presenters in this passage mainly serves to produce a comic effect, the same stance is exhibited by other protagonists throughout the whole novel. Altogether, it may be read as an indication of the constructed quality of 'authentic desiness', which does not rely on any clearly definable facts but rather results from the subjective evaluation of a person's status.

Another element among the recurrent topics of the plot which figures prominently consists in the gang's anxious attempts to delimit their circle from other groups and to affirm their own cultural superiority. Despite being British citizens in legal terms, the members of the gang do not identify with the English nation state or with British institutions but are rather intent on highlighting their being different from English/British society. What is more, no attempts are made to achieve integration into or at least a sort of reconciliation with 'white' society. To the contrary, the group scorn their peers who try to assimilate and decry them as 'coconuts' who have given up their 'real' identity. Hereby, the youths misconceive the fact that, in the last instance, all three groups, i.e. their parents, the alleged 'coconuts', and the 'real' desis themselves pursue the same goal. Each of them tries to acquire lasting affiliations which offer a modicum of security, allow for the construction of consistent identities, and give rise to a sense of belonging, commonality, and coherency. As I have already hinted at in the introduction, there is a decisive difference between first generation and second generation immigrants. While, in the case of the first generation, the 'return myth' still offers a common bond, this possibility is closed off to the second generation. For this reason, the return myth is partially substituted by the notion of real desiness performed in everyday life, i.e. the maintenance of an 'Indian' way of life in a diasporic environment.

To analyse this phenomenon in greater depth, the concept of Sameness provides a helpful tool with which to dissect the gang's strategies and to examine how a collective cultural identity is produced. As the permanent emphasis on the authenticity of their version of desiness reveals, the group has to uphold a clear border between 'us', the desis, and 'them', embodied by both English Establishment as well as the 'coconuts'. In doing so, they draw upon essentialist notions upon in order to retain the division outlined above.[145] According to Wren, this conduct may be considered characteristic of the construction of collective identities in general:

> [T]he most important part of what makes an assemblage of human beings a group is their shared perception of themselves as (1) a collective which is (2) numerically different from other collectives (expressed indexically as: "We are not they") and also (3) qualitatively different, at least in most cases. *Note, by the way, that when this last feature is absent individuals tend to construct such differences for themselves, with the eventual result that the group does in fact take on qualities that differentiate it from other groups.*[146]

It is only against the background of the final scene of the novel that the seemingly constitutional distinction between the group of second-generation immigrants and the 'indigenous' English population grounded on their respective inherited 'ethnic' roots proves untenable. In view of the fact that Jas does not

---

[145] Seeing that Jas's true ethnicity is only revealed at the end of the novel, I deem it justified to use the term 'essentialism' with regard to the group's negotiation of ethnicity since the reader is led to believe that all youngsters stem from the same ethnic background.

[146] Wren, 2002, 252-3, my emphasis.

stem from a migratory background but is rather 'an Englishman born and bred', the foundation of desiness on certain character traits received by birth becomes brittle. Moreover, the 'authentic' version of desi culture praised by the protagonists turns out to be an amalgam of various elements borrowed both from Western pop-culture – especially the styles promoted by rap-stars – and what is perceived as 'real' Indian culture, i.e. primarily Bollywood and bhangra. With regard to the latter component, I would like to point out once again that, on closer examination, the expressions of 'authentic' Indian culture turn out to represent a Westernised version of Indianness since bhangra, in its present popular form, originated in Great Britain and does by no means constitute an import from the Indian subcontinent. Yet, despite these contradictions and tensions, the protagonists themselves cling to the illusion that their way of life (at least as displayed when out on the streets) offers an authentic form of Indian culture. Moreover, it provides them with an important source of pride and self-respect. Seeing that none of the established forms of collective identity seems to cater to their specific needs arising from their 'in-between-status', the youths try to solve this dilemma by creating their own version of British-Asianness, or, to use a term currently rife in studies of the subject, BrAsianness[147].

Another criterion which impacts considerably on the interaction between the characters arises from the differential category of age. Here, boundaries are likewise presented as all but insurmountable. With only a few exceptions, the older generation is depicted as incapable of understanding the problems their children have to face. Especially in the discussions on the value of traditions and the need to respect one's elders, members of the first generation are frequently shown to adopt an unrelenting stance and to insist on the need to comply with customs and rites irrespective of whether their original function persists or not. This predicament is solved in different ways: While the 'real' immigrant children tend to succumb to the intra-familiar pressure and to oblige to their parents' wishes, Jas openly rebels against his parents and refuses to take part in any form of family life except the most inevitable encounters. The collision of values leads to a marked gap between the generations, who, at times, even seem incapable of communicating with each other. This impression is confirmed by the linguistic variances between the different age groups with the parental generation still speaking a form of Indian-English whereas the young have chosen a rap-like style and created their own version of patwa. Surprisingly though, while strains and discords within the family are rife, these altercations do, in the majority of cases, not cause a definite rupture between the parents and their offspring. Despite frequent complaints about their parents' stubbornness and bossy behaviour, the members of the gang immediately perform a

---

[147] For a detailed discussion of this concept and its possible modes of application, see Sayyid, Salman. „BrAsians. Postcolonial People, Ironic Citizens." *A Postcolonial People. South Asians in Britain*. Ed. Nasreen Ali *et al*. London: Hurst, 2006. 1-10.

U-turn in terms of behaviour once they have entered one of the 'Indian' houses. In fact, it is only Jas, who dares to stand up to his parents and to display a disrespectful way of behaviour. The other protagonists, by contrast, almost always give in to their parents' expectations and wishes and conform to the rules within the household. What they fail to realise, though, is the fact that, ultimately, the first generation is likewise intent on cultivating their own variety of Indianness and thus can be seen to behave in a way similar to the way of life adopted by their offspring. Although the novel gives much less space to the discussion of the parents' daily routines, it nevertheless becomes clear that their situation may likewise be analysed as an instance of Sameness. Having settled in a foreign environment, they, too, practise a specific form of Indianness. The differences between the various social groups within Indian society are hereby deliberately suppressed and 'India' or 'Indianness' as such is turned into a new point of reference, not unlike 'Africa' as the ultimate home country in *On Beauty*. Moreover, 'Indianness' serves as an incontestable justification for decisions challenged by the younger generation. By way of reference to Indian customs and traditions, controversies are quickly quelled and counter-arguments immediately rebutted.

Pursuing this line of thought one step further, we detect yet another instance of Sameness in the novel which is exemplified by the 'coconuts'. Like the first generation and the desis, they also search for lasting and stable forms of bonding. In the process, though, they take exactly the opposite path. Instead of constructing a version of Indianness which stresses their being different from English society, they, in turn, try to suppress their alleged foreignness so as to blend in with established society. Even though the outcome of those efforts taken by either desis or 'coconuts' are completely different and result in conflicting positions towards the British Establishment, the goal as such as well as the strategies employed to achieve this aim turn out to be almost identical.

Seeing that the successful adoption of 'English' codes of conduct constitutes a threat to desi identity since it implicitly rebuts the assumption of a 'genetic' or 'inborn' incongruity with English society, it does not come as a surprise that all attempts of assimilation are lampooned as a sign of hypocrisy by the desi protagonists. Moreover, the concept of 'authentic desiness' hailed by the gang only works as long as it can be presented as superior to other concepts and thus be legitimately promoted as a 'more valuable' expression of cultural identity. Nevertheless, the constructed version of desiness which can only be maintained by permanent efforts to assert its validity and to simultaneously ward off potential divisive factors remains fragile. Thus, the element of a temporary limitation – a characteristic feature of Sameness – may likewise be found in the conceptualisation of desiness in *Londonstani*: The group identity promoted by the gang retains its functionality only for a restricted period of time and never reaches a stable state.

In this context, narrator Jas obviously embodies a key figure as it is ultimately he who discloses the degree to which desiness represents a construct lacking any 'biological' or 'natural' basis. As the last pages of the novel reveal, Jas does not have any 'Indian' roots whatsoever but instead hails from an all-white English middle-class background. This 'cultural heritage', however, does not prevent him from adopting the codes of behaviour set up by the rudeboys and from stylising himself as a member of the gang by imitating their conduct. For a short period of time, he even succeeds in being accepted into the group, albeit only in a relatively weak position, which forces him to endure constant nagging from the others as well as repeated remarks on his allegedly poncey ways.

This motive of a protagonist disguising his true ethnic identity in order to gain access to a circle otherwise closed off to him merely on the grounds of his looks has a comparatively long tradition and examples which exploit this plot element for comical purposes abound.[148] Thus, with respect to the plot element as such, *Londonstani* does not introduce any innovations. Nevertheless, when compared to the somewhat dated (Western) tradition of characters assuming a different ethnic identity, a significant change shows. In previous renditions of the topic, we generally detect two basic patterns: The first plotline shows a black figure who tries to hide their blackness so as to succeed in white society. In the second scenario, a white person dresses up as black, a move which almost invariably leads to a welter of comic situations and misunderstandings which are solved once the character discloses their true ethnic identity. *Londonstani*, by contrast, introduces a male, white character who denies his 'whiteness' and forms his self-image on the basis of his 'rudeboy' status. The novel thus traces a reversal of values – at least in contemporary youth culture – in which formerly ridiculed markers of Asian identity (such as a specific register and a particular dress code) are turned into indicators of coolness and street credibility.[149] In addition

---

[148] As a prototypical case, one might cite the minstrel shows. Here, a whole genre relied on this strategy in order to entertain its audiences. Moreover, the topic of dissimulated ethnic roots apparently continues to exert a profound fascination and still serves as subject matter for literary renditions, among them commercially successful publications such as Roth's *The Human Stain*.

[149] This finding is in tune with studies of recent tendencies and trends in popular youth culture and the music industry where a rising popularity of so-called Asian Kool can be observed from the beginning of the 1990s. Hutnyk and Sharma underline that, especially as far as popular music is concerned, ethnic difference is increasingly instrumentalised as a marketing strategy: "We know that popular youth culture has an adroitness for feeding upon/obliterating difference. And that difference – especially ethnic difference – sells in late-consumer capitalism. [...] Via a critique of celebratory cultural hybridity as the *lingua franca* of contemporary multiculturalism, he [Koushik Banerjea] shows how there is perhaps currently no better illustration of how ethnicity as a marker of (exotic) otherness has entered into the realms of a European popular musical culture than the

to that, we detect a deliberate instrumentalisation of exoticism, a phenomenon which chimes in with the recent rise of bhangra and its increasing popularity and integration into 'mainstream' popular youth culture. Here, Asianness is likewise exploited for marketing purposes due to its being perceived as hip and avant-garde. Part of the fascination with bhangra thus arises from its being allegedly moored in a foreign culture. For this reason, both the performers of bhangra music and their listeners, who do have a migratory background, play on their being 'exotic'.

As far as *Londonstani* and its orchestration of adopted or chosen ethnicity is concerned, the signals given by the concluding chapters are quite clear since Jas's attempts to sustain his status as a member of the group of desis ultimately fail spectacularly. Yet, prior to his ousting from the group, both he and the gang become involved in organised crime. At the climactic end of the novel, Jas even has to fear for his life, and, in the showdown scene, is seriously wounded. Against the background of this dénouement, the impression may arise that, ultimately, the two 'cultural spheres' are incompatible. This dire prediction is alleviated, though, by the concluding episode of the narrative which describes a conversation between Jas and the Indian nurse in the hospital. Here, despite their 'cultural' differences, first signs of the possibility of a dialogue and of mutual sympathy are discernible. Due to this final twist of the novel, interaction between ethnic groups is not ruled out entirely. In this context, the very last word of the novel – "Shukriya" [thank you] – may be interpreted as a hint at a potentially more successful form of engagement between the two spheres. While Jas's disguise as a rudeboy has been blown, his 'cultural knowledge' might constitute an asset in the future.

By addressing the relationship between second-generation immigrants and their British peers, *Londonstani* tackles a pressing social problem, which has recently been widely debated both in an academic setting and in the popular media. Seeing the transformation British society has undergone in the last years – not least triggered by the heightened presence and visibility of second generation citizens who do not fit 'traditional' notions of Englishness/Britishness – *Londonstani* sheds light on a cultural milieu which has so far not been covered extensively

---

example of the 'New Asian Dance Music'" (Hutnyk, John and Sanjay Sharma. „Music & Politics. An Introduction." *Theory, Culture & Society* 17(3), 2000: 55-63. 59). In *Critique of Exotica*, Hutnyk furthermore underlines the economical imbalances inherent in the cultural industry's 'Asian' turn: "The difficult fact is that those who are well connected and globally mobile can plunder the cultural resources of the world without restrictions – presently it is Asian dance music that provides the merchandise for resale in the elite salons. Shorn of political roots, toned down and sweetly packaged as exotic magical mystery tourist fare, these transnational flavours do not burn the tender tongues of middle-class liberalism" (Hutnyk, John. *Critique of Exotica: Music, Politics and the Culture Industry*. London: Pluto Press, 2000. 116).

by so-called 'Black British writers'. Although the novel can surely be criticised on aesthetic grounds, it nevertheless provides a significant contribution to the current debate on hyphenated identities and the question of Britishness. Moreover, it offers yet another example of the use of Sameness in the analysis of collective identities and shows how certain differential categories are exploited for the creation of stable self-images while other, contradictory elements, are completely suppressed. Therefore, this strategy may be understood as an example of what Hutnyk terms the benefits "to reconsider difference as something to be reclaimed, not as identity-product but as a grounding for solidarity and unity and a possible way beyond the culture industry"[150].

---

[150] Hutnyk, 2000, 134.

Dhaliwal Nirpal Singh's *Tourism* – A Return to Binary Essentialisms?

In its treatment of differential categories, *Tourism* differs markedly from the two other novels discussed in this section since, contrary to *On Beauty* and *Londonstani*, the narrative pursues a decidedly essentialist approach. Although Nirpal Singh Dhaliwal's novel likewise centres on topics such as ethnic identity, sexual difference, and the value of the family, the stance displayed by the narrator clashes visibly with the attitudes mustered by the protagonists in *On Beauty* and *Londonstani*. In those latter texts, the reader is presented with strategies to bridge differences and to create types of communities that emphasise uniting aspects, thereby highlighting experiences shared by all its members (as well as, in the meantime, suppressing those elements which might rupture this homogeneity). *Tourism*, by contrast, underlines the divisive nature of specific differential criteria – ethnicity[151] in particular – and draws clear boundaries between individual groups.

Narratological Patterns, Generic Influences, and Temporal Structures

In terms of its narratological make-up, *Tourism* follows a comparatively conservative pattern: The story is told from the point of view of an autodiegetic narrator whose perspective unalternatingly dominates the novel. Consequently, the presentation of the events related in the text is limited to the narrator's (biased) perception of the situation. Since Bhupinder attempts to construct a specific persona for himself by explicitly brandishing a detached, aloof, and uninvolved attitude, the entire tone of the narrative is likewise shaped by this stance. What is more, due to the narrator's deliberately harsh, unrelenting, and, at times, even highly offensive and politically incorrect mindset, the text contains several passages which are likely to provoke outrage in a number of readers. The offensive quality of the novel hereby mainly results from its very graphic depiction of sexual intercourse, its dismissive, sexist comments on women as well as its all but racist statements about a variety of ethnic groups.[152]

---

[151] The text itself employs the term race rather than ethnicity. From a sociological standpoint, though, what is described as 'racial' groups or features in *Tourism* would rather be termed 'ethnic' since cultural elements form the main criterion on the basis of which those groups are distinguished from others.

[152] Even though a highly intriguing topic, a detailed examination of audience reactions had to be omitted here due to the scope and general outlook of this chapter. Very briefly, though, it may be stated that readers are strongly divided into two 'camps' with one side dismissing the book as cheap, sensationalist pulp fiction whereas the other side hails it as an expression of a new-found Black-British or Asian-British confidence. In this context, a further interesting aspect consists in

As to the subject-matter of *Tourism*, the text covers a decisive period in the main character's life, tracing the various stages which bring him to a turning point and finally entail a thorough reformation – or at least a state presented as such by the narrator himself. Undoubtedly, *Tourism* therefore displays a proximity to the genre of confessional literature[153]; simultaneously, some parallels to the general plotline of the bildungsroman are discernible. These, however, remain quite faint, especially in view of the outcome of the events, so that they should be treated as comparatively loose allusions rather than a template or paradigm. Nevertheless, the question of the protagonist's development – or possibly also lack therefore, which depends on one's own assessment of the closing scenes of the story – proves worthy of further investigation. While he at first leads a life of excess and indulges in all sorts of 'depraved' pleasures such as drugs, extensive drinking sessions, and sex with prostitutes, Bhuphinder, later on, reaches a higher level of consciousness, so to speak, which makes him realise the true value of the family and in the end reconciles him with his roots. At least this seems to be implied by statements such as "[while doing yoga], I had a vision of my mother. It was nothing spiritual, just an honest realisation of how much she loved me" (Tourism 243) and "I never contacted my family. Thinking of my kid brother, my heart is heavy. Maybe it's the yoga, probably it's just age, but I know the value in them now" (Tourism 245).[154]

---

the question of whether the charge of racism would have been brought forward if comments such as the following one had been uttered by a) a 'non-ethnic' speaker and b) with respect to 'minority groups': "Like the Germans, the Japanese have sublimated their bloodlust into a taste for sport and consumer goods, and were co-hosting the tournament with Korea. [...] Watching white guys play football is like watching them dance: they do it with such gauche and inept gusto. No doubt they fuck just as badly" (Dhaliwal, Nirpal Singh. *Tourism*. London *et al.*: Vintage, 2006. 96-7. Hereafter quoted as Tourism).

[153] Axthelm offers the following characterisation as a very basic definition for the genre of the confessional novel: "The confessional novel presents a hero, at some point in his life, examining his past as well as his innermost thoughts, in an effort to achieve some form of perception" (Axthelm, Peter M. *The Modern Confessional Novel*. New Haven and London: Yale UP, 1967. 8). He continues with a description of the confessional hero as a protagonist who "often introduces himself to the reader at the outset; taken together, these introductions provide a vivid image of this type of hero. [...] This, then, is the confessional hero – afflicted and unbalanced, disillusioned and groping for meaning. He faces many of the same problems which confront every modern hero but is distinguished by his reaction to them. He views his condition not with anger but with a deep internal pain; he rejects external rebellion in favour of self-laceration" (ibid. 8-9). Even though Bhupinder does most certainly not represent the classical confessional hero in the vein of St. Augustine, some parallels are nevertheless perceptible as, for instance, his search for meaning as well as his assessments of his own way of life proffered towards the end of the narrative.

[154] In view of the high number of comparable scenes in which the narrator claims to regret his former way of behaviour towards his family – but subsequently still continues to act in exactly the same ruthless way – the 'sincerity' of these acknowledgements may certainly be doubted. Since such assumptions arise from individual reading practices, though, I will abstain from judgements on the 'truth value' or 'credibility' of the novel's final turn.

As regards *Tourism*'s engagement with the tradition of the confessional novel, the following features prove significant: First, of all, in the process of narration, the reader is, as it were, ascribed the role of the listener or confessor.[155] Provided one follows the assumption that a confession constitutes an 'act of community', though, one may detect a marked difference from the 'traditional' form and set-up of the confessional narrative, which Doody defines as follows:

> A confession is the deliberate, self-conscious attempt of an individual to explain his nature to the audience who represents the kind of community he needs to exist in and to confirm him. Confession is always an act of community, and the speaker's intention to realize himself in community is the formal purpose that distinguishes confession from other modes of autobiography or self-expression.[156]

Understanding 'community' as a group of people linked by a shared 'cultural' background or heritage, the protagonist in *Tourism* does not entirely fit this pattern. In view of his status as a bystander or 'tourist' in established society as well as his initial deliberate self-marginalisation within his own ethnic community which he achieves by actively distancing himself from his family, the narrator cannot be assumed to address members of his own circle. What is more, despite signs of regret and hints at an onsetting 'reformation' – underscored by Bhupinder's professed intention to achieve a reconciliation with his family – the narrator, even in the latter stages of the story, continues to maintain a defiant conduct and repeatedly expresses his pride in being different from white, bourgeois English society. Thus, he apparently does not shed the habit of highlighting his being different from – probably even superior to – both English and average 'Indian' middle class. This assumption is also in tune with the general reception of the novel which (in case of the more favourable reactions) saw it as an indication of a new-found Indian confidence. Consequently, the community the narrator most likely addresses is not the "kind of community he needs to exist in" but rather the circle against which he attempts to set himself off.

As sketched above, the novel depicts various stages in Bhupinder's life. For the portrayal of the narrator's gradual transformation – and his self-stylisation as a 'reformed sinner' – the text employs a series of flashbacks relating episodes

---

[155] Doody defines the confessor as "the one who hears it, the speaker's audience" (Doody, Terrence. *Confession and Community in the Novel*. Baton Rouge and London: Louisiana State UP, 1980. 5). On the roles of the confessor and the confessant as well as the special interaction between the two, likewise see Brooks, Peter. *Troubling Confessions*. Chicago and London: Chicago UP, 2000. Brooks furthermore underlines the religious tradition informing what he calls the 'culture of confession'.

[156] Doody, 1980, 4-5.

from the past. Hereby, the first and the last chapter serve as a frame for the whole story and may simultaneously be considered the two extreme poles in the protagonist's life. Accordingly, in the opening chapter set in Italy and titled "September 2003", Bhupinder is confronted with the worst moment in his life. Having spent all his money, he finds himself broke, alone, and without a place to stay on an Italian beach. The first scenes show him flirting with a girl, trying to establish a relationship with her in order to procure cheap housing. Over the course of the novel, this feature proves a recurrent plot element and may be seen as symptomatic of Bhupinder's itinerant way of life and his failure to settle down permanently and to provide for himself. Due to its being written in present tense, the first chapter conveys the impression of great immediacy. At the same time, it contains a variety of remarks about the narrator's previous travels through several European cities. These are obviously intended to arouse the reader's curiosity as they hint at various adventures coupled with a debauched way of life during the months leading up to the present situation:

> And now I'm broke. I wish I'd had foresight, not flitted and squandered from one city to the next. What was the point of Amsterdam? Months of narcotic indolence, some lechery; nothing of interest nor value. Munich was worse; I was mad to go there in winter, alone and freezing. I thought that in isolation I'd focus myself and write. But every city has its easy pastimes, easier women. Barcelona was better, for its weather and for having suspended my plans: I'd write, so I told myself, when I'd finished scratching my itch. (Tourism 7)

Those initial lines set the tone for the series of episodes to come and list the core activities during the stretch of time related in the main part of the novel: sex, drugs, and excess. Nevertheless, subtle signs of a possible reformation are discernible as the protagonist has come to the conclusion that, in the end, his drifting through European metropoles proved utterly dissatisfying: "Nonetheless, this past year: bullshit! It's brought few rewards, little joy, no peace" (Tourism 7). Especially with regard to this assessment, one has to bear in mind that we are, once again, presented with a subjective account offered from the biased perspective of an autodiegetic narrator. For this reason, it is impossible to decide whether Bhupinder's plans to change his life completely and to become a better person are mere lip service or whether he has in fact undergone a profound change of mind.

Returning to the form of presentation, I would like to draw attention to the extent to which the narrative relies on established structures. As the brief excerpts quoted above demonstrate, the novel employs a conventional opening formula: Showing the protagonist at a turning point of his life, it sets the scene for the

events leading up to this breakdown. Immediately afterwards, an elaborate analepsis follows which, in itself, comprises several moves backwards and for-
wards in time. This analepsis, which constitutes the main body of the plot,
briefly covers the narrator's childhood and teenage days via personal memories.
Those are interspersed into the main narrative which focuses primarily on
Bhupinder's life as a young adult and traces his rise from a comparatively poor
immigrant background to a person frequenting the venues of high society. The
loose thematic connection between the chapters (consisting primarily in the
repeated coverage of the same topics) lends the novel an episodic quality. This
impression is increased by the non-linear progression of the story and its
switching back and forth between various situations and places. This feature
may be seen to mirror the lack of coherence and stability in the main character's
own life. Instead of pursuing a set aim or concentrating on a specific career,
Bhupinder spends his time drifting from one girlfriend to the next, in the interim
earning his keep by writing short, badly researched, and unambitious articles for
lifestyle magazines.[157] This recurrent plot element creates a certain repetitive-
ness which is underscored by the structural connection between the beginnings
of single chapters; accordingly, the first two episodes start in a similar way:

> Luca told me to go to a prostitute; he visits them regularly. Buying sex
> helps him fuck other women; it empties him of sentiment, so he handles
> them with ease. (Tourism 10)

The same attitude towards women – i.e. the perception of females as objects to
be handled in the right way in order to achieve one's aims – is expressed at the
outset of Chapter 2:

> The tip of the redhead's cigarette flared as she took a long drag, her lips
> tight against the filter; her head cocked, her eyes raked over me. I

---

[157] Even though his nickname Puppy allegedly results from a mispronunciation of the Punjabi
"Papi" (Tourism 37), certain associations such as playfulness and a general lack of determination
impose themselves. Tellingly, it is Sarupa, the mature woman (and only female to truly touch the
narrator) who addresses him with his full name and succeeds in pronouncing it correctly. In view
of the fact that Sarupa partly triggers Bhupinder's realisation about the 'true' values in life, this
scene is clearly reminiscent of the topical scene of a calling or hailing. Opposed to the associations of playfulness and a lack of seriousness triggered by the expression "Puppy" is Sarupa's
nickname Super. Quite tellingly, in the passage which reveals this university nick-name, it is
pronounced "'soup-ah', the way upper-middle-class people would" (Tourism 123). This linguistic
feature establishes a connection between Sarupa and the higher realms of society and indicates
that she to some extent embodies the dream-come-true of any immigrant family: Having undergone a classical English formation, she is now fully accepted in the top ranks of society and apparently considered a member of the upper classes.

turned towards her and she looked away, affecting an interest in something or someone else, just as I had a moment before. (Tourism 21)

In general, a new topic is introduced or resumed at the beginning of each chapter. Moreover, the chapters themselves display an associative structure whereby
a certain thought or perception triggers a transition to an entirely different topic
or evokes memories of a specific situation which serves as a starting point for
an analepsis. For instance, while reflecting on the appeal of expensive health
clubs to the newly rich, Bhupinder remembers Sarupa's membership in a club
offering yoga classes. This episode, in turn, raises memories of a drive with her
in the car as well as the ensuing conversation:

> Clubs like this revitalise capitalists, so they can manage capitalism more
> effectively; billions are made worldwide from such ventures. I thought
> of Sarupa. She was a member of an Ayurvedic health club, called
> Bhakti Zone, in Notting Hill. She'd had a yoga class there on Saturday,
> before she met Sophie and I for lunch.

> Hatha yoga was her preferred form; it's less strenuous, placing great
> emphasis on one's breathing. She spoke about yoga for over ten minutes
> as we sat in her car. [...] Her monologue began when we stopped in a
> traffic jam, caused by road works in Kensington High Street. Being po-
> lite, I feigned a mild interest and asked a few questions. The conversa-
> tion, like the traffic, hadn't moved since. (Tourism 77)

At this point, we detect the almost imperceptible transition from the 'present' to
another, earlier point in time. This technique of providing additional information by way of flashbacks renders the chronological structure of the text more
complex as the story does not unfold in a straightforwardly linear way but rather
supplements certain events later on, a tactics which allows the reader only then
to realise the entire significance of a specific event.[158]

---

[158] This holds particularly true for the scenes involving Sarupa since Bhupinder frequently holds
back essential information such as his having had sex with her during the weekend at the Cotswolds. Accordingly, Chapter 7 ends with the unsuspicious announcement: "I pulled myself out of
the water and towelled myself dry. I waved to Ben, Ghislane and Olivia, and said good-bye. It
was nine; I wanted to leave before everyone was awake. I didn't want to be here. I didn't want to
see Sarupa at the breakfast table, didn't need the torment" (Tourism 155). The following chapter
starts with an account of Bhupinder smoking dope with his mate Michael. It is only at the beginning of Chapter 10 that the reader learns about Bhupinder's fling with Sarupa (Tourism 183ff.).
Bhupinder may thus be considered a specific type of unreliable narrator. While he does not deliberately mislead the reader by providing incorrect information, he nevertheless abstains from
mentioning decisive events and thereby guides the reader's assumptions in a wrong direction.

This strategy proves particularly interesting against the background of confessional writing as a genre influencing the novel. Gill makes an important point when she states:

> Confession, then is not a means of expressing the irrepressible truth of prior lived experience, but a ritualized technique for producing the truth. Confessional writing is poietic not mimetic, it constructs rather then [sic!] reflects some pre-textual truth. [...] Most importantly, confession takes place in a context of power, and prohibition, and surveillance.[159]

By way of deliberately inscribing itself into this tradition of confessional writing the origins of which reach back several centuries, *Tourism* cites an established literary genre, which is traditionally associated with a specific (Western) image of man as a rational being endowed with the capacity for agency. This 'Western' convention is now adopted by an 'Indian' character, who thereby, on the one hand, consolidates a connection to this tradition with its Enlightenment-inspired system of thought, but who, on the other hand, simultaneously highlights his distance to English establishment and emphasises his 'Indianness'. Moreover, in the depiction of his sexual escapades and his subsequent reformation via a semi-spiritual or quasi-religious experience (exemplified by the protagonist's taking up yoga), the narrator refers to a further literary topos dating back to early 18th century novels such as *Moll Flanders*.

In view of the subject-matter of the text with its permanent assertions of Bhupinder's status as an outsider or at least bystander in English society, a tension arises from the chosen form of presentation which, structurally speaking, situates him in a Western context. Yet, as far as the engagement with those conventional patterns is concerned, some modifications are discernible. With regard to the interaction between confessor and confessant, for instance, the power balance is clearly shifted in favour of the narrator who stays firmly in control of his story and reveals only those pieces of information he chooses to offer to the reader. It thus seems to be Bhupinder's intention to subtly weaken the confessor's position since he treats the reader more as a listener than as a true 'judge' of the events confessed – even though the protagonist adopts the stance of a

---

[159] Gill, Jo. „Introduction." *Modern Confessional Writing. New Critical Essays*. London and New York: Routledge, 2006. 1-10. 4. On the specificities of modern confessional writing and the particular rhetorical structures of the genre likewise consult Van Zanten Gallagher, Susan. *Truth and Reconciliation. The Confessional Mode in South African Literature*. Portsmouth NH: Heinemann, 2002.

repenting sinner, one may entertain severe doubts about the uprightness of this endeavour since other passages show the hero lying and deceiving repeatedly.

In addition to that, a number of further literary topoi, contexts and motives are cited which cover a broad range of themes and styles; accordingly, they contain the country house idyll in the Cotswolds episode, magazines and newspapers as diverse as *Cosmopolitan* (Tourism 23), *Tatler*, *Guardian* (Tourism 53), and *Glamour* (Tourism 121), a quote by Rushdie (Tourism 105), books by Harold Robbins, Tom Clancey, John Grisham, Jeffrey Archer, Antony Robins and Dale Carnegie (Tourism 126), and, finally, a reference to Nick Hornby (Tourism 160). Via this strategy, the protagonist situates himself into a specific literary and cultural context. Strikingly enough, all of these references are taken from the realm of 'Western' culture which Bhupinder allegedly does not consider his own.

Coupled with these real-life references are fictional titles and provocative suggestions for possible future projects, which fulfil a slightly different function. These imaginary works include, for instance, "*The Black Cock Diaries: My Struggle with Miscegenation*" (Tourism 61), "*Share My Joy*" (Tourism 71), the album Luca releases under his pseudonym White Man, and two installations titled "*Milk and Two Sugars*" and "*Niggers*" (Tourism 158). The choice of these names is obviously intended to poke fun at current trends in the art world and probably also to comment on the practice of using shocking titles and images to gain attention and to promote one's 'products'.[160]

Yet another instance of fictive titles may be found with regard to the newspapers quoted in the text. While some of them refer to truly existent publications such as the *Standard* or the *Guardian*, others prove pure imaginary. This holds true for the "*Barking and Dagenham Gazette*, *Eastern Eye* and the *Caribbean Times*" (Tourism 71-2), "*Blasé*" as well as "*Dazed & Confused*" (Tourism 92), "Cunt!" (Tourism 157), "UK Asian" and the "Afro-Caribbean Monitor" – tellingly belonging to "Ethnic News Ltd" (Tourism 211). Once again, these titles

---

[160] The notion of a product or commodity which gains its value exclusively via marketing strategies is evoked by Michael's explicit comment on his artistic practice which plays on currently 'hip' topics within the art world: "'I just gave them a load of crap,' he [Michael] said, talking about the application process. 'I wrote about how this idea deals with the white paradigm, and its appropriation of the black subject.' – 'What does that mean?' – 'Fuck knows. Evie told me to write it. But they fell for it. Can you fucking believe that?'" (Tourism 159). The passage in question moreover assumes a decidedly ironic note when we consider sponsoring strategies in the art world: While the funds are apparently intended to support 'exploited' black artists, it is actually those artists wittily exploiting the Establishment's (patronising ?) attempt to give the disprivileged a platform to speak out.

may be seen as an ironic comment on current marketing strategies and attempts to reach specific target groups.

With respect to the overarching organisation and the general logics of the text, the connecting thread between individual chapters consists exclusively in the unbroken narrative perspective of Bhupinder as an autodiegetic narrator. Moreover, several thematic links emerge, which lend the text a certain coherency, since the protagonist finds himself repeatedly in comparable situations and offers reflections on a number of selected topics over and over again. As the employment of an autodiegetic narrator limits the information provided to the reader to Bhupinder's perception, there is a very strong focus on his character. Other figures derive their importance, i.e. the space and attention given to them, from their relationship to Bhupinder and from the significance they assume in his life. Accordingly, Sarupa, Bhupinder's true love, is described lively and in great detail, whereas his actual girlfriend Sophie appears somewhat pale and indistinct, a fact which mainly results from Bhupinder's characterising her as a rather blunt person whose behaviour he only tolerates in exchange for sex and housing. Moreover, the specific rhetorical structures create the impression that the narrator tries to establish some sort of rapport with the reader. This effect is primarily achieved by two means: First, the narrator addresses his audience directly. These passages usually serve to provide further background information or to introduce one of Bhupinder's longer digressions on topics such as politics or the art world. Frequently, the illusion is created that the reader (or listener so to speak) serves as a sort of confidant(e). It is here that the protagonist voices particularly strong opinions on subjects such as ethnicity and sexual orientation.[161] Likewise, the reader is led to assume that he is given intimate insights into Bhupinder's 'secret' thoughts, for instance when being informed about his true attitude towards people such as Sophie, whom he lures into believing that he really is in love with her, whereas his true motives – sex, accommodation, and access to high society – are only revealed to the reader.[162] The reader might therefore easily gain the impression of being made privy to a gossipy exchange between friends or peers. This effect is increased by the gen-

---

[161] I have already commented on the potentially offensive quality of these remarks, especially as far as the topics of race and sexuality/sexual orientation are concerned. They undoubtedly constitute one of the features of the book most prone to raise objections and provoke critique.

[162] In the popular press, the depiction of the relationship between Bhupinder and Sophie has attracted great attention because it has been interpreted to mirror the relationship between the author and his former wife. Since the scope of this analysis does not allow for a discussion of the reception situation of the novel as well as concrete public reactions, this aspect has not been taken into account. Moreover, I do not wish to engage in speculations about possible parallels between the author's private life and the contents of his book. Nevertheless, the marketing potential of this possible 'literary revenge' should not been underestimated since it has triggered heated debates between the two camps – i.e. followers of Nirpal Singh Dhaliwal and supporters of his wife – in the yellow press.

eral colloquial style of the text, which mimics the tone of an informal conversation and relies primarily on short, unelaborate sentences and slangy, non-
standard expressions.

Throughout the whole novel, the tone of the narrative constantly shifts between
two styles since the narrator, in his self-orchestration, switches between two
different personas: On the one hand, there are several passages which depict
him in an apologetic stance and show him seeking sympathy for his debauched
actions. By contrast, other scenes portray him in a self-confident pose priding
himself on his superiority over those lacking his own (self-proclaimed) expert
status with regard to the mechanisms of cultural processes and social formations. Moreover, the novel comprises several paragraphs stylised as instances of
deep thought and profound reflection. Here, Bhupinder pretends to question his
own behaviour by tracing the stages which provoked him to indulge in activities
he professedly abhors. Especially in the first parts of the novel, the pseudo-
proximity between reader and narrator is exploited for mock-confessional
scenes in which the main character constructs the self-image of a somewhat
quixotic womaniser, i.e. the eternally misunderstood but nevertheless likeable
tragic hero:

> I've always loved women. Not in the way they want to be loved – ex-
> clusively, with unwavering attention – but in my own selfish, utterly
> sincere way. Even as a child. I hadn't begun school when I stole my sis-
> ter's dolls. I'd kiss their mouths, buttocks and chests; I smelt their nylon
> hair, their plastic skins. Breathtaken by this petting, I'd hide them naked
> behind the sofa, exhilarated. It wasn't just the slim, long-haired Sindys I
> loved, but also the big squat baby dolls who were brunette, red-haired,
> sometimes bald. Some were brown-skinned; one was black with Dionne
> Warwick curls. I loved them all. I loved women, girls; I longed to be
> loved by them. (Tourism 44)

By tracing back his longing for love – as well as his love of women in general –
to inherited or inborn character traits, Bhupinder clearly resorts to essentialist
patterns of explication. Implying that flirting is simply part of his nature, he
covertly suggests that he could not have acted otherwise and is, therefore, ultimately not to blame for his behaviour. Once again, these scenes may be read as
part of his strategy to construct a specific self-image and to convince his audience of his sincerity as he or she is allegedly allowed an insight into
Bhupinder's heart of hearts.

This constant shifting between contrasting positions and stances likewise raises the question of his reliability or rather unreliability. Even though the concept of an 'unreliable narrator' is well established in the academic literary discourse, a precise definition of this term has not been brought forward, yet. Nünning phrases this observation as follows:

> Die weitreichende Bedeutung, die der Frage nach der Verläßlichkeit bzw. Unglaubwürdigkeit des Erzählers allgemein zugeschrieben wird, steht gleichwohl in umgekehrt proportionalem Verhältnis zu den zahlreichen terminologischen, theoretischen und methodischen Problemen, die mit dieser Kategorie verbunden sind und die auf Booths unklaren Begriffsgebrauch zurückgehen.[163]

Despite this lack of terminological clarity, I deem the concept of 'unreliable narration' as such helpful for the characterisation of the narrative structures in *Tourism*. This conviction arises first and foremostly from the fact that there is, at times, a stark discrepancy between the protagonist's professed intentions and his actions. This phenomenon may primarily be detected with regard to Bhupinder's family. Even though he repeatedly proclaims his willingness to change and to stop letting down his family, he, ultimately, fails to realise this project. Moreover, as already indicated above, the protagonist's attitude proves inconsistent since he, on the one hand, exhibits a great perspicacity and acuity with regard to topics such as hybridity or identity politics but, on the other hand, stylises himself into a crude, deliberately offensive playboy.

While these arguments are to some extent informed by subjective reading practices and assessments and might therefore incur the objection of being intuitional brought forward by Nünning, I would like to turn to those more 'objective' textual features which confirm the assumption that we are dealing with an unreliable narrator. Among the textual signals indicating a case of unreliable narration Nünning lists the following aspects: discrepancies between a narrator's statements and his actions, linguistic signals of expressivity and subjectivity, a high number of direct turns to the reader coupled with attempts to guide his reception of the text and, finally, syntactic indicators of a high degree of emotional involvement.[164] Seeing that these criteria are all present in *Tourism*, it seems legitimate to classify Bhupinder as an unreliable narrator.

---

[163] Nünning, Ansgar. „*Unreliable Narration* zur Einführung: Grundzüge einer kognitiv-narratologischen Theorie und Analyse unglaubwürdigen Erzählens." *Unreliable Narration. Studien zur Theorie und Praxis unglaubwürdigen Erzählens in der englischsprachigen Erzählliteratur.* Hg. Ansgar Nünning. Trier: WVT, 1998. 3-39. 3.
[164] Nünning, 1998, 27-28.

At the same time, the illusion of an immediate, 'authentic' report of the events is fostered by the minute reproduction of linguistic specificities such as dialects and different registers since these produce the impression that the reader is directly present at the conversation:

> 'You heard wo' Mickey done? When 'e come dan?'
>
> 'Na.'
>
> 'Dincha?'
>
> 'Na.'
>
> 'Fackin ittim inni'!'
>
> 'Wanka!' (Tourism 11)

This notion of a 'true' picture of London street life is intensified by Bhupinder's comments on various communities of people. On first sight, those descriptions may be seen as an exact reproduction of the ethnic make-up of single London boroughs. On closer examination, though, the characterisations in question turn out to be fraught with essentialising, stereotypical associations which reduce members of all ethnic groups (safe the narrator's own circle) to a limited number of (negative) character traits. In this process, no distinction between individual persons is made but communities are treated as homogeneous entities. Thus, what the narrative in fact offers is a list of clichés maligning all 'cultural' groups except for the narrator's own Punjabi community. What proves astonishing here is the extensive degree to which reductive generalisations are employed. We therefore undoubtedly witness a turn away from strategies intending to reconcile or bridge differences or to search for possible points of fusion. Instead, boundaries based on binary oppositions are erected in order to underline the inherent incompatibility of different ethnic groups. It is probably at this point that the contrast to the two other novels discussed in this section, *On Beauty* and *Londonstani*, becomes starkest. Apart from the rigid stance taken by the protagonist towards other ethnic communities, a further striking feature of the text consists in its general treatment of differential categories since they are likewise essentialised and exploited for the consolidation of demeaning, stereotypical constructions of alterity. Similar phenomena have been widely theorised in Postcolonial Studies; unlike previous occurrences of this procedure, though, the formerly inferiorised 'other' is, in *Tourism*, placed on top of an imaginary hierarchy. Thereby, power relationships are reversed and value judgments are performed in precisely the opposite way with the formerly denounced now being hailed as culturally superior.

Still, the narrator himself denies any deeper affiliations to any cultural circle and, for this reason, distances himself both from the Punjabi community and from established English society. While presenting 'Indian' culture as superior to the Western realm when compared with each other, Bhupinder nevertheless utters caustic comments when speaking about his own family and his peers[165]. One of the first instances of this habit may be found at the beginning of Chapter 3:

> Behold! The Asian family: unit of tradition, moral strength and business acumen. Behold!, my mother: matriarch and fulcrum, proud bearer of sons, stately in her new sari, her one eyebrow draped across her fore-head like a trophy pelt, her moustache downy like an adolescent boy's. (Tourism 34)

As this example demonstrates, vast stretches of the novel are informed by a highly ironic tone, which often verges on sarcasm. In the majority of cases, Bhupinder's sarcasm is directed either towards his peers or towards another, allegedly inferior ethnic group. This stance forms part of the image Bhupinder tries to construct of himself. The attitude of deliberately not getting involved and of remaining aloof and detached is summed up in a self-description brought forward in a conversation with Sarupa. Here, it is striking to note the intensity with which he emphasises his status as a bystander or tourist. In Bhupinder's assessment, this self-positioning as an observer is intended to validate the evaluation of all other groups since – according to his own statements – he is the only one in a position to comment adequately on them because he is not truly involved with any community.

> 'So you're not a socialist, or an anarchist or antiglobalist, even though you think capitalism is mediocre and paranoid?'
>
> 'No.'
>
> 'What are you, then?'
>
> [...] 'I'm a tourist,' I said. 'I'm just a fucking tourist... I just look at the view.' (Tourism 85)

---

[165] In view of the fact that the protagonist was raised and socialised in the context of Western or, more specifically, English society, one may assume that he has acquired and internalised Western norms and values. At least as far his aspirations for life – including a luxurious lifestyle, money, and social prestige – are concerned, Bhupinder seems to endorse a number of 'characteristically Western' values. Nevertheless, he himself obviously succumbs to the illusion that he, by contrast to others, is able to detach himself entirely from this background. This move, in his eyes, allows him to comment dismissively on all other social groups, and places him in the position of the privileged observer with an exclusive inside knowledge of the mechanics of social and cultural processes.

In addition to that, the passage constitutes the clearest reference to the title: Just like a tourist, Bhupinder stays at various dwelling places only as a visitor but not as a permanent resident; moreover, all of his arrangements are temporary and subject to frequent change. The idea of travelling as a means of (self)education is extended by the two chapters framing the embedded narrative.[166] Tellingly, after a prolonged spell of frenzied skipping from one city to another, Bhupinder finally comes to realise that his former way of life has been utterly dissatisfactory. Yet, it is only after leaving Europe that he succeeds in reconnecting to his 'roots' by taking up yoga. The contrast opened up between Europe and India proves remarkably intense. The two geographical realms are set off against each other as two neatly separable and entirely incompatible cultural spheres. Hereby, as will be discussed in greater detail below, Indian culture is implicitly presented as superior to the Western way of life, which, according to Bhupinder, has merely taken to imitating Indian customs and traditions. Apparently, all forms of cultural exchange or fusion are considered as 'dilutions' and are therefore rejected by the narrator:

> They're [the owners of the yoga centre] in their fifties and think they've defied age and transcended the material world. In truth, they're just loopy white people, growing old, underfed and in denial. The West repeats itself in India as farce; India repeats itself in Westerners as tragedy. (Tourism 242)

Bhupinder's scornful stance towards Europe shows even more clearly in his attitude toward the practitioners of yoga in the centre he is temporarily employed at: "White people love doing yoga; with so much bad karma to shake off, that's no surprise" (Tourism 243). By contrast to the (white) owners of the centre, Bhupinder starts his daily yoga routine at mid-morning. Since he is the only one able to bear the heat he, in his own eyes, becomes the sole 'true' practitioner and is singled out from the other guests at the centre who are merely lured by the exoticism of doing yoga. This assumption is confirmed by the highly essentialist notions brought forward towards the end of the novel. The narrator once again draws upon 'nature' as the basis of (ethnic) identity and apparently endorses the idea that a 'preconfigured identity' exists, i.e. that every person is endowed with a 'natural blueprint' controlling their behaviour and

---

[166] This motive clearly draws on the tradition of the bildungsroman, where the protagonist likewise can be seen to start out on a prolonged journey which enables him to develop or discover his 'true self' and which, probably even more importantly, results in his re-integration into established society. The same itinerary may be observed with respect to Bhupinder's drifting around Europe before finally finding his 'authentic' ethnic identity and, via this achievement, his place in society.

rendering them particularly well-suited for life in specific areas: "This [the darkest complexion he's ever had] is how nature meant for me to look, browned under an Indian sky" (Tourism 244). Especially at this point a blatant contrast to the approaches towards the negotiation of difference discussed in the previous chapters unfolds as, in *Tourism*, we witness a clear return to essentialist categories and biologist explications.

Differential Categories in *Tourism*

As already mentioned above, the narrator sets the East and the West in direct opposition to each other and draws firm boundaries which result in seemingly insurmountable binary oppositions. Instead of emphasising potential points of contact or possible overlaps, *Tourism* presents both the 'East' and the 'West' as two entirely different realms with their own cultural background. This practice of resorting to essentialising dichotomies in order to set off individual groups of people against each other may likewise be observed with respect to a variety of other differential categories. Accordingly, the narrator expresses highly generalising notions of male and female behaviour and endorses essentialist concepts of femininity and masculinity. In connection with this topic, we witness the emergence of a specific discourse of masculinity similar to that cited in *Londonstani*. In both cases, the protagonists are highly intent on asserting their 'male' qualities and to confirm their status as 'real' men, i.e. to dispel all allegations of effeminacy or homosexuality. As repeated comments indicate, Bhupinder perceives women as literally the opposite sex and ascribes stereotypical 'female' character traits to 'women' in general. With the possible exception of Sarupa, Bhupinder's interest in women is confined to sex and the advantages in terms of money and social status to be gained from a relationship. In this context, the woman is treated as a mere object. What is more, sexual intercourse is detached from feelings and emotions and thereby reduced to an all but mechanical act intended to provide instant gratification. At least this is the impression conveyed by remarks such as: "I hadn't been laid in a while and I was pissed off, so decided to do as he [Luca] does, treat sex as sex and, as I would a pint of milk, buy it as necessary" (Tourism 10). Further passages portray Bhupinder priding himself on his perspicacity and his ability to see through women's flirting ruses and dating strategies. Accordingly, he comments on Sophie's attempts to bind him by making him dependent on her:

> Women cultivate imbecility in men; infantilised by overindulgence, men become dependent on them. This meets two pathological female needs: martyrdom and security. A woman will tolerate a useless slob, if

> he's predictable and unlikely to leave; that same slob provides copious
> reasons to complain of the sacrifices she's made, proving her stoicism
> and moral perfection. [...] She'd [Sophie] made a gilded cage for me;
> life here was so easy, I was slipping into lassitude, becoming a sort of
> pet. She wasn't the brightest girl, but even dumb chicks can outsmart
> most men. (Tourism 230)

Bhupinder's simplistic statements on the 'nature' of women and his belief in
fixed patterns of 'female' behaviour underscore his essentialist view of masculinity and femininity. Moreover, the narrator resorts to stereotypes in order to
explain characteristic forms of male-to-female interaction and traces these behavioural features back to an inherent masculine or feminine disposition. A
further striking element of the protagonist's stance towards women consists in
the beauty ideal promoted in the text. Instead of following the current 'Western'
ideal of a slim, well-toned body, the narrator praises Sarupa's wide, curvy physique. Hereby, Bhupinder even posits a connection between the perception of
one's own body and the cultural sphere a person belongs to. Once again, the
non-white approach is implicitly judged superior:

> Big white girls, their eyes full of shame and sadness, hide themselves
> under shapeless skirts and long jackets. Devised by pussy-loathing
> queers in the fashion industry, and disseminated by the shit-head fag
> hags who work for glossy magazines, the cult of thinness is set in the
> Western mind. [...] Sophie couldn't bear to be any bigger than she was,
> though she was a week's fast from being skeletal. Did she really find
> that image so compelling? Or was it just Anglo-Saxon masochism?
> (Tourism 195)

The same indiscriminate, essentialist attitude may be detected as far as homosexuality is concerned. In this context, the narrator expresses homophobic notions of characteristically gay behaviour and obviously sticks to the idea that
one single type of 'homosexual identity' or at least a homosexual self-image
(with the concomitant hopes and aspirations) exists. In general, these insights
are presented to the reader in slangy terms, often ranging on the vulgar and offensive. Moreover, the protagonist's use of various terms to describe homosexuality is highly provocative. This holds particularly true with regard to the
term 'queer', which the narrator uses in an insulting way, whereas the expression has, especially in the context of gender studies and identity politics, acquired connotations such as tolerance towards difference and the subversion of
established (gender) norms. As has been demonstrated with respect to male-
female relationships, the narrator here likewise adopts a superior, arrogant attitude and stylises himself as the detached arbitrator who, due to his lack of in-

volvement, is able to recognise the ulterior motives behind certain forms of behaviour and to analyse their 'true' causes. Bhupinder hereby sets himself decidedly off from the allegedly deluded, instinct-driven people surrounding him:

> Behind the DJ's booth was a huge screen, showing the video of his de-but single, 'Pussy Ain't Shit 2 Me'. Overlaying the music from Gloria Gaynor's 1979 dance classic, 'I Will Survive', his voice blared from the speakers, making it impossible to hear much else. [...] It was a catchy tune, and its sentiments were clear; KinQ sought to present a new, mus-cular and assertive queer identity. [...] Michael was on the dance floor, too, trying to ignore the dinge queens who kept bumping into him, wanting to make contact. [...] He was handsome, deeply masculine, and a resolute heterosexual: what more could a fag want? The love homos have for straight guys is the love that dares not speak its name. Like any other girl, the homosexual longs for a *real man*. (Tourism 210-1, orig. emphasis)

The quote is also striking in terms of its rhetorical features as they stress the extent to which the narrator has internalised essentialist clichés. Accordingly, he refers to '*the* homosexual' and apparently assumes the existence of the quintes-sential, i.e. 'real' man.

A third example of this conduct may be found in the treatment of ethnic groups and the discussion of ethnic identity. Again, Bhupinder minutely distinguishes between several communities and ascribes specific characteristic features to each of them. On closer examination, an intricate system of hierarchies and dichotomies unfolds. First of all, Bhupinder opens up an over-simplifying oppo-sition between the East and the West, which are again presented as incompati-ble, separate spheres. This East-West-dichotomy is subdivided into subordinate categories and groups to encompass, on the one hand, the various Indian castes and religious groups and, on the other hand, the different social classes in Eng-land. In terms of power relations and hierarchies, it has to be noted that, in gen-eral, 'Indian' communities are presented as culturally superior to those with a Western background. This professed superiority is traced back to the allegedly higher degree of complexity as well as the more sophisticated forms of internal organisation which, in the narrator's presentation, render them inaccessible to the non-discernible Western mind. What is more, a profound knowledge of Indian customs and traditions is promoted as a cultural asset as it allows the person in question to move securely in two cultural spheres – the East and the West – whereas those only versed in Western traditions fail to grasp the minus-cule distinctions between various Indian communities and, as a consequence, are permanently prone to blunders. Via this portrayal, difference is instrumentalised as an indicator of superior cultural knowledge, which places the initiate on a higher (cultural) level. As outlined above, traditional 'Western' hierarchies are inverted in this process as it is no longer the known and familiar which is presented as civilised and therefore more valued but rather the formerly disregarded exotic other.

Furthermore, this 'cultural capital' is treated as an inborn feature and obviously not considered a skill or capacity to be acquired by learning or by immergence into the other culture. At least this seems to be implied by Bhupinder's conduct when dealing with people ignorant of Indian customs, traditions, and religious groups. In this context, the comments on Sophie's behaviour prove revealing as the narrator's lack of interest and his unwillingness to clarify the function of specific habits show most evidently here. Already at their first meeting, Bhupinder abstains from explaining Sophie the true roots of his nickname Puppy: "I thought of explaining how *Papi* is a common Punjabi pet name – which my friends mispronounced as 'Puppy' – but I couldn't be bothered" (Tourism 29). The narrator continues to display this lack of motivation to introduce Sophie to his cultural background during the entire course of their relationship. At the same time, an understanding of Eastern culture is continuously promoted as a sign of superiority while sarcastic remarks on Sophie's blunders abound. When Ash, for instance, ridicules her by stating: "The occidental mind grappling with the complex Orient. Poor girl's never going to get it" (Tourism 130), Bhupinder immediately chimes in by confessing to the reader: "I was embarrassed by her lack of general knowledge" (Tourism 131).

In my analysis of the individual ethnic communities referred to in the novel, I would first like to discuss the general presentation of established white society. With only a few exceptions, 'Westerners' or 'the West' may be equated with (white) English society. Apparently, individuals stemming from this specific background are perceived as essentially different from members of other 'cultural' groups. This allegation is even extended to defaming speculations about their sexual preferences:

'Listen,' I said. 'The anus is the locus of the Western experience. That's where stuff happens for white people. De Sade, Freud, Foucault, they knew what the deal is with the anus.' […] Crackers aren't like us. Their culture is all about abstraction and rational inquiry. They get so lost in their heads, they only come into themselves when something's being stuck in their behind.' […] 'Our people are innately simple,' I said, lighting our cigarettes. 'We're creatures of the sun. We like to take things easy and not make a fuss. They're the ones who built boats and

went exploring the world, discovering stuff. We didn't give a shit about
what was out there. We were happy moseying along, beating our
women and eating other.' (Tourism 218-9)

Even though the context of this utterance has undoubtedly to be taken into account – Bhupinder is watching girls dancing in a club and talking to his friend
Michael about sex – the passage still proves remarkable inasmuch as it offers
insights into the narrator's judgemental presentation of cultural differences.
Among its most egregious aspects is the terminology used since the narrator
talks about "the Western experience" and "their culture" and thereby draws a
clear boundary between the two spheres. We once again witness a provocative,
simplistic, and biased ascription of characteristic features. While, on the surface,
intellectual abilities such as abstraction and rational inquiry are praised, the
sarcasm at the end of the passage, which reiterates 'Western' clichés on the
seemingly uncivilised East, subvert this acknowledgment. Moreover, the acco-
lade of the West's intellectual prowess is coupled with the reproach to indulge
in 'pathological' sexual practices. Via this stance, Bhupinder implicitly posits a
'healthy' or 'natural' (heterosexual) norm. Hereby, the West is slandered as
silently engaging in 'abnormal' sexual practices while outwardly acting in a
superior, patronising way.

The same strategy is applied in the depiction of female sexuality. Here, too,
clichéd notions are reversed with women being presented as lusting after black
males. Interestingly enough, a further established discourse – traces of which
may be found as early as the Elizabethan Age – is quoted. As in previous instances, though, power hierarchies are inversed with the formerly inferiorised
element now turned against its 'creators':

> He [Michael] was well over six feet tall, and was an interesting Carib-
> bean mix – tar-black skin, hazel, European eyes and sleek, almost Asi-
> atic features, combined with a powerful West African frame, perfected
> by slavery, its harsh conditions of natural selection. It's great to know
> that in his grab for wealth, Whitey created the body his women want to
> fuck the most. (Tourism 62)

This scene likewise demonstrates that we are dealing with a general strategy of
reversing hierarchies in established binary oppositions. While discursive formations in the past (produced in a Western context) tended to present black sexuality as deviant, animalistic, and dangerous, similar qualities are now ascribed to
Western ways of behaviour. A further feature that can also be observed in European constructions of otherness consists in the reference to 'nature' and the

assumption that certain characteristics are inborn, 'biological' qualities which determine an individual's personality. This supposition is confirmed by the end of the novel, where the dichotomy between East and West is opened up again. It is only in a sphere outside of Europe that Bhupinder finds a way to recover his 'true self'; subsequently, he expresses the wish to re-connect with his roots by travelling to India in order to learn the practices and customs of 'his' culture in an authentic, non-Westernised setting.

In the passages explicitly discussing the status of Indians in Great Britain, the notion of 'us vs. them' figures prominently. The narrator deliberately stakes out clear boundaries by, for instance, talking about "our people" (Tourism 180) as opposed to English or British society. Interestingly enough, 'Indianness' is extended to the second generation as well, who are considered a group apart from their English peers despite the fact that the majority of them have been raised in Great Britain and most likely carry a British passport. The distinction between individual communities is obviously performed against the background of 'cultural' affiliations and bloodlines rather than national ties and citizenship.

Nevertheless, even though he continuously praises the higher level of 'Indian' culture, Bhupinder is, at the same time, intent on setting himself off from fellow Indians and to highlight the differences between himself and other people from his age group. At this point, internal differences show. While the narrator treats 'East' and 'West' as homogeneous realms when opposed to each other, he distinguishes among different circles when discussing these spheres uncoupled from each other. Accordingly, Bhupinder comments dismissively on the backward habits of some members of the first generation and slanders the over-assimilationist behaviour of the second generation. As far as he himself is concerned, Bhupinder claims a superior position, a pose which I have already analysed and commented on above. When compared to the way of life of his countrymen, he even ascribes a certain subversive potential to his own lifestyle:

> They'd lived by the tenets of our people; they were cosseted, neurotic and profoundly afraid. I'd talk about my life – what I wrote, what I'd read, the places I'd been and the girls I was seeing – and their eyes would glaze. Any suggestion at a world beyond their jobs, their families and their old man's precepts discomforted them. My life was a dangerous example; it contravened the logic behind their achievements. Bland and assiduous Indians were now the backbone of this country; the NHS, the legal system, the technocracies of commerce and the state were diligently upheld by men like Hanesh. To him I was somewhat outré, and best kept at a distance. (Tourism 180)

The passage quoted above constitutes but one example among many others of the narrator's frequent derogatory and scornful comments on the streamlined behaviour of Indians in England. According to Bhupinder's account, for the overwhelming majority of first generation immigrants, the main purpose in life consists in the back-breaking task of establishing a small business solely intended for the purpose of providing a living and endowing their offspring with the opportunity to participate in the British educational system so as to reach a higher social level than their parents.

As far as the presentation of non-whites is concerned, the categories employed by the narrator prove remarkable inasmuch as he does not stick to widely used labels such as black or Asian[167] but also draws attention to ethnic groups frequently not included in these discussions such as the Japanese. It is striking to note that the narrator, in this case, relies exclusively on national affiliations whereas he abstains from doing so with respect to second-generation immigrants in Britain. Again, Bhupinder displays a supercilious, patronising attitude when commenting on the assimilative skills of the Japanese:

> The first non-white people to wholly commit to the project known as 'the West', the Japanese have always fascinated me. [...] The Japanese are obsessed with Western culture – the people next to me adhered to Western fashion, its code of being cool – and never seem out of place in London, 12,000 miles from home. Indians, even when born here, are rarely so at ease. The West jars with them, and they cocoon themselves within religion, arranged marriages and extended families. (Tourism 104-5)

By contrast to this generalising description, the protagonist, with regard to 'Indianness', acutely distinguishes between individual groups and ascribes specific intellectual, physical, and behavioural features to each of them. As in the case of the East-West-opposition, those distinctions serve as a basis for the establishment of hierarchical structures. Again, the narrator posits a close connection between ethnic identity and outer appearance which underlines his essentialist notions. Thus, Bhupinder explains his own looks by a reference to his Punjabi descent and traces further influences combining in his physique:

---

[167] Quite recently, there have been increasing discussions about whether 'Asians' should be included under the label 'black' and whether they are adequately represented by this category. Seeing that this debate is not immediately pertinent to my analysis of the novel, I will not present it in greater detail here. Nevertheless, the question as such, i.e. the current debate about 'ethnic labels' and attempts to establish new categories such as BrAsian, is undoubtedly worthy of further investigation.

> Punjabis are a hairy people, and I now had a full beard. [...] The Punjab
> overlaps India's border with Pakistan, and was the historic gateway for
> migration in and out of the subcontinent: Greeks, Persians, Afghans,
> Moguls and Aryans have all entered the region through the Punjab. [...]
> I looked at myself in the mirror, tracing the ethnicities in my face: thick
> Eurasian eyebrows; a round Tatar face; fine black oriental hair; a Medi-
> terranean nose; full Indic lips and wide Asiatic eyes. My parents
> weren't attractive people; somehow, in the collision of DNA at my con-
> ception, their genes combined in a harmonious sequence. (Tourism 139)

Despite this hybridity in terms of his looks, the main character obviously does
not entertain any feelings of being 'mixed race' as far as his cultural background is concerned. To the contrary, he clearly defines himself as Punjabi.[168]
Moreover, this passage seems to imply that Bhupinder considers himself a
combination of the best elements from a variety of ethnic influences converging
in the Punjab.

Apart from these comments on racial/ethnic divisions which are triggered by
concrete events and situations, the text likewise offers a number of theoretical
reflections on the concept of ethnic identity as such. In addition to that, various
passages deal with the exploitation of exotic otherness for both political and
financial purposes. Here, the media and the arts are cited as two areas in which
an exotic ethnic identity is treated as an asset and aggressively promoted as a
marker of quality. Bhupinder himself openly admits to the fact that the 'ethnic'
newspaper he used to work for achieved its prominent place and quick success
mainly by way of conforming to the zeitgeist. Moreover, a considerable benefit
was derived from the current political climate as well as from policies in the
distribution of government funds. Despite having profited from government
programmes himself, Bhupinder comments scornfully on them and tries to dismantle these projects as mere political ruses for self-promotion and for the dissemination of an open, tolerant, and 'multicultural' image. Seeing Bhupinder's
essentialist and over-generalising attitude voiced in other instances, the comparatively high level of awareness and perspicacity with respect to concepts
such as ethnic identity as they can be found in current discursive formations in
cultural politics and in the art world undoubtedly comes as a surprise. What is

---

[168] Interestingly enough, the notion of desiness plays a far less important role in the construction
of Bhupinder's self-image than is the case in *Londonstani*. Here, the protagonists constantly
affirm their desiness and are intent on highlighting the 'authenticity' of their version of Indianness
as opposed to the mode endorsed by the so-called coconuts. In *Tourism*, by contrast, Indianness –
the equivalent to desiness – is treated as an inborn feature. Even though immigrants are criticised
for their over-assimilationist stance, their basic Indianness is never questioned.

more, the novel adopts a critical stance towards sponsorship policies aiming at the advancement of 'disprivileged' artists and implies that public funds are distributed on political grounds rather than granted because of artistic merit. It is thus claimed that a sufficient knowledge of the decisive keywords can make up for a lack of artistic talent or professional formation. This strategy is presented to work particularly well for black artists seeking support for projects allegedly subverting white supremacy and hegemony:

> Identity was a hot topic in today's society and Michael was keen to jump on the bandwagon. With Evie's help, he'd taken his first steps towards becoming a contemporary artist. [...] 'I just gave them a load of crap,' he said, talking about the application process. 'I wrote about how this idea deals with the white paradigm, and its appropriation of the black subject.' – 'What does that mean?' – 'Fuck knows. Evie told me to write it. But they fell for it. Can you fucking believe that?' (Tourism 158-9)

This parallelisation of two levels of reflection – i.e. the protagonist's provocative and often offensive ad-hoc comments on concrete situations juxtaposed with (sometimes nonetheless challenging) theoretical reflections on the same topics – creates a tension as the portrayal of the narrator becomes slightly incongruous. On the one hand, he is presented as a person capable of abstraction, who possesses the necessary intellectual skills to comprehend and adjudicate on the strategies of identity politics and to comment critically on them. This image of the protagonist as the subversive intellectual clashes, on the other hand, with the impression that might impose itself in view of Bhupinder's endorsement of essentialising stereotypes and the repeated utterance of truisms and over-generalisations. What is more, by citing current models on the theorisation of ethnic identities in, for instance, cultural studies, the narrator seems to deliberately engage with a specific discursive formation and to ironically comment on it. This assumption is suggested by his inconspicuous insertion of various theoretical approaches into the text as is the case when he comments on Sodhilal's business creed:

> He was formulating a model of corporate and global capital management, based on the principles he'd discerned in Vedic scripture. The ancient Hindus, he believed, had an uncanny insight into *the dynamic of postmodern political economy*. (Tourism 193, my emphasis)

In a similar fashion, Bhupinder exhibits a dismissive stance towards the literary establishment and its value judgements. Here, likewise, topical concepts such as postcolonial literature are quoted off-handedly. Once more, a tension arises from the fact that the narrator's explicit self-positioning proves blunt and provocative to such an extent that one might speculate about whether he intentionally adopts this controversial attitude in order to criticise or subvert the concepts and theories he, allegedly, is unable to grasp due to his lack of education. What is more, his ignorant stance chimes in well with the explicit political incorrectness and the persona of a distanced bystander.

> I knew she [Sarupa] liked tiresome, canonical writers like E.M. Forster and Virgina Woolf, and hip contemporary ones like Haruki Murakami. I'd read something by him once, *The Wind Up Bird Chronicle*; it was about some guy whose wife was lost in a sort of spirit world. He didn't do a lot about it, other than smoke cigarettes and gaze into his navel – the kind of lame thing I'd do, if that happened to me. The book was complex, its narrative convoluted and taxing; I gave up after a couple of hundred pages. I hated paying good money and being made to feel dumb. Sarupa used the term 'post-colonial' to describe a lot of the books she was into; she thought Toni Morrison was a genius. I said I liked Iceberg Slimm; he was a cool black motherfucker who'd pimped a lot of chicks and been hooked on smack. (Tourism 196)

This impression of Bhupinder's merely putting on the disguise of the wanton, non-literary – and therefore probably all the more masculine – playboy is confirmed by the subsequent conversation with Sarupa. Here, the protagonist professes to be reading Bataille, a choice of book which bespeaks a certain interest in literature. Tellingly, though, Bhupinder classifies Bataille's *Story of the Eye* as "a piece of fin de siècle French pornography" (Tourism 197). Nevertheless, towards the end of the passage, a break in this deliberately maintained façade shows. Hereby, it is worthy of note that Bhupinder apparently does not want to be considered as a reader of cheap pornography, a stance which has him defending the literary merit of Bataille after all: "It's more than just filth. It's very fevered, very condensed writing, a bit like Faulkner" (ibid.).

A comparable incongruity arises in connection with the narrator's explicit declarations on national identity and the debate about a possible need for a redefinition of the concepts Englishness and Britishness. Once again, it is hard to assess whether the protagonist's decidedly provocative statements are intended to ridicule and to thereby subvert established notions or whether, within the logics of the text, they must be considered as expressions of his 'true' opinions.[169]

---

[169] It is especially at this point that the problem of the narrator's reliability arises once again. In view of the signals given by the text, the *possibility* of reading Bhupinder's comments as an at-

As has been demonstrated with regard to the discussion of recent discursive formations in the realm of modern art, the narrator here likewise re-iterates key positions in the negotiation of Britishness. It is for this reason that Bhupinder's statements allow for a reading which understands them as a cynical description of the present state of Britishness and an implicit critique of academic positions. In this context, the late 1990s are in the limelight of attention as the story focuses on the time in which Bhupinder's early adulthood is set. This period coincides roughly with the duration of the Blair government. Among the catch phrases taken up from political discourse in *Tourism*, is, for instance, the idea of 'Cool Britannia', a campaign intended to create a more modern, outgoing, and vibrant image for Great Britain:[170]

> When I first moved to Hackney, in 1996, Hoxton was aflame with ambition and ideas. It was the Mecca of 'Cool Britannia'. [...] This was its attraction: white people gauge their cool and creativity by the degree they tolerate being in proximity to blacks and Asians. [...] 1996 was the era of Britpop, and the final year of two decades of Tory government. The idea of what it was to be British was up for grabs; people's vision of things was loose, carefree. (Tourism 173-4)[171]

When the protagonist visits Hoxton a couple of years later, the former openness and tolerance turn out to have been a mere flash in the pan. Previously one of the in-quarters frequented by up-and-coming artists as well as by the hip and the cool, the area is now depicted as almost abandoned by the better off and seems to be on the verge of lapsing into a state of degradation. This passage may therefore be seen to imply that white people's engagement with black and Asian cultures resulted from a mere temporary fad rather than a profound interest.

In view of both the explicit distinctions the narrator makes between the numerous ethnic groups within British society and their representation as incompatible units, passages such as the one quoted above may likewise be seen as an im-

---

tempt of ironization or subversion is certainly embedded within the structure of the novel, irrespective of the highly offensive quality of certain statements.

[170] Even though the term itself was by no means invented by the Blair government and although it is in fact sometimes claimed that the idea for the campaign originated with the Major-Government, the concept of 'Cool Britannia' and the ensuing projects such as the Millennium Dome are by now firmly associated with New Labour under Blair.

[171] This passage likewise proves interesting in terms of its reference to specific spaces. The significance of place/space in the novel – although a highly intriguing topic with regard to the analysis of *Tourism* – had to be omitted here due to the scope of this study. Moreover, it did not seem immediately pertinent to the present discussion of differential categories.

plicit comment on the whole project of a 'multicultural' Britain. At least the account given by Bhupinder feeds doubts about the possible success of the endeavour as such; this impression is confirmed by the end of the novel which indirectly claims that, for a second-generation immigrant, the only possible way of creating an 'authentic', satisfying identity consists in re-connecting with his roots. Against this background, it proves striking that the narrator himself – despite his self-orchestration as the neutral bystander – has internalised various quintessentially 'English'[172] ideas and clichés. Among the most prominent examples is his adoption of the myth of the English countryside. Hereby, he likewise lapses into essentialisms, for instance when positing the existence of "real England" (Tourism 119). Even though Bhupinder continuously prides himself on having maintained his 'tourist status', i.e. the ability to see through social constructions, he has evidently internalised the association of Englishness with a specific type of scenery. For him, vast, seemingly untouched rural landscapes constitute a representative image of 'England proper':[173]

> England is a beautiful country and Chipping Campden is the epitome of English rural beauty. The buildings are historic artefacts, protected by law; shops and offices are located in pristine honey-coloured terraces, built with lime-rich Cotswold stone – many have their original doors and wood fittings. (Tourism 120)

Thus, in the definition of Englishness brought forward by the protagonist, we find another instance of the consolidation of clichéd notions and the construction of homogenous, unified spaces, which are promoted as the embodiment of specific values and cultural communities.

---

[172] Seeing that the narrator draws his examples from a variety of geographical areas and, for instance, ascribes the same features to Blacks in America as he does to black people in Britain, it is at times almost impossible to decide whether the narrator refers to Englishness or Britishness. This question is complicated even further since, as has been variously noted, the boundaries between Englishness and Britishness have become blurred and definitions are far from unambiguous. In the case discussed above, though, we are clearly dealing with an 'English' myth.

[173] Aptly choosing "Our England is a Garden" as a chapter heading, Aslet points out the emotional qualities attached to 'English countryside' and the notions generally associated with it: "The countryside is more than just a place, with a physical shape and existence; it is a cultural construct, a product of the imagination, which both lives in the English psyche and helps define it. Even to people who do not dwell there, who may never dwell there, it has traditionally offered the hope of a more wholesome, safer, less regulated way of life than available in cities. It could be argued that this way of life, which finds its fullest expression in the country house, is more completely civilised than most others in the world, being the result of centuries of careful study" (Aslet, Clive. *Anyone for England? A Search for British Identity*. London: Little, Brown, and Company, 1997. 173). On the significance of rurality with respect to the construction of English identity, see also Howkins, Alun. „Rurality and English Identity." *British Cultural Studies. Geography, Nationality, and Identity*. Eds. David Morley and Kevin Robins. Oxford: Oxford UP, 2001. 145-55.

A further differential category which Bhupinder re-strengthens or even re-activates is class. Even though, in recent sociological discourse, this category is considered to have lost some of its initial thrust and is often perceived as less significant in the organisation of people's lives than it used to be, the narrator in *Tourism* divides people precisely along these lines. He openly voices a strong aversion to the white underclasses, which, as he claims repeatedly, even provoke physical unease in him: "Watching Rory, I felt the shiver of disgust I sometimes feel when I look at white people" (Tourism 236). This rejection of disprivileged white people is coupled with Bhupinder's particular conception of ethnicity. In tune with the practice of ranking specific ethnic groups higher than others, he even ascribes a kind of reforming or improving quality to 'ethnic' genes:

> The magic of miscegenation: genes alchemised by a slap of the tar brush, even the ugliest honky can have enchanting offspring. This, I thought, is why white women go out of their way to have mixed-race babies, especially the poorest. If you've got fuck all, having beautiful kids is a great way to feel less shit about yourself. (Tourism 209)

Bhupinder's disdain is not confined to white lower classes but also covers black working classes. Yet, by contrast to the 'white trash', a stratum of society Bhupinder openly slanders, he displays a far more sympathetic and understanding attitude towards (lower class) black people and their historical plight:[174]

> The cruelty and imbecility of the working class is limitless […]. I hate poor white people. No one is more stupid or useless. […] Blacks are forever angry. In America – vexed by their own enduring mediocrity and inability to progress – they vent their spleen at Koreans or Jews, or whoever else happens to own the local corner store. In Greenford they hated Indians. […] In time I learnt to sympathise with black people, not judge them for their failures. They'd been fucked by slavery: plantations don't foster an ethos of erudition, commerce and deferred gratification. (Tourism 115-6)[175]

---

[174] Once again, it must be pointed out that the narrator apparently does not consider himself as black even though this label is, especially in the field of identity politics, frequently extended to encompass citizens from Asian communities as well.

[175] This particularly harsh statement reveals another 'value' to which the narrator attaches great importance: money. As will be demonstrated in greater detail below, sufficient financial resources are apparently seen to make up for a number of other shortcomings and, in the narrator's eyes, increase a person's status considerably.

In his references to black culture, the main figure cites an appeal currently also rife in popular music: the notion of 'keeping it real'. This idea of an 'authentic' display of black culture which can unambiguously be set off from 'fake' versions – usually embodied by those performers who have succumbed to the lures of commerce and are therefore accused of 'selling out' – figures prominently in the contemporary US-American rap scene but has by now been taken up in other circles as well. Although references may still be found primarily in the field of popular music, other forms of creative expression (popular fiction being among them) have by now come to quote the concept as well. In literary examples, the specific forms of engagement with 'black' culture prove intriguing especially as far as the protagonists' self-positionings are concerned. While the main characters in *Londonstani* proclaim a certain proximity between desiness and 'black culture' – at least with regard to role models and preferred styles in music – Bhupinder draws a clear boundary between 'blackness' of the US-American veneer and his own 'Indianness'. In the ensuing assessment of 'black' culture and music, black rappers are repeatedly scorned since they, in the narrator's eyes, have let themselves become instrumentalised as projection screens which are meant to trick audiences into believing that a homogeneous, unified black community with shared experiences and the possibility of social mobility exist: "By believing in Will [Smith, a.k.a. the Prince of Belair], America's black bourgeoisie and sub-proletariat can still believe in racial unity" (Tourism 65).

As far as the upper-classes are concerned, similar distinctions are made. In the stereotypical listing of their characteristic features, (white) English upper-classes are portrayed as a homogeneous group with fixed patterns of behaviour displayed by all members and passed on over generations. In this case, the protagonist's spite is mainly directed at members of his own peer-group:

> I'd met a lot of rich white kids who were set on acting, modelling or music; Cecily would no more become a singer than Sophie had become a model. When a rich white kid tells you they're acting, modelling or making music, it means they're doing fuck all. (Tourism 134-5)

This remark chimes in with the general description of young people hailing from the upper classes as lazy and ungrateful. The majority of them are presented as wasting their time spending their parents' money. The repeated discussions about a person's wealth indicate that, for Bhupinder, class as a differential category is obviously supplemented by 'money' as a decisive factor since the crucial issue in his assessment of a person's social position does not consist in their belonging to a specific stratum of society in 'cultural' terms but rather

results from an evaluation of their financial means. The power of money is presented as so strong that it may even flatten racial differences: "Everyone else
belonged to a milieu of metropolitan wealth, their differences in colour subsumed within *a shared order of money*" (Tourism 189, my emphasis). The same
impression of the very well-off forming a class of their own with ethnic and
cultural differences retreating into the background is implied by the following
observation:

> Money alchemises people, the mere suspicion of it changes *everything*.
> The gentillesse of Sophie's street – people sharing glances and smiles,
> stepping aside for one another on the pavement – came from the mutual
> assumption of wealth. They were a beloved elect: Europeans, Arabs,
> Americans and Jews; each saw the other through a prism of money, and
> loved what they saw. (Tourism 52-3, orig. emphasis)

In other contexts, though, a clear parallel is drawn between a specific ethnic and
religious background and (financial) success within English society. Bhupinder
here even goes so far as to claim that the British economy and its social system
were in fact maintained by Indians displaying an all but Puritan work ethos:
"Bland and assiduous Indians were now the backbone of this country; the NHS,
the legal system, the technocracies of commerce and the state were diligently
upheld by men like Hanesh. To him I was somewhat outré, and best kept at a
distance" (Tourism 180). At the time of the Blair government, the significance
of Indians in England has, according to the picture drawn by the narrator, increased to such an extent that Cherie Blair even starts to 'assimilate' by wearing
a sari at the award ceremony of the Asian Business Awards. While the Blairs'
adaptation is limited to their dress code, the 'Indian spirit' and system of values
are presented as embodied by prime minister Margaret Thatcher. As Sarupa puts
it in a conversation with Bhupinder:

> 'She's the best thing that ever happened to this country. She was *Brit-
> ain's first Indian Prime Minister.*' [...] Her life and values are totally
> consistent with *ours*... She believed in hard work and ambition, and
> created an economic environment in which people with those values
> could flourish.' [...] 'Thatcherism did attract a vulgar nationalism, but
> its essence always resonated with Indians. Tony Blair has a lot of sup-
> port among Asians, because he's a Thatcherite without racial preju-
> dices.' (Tourism 151, my emphases)

Strikingly, while Bhupinder himself permanently asserts his 'quintessential'
difference from English society on the grounds of his Indianness, he, in this case,

posits an overlap between Indian and Thatcherite values which render the two all but congruent.

It is interesting to note that judgements on individual forms of behaviour – especially with respect to members of Bhupinder's own ethnic community – obviously depend on an individual's financial status and that, for instance, despised forms of behaviour such as an (over)assimilation to English society are all of a sudden silently endorsed. What is more, despite his own habit of being kept by his girlfriend, he does not accept this stance when exhibited by other people. While Bhupinder disdains his peers who live off their parents' money and have not achieved anything by their own skills and talents, he appreciates Sodhilal's rise to the upper echelons of English society.

In the process of establishing a large company, Sarupa's father has forged close ties to leading politicians and has apparently acquired the tastes and habits of English establishment. Moreover, he clearly displays 'Western' notions of cultural capital. His 'English tastes' are exemplified best by the décor of his home in the Cotswolds (a renowned dwelling place for the rich) as well as by the choice of books in his library. Apart from popular US-American authors and self-help books, the walls in his holiday home are shelved with 'culturally valuable', i.e. mostly canonical texts such as the *Encyclopaedia Britannica* and works by W.H. Auden, Shakespeare, and Jane Austen (Tourism 128). The chapters dealing with Sarupa's family do not only imply that complete acceptance in the world of the upper classes is merely possible on condition that a certain degree of assimilation takes place and that former, purely 'Indian' values and traditions are shed in favour of habits and tastes characteristic of the English upper-classes.[176] As a closer examination reveals, Sodhilal in fact judges his Englishness as even more authentic than that exhibited by the 'indigenous' English. Again, Bhupinder's assessment of relationships and hierarchies within this family carries a pronouncedly caustic and sarcastic note. What is more, a specific discourse of masculinity shows which is informed by misogynic attitudes towards women in general and a patronising stance towards 'traditional' Indian women in particular:

> Sarupa was the baby of the family, adored and indulged by her father and brothers. Her mother was traditional, selfless, dutiful and pious; *religion gave her something to do in old age*, now the children had been raised and their fortunes made. She spoke limited English, and was Sodhilal's firm and unquestioning ally. Sarupa and the younger of her

---

[176] Undoubtedly, this assumption may be read to mirror Bourdieu's theory on cultural capital, which is exemplified by Sodhilal and his home in the Cotswolds.

brothers went to public school as soon as their father could afford it.
He'd been to one himself, an old colonial boarding school, on the coast
of Lake Victoria. He was an Anglophile who'd studied in London in his
twenties; he loved P.G. Wodehouse and Evelyn Waugh. He loved their
subtle wit and turn of phrase; *he lamented that one now has to go to In-*
dia to hear English spoken like that. (Tourism 193, my emphases)

Yet, despite her father's high degree of assimilation, Sarupa has not entirely
forfeited her 'Indian' identity, a fact which shows, at least in the narrator's estimation, in her attitude towards her body and in her practising yoga not merely
as a new fitness trend but rather as a 'spiritual' activity. Therefore, on closer
examination, the seemingly 'naturalness' of the delimitations set up by the narrator begins to become dubitable. This blurring of boundaries, however, is only
visible when the categories themselves are questioned and the constituent elements are analysed meticulously, a step the protagonist fails to take. Therefore,
'natural' divisions or groupings may be disclosed as subjective constructions on
the level of the reader but are not recognised or presented as such by the narrator himself.

The Family – A Source of Stability and Support?

Throughout the novel, the reader is presented with a series of diverse types of
families.[177] Despite the different backgrounds in terms of social class and level
of education, all those families share one characteristic element which consists
in a certain degree of dysfunctionality. Even though the extent of this dysfunctionality varies, the cause for the weakening of family ties can be traced back to
the same source: In all cases, the destabilisation results from the fact that one
member fails to meet their duties. This neglect unsettles the structure of the
entire family and, sometimes, even ruptures the bonds between individual
members completely.

A first instance of this pattern may be found in the frame narrative of the novel
with its depiction of the Italian gentleman and the young girl, who, later on,
turns out to be his niece. Apparently – as is claimed at the end of the novel – the

---

[177] As mentioned before, from a sociological standpoint, the definition of the term 'family' is
highly controversial. Especially more recent studies acknowledge the need to extend the concept
of the family so as to cover 'non-traditional' families as well, i.e. include those types of relationships which do not conform to the model of the nuclear family. Seeing that this debate is not
pertinent to the present analysis, the decision to stick to the conventional definition of a family as
a heterosexual couple and their offspring appears legitimate.

old man shows no intention of taking care of the girl in his charge but rather seeks the utmost amount of pleasure (i.e. sexual gratification) for himself. Bhupinder comments disparagingly on the Italian's behaviour: "The dirty wop kept trying to suck me off; when he figured I wasn't interested, he wanted me to fuck his niece while he peeped through a hole in the wall" (Tourism 242). Seeing that Bhupinder persistently expresses very strong and frequently derogatory value judgements on other characters (especially when they are homosexual), the truth value of this assessment is undoubtedly open to debate.

Over the course of the novel, the narrator introduces further examples of dysfunctional families. Hereby, we may distinguish between two different types, which are separated along ethnic lines. With respect to families hailing from a migratory background, it is primarily the first generation who are dissatisfied with their situation. Having spent most of their lives with back-breaking drudgery, they have forfeited the chance of benefiting from their efforts before old age strikes and can only put their hopes on the next generation. Their sole reward is the knowledge of having provided their offspring with better opportunities. This situation is also drawn upon as an explanation of the eagerness with which they spur on their children to achieve a higher level of education, to get better jobs, and to improve their general standard of living. A characteristic example of this attitude may be found in the family living opposite Bhupinder's family home.

By contrast to the stereotypical high-achieving members of the second-generation, the young white upper classes, epitomised by Bhupinder's friend Luca, do not take advantage of the head-start they were given by their parents but rather waste their time idly spending their parents' money, and pass their lives mostly in bars or clubs where they consume large amounts of alcohol and drugs. In descriptions of their careless ways, the question of who should be blamed for this type of behaviour is not addressed directly. Nevertheless, the narrator's disapproval demonstrates that, for him, this lack of gratitude and the unwillingness to earn one's own keep must not be traced back to a shortcoming on the parents' side but rather constitutes a character flaw in their spoilt children.

One possible exception to this pattern is embodied by Sarupa's family as, in her case, we are dealing with both a successful, satisfied parental generation and a high-achieving daughter. Seeing Sodhilal's internalisation of Western tastes and habits, one could argue that his success in building up a large business empire and in having his children contribute to it derives from his fusion of Western values with an 'Indian' education. Having instilled specific values such as respect for one's parents and the duty to obey in his offspring, Sodhilal has managed to turn Sarupa into an able, intelligent, and hardworking young woman who does not display the 'shortcomings' of her white peers.

Yet another type of family is represented by Sarupa's friends Ghislane and Ben. Even though successful in terms of professional career, the couple's relationship can allegedly only be maintained at the cost of Ben's masculinity and due to his renouncing a career in order to support his wife. The narrator's assessment of their situation reveals that he has internalised 'bourgeois' norms on gender roles which still posit the man as main breadwinner; moreover, he considers the fact that Ben's wife has obtained a higher professional position than her husband as a sign of failure and lack of masculinity on Ben's side[178]:

> For a man of his size, Ben had little masculine presence. [...] They were a few years older than me, but their faces were hardened by lack of sleep and constant worry: people age so much faster once they've had children. Ghislaine wore a knee-length black dress. I looked at her slim stockinged calves, her tidy little ankles, and asked what she did for a living. She was a director at a publishing house; she read submitted manuscripts, decided which might be developed, and helped shape ideas with their existing writers. Ben wore black trousers, an unironed shirt and scuffed black shoes; he was a teacher at a state comprehensive in Lambeth. (Tourism 141)

Even though the narrator cites almost exclusively 'negative' examples of family life, thereby underscoring cases in which individual members suffer or are dissatisfied with the outcome of their lives, he nevertheless episodically expresses his regret to be letting down his own family. Once again, the narrator's stance proves ambiguous and unreliable. While, on the one hand, he professes to be unable to bear his mother's presence for a longer period of time, he, on the other hand, tries to find excuses for her behaviour. Accordingly, he accuses his father of having failed to provide for the family and of having neglected his duties as head of the household, which renders him in Bhupinder's eyes responsible for his mother's exaggerated turn to religion and led her to follow religious rules in a far stricter fashion than she had done in her home country (Tourism 34-5). Moreover, the narrator is acutely aware of the fact that his mother belongs to the same age-group as other first-generation immigrants and shares their hopes and aspirations so that Bhupinder's failure to earn a university degree and to follow

---

[178] It is interesting to note that Bhupinder himself actually falls short of his own definition of masculinity or 'manliness' since he is kept by his girlfriend Sophie. One might speculate that the passages in which the narrator prides himself on his sexual prowess constitute an attempt to contradict this assumption and to consolidate his masculinity. Moreover, Bhupinder continuously highlights the fact that it is him exploiting Sophie rather than the other way round.

a career means a major disappointment to her. As a result, a tension arises between Bhupinder's disregard for his mother's old-fashioned, superstitious conduct and his permanent guilty conscience for having marooned his family. While the narrator maintains a detached façade for most of the time, his qualms at several occasions overcome him in violent bouts: "I cried for my desperate, backward and abandoned mother, and for my desperate no-good bastard father. Most of all, I cried for me, the desperate first-born son who'd now have to pick up the tab, but couldn't afford the bill" (Tourism 138). Seeing that such outbreaks always take place in the absence of his mother, their profundity may appear slightly dubitable so that one may speculate whether the attitude of the redeemed sinner simply fits the image Bhupinder intends to create for himself at this specific moment. It is only by way of picking up yoga and thereby recovering his 'roots' that the main character seems to find a way of re-establishing a connection to his family and to realise the true value of family bonds:

> Lying in Savasana – 'corpse pose' – at the end of class, exhausted after practice, eyes closed and breathing deeply, I had a vision of my mother. It was nothing spiritual, just an honest realisation of how much she loved me. I felt her love in its purity, freed from her fear and confusion. I felt her pain at never having given me this, and at not knowing where I was. I've done yoga every day since. I often think of her during practice; sometimes I hear her voice, speaking to me when I was a child, or quietly reciting *kirtan*. I feel I know her a little more each time, and the urge to see her grows. (Tourism 243)

Undoubtedly, the motive of the family as a source of stability, support, and affiliation figures less prominently here than is, for instance, the case in *On Beauty* or *Stone Cradle*. Nevertheless, the potentially uniting and binding force of the family is clearly visible here even though most families actually portrayed do not represent a safe haven or possible retreat but rather find themselves in varying states of disintegration. Since the reason for this disintegration is traced back to the shortcomings of individual members, one may nevertheless argue that the fault does not lie with the institution of the family per se but rather results from the failure of individual persons to fulfil their duties. Thus, *Tourism* outlines the unificatory potential that may be derived from the family once its 'stray' members have so to speak recognised their faults and rectified their neglects.

As could likewise be ascertained with regard to the depiction of family relationships in the previous analyses (especially in the discussion of *On Beauty*) love figures as the ultimate redemptive force. Accordingly, it is by way of love that formerly estranged members of a family may become reunited. Moreover, love serves as an important means to get individual family members to understand each other and to appreciate the other's intrinsically good intentions. This observation likewise holds true with respect to Bhupinder's immediate kin. Thanks to the 'reforming' effects yoga exerts on him, he claims to have discovered what his family really means to him and wishes to be reconciled with his mother and his brother. As far as his potentially newly-founded own family, i.e. the relationship with Sarupa, is concerned, the issue remains more complicated: Seeing the date of her daughter's birth, the assumption that Bhupinder might be the father after all imposes itself. Moreover, Sarupa's announcement – "we have a beautiful daughter" (Tourism 245) – certainly allows for the interpretation that she is referring to herself and Bhupinder rather than to herself and her husband. Even though the novel ends with Bhupinder anxiously waiting for the file with his (?) baby daughter's pictures to download – a gesture which leaves the reader in a state of suspense as the question of fatherhood is not solved – there are certain hints which may be read as first signs of an imminent change in the narrator's behaviour towards a more reliable conduct. Even though no complete integration into established society is achieved, the 'hero' nevertheless seems to finally have found 'his' place and to have realised the significance of certain socially accepted values such as the family.

After Fusion and Bonding – The Proclamation of a New Biologism?

With regard to the treatment of differential categories in *Tourism*, the following aspects are especially worthy of note. First, we witness a return to a generalising, essentialist approach towards difference which aims at drawing clear boundaries and relies on binary dichotomies established on the basis of allegedly 'natural' or inborn features. Both gender and ethnic differences are hereby posited as clear-cut categories which allow for a neat separation between individuals in terms of personal and collective identity. The two 'poles' or sides of a binary opposition are thus treated as fixed entities, a move which leaves no space for in-between positions or dynamic processes (as is, for instance, the case with the oscillating movement described by transdifference). This move constitutes a turn away from 'postmodern' approaches since there is no attempt to either fuse the poles of a binary opposition or to reveal the concepts as untenable in such a stark, essentialist form and to thereby deconstruct hierarchical dichotomies. At the same time, however, the way of dealing with difference adopted in *Tourism* likewise differs from the late or 'post-postmodern' strategies discussed in this study so far inasmuch as it presents differences as insurmountable barriers. What is more, the narrator even repeatedly voices the idea that certain character traits and features are inherited and that a person's character and conduct are therefore determined by their 'nature'. This stance has several implications. First of all, it proves highly convenient for labelling ethnic or social groups. When taking the conviction of people being determined by their biology to an extreme, there is no need to deal with individual differences since everybody can be pigeonholed according to their social class and cultural background. The same approaches may be witnessed with regard to gender differences, which are likewise seen to arise from 'nature'. In academic discourse, this practice of positing a direct link between biological features and the forms of behaviour exhibited by a person is in general referred to as 'New Biologism'. Ironically, *Tourism* couples these biologist assumptions with economic aspects, for instance when Bhupinder comments that "upper-class women look the best, their genes refined by generations of monied men marrying attractive women" (Tourism 157). Once again, a tension arises from the fact that the narrator cites discussions from academic discourse but places them in a different context and thereby implicitly subverts, or at least comments ironically on them.

Another instance of this phenomenon may be found in the portrayal of ethnic difference, where it is likewise all but impossible to ultimately decide whether Bhupinder truly subscribes to the essentialist notions brought forward in comments on individual groups or whether he, in fact, cites biologist discourses in an ironic or sarcastic fashion. This holds particularly true for inter-cultural relationships. With regard to this topic, the novel abounds with caustic remarks on 'interethnic' dating such as the following one:

> It [Portobello Road] was a miscegenist heaven: white women clung to well-wrought ethnic studs who pushed tricycle pushchairs laden with fat brown babies; demure young white men guided Asian girlfriends through stalls selling hookahs, avant-garde sneakers and sun-dried tomatoes. […] I hated the area: a vapid would-be bohemia, it was too fey for imagination and radicalism, but had odd pockets of deprivation, the remnants of the old West Indian quarter. (Tourism 52)

For the reasons outlined previously, *Tourism* may be considered 'non-postmodern' in at least two regards: First, identity is described as a fixed set of characteristic features inherited by birth. This position on identity formation clearly clashes with 'postmodern' notions which highlight the changing, fragmentary, and unstable quality of all types of identity and frequently perceive identity as the product of discursive formations rather than the outcome of a specific genetic or biological disposition. The deterministic and essentialist concept brought forward in *Tourism* is therefore obviously not in tune with 'postmodern' theorisations. Secondly, the narrator in *Tourism* depicts individual ethnic groups and social classes as homogeneous units. This may be derived both from linguistic specificities and from thematic foci. Accordingly, the narrator offers generalising comments in which he refers to "*the* white underclasses", "*the* upper-classes" or "*the* Blacks". Via this strategy of filing people into neatly separable slots, each of the resulting groups is represented as a unified entity since, in a pars pro toto fashion, a single member is considered to stand for the whole community. On a thematic level, the end of the novel proves highly revealing. Here, Bhupinder finally seems to succeed in recovering his 'true' self by taking up yoga and thereby claims to reconnect with his roots (even though, in view of the narrator's unreliability, it is subject to doubt whether this reconciliation truly takes place in the end). This may be interpreted as an ultimate indication of the narrative's endorsement of the notion of an 'inner core' which, in certain cases, has first to be 'unearthed' but exists nevertheless.

A further important aspect in this context is the narrator's refusal to assimilate or integrate himself as well as his lack of interest to become part of English society. To the contrary, a number of passages portray him priding himself on his status as a bystander emphasising his 'cultural' superiority. What Bhupinder completely neglects, however, is his unconscious adoption of several features of the 'Western' way of life. Despite proclaiming to be a Punjabi and to have strong affiliations to this community, the narrator nevertheless does not abstain from alcohol or drugs; likewise, he does not show any moral qualms when having sex with prostitutes or when exploiting his girlfriends. Moreover, allegedly 'Western' values and status symbols such as fast cars, luxurious homes, and visits to hip restaurants or nightclubs play a major role in his life and he indulges in them excessively. Similarly, the protagonist operates in a highly eclectic fashion when selecting the 'ethnic' features he chooses to display. Having been discriminated against by his peers at school due to his apparel and his long hair resulting from the Sikh ban to have one's hair cut, the main character sheds these immediately recognisable markers of his religious and cultural affiliations on entering college. Nevertheless, he continues to pride himself on his good looks resulting from his 'exotic' background, which single him out from other people. Apparently, Bhupinder feels completely at ease with selecting those elements of his parents' religion and culture which fit conveniently into his own Westernised lifestyle while simply abandoning other, less convenient ones. Moreover, he permanently underscores his not blending in with his environment. Even though he readily accepts the advantages gained by the relationship with Sophie, he is anxious to underline that he issues from a different cultural context and does therefore not succumb to the 'depraved' ways of the old-established upper classes. This attitude as well as the great pride he repeatedly expresses in stemming from a non-Western culture prove remarkable inasmuch as his 'original' tradition has only been handed down to him via his mother and that he has never experienced the 'real Indian way of life' at first hand. In the end, he at least intends to travel to India. Yet, these plans are far from being final as, at the closing moment of the novel, Bhupinder still lacks the necessary financial means.

On a supra-individual level, i.e. in a national context, the protagonist's stance may be considered problematic as he claims that a satisfying identity and sense of one's 'real' self may only be found in the cultural background of one's ancestors and that 'authenticity' may only be achieved via a return to one's roots. Nevertheless, this attitude displays a certain connection to current social developments. As Ellis observes, we presently detect a tendency among ethnic groups to point out their being different from 'indigenous' English society. Coupled with these assertions are attempts to strengthen ethnic identities by deliberately stressing their characteristic features:

> After protests and a period of time when consciences were raised about ethnic stereotypes, ethnicity is back. The melting pot is out; ethnic identity is in. Groups assert themselves, take pride in ethnic cultural expressions and demand that their language and communication be recognised and respected.[179]

Taken literally, this assumption bars all possibilities of integration and erases the chance to reach successful hyphenated identities. In an extreme version, the conviction of the incompatibility of an 'ethnic' parentage with a British identity means that the whole project of integration and a concomitant re-definition of Britishness so as to encompass second-generation immigrants or people with a 'mixed' background are practically doomed to failure. With respect to the depiction of the protagonist's self-positioning in *Tourism*, it is striking to note that he does strive for wealth and access to the higher levels of society but does not seek to be recognised as an English or British citizen.

When compared to the other two novels in this section, it becomes clear that *Tourism* obviously offers a highly divergent view on difference and that the strategies used differ markedly from those adopted by the protagonists in both *On Beauty* and *Londonstani*. Furthermore, *Tourism* may be considered a counter-example to Schabert's observation of a general tendency in the contemporary novel which employs the process of narration as a tool to bridge the potentially divisive quality of difference. This element is clearly not present here. Still, the aspect of community building referred to by Schabert does figure in Singh Dhaliwal's text, albeit in a different version than the one described by her. While Schabert focuses on the possibilities of bonding arising from affilia-

---

[179] Ellis, 2007, 39.

tions created by narrative means, *Tourism*, by contrast, displays a much stronger emphasis on the fragmentarising quality of difference between individual groups. Thus, while Schabert highlights the potential for strengthening intra-cultural ties, *Tourism* underscores the gaps forming between various social and ethnic formations. As outlined above, those groups are perceived as homogenous units with little chances of blending successfully with each other. What is more, the individuals filed into these rigid categories do not necessarily derive strength or support from the group they are affiliated with. Whereas, in other cases discussed in this thesis, narrative constructions of Sameness serve to consolidate in-group identities and offer a feeling of belonging and commonality to its members, *Tourism* depicts differential categories such as ethnicity and class as determining for an individual's life and behaviour; the affiliations arising from those bonds are hereby presented as fate rather than a potential source of empowerment and support.

Despite the fact that the strategies drawn upon in *Tourism* for the negotiation of difference (as well as the ensuing construction of both personal and collective identities) exhibit a certain proximity to the strategy of Sameness, the means to which they are employed turn out to be disparate. Although each of the approaches applies narration in a "sinnstiftend" or meaning-generating way as Schabert calls it, the instrumentalisations of difference to this purpose pursue divergent aims. While texts such as *On Beauty* seem intent on opening up possibilities for bonding and emphasise the support potentially to be derived from 'difference-based' communities, *Tourism* establishes hierarchies and mainly uses differences in order to set off individual groups against each other. What is more, by stressing their 'essential' discrepancy, the narrator presents them as incompatible, separate units which, if ever, only mingle so as to enhance the 'gene pool' of the allegedly inferior group. The project of a successful, practicable version of multiculturalism – or any form of closer interaction between the different strata of society whatsoever – is therefore dismissed and reduced to another instance of topical rhetorical spiel in cultural and identity politics.

Section II – (Covert) Same- and Otherness Within

The second set of analyses likewise deals with the construction of collective identities among groups of people within British society who are to some extent marginalised or, in general, not considered 'indigenous' English or British citizens. In contrast to the texts covered in Section I, though, one may observe a slight change of perspective with respect to the categories highlighted by this group of novels. While a strong focus is still placed on the aspect of 'deviancy', i.e. a non-conformity to an implicitly posited (white, middle-class) English or British 'norm', the 'ethnic' component proves less pronounced since further differential categories are taken into account and shown to be equally important in the construction of so-called hyphenated identities. One of the key aspects guiding my reading of the following texts will therefore consist in the question of whether a shift of perspective is performed inasmuch as ethnic difference is treated as just one marker of identity among many others and frequently only serves to supplement more prominent categories such as class or age. Thus, while ethnicity figured as the most decisive element in the narratives in Section I, which presented this feature as the ultimate basis for the construction of collective identities, this privileged status is, in the following texts, challenged and discussed from a different angle.

In this context, Evaristo's *Soul Tourists* may be considered a 'bridging' text between the first group of novels and the second one since the protagonists – due to their skin colour – have a visible 'migratory' background and are in search of their cultural and, for that matter, to some extent also their ethnic identity. However, the solution offered in *Soul Tourists* does neither involve a return to 'generic' or 'ancestral' roots, nor is a specifically black British ethnic identity arising from an imaginary shared homeland promoted as is the case in Smith's *On Beauty*. In Evaristo's novel, the main characters find a way of reconciling their 'black' heritage with a seemingly clashing European tradition. Seeing that the story is set in a European rather than a British context and therefore deals with the larger formation of 'European' culture, one of the main points of interest consists in the function ascribed to Englishness and Britishness and its possible inclusion into the notion of a 'European identity'. Moreover, I will examine whether the discussion on the formation of European 'cultural' identities constitutes an extension of the concept of national identity. This aspect proves particularly intriguing against the background of current socio-political developments, especially as far as the decreasing significance of national boundaries and the nation state as such are concerned. What is more, in view of political attempts to create a united Europe with shared institutions and specific laws and guidelines binding for all member states, the discussion of 'Europeanness' offered in *Soul Tourists* might open up new perspectives inasmuch as the text sheds light on the orchestration of a 'European' history. In addition to that, it provides a starting point for a reflection on the activity of historiography as such as well as its instrumentalisation for the construction of collective identities. Whereas most sociological or political studies on the topic of Europe and the possibilities of a European identity focus on inter-national differences, Evaristo highlights the diversity within individual nations. Moreover, she demonstrates that, while a homogeneous, white 'European culture' has always been a construct deliberately maintained by the ruling classes, possible re-writings of official history are potentially likewise fraught by subjectivity and biased notions. As I aim to illustrate in the respective chapter, what, in her account, ultimately seems to constitute the decisive aspect for the individual person is neither the factual verifiability of historical influences nor the definitely assessable importance of single figures but rather the possibility to enter into a rapport with one's own past and to find ways of integrating personal life stories into the larger framework of (national) h/History.

The take offered by the narrative also clashes with many current studies on the topic in terms of its focus on intra-societal discrepancies. While the subject as such has gained prominence in the wake of attempts to forge a strong European Community, efforts in community-building were most frequently directed at inter-national differences. As a result, the last years have seen various programmes intended to create a feeling of commonality by, on the one hand, the establishment of legal standards and practices and, on the other hand, the promotion of icons to serve as markers of a specifically European culture. In this process, next to the standardisation of legal and administrative proceedings, one central aim pursued by EU-officials seems to consist in creating a sense of 'Europeanness' and in improving the reputation of 'Europe' as a cultural entity among the citizens of the respective nation states included in the Union. For this purpose, studies have been conducted on possible means for the integration of national identities[180] into the larger framework of a European community, which transcends national boundaries.[181] While the problem of the heterogeneity of this geographical area has been acknowledged, the distinctions are first and foremost seen to arise from the diversity of the nation states located within the area. This comparatively simplistic recognition of the differences between national cultures – an assumption which presupposes the existence of

---

[180] On the concept of national identity as well as the development of the notion of the modern nation state see Greenfield, Liah. „Types of European Nationalism." *Nationalism*. Eds. John Hutchinson and Anthony D. Smith. Oxford and New York: Oxford UP, 1994. 165-71.
[181] On the specificities of a 'European' identity and the consequences arising from the lack of an unambiguous geographical definition of 'Europe', see Schlesinger, Philip. „Europeanness: A New Cultural Battlefield?" *Nationalism*. Eds. John Hutchinson and Anthony D. Smith. Oxford and New York: Oxford UP, 1994. 316-25. Brewin raises a similar point with respect to the significance of physical geography for the formation of a European identity. See Brewin, Christopher. „European Identity." *Why Europe? Problems of Culture and Identity*. Eds. Joe Andrew, Malcolm Crook and Michael Waller. Houndmills, Basingstoke and London: Macmillan, 2000. 55-73.

culturally homogeneous nation states – frequently results in a reiteration of truisms and highly generalising conclusions with little heuristic value for the theorisation of a 'European identity'. An illustrative example of this procedure may be found in Green's essay:

> Schlesinger notes the lack of common culture across the European continent, which leaves the integrationist reaching for certain "core values" around which to unite disparate nations: [...]. This stretch is required because, unlike in traditional nation-states, European integration "cannot be based upon the classic simplifying nationalist criteria of ethnicity, consanguinity, language, or religion. *For Europe is simply too diverse.*[182]

Despite a general consensus on the need to base a 'European' identity on a broad range of features so as to include individual 'national cultures'[183] most accounts neglect the fact that the respective nations themselves constitute highly hybrid entities. The problem of how to integrate those internal differences is, however, not addressed in the majority of cases since many studies consider the Enlightenment tradition (or, moving back in time even further, the Christian-Roman heritage) as the decisive element on which to ground 'Europeanness'.[184]

---

[182] Green, Michael David. *The Europeans. Political Identity in an Emerging Polity.* Boulder CO and London: Rienner, 2007. 37, my emphasis.

[183] In this context, I use the term 'culture' to denote the individual habits, practices, and ways of life considered characteristic of a particular people. Even though I am aware of the fact that the notion of a homogeneous 'national culture' constitutes a social construct, I deem usage of the term adequate in the present case as the concept of national cultures still circulates in official discourse and seems to inform public opinion to a considerable degree.

[184] This phenomenon may likewise be observed in Depenheuer's discussion of the potentially binding or integrating power of the European Union: "Wurde die Frage der nationalen Identität bislang vor allem unter dem Gesichtspunkt gesehen, ob sich die nationale in eine europäische überführen lasse und die letztere die erstere überwölbe, so soll in den nachfolgenden Überlegungen die These begründet werden, dass es die weiterbestehenden nationalen Identitäten der Mitgliedstaaten sind, die über Erfolg oder Misserfolg des europäischen Einigungsprozesses entscheiden" (Depenheuer, Otto. „Nationale Identität und europäische Gemeinschaft. Grundbedingungen politischer Gemeinschaftsbildung." *Nationale Identität im vereinten Europa.* Hg. Günter Buchstab und Rudolf Uertz. Freiburg, Basel und Wien: Herder, 2006. 55-74. 57). Strikingly enough, Depenheuer refers to individual 'national identities' as seemingly coherent and homogeneous entities and, on a European level, deems the main problem the integration of those entities into a larger whole rather than the formation of firm national identities as a first step and necessary precondition. He moreover suggests that the creation of a truly united Europe may only happen on the basis of a European identity; remarkably, the author abstains from outlining the concrete realisation of this European 'umbrella' culture. While Oexle's study "Mittelalterliche Grundlagen des Modernen Europa" displays a certain awareness of the inherently hybrid nature and the existence of contradictory tendencies within the geographical realm generally referred to as Europe, he subsequently likewise focuses on the tensions arising from sources such as institutions, estates, and social groups (29) rather than discussing the presence of 'foreign' elements within European

Another feature of these sociologically or politically oriented accounts consists in their instrumentalisation of difference in order to distinguish Europe from a seemingly incompatible Arab or rather 'Islamic' world. Although there is no denying the fact that cultural or, to be more precise, religious differences between those two realms exist, the value judgements performed in the following quote with its ascription of specific qualities to both spheres serve to strengthen binary oppositions and essentialising dichotomies. Moreover, they are reminiscent of dated constructions of alterity which presumed an irreconcilable contrast between the European and the Islamic world and thus made way for the construction of hierarchical binary oppositions as well as for the production of essentialist auto- and heterostereotypes. We witness the same procedure in Kocka's account, who (in a study co-edited by the former German minister of culture Julian Nida-Rümelin) states:

> Doch im Übrigen ist der Unterschied zwischen dem weitgehend säkularisierten, durch Aufklärung geprägten, auf individuelle Freiheit und Entfaltung setzenden, die gleichen Chancen von Männern und Frauen betonenden, liberalen Grundsätzen nahen Europa und den islamischen Gesellschaften mit ihrer Distanz zu modernem Wissen, moderner Bildung und modernen Werten stark ausgeprägt, so verschieden islamische Gesellschaften untereinander zweifellos auch sind.[185]

While I do by no means wish to deny the existence of historical, social, and possibly even 'cultural' differences between the geographical areas of Europe and say, Asia or Africa, a crass contrasting of these realms as in the quote cited above does not appear conducive to the project of establishing a peaceful and tolerant relationship. At this point, it proves striking to note that a number of literary engagements with this topic apparently tend to place less emphasis on the disparity of these diverse cultural contexts but are rather intent on unearthing ways of reconciling them. In the following, I will therefore focus on the question of how 'foreign' or seemingly 'Non-European' elements are integrated into the notion of a European identity. Hereby, *Soul Tourists* seems particularly well suited to demonstrate in which way allegedly contradicting aspects and traditions may, on an individual level, be merged and thereby made compatible with each other and how, as a result, the perception of 'established European-ness' is simultaneously changed.

---

culture (Oexle, Gerhard Otto. „Mittelalterliche Grundlagen des Modernen Europa." *Was ist der Europäer Geschichte? Beiträge zu einer historischen Orientierung im Prozess der europäischen Einigung.* Hg. Jörg Calließ. Rehburg-Loccum: Evangelische Akademie Loccum, 1991. 17-60).
[185] Kocka, Jürgen. „Europäische Identität als Befund, Entwurf und Handlungsgrundlage." *Europäische Identität: Voraussetzungen und Strategien.* Hg. Julian Nida-Rümelin und Werner Weidenfeld. Baden-Baden: Nomos, 2007. 47-59. 51.

A further problem with regard to the concept of a supra-national identity which is to include a number of separate nations arises from the treatment of distinctions among the various groups present within this wider formation. To some extent, the impression imposes itself that the general awareness of the intra-communitarian differences is higher in literary disputes of the topic which usually abstain from offering cure-alls for integration allegedly applicable to the majority of cases. For instance, narrative renditions of the subject seem more often to take into account that, despite all efforts to unite Europe's citizens and to create a feeling of commonality, regional disparities will most probably persist and will have to be bridged, yet without erasing the existing variety. In view of the sheer territorial size of the area, the emergence of an entirely homogeneous cultural unit seems illusory and, in view of the concomitant suppression of diversity which such a development would inevitably entail, not even desirable. For these reasons, a potential 'European' identity must, by necessity, acknowledge the lasting presence of 'internal' differences and try to incorporate those into any successful conceptualisation. This element differentiates the construct of a 'European' identity from previous constructions of collective formations such as national identitie,s which were intended to create the feeling of a high level of similarity and, especially in the heyday of nationalism, were exploited for the strengthening of a political system. Seeing that attempts to delimit intra-differences, i.e. differences among people within one nation, have never been successful or, respectively, have only been achieved at the cost of warfare and bloodshed, a 'European' identity has to be founded on broader terms than national identities and must allow for more variations. Veen confirms this assumption when he states that

> [a] political European identity therefore will always remain an identity in a restricted sense, confined to the common political objectives of European integration, alongside which other identities, just as national identities will always continue to exist. European integration must not be taken too far. The idea of an all-embracing identification with a united Europe would not only be remote from everyday life, but, in my view, would be a highly problematic aspiration, one, indeed, from the realms of ideology.[186]

What is controversial about this statement – and, in fact, jars with dominant opinions in most branches of Cultural Studies – is Veen's presupposition that clear-cut national identities exist. Moreover, he fails to take into account the

---

[186] Veen, Hans-Joachim. „Towards a European Identity: Policy or Culture?" *Why Europe? Problems of Culture and Identity*. Eds. Joe Andrew, Malcolm Crook and Michael Waller. Houndmills, Basingstoke and London: Macmillan, 2000. 41-7. 46-7.

recent changes with regard to the status of national identities in present societies. Over the last decades, many theorists have come to question the viability of
the concept and now tend to treat national identities as cultural constructs,
which are frequently deployed for political purposes. This approach likewise
seems to inform literary treatments of the topic, an aspect I will discuss in further detail in the respective analyses.

Within the debate on the 'ontological' status of various types of collective identities, and, to be more precise, the status of a specifically 'European identity' the
nexus between power and 'truth' constitutes an important subject:

> Discourse is power, therefore, and not only is power the ability to de-
> termine the 'truth' but also, as some of the contributors to this volume
> show [...] 'truth' *is* power. Historically, sermons, political speeches,
> school books, newspapers, etc., have allowed those in power – from the
> medieval Catholic Church to the Soviet *nomenklatura* – to construct so-
> cial categories to fit their interests, presenting them as superior and
> natural. [...] Today, television, the Internet and, in particular, the proc-
> esses of globalisation – regional integration, on the one hand, or large-
> scale immigration, on the other – make it far more difficult to exercise
> this control. As a result, hegemonic discourses and meta-narratives are
> undermined, identities are recast and the elites' control over their pro-
> duction and meaning – by which they are nevertheless constrained –
> lessens, with the result that alternative truths jostle for audiences and le-
> gitimacy.[187]

Seeing the subject-matter of the novels covered in Section II, this element had,
by necessity, to be included in the discussions of the single texts: While *Soul
Tourists* examines primarily the power relationships in historiographical writing
as well as their implications for individual identity constructions, *Stone Cradle*
addresses the question of authenticity and the authority to speak. Even though
the connection between power and discourse is less pronounced in *Saturday*, it
nevertheless becomes an issue pertinent to the interpretation of the story since
the novel implicitly raises the question of authorship and the status (and function) of a written text.

In *Stone Cradle*, the second novel chosen for analysis in this section, established notions on national or even supra-national identities are scrutinised. By

---

[187] Mole, Richard and Felix Ciută. „Conclusion: Revisiting Discourse, Identity and 'Europe'.
Discursive Constructions of Identity in European Politics. Ed. Richard C. M. Mole. Houndmills,
Basingstoke and New York: 2007. 208-12. 210-11. orig. emphasis.

contrast to the foregoing texts, though, Doughty's novel does not focus on one of the minority groups presently in the centre of public attention. It rather sheds light on the way of life of a community within British society of whose presence the general public displays a comparatively low level of awareness: the minority of the Romany or, as they are likewise referred to, the Travellers[188]. Currently, 'official', i.e. institutionalised British identity politics as well as the predominant multiculturalist discourse tend to focus on 'visible' minority groups. Hereby, particular attention is paid to the status of the second-generation.[189] As the so-called Parekh Report points out,

[188] With respect to adequate terms of reference, great controversies exist even among the Romany community itself. While, in *Stone Cradle*, the expression 'Travellers' is used as a self-description by the group, publications by the Central Council of German Sinti and Roma reject this label on the following grounds: "In the same manner existing clichés about the minority are amplified and their segregation is intensified by the striking equation of Roma and Sinti with "Travellers" ("Fahrendes Volk") or by comparison with the situation of migrants in reports or resolutions of the EU or the Council of Europe" (Central Council of German Sinti and Roma. „Realising Equal Treatment: EU Directive for the Improvement of the Situation of the Roma and Sinti Minorities in Europe". *Zentralrat Deutscher Sinti und Roma*. Nov. 2006. 11.08.08 <http://zentralrat.sintiundroma.de/content/index.php?navID=25&tID=14&aID=0>). The same problem is highlighted by Clark. Other than the report cited above, however, Clark does not out-rightly dismiss any of the terms used to refer to the ethnic minority of the Sinti and Roma. By contrast, he points out that the usage of these terms proves context-dependent; moreover, he draws attention to the fact that, comparable to black identity politics, the perception and assess-ment of a specific label results primarily from the speaker's position: "Whereas it seems to be true that some groups, families and individuals will define themselves in general terms as 'Gypsies' (with the possible addition of Romani; this is especially true of English Gypsies), others will prefer the term 'Travellers'. It is important to be aware that the terms 'Gypsy' and 'Traveller' can *both* be perceived as pejorative depending on who you are speaking with and in what situation. Time, space and place are also important contexts in which to appreciate this question of usage" (Clark, Collin. „Who are the Gypsies and Travellers of Britain?" *Here to Stay. The Gypsies and Travellers of Britain*. Eds. Colin Clark and Margaret Greenfields. Hatfield: Hertfordshire UP, 2006. 10-27. 13, orig. emphasis).

[189] The impression that examinations both in sociology and in cultural studies are to a certain extent informed by thematic fashions is backed by Song's finding that "[i]n recent years, there has been a great deal of attention, both academically and popularly, to the meanings, experiences, and politics surrounding ethnic identity. "Ethnicity" and notions of cultural difference and marginality are "in", as shown by the proliferation of studies concerning ethnic identity from the 1990s on-wards [...]. In part, this is due to the fact that the racial and ethnic landscapes of many Western societies such as the USA and Britain have been undergoing major changes in the late twentieth and early twenty-first centuries" (Song, 2003, 6). The assumption that a comparatively low level of awareness exists among the general public with respect to the presence of Travellers or 'gyp-sies' is confirmed by Doughty herself. She states that most reports focus on European Roma coming over to Britain as well as on Irish Travellers; apparently, news coverage on this topic is frequently biased with the Travellers being presented in a negative light especially by the tabloids. As a result, vast parts of the British population are ignorant of the history of English Romanichals and their general perception remains shaped by stereotypes and prejudices (03.09.07, personal correspondence with the author).

> they [Gypsy and Traveller communities] are often neglected in consid-
> erations of Britain as multi-ethnic society, or included only as an after-
> thought. But they too were defined in the past as an inferior race and are
> part of the history of British racism. [...] Despite the great diversity be-
> tween and within travelling groups, all are lumped together in the minds
> of settled communities. They suffer from high degrees of social exclu-
> sion, vilification and stereotyping. Anyone who does not fit the tradi-
> tional stereotype (painted wagon, campfire, swarthy complexion, much
> gold jewellery) is assumed to be a mere traveller, to be feared and de-
> spised.[190]

While the group of English Travellers is considerably smaller than, say, the
Indian or Pakistani community in Britain, the general observation that certain
differences exist in the public perception of and engagement with this group is
nevertheless relevant.[191] When we compare the status of the Travellers in British society with that of second-generation immigrants from the Indian subcontinent, a clear contrast unfolds. The predicament of young people with an Indian,
Asian or black migratory background has been extensively discussed and recent
years have seen repeated attempts to establish programmes for the integration of
those youths, whereas the Romany have usually not been included into projects
aiming at the integration of 'ethnic' minorities into British society. This lack of
recognition as a national minority has likewise been noted both in sociological
studies and in political investigations on the topic. Accordingly, Clark states
that

> English Gypsies, since 1988, and Irish Travellers, since 2000, have been
> regarded as ethnic minority groups in the eyes of the Commission for
> Racial Equality and the Race Relations Act of 1976 [...]. The problem
> has been that *in general terms*, amongst the *majority* of the settled
> population and those people working for local authorities and other
> agencies who deal with Gypsies and Travellers, this legal status has
> largely not been recognised or the implications fully appreciated.[192]

---

[190] Parekh, 2000, 34.

[191] Of course, it is impossible to define people's 'true' attitudes or to establish a 'general public
opinion'. Nevertheless, sources such as news coverage on the topic or sociological studies in the
field seem to imply that a certain hostility towards Travellers remains a persistent problem. This
phenomenon may likewise be observed in other nations where the Romany have likewise repeatedly been confronted with clichéd notions and been discriminated against. For an assessment of
the general situation in Europe, consult, for instance, the homepage of the German Council for
Sinti and Roma
(http://zentralrat.sintiundroma.de/content/index.php?navID=25&tID=14&aID=0 07.08.08).

[192] Clark, Colin. „Conclusion." *Here to Stay. The Gypsies and Travellers of Britain*. Eds. Colin
Clark and Margaret Greenfields. Hatfield: Hertfordshire UP, 2006. 281-9. 283, orig. emphases.
With regard to the political context, see the report on the status of Roma in the European Union

In addition to that, the itinerant way of life of the Romany is generally not met with tolerance.[193] Legislation in the last decades has first and foremostly aimed at the limitation of possible camping sites in order to suppress the activity of travelling as such. Since these problems are extensively dealt with in *Stone Cradle* via discussions among the protagonists, the novel proves to be an interesting example of how concrete social problems may inform narrative texts and in how far fictional writing does engage with difficulties encountered by people in 'real life'.

Although it is hard to estimate the precise level of awareness of the Travellers' presence in England among the general public or to assess majority attitudes, the disprivileged status and the persistent discrimination seem to be a 'felt' reality among the group even today. While *Stone Cradle* is largely set in the late 19th and early 20th century – i.e. in pre-Holocaust times – core problems such as discrimination and harassment are apparently still far from being solved. Accordingly, in a publication demanding equal rights for the Roma and Sinti as Europe's largest minorities, it is argued that

> [a]s a consequence of the Holocaust, the international political system is now extremely sensitive to the various forms of anti-Semitism, whose rise we have observed with great concern in recent years. In contrast to this, there is neither an awareness of the historical dimension of the crimes of genocide committed against our minority nor of the present-day racism which Roma and Sinti are subjected to in many countries.[194]

---

published by the European Commission in 2004 (European Commission Directorate-General for Employment and Social Affairs. *The Situation of Roma in an Enlarged European Union*. Luxembourg: Office for Official Publications of the European Communities, 2004). On recent legislation, likewise consult Resolution P6_TA(2005)0151 by the European Parliament.

[193] This aspect is likewise pointed out by Clark. The treatment of the Travellers in comparison to, for instance, the 'Black British' constitutes an excellent example of the highly diverse forms of engagement with minority groups within British society. What, in my opinion, proves particularly striking in this context is the aspect of lobbying and the 'power of speech'. While black groups, for instance, do by now have certain renowned spokespersons and have also produced highly eloquent members from their own ranks, hardly any representatives of equal status and influence can be found within the Romany community. Moreover, while public pressure to integrate the second-generation is high – in particular after the London bombings in 2005 – lobbyism to fight the disprivileging of Travellers exerts a far less pronounced influence.

[194] Rose, Romani. „Europe's largest Minority - Roma and Sinti demand equal rights." *UN Chronicle* No. 4, 2006. 10.08.08.
<http://zentralrat.sintiundroma.de/content/index.php?navID=25&tID=14&aID=0>).

Doughty's novel, therefore, adds a new dimension to the discussion of the problems faced by minority groups and addresses the question of their status in English society inasmuch as it highlights the specific predicament of a group frequently neglected in debates on the topic. What is more, the narrative may be considered to open up a new angle on ethnic difference. It is at this point that the connotations of the term 'ethnic' become worthy of further reflection since, in public discourse, the minority groups singled out as 'ethnic' are usually those with an 'exotic', i.e. for instance Indian or Caribbean background, whereas the comparatively 'invisible' Romany are usually not included under that label (unless they, too, display a 'visible' alterity such as a non-European dress code or a darker complexion). Despite all tensions and fears of an 'Indianisation' or 'Pakistanisation' of certain quarters or even whole cities, the impression arises that those 'new' ethnic communities likewise exert a marked fascination due to their 'foreignness' and the possibilities they offer for an 'authentic' exotic experience in a comparatively 'safe' environment. Contrary to the efforts currently taken to improve relationships between 'indigenous' British citizens and 'newcomers', attitudes towards the Travellers continue to be tainted by dated prejudices and clichéd notions such as their alleged laziness, treacherousness, and general inclination to petty crime.[195] Seeing the recent preoccupation with the status of hyphenated Britons, one of my prime research interests in the analysis of *Stone Cradle* consists in the question of whether present conceptualisations of Britishness can be stretched to cover this under-acknowledged group and which repercussions such an inclusion might possibly have on the definition of Britishness itself. In view of the ongoing debate about the legal situation of Travellers who stick to their traditional way of life as well as simultaneous tendencies among them to settle more or less permanently, my analysis will tackle the problem of whether the Romany community is portrayed as a group apart and in how far *Stone Cradle* identifies potential points of contact and similarities between the two seemingly disparate realms. In my reading of the text, I will likewise try to analyse to which extent the Travellers are positioned as a 'parellel' society, an impression which might impose itself in view of some seemingly bizarre cultural practices and traditions described in the novel as well

---

[195] With respect to the German context, a survey carried out by the Central Council of German Sinti and Roma confirms the persistence of prejudices and racism (Zentralrat Deutscher Sinti und Roma. „Ergebnisse der Repräsentativumfrage des Zentralrats Deutscher Sinti und Roma über den Rassismus gegen Sinti und Roma in Deutschland." *Zentralrat Deutscher Sinti und Roma.* Oct. 06. 07.08.08.
<http://zentralrat.sintiundroma.de/content/index.php?navID=25&tID=14&aID=0>).Clark discusses the general situation of Sinti and Roma in Europa as well as the effects of recent EU-legislation in Clark, Colin. „Europe." *Here to Stay. The Gypsies and Travellers of Britain.* Eds. Colin Clark and Margaret Greenfields. Hatfield: Hertfordshire UP, 2006. 259-80. On the persisting legal problems the Travellers are still confronted with in Great Britain, see Greenfields, Margaret. „Gypsies, Travellers and legal matters." *Here to Stay. The Gypsies and Travellers of Britain.* Eds. Colin Clark and Margaret Greenfields. Hatfield: Hertfordshire UP, 2006. 133-81.

as the incomprehensibility of their language to outsiders which constitutes a further obstacle to the non-initiated.

Moreover, I will deal with the interaction between Romany and 'indigenous' English/British persons. Hereby, it is striking to note that publications by institutionalised bodies such as Rose's essay in the *UN Chronicle* assume the existence of an autonomous Romany culture and a corresponding autonomous cultural identity. Accordingly, Rose argues that

> members of our minority have been integrated in and citizens of their respective countries of nationality for many centuries, particularly in the European countries. For this reason, most of the European governments have in the meantime recognized Roma and Sinti as national minorities, who, in addition to the national culture of the majority, also cultivate their own cultural identity, which above all includes the minority language, Romany.[196]

As this quote demonstrates, Romany habits and traditions are frequently perceived as a culture in its own right and seen to provide the basis for the formation of an independent cultural identity set apart from 'majority' culture. This impression is confirmed by book publications with titles such as *Romani culture and Gypsy identity*[197] which imply the existence of a specific 'Gypsy' identity. Other theorists, however, point out the great heterogeneity of the group: Fraser, for instance, states that, even for the relatively confined realm of former Yugoslavia, "some 20 principal tribes have been identified [...], and many of these can be further subdivided"[198]. Nevertheless, most studies seem to agree on the fact that, despite this internal diversification, an overarching Gypsy identity with a number of characteristic features exists. As Liégeois and Gheorghe emphasise,

> Roma/Gypsy reality is enormously varied. [...] Roma/Gypsy life is characterized by continuous adjustment and adaptation to a changing environment. Roma/Gypsy society has thus been characterized, throughout its history, by the invention and development of strategies of

---

[196] Rose, 2006, 5.
[197] Acton, Thomas and Gary Mundy (eds.). *Romani Culture and Gypsy Identity*. Hatfield: Hertfordshire UP, 1997.
[198] Fraser, Angus. *The Gypsies*. Oxford: Blackwell, ²1995. 294.

adaptation and negotiation. The result is a tradition of change and innovation.[199]

For this reason, one focus of my interpretation of *Stone Cradle* will be placed
on the interaction between 'minority' and 'majority' culture as depicted in the
novel. Hereby, special attention will be paid to the rhetorical structures of the
text since, due to a specific narratological make-up, the novel manages to combine two perspectives and to relate the story both from the point of view of a
Romany woman and from the position of an 'indigenous' Englishwoman.

Apparently, this juxtaposition of narrative voices is connected to the treatment
of (internal) difference. Hereby, one of my prime interests lies in the question of
how alterity is perceived and dealt with. In this context, I deem it particularly
important that the classical 'us-vs.-them' dichotomy has been replaced by a
formation which might be characterised as the 'Other within'. Thus, metaphorically speaking, one might argue that we are confronted with a part of the English or British 'personality' which is only grudgingly acknowledged and constantly kept at bay with all negative features (such as laziness or an inclination
to crime) being transferred to this 'Other'.

A last point which I will examine in greater detail is the 'meaning-generating'
function ascribed to the act of narration. Seeing that the novel is obviously
meant to provide insights into the habits, customs, and traditions of a specific
minority group in British society, I would like to suggest that the process of
narration does not only serve as a way to produce meaning on an intratextual
level but that a certain degree of 'meaning-generation' likewise arises from the
interaction between reader and text since it is left to the recipient to draw connections between the two narratives and to thereby piece together the entire
story. Moreover, the novel may be considered to pursue a 'political' or at least
consciousness-raising aim. Although it is certainly open to debate whether
comments by the author should be taken into account in the analysis of a literary
text, doing so appears legitimate in this case. This assumption arises mainly
from the prominent position of the acknowledgements immediately after the
title page where Doughty explicitly states that, in the creation of her characters,
she has drawn upon real-life sources. The implications of this statement and its
repercussions on the assessment of the 'authenticity' of the story will be addressed in the relevant chapter.

---

[199] Liégeois, Jean-Pierre and Nicolae Gheorghe. *Roma/Gypsies: A European Minority*. London:
Minority Rights Group, 1995. 29.

The same logics of inclusion and exclusion – supplemented with the consolidation of both auto- and heterostereotypes – also figures prominently in *Saturday*, the third novel under discussion in this section. In view of the oppositions opened up in the text, one may conceivably argue that, juxtaposed to an 'us-vs.-them' opposition embodied by the East-West dichotomy, the narrative offers a further example of the phenomenon of the 'Other within' which may also be found in *Stone Cradle*. Yet, while Doughty focuses on a group discriminated against on 'ethnic' grounds, the 'Other within' in *Saturday* is personified by the lower classes. It is for this reason that the term 'minority group' does not truly apply in this context since we are not dealing with a group which is marginalised on the grounds of the small number of its members but rather due to social, financial, and cultural reasons.

In its presentation of the lower classes, *Saturday* depicts this stratum of society as a comparatively homogeneous unit. In my analysis of the novel, I will discuss potentially controversial aspects in the assessment of class differences especially as far as implicit value judgements are concerned. In this context, it seems particularly important to take into account the values and qualities – both negative and positive – ascribed to each of the social classes. In addition to that, I will address the question of whether the portrayal of the lower classes may be perceived as biased and possibly even degrading. Turning away from the subject-matter of the book treated explicitly in the story-line, I will also examine class as a differential category and try to situate McEwan's text within current discourses on class in cultural studies and sociology. Hereby, my main interest consists in the evaluation of class as a criterion structuring everyday reality and the renewed interest in class presently to be witnessed in certain subdisciplines.[200] It is striking to note that, in the last decades, studies on difference tended to focus primarily on elements such as ethnicity, sex, and age, whereas class nowadays seems to be re-entering theoretical discourse. Roberts explains this temporary decline in the attention paid to class by the fact that "in former decades, in most of the UK, other divisions [such as race and gender] could simply be taken for granted"[201]. Due to social transformations triggered, among other things, by feminism and the concomitant change in the perception of gender-roles as well as by the need to acknowledge 'ethnic' differences among British citizens, the tensions arising from class differences were sometimes estimated as less pressing. Additionally, repeated claims about Britain turning into a 'classless society' brought forward by, for instance, the Blair government aimed at furthering the illusion that class had finally become an issue of the past

---

[200] On definitions of the term class as such as well as attitudes towards class as an analytic category, see Day, Gary. *Class*. London and New York: Routledge, 2001. An insightful account on this topic may also be found in Adonis, Andrew and Stephen Pollard. *A Class Act. The Myth of Britain's Classless Society*. London: Hamish Hamilton, 1997.
[201] Roberts, Ken. *Class in Modern Britain*. Basingstoke: Palgrave, 2001. 17.

and had thus lost its significance in the organisation of people's daily lives. Against the background of several surveys on the topic, though, it appears that class has by no means become an entirely meaningless category and continues to be perceived as a major element in the formation of collective identities. What has changed, though, is the reputation of certain affiliations. In addition to that, the number of citizens labelled as members of the middle classes has grown considerably because of a general improvement in the financial situation of many households. Consequently, former boundaries have shifted and the term 'middle-class' has lost some of its precision as it, by now, encompasses too large a number of people to allow for general statements about characteristic features or to identify a homogeneous system of values:

> As more and more people benefit from increased opportunities by moving into new professional occupations and thus leave working-class incomes behind, a new swelling middle class has emerged. However, the new arrivals do not identify with the value system of the traditionally despised petite bourgeoisie. As a result, a noticeable exchange of class-related values has occurred which gives preference to working-class ethics while at the same time ridiculing middle-class habitus. The fact that subjective class consciousness operates as a stronger bond than financial status is a clear indication that the traditional principle of solidarity within one's class is still intact.[202]

While class consciousness has never ceased to exist and class as a category did and does constitute an important marker of the social status of an individual, it is only more recently that academic discourse has returned to the question of class. This assumption chimes in with the outcomes of the 13th Cultural Studies Conference held at the Technische Universität Dresden.[203] As a survey of the main propositions brought forward in the respective papers indicates, a certain shift in the perception of class is discernible. With regard to the general findings of the conference, Stratmann states in his "Conference Report":

> Though "class" is definitely returning; [sic!] it seems to have lost, as most of the speakers confirmed (with explicit regret or implicit approval) both its political connotations and the leading place on the list of identity markers it had held during the 1950s and 1960s.[204]

---

[202] Kamm, Jürgen. „New Labour – Old Classes? Recent Trends in Britain's Social Transformation." *New Britain. Politics and Culture.* Ed. Bernd Lenz. Passau: Karl Stutz, 2006. 55-73. 69.
[203] The results of this conference have been published in a special issue of the *Journal for the Study of British Cultures* (*JSBC* Vol. 11, No. 1/04).
[204] Stratmann, Gerd. „The Return of Class: A Conference Report." *JSBC* 11, 1 (2004): 89-90. 89.

While the publications referred to above consider class from a sociological standpoint, *Saturday* offers a creative form of engagement with the topic. Nevertheless, it is interesting to note that the two discourses – i.e. the sociological approach and McEwan's literary take on the topic – obviously inform each other to a certain extent and display signs of an overlap. In my interpretation of the novel, special attention will be paid to the description of the interaction between individual social classes and the values and characteristic features associated with each of them. In addition to that, I will address the question of whether the homogenisation of these two social groups may be seen as another instance of the re-emergence of essentialist tendencies in the depiction of social formations. Another issue arising in connection with this problem is the assignment of values and value judgements implied by the text, a problem I will return to in the respective chapter.

Furthermore, my analysis of *Saturday* will be guided by the observation that the novel does not only highlight the issue of class but that it, at the same time, covers the topic of ethnic differences in Britain. In this context, a number of clichéd notions on specific circles are quoted with individual characters either defending or trying to dismantle them. Hereby, it is clearly discernible that the novel was written under the impression of the 9/11 attacks and the general climate of fear prevalent at this time. Accordingly, in its initial chapters, *Saturday* focuses on the widespread fear of another terrorist attack. Describing the great anxiety among the British population, a dichotomy between a civilised, peaceful West as opposed to a potentially hostile and malevolent East emerges. For this reason, special attention will be paid to the description of the two spheres which are identified with specific sets of values: While the 'West' is associated with qualities such as openness and democracy – i.e. 'positive' connotations, the (Islamic) 'East' is presented as threatening and dangerous. In this context, I will also scrutinise the narratological structures of the novel and discuss the implications of inscribing the text in specific generic traditions.

In view of the fact that the perception of difference in *Saturday* is linked to the anxiety and fear resulting from the 'other' which is seen to pose a threat due to its being foreign (and therefore hard to understand), the strategies by which the narrative deals with the 'culturally' or 'ethnically other' prove worthy of further study. Hereby, it is interesting to note that McEwan's novel obviously contains a feature which distinguishes it from other constructions of alterity inasmuch as it posits an implicit link between the 'other without' and the 'other/Other within'[205]. In doing so, the narrative establishes a thematic connection as the

---

[205] Depending on the perspective one chooses to adopt, the other within can both be understood as the Other in Lacanian terms and as the other as a counterpart to the religiously/ethnically other or

two allegedly menacing and terrifying elements are not merely juxtaposed to each other but presented as two sides of the same coin and shown to trigger the same reaction. After the defusion of the danger arising from the 'ethnically other', the external threat is replaced by the fear of the 'other/Other within', this time embodied by a member of the working classes. In the ensuing discussion of alterity, *Saturday* presents a strategy of coping with difference that is employed in both contexts.

A last peculiarity with regard to McEwan's narrative consists in the fact that the text allows for two highly divergent interpretations. Since there are strong arguments recommending each of them, I decided not to limit my reading to one possibility but to present both views and to set them off against each other. This decision seems legitimated by the fact that the contextualisation of McEwan's text and its comparison with the other novels covered here can be performed in two entirely different ways. Accordingly, *Saturday* can either be read as an endorsement of a bourgeois system of values or it may be understood as a subversion of those selfsame values.

This overview of the themes dealt with by the texts in the second set of analyses already indicates the breadth and variety of the topics covered here. Despite the great heterogeneity with regard to the styles adopted by individual writers, the novels are nevertheless linked by certain features which suggest the gradual consolidation of a new line of contemporary British fiction characterised by novel approaches in the treatment of difference. These methods differ from 'postmodern' strategies inasmuch as they, for instance, focus on the potentially meaning-generating quality of difference or even resuscitate (seemingly) essentialist notions. Moreover, the impression arises that a return to pre-postmodern positions is taking place. This turning back, however, does not constitute a mere re-establishment of former strategies. In contrast, I would like to suggest that 'traditional' narrative patterns and genres are cited but used creatively so as to produce new strategies which provide an alternative angle on specific differential categories. While the concrete employment of these strategies as well as their effects will be outlined in the respective analytic chapters, I would, by way of a preliminary conclusion, like to draw attention to one of the most intriguing features of this emerging body of 'post(?)-postmodern' literature. While all narratives chosen for examination tackle the problem of coping with difference, individual solutions are highly divergent so that a range of tactics with an enormous variety is offered to the reader. As a result, especially the novels in Section II differ considerably in terms of style and subject-matter. Nevertheless, as

---

"other without". Further clarification of this problem will be offered in the chapter on McEwan's *Saturday*.

a uniting feature, they all present innovative ways of coping with difference and can be seen to open up new perspectives on the subject.

Bernardine Evaristo's *Soul Tourists* – Black Britishness via a European Detour

As outlined in the introduction to this second set of analyses, Evaristo's novel *Soul Tourists* may be considered the thematic bridge between the two parts of this thesis. While the topic of ethnic identity continues to play a decisive role, the issue is extended considerably so as to encompass the notion of 'European-ness'. In this context, the novel traces potential 'black' influences within the extensive field of a shared 'European' tradition, a concept, which is usually associated with 'white' culture and frequently set in opposition to the African, Asian or Muslim world. Nevertheless, we still discover a clearly discernible link to *On Beauty* and *Londonstani*, since *Soul Tourists* offers yet another form of bonding inspired by ideas such as a common cultural heritage arising from the ethnic group an individual was born into. Simultaneously, though, *Soul Tourists* differs from the novels examined previously inasmuch as it does not exclusively focus on black and white as the two poles of a differential category in its en-gagement with the topic of race and ethnicity but, metaphorically speaking, presents them as the two sides of the 'European coin' instead. Concomitant to this transformation of an established binary is the introduction of a historical dimension, an element which the other texts – apart from the occasional refer-ence to history in terms of shared roots and an imaginary homeland – lack. *Soul Tourists* rather focuses on 'Europe' both as a geographical realm and a specific historical and cultural unit. In the process, the novel pays particular attention to potential loopholes for the inclusion of black characters within the exclusively white master narrative. Still, as I will examine in greater detail below, the narra-tive does not aim at rectifying previous imbalances or even re-writing historical events. By contrast, it illustrates the attempt of one individual character to come to grips with what is perceived as an incongruous cultural heritage. This the-matic outlook is coupled with a reflection on the relationship between members of different generations; likewise, it serves as a starting point for a discussion of the importance of personal roots, or, to be more precise, a detailed knowledge of one's family background. The plights caused by a lack of this information are exemplified via Jessie, who, as an orphan, is ignorant of both her parents and her genealogical background; she therefore (even though not admittedly) suffers deeply from her lack of roots and a family history. As a second example of strained ties within a family, the novel introduces Stanley, who, in his early adulthood, entertains a highly tensioned relationship with his father and wishes to break off all bonds to his former life. Yet, he, too, finally comes to realise that he can only reach a satisfying way of life and a satisfactory self-image once he has become reconciled with his immediate ancestry, i.e. the not-so-distant past (a goal finally achieved via a detour through several centuries). Lastly, *Soul Tourists* stands off from the works analysed previously with respect to its treat-ment of gender differences. By contrast to the essentialist notions endorsed by *Londonstani* and *Tourism*, Evaristo's novel explicitly addresses the question of what should ideally form the basis of a love relationship and to what extent each of the spouses should abandon their own personality in order to fuse with their partner and thereby 'vanish' as an individual in favour of an entirely homogeneous unit. This move constitutes a shift in focus inasmuch as it does no longer discuss the question of 'adequate' male and female behaviour but rather challenges conventional ideals of partnership and examines the significance of gender roles in the construction of personal identities.

As could likewise be observed in the foregoing chapters, *Soul Tourists*, in its selection of categories, once again returns to the established criteria of gender, race/ethnicity, and age. Consequently, the innovative potential of the novel does not lie in this choice but rather in the narrative's creative engagement with established concepts and the new perspective on dichotomies which appear familiar or even 'natural' due to their having been essentialised over a long period of time. In view of the vast number of changes of location, which render *Soul Tourists* a type of travelling narrative or roadmovie, as well as its great diversity in terms of style, genre considerations will likewise take substantial space in the following analysis.

Narratological structures in *Soul Tourists*: The Blending of Narrative Voices

A first striking aspect with regard to the textual strategies employed in *Soul Tourists* consists in the novel's intricate narratological structure, which is composed of a maze of intercepting perspectives. As a result, a complex web unfolds which comprises a welter of different registers and styles. This elaborate and varied structure primarily arises from the juxtaposition of numerous genres coupled with a series of narrative voices in quick alteration. In addition to that, the novel exhibits a purely visual component as its single, rather episodic chapters are grouped into larger sections preceded by an icon which functions as a graphic title. In tune with the narrative's main topic – the activity of travelling – those icons are all reminiscent of road signs. Basically, the 'title images' fulfil two functions. On the one hand, they allude to the further development of the story. This is, for example, the case with the roundabout sign[206], which announces a repetitive, monotonous spell of beach life, and the sign warning of heavy snow fall shortly before Stanley and Jessie cross the Alps. On the other hand, a second group of pictograms can be read as ironic comments on Jessie's and Stanley's relationship. Accordingly, a sign indicating the danger of gusts

---

[206] Evaristo, Bernardine. *Soul Tourists*. London: Hamish Hamilton, 2005. 133. Hereafter quoted as Soul Tourists.

(Soul Tourists 41) precedes Jessie's and Stanley's arrival at windswept Broadstairs (and the start of their tumultuous relationship).

The use of several 'media' or, strictly speaking, genres is perpetuated throughout the novel as we are presented with a variety of different styles and generic conventions. The use of particular forms and the distribution of these structures within a larger framework, however, is far from arbitrary. To the contrary, on deeper analysis, certain rhetorical moves and generic features prove to be recurrent so that a sophisticated pattern unfolds: We, for instance, observe that the narrative perspective continuously shifts from passages narrated by Stanley to episodes told from Jessie's point of view. These scenes are combined with sections featuring an extradiegetic narrator, who offers further (often ironic) comments on the action. In addition to that, the novel comprises chapters which display hardly any graspable narrative transmission as is the case in conversations mirroring the transcripts of interviews or scriptbooks for plays (i.e., in Genette's terms, all but prototypical examples of external focalization). This oscillation between passages with a highly noticeable narratorial presence and sections in which the narrative voice recedes so far into the background that the visibility of a narrative instance is almost reduced to zero may be considered one of the characteristic features of the text.

A further narratological peculiarity of *Soul Tourists* consists in the fact that the transitions from one type of narrative transmission to another are frequently performed in quick succession. Accordingly, the story starts with a chapter in which Stanley acts as an autodiegetic narrator. Already on the second page, though, the narrative voice becomes less tangible as Stanley's memories of his late mother Pearline blur with his father's reminiscences. Thereby, an intricate structural link between the two characters is established albeit Stanley's perception of this bond is, at this stage, still overlaid by his concentration on the divisive elements between him and his father, a stance which provokes mainly disgust for the old man in him and suppresses any feelings of proximity. Although both father and son are apparently still unable to cope with Pearline's death, neither of them manages to share his thoughts or to find comfort in the other's presence (Soul Tourists 6). The sequence of impressions presented from Stanley's autodiegetic perspective ends abruptly by the insertion of his father's death certificate from the coroner's office, which is provided without any narratorial comment or transmission. Subsequently, the text continues with a scene presented by a clearly identifiable extradiegetic-heterodiegetic narrator who sarcastically describes Clasford's new place of residence:

> Stanley is burying his father, in a field of dumb bedfellows whose sole purpose is to provide balanced nutrition for the more vulnerable members of the animal kingdom: [...].
>
> Mr Clasford Williams is the newest, fully paid-up resident of Tower Hamlets' community of gourmet cadavers, whose social relationship to each other is defined only by proximity and the fact that their hearts, in one breathtaking moment, had stopped. (Soul Tourists 19)

This almost shockingly detached account quickly fades and turns into a more melancholic tone. At this point, it becomes impossible to clearly attribute the voice to a concrete speaker and it is thus left to the reader to decide whether Stanley is employed as a focalizer in this passage or whether we are still dealing with an extradiegetic narrative voice, i.e. a case of zero focalization. This movement between a heterodiegetic narrator and Stanley's homodiegetic perspective is maintained right until the end of the chapter. With only slight alteration, it is resumed in the next passage. However, now it is Jessie who acts as a focalizer, whereas Stanley's thoughts are presented in a drama-like fashion without any mediating instance:

> Stanley: I'd been hijacked after work and frog-marched by the guys to this bunker called Mingles, where I squinted in the searchlight of a crazed strobe, my laced-up brogues stamped on by feet hopping to detonating beats that ricocheted around the fragile, membranous chamber encasing the one solid asset I was purported to own: my brain. (Soul Tourists 25)

The following chapters repeat the pattern described above with little variation. Vast stretches of the text are narrated by an extradiegetic-heterodiegetic narrator with Stanley and Jessie alternatingly serving as focalizers; at times, the scenes are interspersed with passages in which Stanley returns to his role as autodiegetic narrator. A striking feature of this scheme consists in the fact that personal reflections, which the protagonists are unwilling to share with each other, and which, for this reason, are only revealed to the reader, are usually offered in the form of a poem. This strategy sets these parts off from the rest of the narrative both in terms of style and in terms of typography. The poems are apparently intended to evoke the impression that the characters now 'speak their true mind' since the ideas brought forward prove highly intimate and personal. In general, they offer a new view on the events and disclose attitudes and aspirations anxiously concealed in open conversation; at times, they even contradict the protagonists' previous utterances. This holds, for instance, true for the scene in which the reader is informed about Jessie's insecurities and her fears. This revelation jars with the overly self-confident, easy-going façade Jessie maintains when dealing with other people. Significantly, the pattern is broken when the protagonists first have sex with each other. At this moment, their conversation switches to the interview or drama style which had previously been exclusively reserved for personal reflections. Even though they do not utter their thoughts loudly, the statements in their minds combine to form a homogeneous text with each of them taking up the other's cues:

> S When I'm inside her, shall we say, tropical lushness, I feel so… male
>
> J When he's inside me, I want to pull up the drawbridge and bolt it
>
> S Wanted comfort (100%). Wanted contrast (100%). Wanted to come (100%)
>
> J Come with me, Stanley, dear. Wake up to wide open fields and driving on a road that leads up and away into heavens
>
> […]
>
> S We've found each other, Miss O'Donnell
>
> J Yes, we have, Mr Williams
>
> S She rolls on top of me and I completely disappear
>
> J Dissolve into me, for eternity… (Soul Tourists 59)

This impression of a perfect, harmonious, and homogeneous union is amplified by the lack of punctuation marks in this passage. Instead of ending each sentence with a full stop, Evaristo allows the statements to blend into each other and to thereby create a continuous flow. The feeling of proximity and utmost closeness experienced by the protagonists at this point of the story is thus not only expressed by the content of their (mental) utterance but also communicated via a specific rhetorical and stylistic make-up. Consequently, the narrative structure serves to underline the great intimacy of the moment and implies that, during this brief period, Stanley and Jessie form an inseparable unit in which sex does no longer constitute a divisive element but rather acts as a complement to the other. While having sex, Jessie and Stanley all but merge into each other – both in linguistic and in more material, bodily terms – and thereby achieve a state of unconditional belonging, albeit only for the time being since their impression of extreme closeness is dispelled immediately after this scene. Tellingly, the rupture is triggered by Stanley's first encounter with a ghost from the past. As the following chapters show, this plot element constitutes a repeated figure with the ghosts gradually turning into an impediment which prevents a restoration of the previous intimacy between the protagonists.

In terms of style, Stanley's contacts with the ghosts likewise display a specific-ity since the ghosts invariably resort to verse in order to communicate with Stanley. This fact may be interpreted as an indicator of their being located on a 'semi-real' level. In view of the phenomenon that only Stanley is able to see the ghosts and to talk to them, the impression arises that they might only form part of his own mind, even though he himself is apparently not conscious of this part of his personality yet.[207] It is already at this early stage in the relationship that the apparitions open up a gap between Jessie and Stanley and constitute a first bone of contention. This assumption is confirmed by the observation that Stanley is only able to communicate with 'his' ghosts when Jessie is absent, or respectively, while she is asleep. As soon as Jessie wakes up, the spell is broken and the connection to the past is interrupted.

Despite these discords, however, the protagonists nevertheless continue to share moments of closeness and proximity. The first chapters of the novel are there-fore characterised by a constant shuttling between scenes in which they are pre-sented as drifting apart followed by subsequent rapprochements which usually result in a state of temporary satisfaction and mutual understanding. This ele-ment likewise finds its expression on a stylistic level. Usually, indications of a (potential) rupture are subsequently followed by a passage in verse in which Stanley and Jessie once again supplement each other. Tellingly, these sections in verse – the medium of intimacy – mainly revolve around the topic of sexual-ity. Although potential disagreements and triggers for disharmony abound al-ready in this early period of the relationship (with Stanley, for example, being put off by Jessie's slovenly habits and her occasionally overbearing presence), the protagonists still rejoice in the bliss of sexual union. These instances are portrayed as times of utmost belonging and oneness, in which all differences and divisive elements are temporarily suppressed.[208]

Yet, as the journey proceeds, tensions between the couple begin to mount up; in general, quarrels between the protagonists result primarily from their incom-patible ideas on the 'right' way of travelling and from their clashing expecta-tions and needs in terms of personal space. The narrative reflects this develop-ment by employing the stichomythic line-per-line style which had previously been used as a sign of great intimacy for the negotiation of these contrary de-mands. Again, the protagonists' thoughts are not openly spelled out. By contrast to the earlier scenes, though, in which individual statements complemented each

---

[207] As all of the ghosts are black figures who have been suppressed in official historiographical accounts and thereby have been more or less erased from History, their return can be read as a symbol for Stanley's own inhibitions to face the past and his problems in reconciling his 'black' heritage with his national identity as an Englishman.

[208] This choice of image may be seen as a variation on the topic of love as a uniting and binding force which can, in a slightly different form, also be found in *On Beauty*.

other to form a homogeneous text, the reader is now presented with two different perspectives on the situation, a technique which indicates an incipient disharmony. Accordingly, the storyline offers various comments which imply that especially Stanley is not happy with the arrangements of the journey anymore. The protagonists' growing alienation is furthermore highlighted by a specific typeset. While, in the preceding chapters, they both took turns in adopting the position of the speaker – with one account supplementing the other – their comments are now set in opposition:

S   J

old town, narrow streets

boutiques, Arab wall

how I *long* to be a tourist

                                                     my little caravan

                                                     now it's gone, my

                                                     summer second to none

rain

missionary of the skies

cleansed

                                                     trauma's supposed to bond

                                                     like cement, not sink

                                                     like subsidence

                                                     (Soul Tourists 147)

Thus, as can be derived from this passage, both form and content serve to highlight the increasing dissent between the partners.

Towards the end of the novel, the presence of an extradiegetic narrator becomes increasingly palpable. While, in the first chapters, it is frequently not possible to ultimately decide whether the text presents an event through the perspective of a focalizing figure or whether we are dealing with the narrator's assessment of a situation, there can, in the later stages of the text, be no doubt that an extra-diegetic-heterodiegetic voice comments on the events. This is, for instance, the case in the following passage on the burdens arising from the protagonists' personal experiences in the past as well as from their respective (cultural) 'heritages':

> [T]hey brought saffron, spices, sperm, slaves, silver, stories, ivory, songs; they wore gems and germs; they traded gunpowder, gold, glass; Jessie brought the convent from high up the hills of Leeds, it was the stone mansion with which she had been clad, the task of excavation awaited her; Stanley brought the visitors who'd come and gone, yet still lingered on;

> they brought religion and refugees, ideas and medicine, myths and music, melanin by the caravan-load; Stanley brought Pearline and a love that would never die; Jessie brought a longing for her son that just wouldn't bloody abate; (Soul Tourists 204)

Again, the tone of the novel is imbued with the sharp irony which is characteristic of the heterodiegetic narrator – a feature which can be detected already on the first emergence of this voice in one of the initial passages of the story. The extradiegetic-heterodiegetic narrator may be immediately recognised by this preference for puns as well as by the strategy to connect unrelated objects or, rather, objects not linked in terms of subject-matter but rather by linguistic means such as alliterations. Yet, despite the characteristic tone of these scenes, the sections told from an external point of view at the same time contain expressions which form part of the register of one of the protagonists such as Jessie's love that "wouldn't bloody abate". Thus, via the use of typical formulations, the main characters are indirectly given a voice as the choice of certain words implies that we are confronted with their view on the situation.

As the story unfolds, signs of an imminent split-up begin to show more and more clearly. Accordingly, the chapter titled "Letter from the Court of Jessie at Ölüdeniz" is aptly introduced by the sign "emergency exit" (Soul Tourists 207). As Stanley turns out to be the writer of the letter immediately following this icon, there can be no doubt of his seeking a way out of the relationship, or, metaphorically speaking his taking the emergency exit. At this stage of the story, Stanley's observations have lost their ironic tinge and come to be replaced by sarcastic, at times even caustic, comments. In order to underline his feeling of being smothered by Jessie's domineering, overpowering presence, he signs his letter with the word "Whatsisname?" (Soul Tourists 214). The novel proceeds with two lists of expenditures headed "Summer of 1989: Court Budget". The two budgets, calculated by Stanley and Jessie respectively, are set off against each other so as to contrast their clashing attitudes towards the trip in general. While Stanley concentrates on the material, calculable costs of the journey, Jessie exclusively points out the 'spiritual' improvement as well as the benefits offered to Stanley for free. As before, typographical features are used to visually set off the two lists from the previous chapter. It is at this moment of great tension that their differences in terms of education and profession come to the fore again, a feature indicated by the respective signatures: "Stanley Orville Cleve Williams, B.Sc. (Quant)" vs. "Jessie O'Donnell, Ph.D. Univ. Hrd Knks (Orphan)" (Evaristo 216-7). Although Jessie had been ridiculing Stanley's professionalism and his City habits throughout their travel, it is only at this point that she comes to consider their different levels of education – and the superiority Stanley allegedly derives from it – as a major barrier. The sequence ends with a further letter from Stanley. Dissimilar to the first one, however, this letter is directed at a real recipient since it informs Jessie about his decision to leave for a limited period of time in order to regain some space of his own.

The subsequent section entitled "Eighteenth-century Slave Market" confronts the reader with a deviation from the usual structure as it starts immediately in the past without any moment of transition. By contrast to previous encounters with an apparition, which were all introduced by Stanley's suddenly becoming aware of another presence in his vicinity, he now finds himself plunged into the sphere of eighteenth century's Constantinople right away. Remarkably, Stanley even seems to seek the ghosts' company so as to interact with them, whereas before they had been treated as intriguing occurrences belonging firmly to the past. Clashing with his former behaviour Stanley thus begins to display a growing inclination to immerge himself into the past and shows a reluctance to return to what he perceives as an over-complicated, problem loaded present. This desire to flee his real life reaches such a degree that he runs the danger of losing himself in the past and finally has to be persuaded to return by one of the ghosts.

During Stanley's trip to both present and past Istanbul/Constantinople, Jessie undergoes a sequence of intensive emotional states. In stylistic terms, these are orchestrated in a hybrid genre reminiscent of drama as well as verse narrative. In a very brief, concise fashion, Jessie's thoughts and feelings are listed, a procedure which implicates that the reader is given direct access to her mind. Despite all wounded pride, the passage still musters a certain degree of irony, especially when Jessie talks about her anger and her plans on how to treat Stanley on his return. Due to the quick rhythm of the passage as well as the use of brackets to supplement sarcastic comments on each of the plans, this scene – irrespective of its serious content – assumes a markedly entertaining and comic note:

Stabbing

(messy).

Drowning

(he's stronger than me).

[...]

Poison, chop into manageable portions,

make mincemeat sausages,

preserve in deep-freeze of camp kitchen

and sell as hot dogs in Fethiye all winter

(most sensible, creative and profitable).

(Soul Tourists 247)

Her self-ironic stance, however, quickly lapses into melancholy and regret; this state is, in turn, followed by the emotional stages three and four titled recovery and revenge. In view of the dramatic quality of this presentation, one may argue that, in order to complete the classic tragedy, a fifth act comprising the great showdown is still to come. This fifth and final act commences with Stanley's return to the campsite and the ensuing argument between him and Jessie which ends in yet another furious split-up. Moreover, the close bond between them seems to have been ultimately ruptured by Stanley's revelation that he is able to see ghosts. This assumption is confirmed by the sequence "Güle, Güle, Ölüdeniz", which once more sets the two protagonists' thoughts in (typographical) opposition to each other (Soul Tourists 254).

Immediately after their break up, Stanley seeks to escape again. This time, however, he does not retreat into the past but rather resorts to some imaginary underwater world on the ocean floor where he ultimately succeeds in being reconciled with his father. This passage proves remarkable in narratological terms inasmuch as it is designed as an answer-less conversation between Stanley and his father. Moreover, as far as the typescript is concerned, it is presented as a poem, whereas the rhetorical make up of individual sentences is very close to plain prose. Seeing the previous instrumentalisation of verse passages, this configuration may be read as an indicator that what is presented here constitutes a scenario in Stanley's mind and reveals some of his most intimate thoughts.

In the following chapter, the combination of drama-like speeches with passages told with an alternation between zero focalization and internal focalization is resumed. It is only in the section entitled "The Supreme Court of 'Justice'" that we encounter a new narratological form. Similar to the passage after Clasford's death, an 'official' document is inserted into the text. By contrast to the death certificate, though, we are this time not dealing with a 'real' document but rather with a mock charge brought forward against Stanley by Jessie. In this accusation, she complains about having been unjustly abandoned and been left "*Emotionally Bankrupt*" (Soul Tourists 274, orig. emphasis). In her charge, Jessie uses a variety of legal terms but applies them to an 'emotional' crime. This strategy fulfils several functions. First, it demonstrates her ability to use an 'educated' register and to prove that, despite her lack of institutional formation, she is not inferior to Stanley on an intellectual plane. Secondly, the form chosen shows that Jessie feels deeply wronged and treated unfairly. At the same time, a comic effect evolves since, as the charge unfolds, juridical language is taken ad absurdum.

At the end, the novel features a last verse-like episode from Jessie's perspective followed by a first-person narrative in which Stanley acts as an autodiegetic narrator. The epilogue, by contrast, introduces a new narrative voice. Here, the action is partly presented from the viewpoint of Queen Charlotte of England, who is employed as a focalizer. The narrator's humorous description, coupled with Charlotte's own comments on her situation, lend a light, funny note to the concluding passages of the story:

> Charlotte was still missing such basic earthly delights as riding side-saddle round the thousands of acres of Windsor Great Park, her dogs, her jewellery, the occasional soirée, her elephants that were housed in a paddock at Buckingham Palace, and O, how she had loved painting, playing the harpsichord, dancing 'The Hempdresser', reading books and going to the theatre.
>
> Georgie was asleep as usual. He rarely woke up these days. It was such a tragedy that he should die blind, deaf and mad. (Although such a relief that at least he couldn't expose himself any more.) (Soul Tourists 285)

This quote provides an excellent sample of the almost imperceptible movements between two speakers. While the beginning of the passage is clearly related by an extradiegetic-heterodiegetic narrator, the perspective switches to Charlotte as a focalizer (indicated by the "O, how she had loved painting") with the 'external' narrator gradually receding into the background. The portrayal of Charlotte's ennui, her troubles arising from her husband's forgetfulness, her musings on her own status, and her final decision to "realign [her] bones" (Soul Tourists 288) constitute an exemplary take of the tone pervading the whole novel.

Space, Place, and Personality

As mentioned in the introduction to this chapter, *Soul Tourists* may, apart from its account on identity formation(s), be likewise read as a travelling novel or roadmovie. For this reason, the depiction of places and spaces[209] naturally assumes special significance. In general, we can differentiate between three types of setting. These are (in chronological order as they appear in the text), first, places of residence, i.e. fictive locations described in a 'realistic' way, secondly, geographical sites or tourist venues with a referent in the 'real' world, and, thirdly, purely imaginary spaces, such as the bottom of the sea.

The novel opens with a reflection on spaces and living environments as Stanley delineates the way from his pristine place of residence to his father's filthy flat. The two realms are obviously perceived as the foil to each other since Stanley even likens his journey to the process of giving birth, hereby describing the Blackwall Tunnel as "the birth canal forcing me underneath the pressurized gallons of the river that splits the city into north and south" (Soul Tourists 3). The river thus serves as a border line between Stanley's minutely organised and neatly ordered life, which is opposed to the chaos his father's flat has sunk into after Pearline's death. Personal places, in particular the living arrangements a figure chooses for their home, are presented as an expression of this figure's character traits and general ways of behaviour. Accordingly, Clasford's house is clustered with items heavily loaded with memories:

> official documents from the years of marriage, houses rented, bought; letters dating back to the 1940s; the passport dated 1956 that he was always going to get renewed for that migration back home that was always 'next year' away; the birth certificates, medical cards and dental cards; and somewhere, a death certificate.[210] *The weight of it all bearing down on us*. (Soul Tourists 6, my emphasis)

Stanley's home, by contrast, is characterised by its conspicuous lack of any superfluous objects and the absence of any personal items. His rejection to get

---

[209] According to Carter, space is turned into place by the process of attaching a name to it: "How then does space become place? By being named: as the flows of power and negotiations of social relations are rendered in the concrete form of architecture; and also, of course, by embodying the symbolic and imaginary investments of a population. Place is space to which meaning has been ascribed" (Carter, Erica *et al*. „Introduction." *Space and Place. Theories of Identity and Location*. Eds. Erica Carter *et al*. London: Lawrence and Wishart, 1993. vii-xv. xii).

[210] It is striking to note that at least a minute part of this documentary heritage 'lives on' as Stanley, in turn, receives his father's death certificate a couple of pages later on.

involved with the past and his attempt to block out painful memories are symbolised by the ubiquity of the colour white, with which Stanley almost obses-
sively surrounds himself. His flat therefore assumes a sterile atmosphere in
which even organic items merely serve as accessories:

> In my narrow kitchen everything is hidden in white cupboards, except a
> Chinese-white porcelain bowl of oranges, pears, apples and grapes. And
> when they go mouldy, brown or bruise, what is it? Pure modern art,
> man. The whole flat is a gallery and I am but a walking sculpture inside
> it. A solitary sculpture, yet to find its perfect match. And she'd have to
> look good lounging on my sofa. No one ever does – they just mess it up.
> (Soul Tourists 12)

Via Jessie, colour and disorderliness enter Stanley's life: Gone are the times of
minute plans, precisely calculated budgets, and perfectly tidied up flats. Seeing
the transformation Stanley undergoes after having met Jessie, the impression
arises that his almost empty, faceless living space has been a reflection of his
'lack' of personal identity up to this point and that his abstaining from displaying any personal items resulted from his fear to give anything away about his
'true self'.

In view of the fact that the relationship between Jessie and Stanley mainly develops during the time the two spend travelling together, spaces necessarily
continue to play a prominent role. By contrast to the initial sequence, in which
the reader is introduced to the fictional venues and locations forming part of the
diegesis, the text now presents clearly locatable places as the protagonists visit
'real' geographical sites. In view of the high number of place names and references to touristic venues, the reader may trace the protagonists' itinerary
throughout Europe with comparative ease. In this context, the sites visited are
indicative of the characters' clashing ideas of travelling and their different notions of places worthy of being seen. Accordingly, Jessie endorses the ideal of
experiencing 'real' life, whereas Stanley is eager to explore classical historical
sites, i.e., from Jessie's point of view, the stereotypical tourist attractions. From
the start, these different expectations lead to considerable tensions between the
protagonists. The couple's visit of Versailles offers a typical example of their
opposing attitudes towards tourism and travelling:

> Upon entering the forecourt, Stanley's mouth released silent exclama-
> tion marks. Jessie's mouth clamped shut as she swept up the vista with
> a reluctant glance, then dumped it right back down again. […] Jessie
> and Stanley hooked fingers within the maze of gardens, which spun out

geometrically around a main axis with radiating pathways, pools and arbors. Versailles, Stanley decided, with its two thousand windows, seven hundred rooms and two thousand acres of park, was simply the most spectacular place he had ever visited. [...] [Jessie] wanted Stanley to notice her mood. Great houses reminded her of St Ann's Children's Home, the Victorian mansion high up in the hills of Leeds run by the Sisters of Mercy, whose greater love was for God but with a generic love for all mankind. (Soul Tourists 91-3)

Increasingly, the quarrels about the importance of geographical space are supplemented by clashes arising from the longing for metaphorical space, and, more precisely, the (one-sided) wish for a reduced degree of proximity. Hereby, Stanley feels smothered by Jessie's permanent, overbearing presence and her bossy behaviour. The way he chooses to finally communicate this desire to her (i.e. his decision to write a letter rather than to talk to her in person) hints at his guilty conscience. Moreover, it reveals his awareness that Jessie will most certainly not understand his wish to get away from her for some time, an assumption which is backed by the actual phrasing of the letter: "All I can say is that I need some, yes, I know it's a dirty word, space" (Soul Tourists 218). These contrary desires for proximity or, respectively, personal freedom translate into jarring idea(l)s of what a successful and satisfying relationship should look like. While Jessie promotes an all-inclusive union, Stanley favours a form of partnership which leaves space for each of the spouses and is not intended to blend their personalities completely. It is for this reason that notions of space are closely related to the issue of gender roles and gender identity.

Gender relationships in *Soul Tourists*

On the surface, *Soul Tourists* may be read as a love story with a comparatively conventional plot structure: A man and a woman get to know each other, fall in love and, finally, split up after having realised that they are, ultimately, incompatible. At the progressive stages of their relationship, the protagonists experience various degrees of happiness, from ultimate bliss to painful alienation. A deeper analysis of the novel, however, shows that the narrative simultaneously provides an insightful discussion of gender roles and negotiates different concepts of masculinity and femininity.

Unsurprisingly, Jessie is, at the beginning, depicted as Stanley's dream-come-true, the woman who will rescue him from his ordinary, monotonous life and help him discover his 'true' self. Contrary to his usual behaviour and his habitual reticence, Stanley is immediately besotted with the big, over-confident, and flirtatious woman even though her way of life does not fit in at all with the arrangement he has made for himself. It is already on the evening of their first encounter that the two enter what later on turns out to be a tension-ridden love relationship. Briefly after their first encounter, the couple sets off for a trip to Australia in order to achieve a reunion between Jessie and her son. This turn of the plot constitutes a first hint that not only Stanley is searching for the right partner but that Jessie is likewise in urgent need of support and anxiously seeks a person to rely on – a fact which she cautiously conceals from Stanley and only discloses to the reader via a sort of interior monologue:

> Maybe she wouldn't have to fight this one. She was so tired of fighting.
> [...]
>
> So I got a doctor's certificate, a visa
>
> allowing me to leave a country
> called Clinica Depressia
>
> for a paradise island called Valium –
> were a lovely holiday, went away for years.
>
> Won't be telling Stanley any of this,
> Whatever you tell them at the start
>
> will be used as evidence against you
> at the end, your honour... (Soul Tourists 34-5)

While Jessie brandishes a self-confident, independent stance when in the company of others, she, as the passage quoted above discloses, secretly searches for a substitute for the family[211] she has never had due to her growing up as an orphan. The long series of husbands and former partners may consequently be

---

[211] Jessie's desperate longing for a family of her own is likewise suggested by a scene in which she reflects on the relationship to her son: "Were made for each other, / me and thee, / out of nothing / but an escaped seed / finding its way *home*" (Soul Tourists 30, my emphasis). Even though the passage clearly plays with the image of an ovum being inseminated, the wish for a warm, welcoming home, which the orphanage could never provide, undoubtedly is alluded to as well.

seen as the outcome of increasingly despairing attempts to compensate for a lack of roots and to overcome the feeling of alienation provoked by being raised as the only black person in an all-white environment. Furthermore, the impression arises that – as far as her relationship with Brewster Montgomery is concerned – Jessie agreed to the marriage on purely pragmatic grounds. At the same time, though, the marriage to this considerably older man may, from a psychoanalytic perspective, be likewise interpreted as an attempt to make up for the lack of a father figure in her life.[212]

Stanley, in contrast, hails from a completely different background since he was raised in a 'functional' and, to all indications, happy family. It is possibly due to this reason that he also adopts a different attitude towards life in a partnership. Although stemming from a 'complete' family and thus having made experiences closed off to Jessie, he still shares some of her concerns and problems. Accordingly, Stanley, too, struggles with the plight arising from family ties and first has to learn how to cope with the 'family heritage' imposed on him. Moreover, as his reflections on the past reveal, the relationship towards his parents has obviously exerted – and to some extent still continues to do so in his adult years – a strong influence on his choice of a partner. While, as a teenager, he relied heavily on his parents' judgement and was highly anxious not to disappoint them in bringing home an 'unacceptable' girlfriend, he later on all but gives up his aspirations towards a relationship based on mutual understanding and love. Therefore, in his later life, the previous efforts of finding a partner for a 'conventional' relationship are replaced by temporal arrangements intended to provide sexual gratification but not considered suitable for a more permanent relationship:

> Yet, somewhere along this high street of relationships, with its, shall we say, takeaways, supermarkets, beauty parlours, pound-shop emporiums, cordon bleu restaurants, banks, libraries and designer boutiques, all of which I have known *intimately*, I gave up on both – marriage and love.

> I became the kind of man who succumbed only to the carnal. (Soul Tourists 45, orig. emphasis)

Despite these different expectations towards a love relationship (at least as displayed on the surface)[213], Stanley and Jessie feel immediately attracted to each

---

[212] After the marriage has come to an abrupt end due to Brewster's death, Jessie unwittingly 'succeeds' in re-establishing a contact to her real family by starting a relationship with her cousin, a fact which is revealed to them only later on and leads to the couple's split-up (Soul Tourists 35). Thus, Jessie's family ties constitute a permanent source of tension and anxiety.

[213] In fact, Stanley's comment about his being at ease in Jessie's company is quite striking as he likens being with her to being with his mother (Soul Tourists 47). Thus, he, too, obviously seeks

other and seem to complement one another's personality. Moreover, when trying to break out of their former routines, they come to heavily rely on each other since, on their own, neither of them has the courage or the necessary means to abandon what has become an unsatisfying way of life: While Stanley does not dare to leave the safety of his secure job and regular pay-check, Jessie cannot start out on her journey without a travelling companion. Providing precisely the qualities the other lacks, Jessie and Stanley at first seem to form the perfect couple. This impression is strengthened by the scene depicting the first night the two spend together in which their sexual intercourse is likened to a fusion of their two bodies into an all but seamless union (Soul Tourists 57-9). A further remarkable feature of this scene consists in the differential categories emphasised. Apparently, all divisive elements between the protagonists are overcome for the moment which leaves them in a state of absolute congruence of emotions. Nevertheless, both explicitly refer to their gender and Stanley even states to feel extremely "male" thus foregrounding the gender differences between the two of them. Moreover, they address each other with "Miss" or, respectively, "Mr", two equally gendered terms.

Over the course of the relationship, however, the protagonists' ideals of a partnership prove increasingly divergent. While Jessie still hopes for unconditional love and a partner who is willing to form a very close, impenetrable unit with her, Stanley feels oppressed and smothered by Jessie's permanent presence and her overbearing stance. Nevertheless, his attempts to create some distance between himself and Jessie in order to retain his own personality are not met with sympathy at all. In fact, the clashing degrees with respect to their individual desires for proximity turn out to constitute one of the main bones of contention in the long run. At one point, Stanley even feels that he has all but lost his own self and instead been transformed into a persona shaped by Jessie's wishes and expectations:

> S I've started to long for a walk alone, along the beach at sunset, to collect my thoughts before they go completely awol
>
> J Space? Look at the sky overhead. Look at the sea yonder. Look at the mountains behind us. There's space if you want space
>
> S There's not one of me any more. I'm a proper twosome
>
> J We're knuckle and joint; separate and we'll dislocate
>
> S Gibraltar is only down the road; I'll be gone a few hours

for the warmth and emotional support that disappeared from his life with his mother's death. Therefore, Jessie and Stanley are not as incompatible in their desires as it might seem on first sight even though neither of them openly admits their true longings to the other but rather tries to maintain the image they have constructed for themselves after several previous disappointments.

J We'll go together. When the season's over and the weather's cooler

[...]

S I listen to the radio wittering on all day long: Jessie FM

J If it's one thing I'm good at, it's communication

S She clings to me while sleeping; there's a sticky film of sweat between us, but if I try to budge, she grips tighter

(Soul Tourists 139-40)

While Jessie appears to be perfectly happy with this situation, Stanley tries to
break away from what he perceives as exaggerated closeness. He, by now, longs
for the luxury of spending some time on his own and for being once again able
to make his own decisions without consulting Jessie first. In the end, Jessie's
constant complaints about his needing more space provoke Stanley to move
away for a period of time and finally result in the couple's split up. In the final
instance, however, this incompatibility does not result from issues arising from
gender-specific problems but is rather triggered by the incongruence of the main
characters' personalities as well as their expectations and wishes. Apparently,
Stanley feels put off by Jessie's overanxious behaviour and tries to flee her almost hysterical fear of losing him as well as her subsequent attempts to bind
him closer and closer. This is illustrated by Stanley's following reaction:

> Your opinion is my opinion because I have none of my own. Well, you
> listen to this: I am so much more than your all-encompassing 'we'. And
> you, Jessie O'Donnell, as I have discovered, are not much more than a
> series of bold exclamation marks. (Soul Tourists 262)

Thus, potentially clashing ideas of masculinity and femininity do apparently not
pose the main problem in the relationship. By contrast, both protagonists feel
perfectly at ease in their respective gender roles at the beginning[214]; tensions
only arise when Jessie begins to dominate the union, starts to deny Stanley any
room for his own decisions and, ultimately, tries to change his personality.

---

[214] This depiction obviously contradicts the strand of feminist writing which assumes an intrinsic
oppressive quality of all heterosexual relationships due to established hierarchies and claims that
male-female-relationships are first and foremostly to be traced back to a socially enforced heteronormativity rather than to a true desire on the individual's side. Contrary to this assumption, if we
encounter any form of oppression in *Soul Tourists* at all, it is the female protagonist trying to
dominate her male counterpart rather than the other way round.

The 'Authenticity' of Culture and a New Concept of 'Europeanness'

With regard to the protagonists' identity formation, their ethnicity as well as its alleged incompatibility with the (white) society they live in obviously constitutes an important factor. As far as their 'cultural heritage' or ancestry is concerned, both characters are confronted with the problem of how to combine two contrasting cultural influences since each of them hails from a 'black' background but was raised within British society. From the start, casual comments and reflections (usually not uttered openly but presented to the reader by 'mind-dramas') imply that the main figures perceive their skin colour as a feature which sets them off from established English society and marks them as 'different'. This may clearly be observed with respect to Stanley's self-perception:

> His was an archetypal Caribbean face, which others found attractive but at which he could not look without being appalled at how dull it was. A face waiting for someone to move in and mess it up a bit, he thought, not realizing it was already loaded with the cargo of many seafarers. Bright slanting eyes, inherited from some hapless boy who had sailed from the island of Macao to decades of indentured labour on a sugar plantation in the faraway West Indies. A broad, shining forehead was the legacy of an ancestor who had lain in the hold of a galleon that sailed due west, cutting a swath between waves that rose like Turner's white flames. And the thin mouth of an aristocratic Scottish planter, vulnerable top lip rising like the tip of a wave over his slipstreamed bottom lip, indicating just a hint of self-pity. (Soul Tourists 29)

Especially the latter part of the quotation points out the various historical influences having potentially formed the protagonist and indicates that he himself is, as yet, not entirely aware of them. It is only at a subsequent stage in the novel that Stanley begins to perceive the flickering but all the same lasting presence of black people in Europe. While this presence comes to assume a great significance for Stanley himself, the precise impact of those figures on the formation of European history remains dubitable, since we are almost exclusively dealing with marginal, in the case of Shakespeare's black lady probably even fictional figures. One might therefore argue that the decisive function of those ghosts from the past does not consist in their offering a re-writing of established historiography with a concomitant introduction of previously 'hidden' black influences. Rather, they serve to reconcile Stanley with both his 'cultural' heritage and his more recent past, especially in terms of the relationship to his family or, to be more precise, the strained rapport with his father. Hereby, the actual 'truth value' of the ghosts' accounts does not appear of major import; to the contrary, these occasionally bizarre personages with their at times frivolous, cheeky, and disrespectful behaviour do by no means come across as reliable sources of information on past events. Nevertheless, they help Stanley realise that, even as a black person in 'white' Europe, he must not necessarily remain an outsider, but that it is up to him to find ways of reconciling the various influences he was subjected to in his life.

On first sight, Jessie seems to feel much more at ease with her skin colour than Stanley does; occasionally, she even exploits reified clichés by deliberately conforming to stereotypical (white) notions, for example when setting up Mama Hortense's Singing Kitchen or when luring Turkish custom officers to let her cross the border (Soul Tourists 198-9). Nevertheless, on closer examination, she, too, struggles with being 'different' and suffers from the recurrent ostracism on the grounds of her looks. Even though Jessie reprimands Stanley for suspecting racism everywhere and tends to trace hostile behaviour back to causes other than xenophobia (Soul Tourists 43), she feels hurt by being treated differently because of her skin colour. In this context, it is especially the memory of her upbringing in the all-white environment of St Ann's convent that continues to form a major burden for Jessie in her adult life.

Due to their experiences and the troubles they have encountered when trying to come to grips with their cultural heritage, both protagonists face difficulties in positioning themselves in English society. While Stanley's father turned into the stereotypical embittered immigrant, an eternal foreigner never accepted by or integrated into English society[215], Jessie is ignorant about her family roots, a void that obviously continues to cause her pain even after decades: "I *was* unloved, proven fact, no parents, / just a house full of frustrated elderly virgins / what hadn't a clue how to love the seventy-odd / waifs and sad strays at their mercy" (Soul Tourists 106, orig. emphasis). Jessie's attempts to maintain her self-confident façade and to downplay the extent of xenophobia in British society cannot conceal her preoccupation with the topic of race and her longing for lasting ties and affiliations. Stanley likewise feels troubled by the seeming incongruity between his cultural/ethnic identity and his nationality. At a comparatively early stage in their relationship, Jessie and Stanley discuss this problem:

---

[215] Apparently, the problem of immigrants not being given the opportunity to practise their former jobs constitutes one of the prime concerns of many writers dealing with the burdens faced by immigrants in their new homecountry. The problem of being prevented from working in one's former profession is explicitly raised in publications as diverse as Evaristo's *Soul Tourists*, Phillips' highly political *A Distant Shore*, and Neat's private-eye-novel *City of Tiny Lights*, to name but a few.

'You're just another Englishman, don't kid yourself. You think like an Englishman, walk like an Englishman, talk like an Englishman, eat like an Englishman and most likely you dance like an Englishman. You've spent all your life in England, Stanley, so what does that make you? Mongolian? Peruvian? Egyptian?'

Did it make sense? Maybe. But I wasn't going to be crushed like a can of Coke.

'I don't have any real roots here. None of us has.'

Was I really just like him, hanging on to a state of statelessness? *We don't belong, Stanley.* So why did he never make it back home, where presumably he did belong? (Soul Tourists 51, orig. emphasis)

Here, the narratological structure creates an interesting tension between the stances adopted by the characters in their conversation and the uncertainties which are left unvoiced. While both doggedly stick to an unambiguous, straight-forward opinion when talking to each other, they secretly entertain doubts about whether the problem is really as clear-cut as it appears on the surface. Still, the protagonists obviously feel that admitting to their doubts in this situation equals weakness. As discussions between them almost always turn into implicit nego-tiations of status and power, each of them increasingly grows reluctant to give in even on minor points.

In the end, though, both of the main characters find a way of dealing with the past, an achievement which reconciles them with their roots and allows them to feel part of a family line. With Stanley's help, Jessie manages to reach Austra-lia, where she is reunited with her alienated son (Soul Tourists 277). Contrary to their initial plans, however, each of them ultimately pursues their own path since their conceptions of life prove incompatible after all. Even though "The Supreme Court of 'Justice'" suggests that Jessie is deeply hurt and desperately wishes for a reconciliation, the chances that the rupture will be overcome are minuscule as Stanley's plans, which are laid out in the last chapter, obviously do not include Jessie. While she finally finds her inner peace by being reunited with her son, the only member of her family she has ever known in person, Stanley reaches a reconciliation with his 'cultural heritage' and the more recent past via his 'historical detour'. Strikingly, Stanley's encounters with figures from the past frequently mirror the respective state of his relationship with Jessie at a particular moment in time. This especially holds true for the very first meeting with a ghost, i.e. his encounter with Lucy Negro, Shakespeare's dark lady. Just like Jessie, Lucy Negro has been cut off from her roots and been left to fend for herself at a comparatively early age. Moreover, not unlike Jessie, Lucy displays an outgoing, self-confident stance and presents herself as a strong and independent black woman. This feature may be read as an indication that, as far as Lucy is concerned, the meeting between her and Stanely is less about 'the Past' in terms of History/official historiography but rather pertains to Stanley's and Jessie's still comparatively short common past as well as their own personal histories.

When we trace the sequence of spectres occurring in the text, a specific design unfolds. Each time, the intention of the ghost talking to Stanley is to reveal another, allegedly suppressed aspect of 'official' European past and to thereby disclose the, quite literally, 'dark' secrets in the lives of Europe's leading classes. Apparently, this feature introduces a distinct element of gossip. Even though the ghosts claim to unearth some of the lapses and scandals amongst European high society of yesteryear, their own role in shaping 'European' culture must be assessed as minuscule at best. Nevertheless, to Stanley, they seem to prove that black persons have been part of European society over the centuries and that he, therefore, might likewise find his place in life. As a result, the protagonists' journey turns into a two-fold quest with Jessie searching for her son and Stanley exploring the past. Reflecting on his encounter with Lucy, Stanley immediately draws a comparison to his father's situation so that, next to the parallel between Jessie's character and the dark lady's stance, a further similarity is established between Lucy Negro's and Stanley's experiences:

> *Grief fills up the room of my absent father.*
>
> Took leave of absence in his last years,
>
> the woman he belonged to – gone.
>
> He felt he never, ever belonged – here
>
> was black Lucy in Elizabeth's England
>
> a dream witnessed by your son
>
> whose dreams had been deferred
>
> in deference to you – Father? (Soul Tourists 70, orig. emphasis)[216]

The second ghost to approach Stanley is the Black Nun of Moret, Queen Marie-Thérèse's illegitimate daughter, who claims to have been ousted from life at court because of her conspicuously dark skin colour, which betrayed her being a

---

[216] Another remarkable aspect concerning Stanley's encounters with the ghosts consists in the fact that they were all but predicted by his mother who told Stanley that he had "inherited The Gift, passed down through generations of her mother's family: to see what others could not *They'll find yu in time, Stanley*" (Soul Tourists 4, orig. emphasis). In a certain respect, Stanley is therefore not only re-establishing a connection to his father but simultaneously inscribing himself in a tradition passed on to him from his mother's side.

'bastard'. Next in line follows Joseph Boulogne, Chevalier de Saint-Georges[217], who enters the scene in conversation with his biographer outlining the planned portrayal of the former's achievements. Joseph Boulogne is the first character to express the wish that his fate be made known to a broader public so as to re-activate it as part of the European collective memory[218]. In the last moments before vanishing into oblivion again, the Chevalier assigns this task to Stanley: "I beg of you, make of me a memory once more / Let me be known" (Soul Tourists 121). This statement hints at the quintessential function ascribed to the act of narration or story-telling in the creation and preservation of cultural memory. Obviously, only those personages whose memory is actively kept alive become inserted into the stock of collective memory circulated within a given society. As soon as a person's life story is no longer preserved they, as it were, lose their identity due to their absence in one of the grand narratives so that an awareness of their presence is not passed on to future generations.[219] At the same time, this aspect denotes the unreliability and, ultimately, subjective quality of historiography as such. Seeing that figures can be included and de-leted from history more or less arbitrarily, we realise that a neutral, impartial account of History constitutes an illusion. As to the implications of this phe-nomenon with regard to *Soul Tourists*, one might reflect on the value ultimately

---

[217] Interestingly enough, the composer's skin colour is now exploited for marketing purposes. The afrikanet homepage, for instance, promotes him as "Der schwarze Komponist, mit dem Mozart nicht spielen wollte" (Inou, Simon. „Schwarze Komponisten: Joseph Boulogne Chevalier de Saint George." *afrikanet.info*. 12. Feb. 2006. 05.07.08
<http://www.afrikanet.info/index.php?option=com_content&task=view&id=316&Itemid=105>).

[218] In recent years, the concept of collective memory has been extensively discussed. Especially in a German context, it has become an established category which is frequently drawn upon in con-ceptualisations of forms of cultural memory and in the discussion of the selection processes in-volved in its formation. On the role of culture as a "nicht vererbbares Gedächtnis eines Kollek-tivs", see Lachmann, Renate. „Kultursemiotischer Prospekt." *Memoria. Vergessen und Erinnern*. Hg. Anselm Haverkamp und Renate Lachmann. München: Wilhelm Fink, 1993. XVII-XXVII. For a detailed definition see Assmann's seminal essay "Kollektives Gedächtnis und kulturelle Identität" (Assmann, Jan. „Kollektives Gedächtnis und kulturelle Identität." *Kultur und Gedächt-nis*. Hg. Jan Assmann und Tonio Hölscher. Frankfurt a. M.: Suhrkamp, 1988. 9-19).

[219] In this context, however, it has to be pointed out that history, as an academic discipline, has undergone considerable changes. Hereby, some of the most important developments are the turn away from an unreflected reiteration of master narratives as well as the emergence of alternative models of theorising the past. Moreover, the impact of the researcher's positioning within the social context of his own living environment and time is now taken into account. Similarly, there seems to be a general consensus on the impossibility of 'making the past accessible' or of giving one 'true' version of it. On the general development of the discipline and its methodologies see Lambert, Peter and Phillip Schofield (eds.). *Making History. An Introduction to the History and Practices of a Discipline*. London and New York: Routledge, 2004. An insightful account on the treatment of master narratives as well as a detailed overview of individual approaches towards the study of history may be found in Eibach, Joachim und Günther Lottes (Hg.). *Kompass der Ge-schichtswissenschaft: ein Handbuch*. Göttingen: Vandenhoeck und Rupprecht, 2002. On general problems in theorising both present and past 'reality' see Goertz, Hans-Jürgen. „Geschichte – Erfahrung und Wissenschaft. Zugänge zum historischen Erkenntnisprozeß." *Geschichte. Ein Grundkurs*. Hg. Hans-Jürgen Goertz. Reinbek bei Hamburg: Rowohlt, 1998. 15-41.

attributed to objectivity and impartiality. Especially in view of Stanley's development, the impression arises that factuality turns out to be less significant for the construction of a satisfactory personal identity than an imaginary belonging and continuity irrespective of its truth value in terms of historiographical accuracy.

Tellingly, the figures from the past approach Stanley solely when he is on his own. Jessie, who ridicules her companion for talking to ghosts, remains unable to see the apparitions, who even seem to fly her because they always disappear as soon as Jessie turns up. As the Epilogue finally reveals, only Stanley is endowed with the gift of talking to the dead, a skill interpreted as a sign of great empathy. This fact might also be read as an indication of Stanley's greater willingness to engage with the past and his readiness to get involved with the more problematic aspects of his (cultural) roots.

Finally, the ghosts come to adopt a symbolic quality inasmuch as they reflect the widening gap between Stanley and Jessie:

> 'Ghosts!' I blurted out. 'Have you ever seen one?'
>
> Jessie emitted a vulgar, scoffing laugh, prolonging its initial impulse until it rang hollow and fake. It was then that I had a little revelation: she didn't really know me; nor I, her.
>
> […]
>
> *Got my own ghouls, Stanley, dear –*
>
> the nameless mother who shamelessly left me,
>
> the named father who could have rescued me,
>
> the son who selfishly deserted me –
>
> getting in my way when I'm walking,
>
> popping in my head when I'm talking,
>
> creeping around me, stalking. (Soul Tourists 129, orig. emphasis)

The scene may be interpreted as a signal that Jessie remains unable to cope with the past, whereas Stanley has apparently found an effective strategy in dealing with his personal history. With him reflecting in more and more depth on the information provided by the ghosts, the feeling of alienation between the couple expands as they are becoming aware of the growing lack of mutual understanding. It is in these moments that differences with respect to education resurge, for instance, when Jessie accuses Stanley of showing off and deliberately belittling her by demonstrating his intellectual superiority (Soul Tourists 132). Strikingly, during the prolonged period of time spent at the Spanish seaside, no further ghost appears and Stanley grows increasingly restless. Only when he sets off for Gibraltar on his own is the connection with the past re-established. At this point, however, Stanley is still not ready to tackle his cultural heritage head-on, despite the great temptation the idea of crossing over to Africa for the first time exerts on him:

> It was a trip lasting all of two hours, but one that would place him for the first time in Africa – the continent where some of his family tree had begun one, two, maybe four centuries ago. It would be a momentous decision, yet he was afraid that if Europe was opening little skylights, through which he could see that its history was more than he'd ever realized, then surely Africa would open whacking great doors, through which he might never return. […] He decided that Africa would be for another time. (Soul Tourists 153)

The decision not to cross the sound is also influenced by the realisation that a trip to Africa might ultimately sever all bonds with Jessie, a step which Stanley, at the current stage of the relationship, is still not willing to take. Thus, once again, Stanley's engagement with the past comes to mirror the state of his love affair with Jessie and their common (hi)story. Despite the decision against going to Africa, a change in Stanley's behaviour becomes discernible which grows increasingly pronounced. After repeated altercations about whether to travel as an ordinary tourist (Stanley's preference) or as a 'soul tourist' (Jessie's ideal), the main character begins to set out on his own more and more frequently. It is on one of his solitary trips to the formerly Moorish settlements in Spain that he realises the true cause of his desire to visit these sites: "As he explored the past, he became aware that the past was exploring him too, in its own spooky way. Life on earth was just the beginning, he now understood" (Soul Tourists 155). Consequently, we observe a direct interaction between Stanley's perception of the past and his self-image. While the past itself adopts a new guise due to the information disclosed by the ghosts, Stanley likewise acquires an altered sense of his own personality.

In view of Stanley's hesitations to cross over to Africa, it does not come as a surprise that the next voice from the past tells him about Jabal al-Tariq's passage to Gibraltar (Soul Tourists 155). Moreover, the voice admonishes him to return to Jessie in order to complete their endeavour. It is interesting to note that the voice refers to their travelling together as a mission, a fact which can be read as another indication of the imminent split-up once Jessie has been reunited with her son (the mission being thus completed). Subsequently, the voice materialises into Zaryab, a Mesopotamian musician abducted to Andalusia and the self-proclaimed creator of the local civilisation (Soul Tourists 157). According to his account, civilisation in Spain did not originate on the continent but was rather introduced to Andalusia by the allegedly 'barbarian' moors, a fact ironically summed up in Zaryab's statement: "I often come here, to remember the time when Africa began at the Pyrenees" (Soul Tourists 158). In sharp contrast to Stanley's initial assessment of his cultural heritage, Zaryab displays a strong pride in his Mesopotamian ancestry and places his original cultural context above 'backward' Europe. Undoubtedly, this reversal of established assumptions about mutual influences between Africa and Europe allows for a reading as a parody or at least as an ironic comment on widespread practices of historiography. Again, however, as far as the level of the diegesis is concerned, the implication for Stanley's personal history proves most significant.

Having left Spain, Jessie and Stanley tackle the Alps, an almost fatal enterprise because of the adverse weather conditions. In tune with his own agony, Stanley is suddenly struck by the sight of elephants which form part of Hannibal's track across the Alps. This passage sheds a new light on the renowned Carthagian leader as he is described as an easy-going, ironic, and highly self-confident youngster:

> I was born Hannibal of Carthage,
>
> son of Hamilcar 'The Lightning' Barca,
>
> 250 years before your Jesus Christ.
>
> And it was my life's duty to honour
>
> my dad's intent to take the army of Rome,
>
> who patrolled the Mediterranean
>
> with their flash ships and falsetto sailors
>
> as if they owned the very sun itself,
>
> […]
>
> But the Alps were not the desert
>
> […]
>
> Need I tell you, Mr Second-in-Command,
>
> no one had effing done it [crossing the Alps] before. (Soul Tourists 177)

With the situation growing more and more precarious because of the heavy snowfall, Stanley turns to Hannibal's ghost for help. Curiously, time as it were stops and Hannibal and Stanley suddenly find themselves on the same chronological level or, rather, outside of time. Hannibal's presence assumes an almost fairy-tale like quality as, immediately afterwards, Stanley and Jessie return to the safety of less mountainous terrain. For the first time after a long period of tensions and disagreements, some commonality between both figures unfolds as Jessie subconsciously seems to have been aware of Hannibal's attempts to encourage them. In fact, the meeting with Hannibal constitutes the first instance of Stanley's being approached by an apparition in Jessie's presence. When he inquires about her knowledge of Hannibal, however, Stanley has to realise that Jessie does not share his ability to interact with ghosts after all as she succinctly tells him that "*[e]veryone* knows about Hannibal" (Soul Tourists 181, orig. emphasis).

For this reason, the state of rapprochement does not last for long. On their arrival at Florence, a further rupture ensues which is once again caused by different ideas on how to explore a city. In the aftermath of the quarrel, Stanley, on one of his lonely trips, meets another figure from the past, Alessandro de Medici, who is presented as a self-righteous, rash character. Nevertheless, the conversation with him leads Stanley to a further insight which adds considerably to his understanding of the complexities of belonging and cultural affiliations:

> Was he, Stanley, really an outsider? Maybe you didn't have to blend in or be accepted to belong. You belonged because you made the decision to and if you truly believed it no one could knock it out of you. These visitations came from inside the body of history, turning its skin inside out and writing a new history upon it with a bone shaved down to a quill dripped in the ink of blood. Europe was not as it seemed, Stanley decided, and for him, at least, Europe would never be the same again. (Soul Tourists 189)

This passage offers an interesting new perspective on the question of 'European identity'. Clashing with essentialist notions of cultural identity, the strategy Stanley decides to adopt at this stage does no longer rely on 'biological' features but bases belonging and cultural affiliations on a deliberate and conscious decision, thereby abandoning established points of reference such as place of birth or race. This possibility of actively choosing one's affiliations instead of merely being born into a specific milieu and subsequently being – almost by default – subsumed under certain labels arising from social conventions transforms Stanley's view of Europe considerably. His new outlook on Europe and European identity finally allows him to combine his 'black' heritage and the Western context he was raised in without, so to speak, betraying either of them. Likewise, Stanley realises that his father's misery can ultimately be traced back to his doggedly clinging to an outsider status and his self-perception as a victim.[220]

As the journey continues, Stanley is unable to conjure up any further apparitions as long as Jessie is by his side. It is only when he decides to temporarily leave her again that he meets Mrs Mary Jane Seacole, the black counterpart to Florence Nightingale. In the following conversation, Stanley for the first time comprehends the impact of his father's personality on his own character. Moreover, he is forced to acknowledge that he might unconsciously have adopted a number of those character traits which he had always despised in his father, a realisation which triggers a moment of profound self-questioning:

> As Stanley had never been accused of this [being a judgemental person] before, he was taken aback. Was she right? Instant appraisal, instant dismissal? Had he been wrong about Alessandro? Was he really just like his father? Lashing out with his thoughts, if not always his tongue? Was he judgemental about Jessie? Was no one ever good enough for him? Was he just a self-righteous prig? (Soul Tourists 225)

On his arrival at Istanbul, Stanley reaches the 'frontier' of Europe, a symbolic moment heralding the imminent end of both the journey with Jessie and of his exploration of European history and culture. The pictogram at the beginning of the chapter "Old Istanbul" underlines this impression:

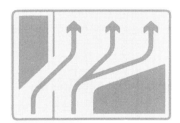

This icon obviously suggests that the formerly united routes are about to separate and to take different turns so that each of the protagonists will continue the trip on their own, pursuing their respective aims.

At Istanbul, Stanley enters the world of the Ottoman Empire with its slave market, the palace, and, finally, the seraglio. In this environment, he meets Major-General Ibrahim Gannibal accompanied by his grandson Alexander Pushkin.

---

[220] This presentation may be considered progressive inasmuch as it blames both sides, immigrants and the population of the host country, for the lack of integration of 'foreigners'.

Again, a figure numbered among Europe's cultural elite is shown to have a, metaphorically speaking, 'black side'. To highlight these affiliations, Pushkin's Ethiopian roots are accentuated. Moreover – a gesture heavily scratching at his status as an established, authoritative literary grandmaster – Pushkin is depicted as a lovable but loutish youngster strongly influenced by the impact of Americanisation (Soul Tourists 238). Now, Stanley himself finally recognises the transforming power of the apparitions on his own life:

> In that moment, Stanley saw that the journey from England, with all its characters and happenings, had not only freed him from the bondage of his early years but also opened up the history of his country and continent to him. (Soul Tourists 239)

Strikingly, it is Pushkin, the 'godfather' of Russian literature and one of the great names of canonical European fiction who, by disclosing his Ethiopian roots, succeeds in reconciling Stanley with his Jamaican cultural heritage. Seeing Stanley's initial unease about his origins and his attempts to over-assimilate, this sudden declaration of being Jamaican signals a major transformation. At this moment, though, a different, unexpected type of danger arises because Stanley begins to feel loath of returning to 'his' time and is tempted to immerge into the past.

Towards the end of the novel, the apparitions cause a final rupture between Jessie and Stanley. When Stanley tells her about his ability to see ghosts, Jessie does not show any signs of sympathy or understanding. In the scene leading up to their separation, Stanley's way of introducing the topic hints at his emotional detachment from Jessie:

> S Jessie, we've not been on the same journey
>
> [...]
>
> J Stanley, that is the most pathetic excuse for cheating on a woman that was ever invented! Truth is, you went off with some young bimbo you met on one of your *long* expeditions to the toilet!
>
> [...]
>
> S She loses it and starts frothing as insults fly out at falsetto operatic pitch and, I must say, with little regard for correct syntax. *Like Ibrahim with the boy Menelik, I can see her, but I can't feel her any more.*
>
> (Soul Tourists 252, second emphasis mine)

Stanley's sarcastic stance paired with his admission of no longer "being able to feel her" demonstrates the degree of alienation between the partners. Finally, by way of parting gesture, the protagonists both take leave of those elements of their journey that have become valuable to them. Hereby, Stanley lists the apparitions that he has met on his journey: "*Lucy, Louise-Marie, Joseph / Zaryab, Hannibal, Alessandro / Mary, Pushkin, Gannibal*" (Soul Tourists 254, orig. emphases). Thus, all in all, Stanley's encounters with the past cover a period of more than 20 centuries reaching from Hannibal to Pushkin and including both historically documented as well as invented characters. For Stanley, those figures fulfil a three-fold function: First, the ghosts hint at the possible existence of 'black' elements within European history throughout the ages even though the examples cited are mostly limited to marginal, forgotten figures. More importantly, though, they, as a second function, bring Stanley closer to his own past by forcing him to reflect on the relationship between him and his father, an important pre-condition for him to finally reach closure as far as the conflict within the family is concerned.[221] Thirdly, the apparitions' accounts of European history enable Stanley to inscribe himself into this tradition, which he formerly had perceived as alien and inaccessible, without having to abandon his 'black' cultural roots.

In combination with Jessie's silent reflections, the spectres furthermore add a new perspective to the discussion of 'cultural authenticity'. While the ghosts themselves challenge the authenticity of European culture only implicitly (at least as far as the 'pure' version offered by established historiography is concerned), Jessie spells out her doubts openly:

> When the Black Power Movement jetted
>
> across the Atlantic, […]
>
> […] it brought a shipment
>
> of unprocessed hair in the shape of an Afro,
>
> the shocking slogan Black is Beautiful
>
> and a longing for 'Our African Culture',
>
> which my BPM mates from the Caribbean,
>
> with their kente cloth headscarves and stick-insect

---

[221] In view of the fact that a reconciliation with Clasfield can no longer take place due to the old man's death, I deem it significant that Stanley is approached by ghosts, a phenomenon which allows him to enter into an interaction with the past and to make his peace with his father after all.

Masai-goat-herder-sculptures-on-the-sideboard,

said was my *authentic* one. But the only culture I knew

wrapped greasy chips in dirty old newspaper

with battered fish and squashed peas,

and better the devil you know anyway.

Africa's a continent, not a country,

so which of its cultures, thousands of tribes

and languages is mine, exactly?

[...]

but I'm a Yorkshire woman, and reet proud of it.

(Soul Tourists 197-9, orig. emphasis)

Interestingly, Jessie – just like Stanley – suffers from a feeling of alienation and a perceived lack of reliable affiliations. By contrast to the situation with which Stanley is confronted, however, Jessie's problems do not primarily result from her inability to reconcile her 'origins' with 'majority' culture since she clearly identifies herself as British. To the contrary, she is first and foremostly troubled by the permanent rejections and the suspicions as to her nationality, issues which she has to face on a regular basis. Furthermore, Jessie feels unable to identify with the Black Power Movement, an initiative originally launched to fight precisely those predicaments faced by black people. These complex affiliations, or respectively, the lack thereof, demonstrate that, in the end, all-encompassing labels such as Englishness, Britishness, Europeanness, and Africanness represent constructed categories, which imply a homogeneity among the people grouped under these labels that does not exist in reality. What is more, felt or chosen affiliations result only to a minor degree from place of birth or skin colour.

This observation it not limited to literary engagements with the topic, though. Accordingly, we may at present detect a comparable challenge to notions on national and cultural identity in sociological studies. These studies often assert an increasing need to include seemingly heterogeneous and incongruent elements into conceptualisations of collective identities so as to adapt the present categories to the changing living conditions and newly emerging social formations individuals are confronted with in their daily lives. Tomlinson, amongst others, describes the effects which globalisation exerts on national identity and characterises the concomitant changes in theories on cultural identity as follows:

> [C]ultural identity is not likely to be the easy prey of globalization. This is because identity is not in fact merely some fragile communal-psychic attachment, but a considerable dimension of *institutionalized* social life in modernity. Particularly in the dominant form of *national identity*, it is the product of deliberate social construction and maintenance [...]. Of course this is not to deny that nation-states are, to varying degrees, *compromised* by globalization in their capacity to maintain exclusivity of identity attachments, just as they are in their capacity independently to regulate national economies within a global market.[222]

Soul Tourists mirrors these changes and transformations inasmuch as it aims at dismantling the 'master narratives' of Western culture via the introduction of allegedly ill-fitting (black) characters. What is more, the text offers a new, alternative perspective on the topic of national identity by, on the one hand, extending it to the geographical area of Europe and, on the other hand, by highlighting the constructed quality of seemingly natural borderlines between 'Western' and 'immigrant' cultures.

Soul Tourists – Going Beyond Established Boundaries

As the analysis of Evaristo's novel demonstrates, *Soul Tourists* transcends several established boundaries in its engagement with differential categories. Moreover, the text reveals that certain oppositions prove impossible to uphold in a purely dualistic, binary form. Hereby, the most prominent of the differential categories dealt with in the novel are sex/gender and race/ethnicity. While these categories likewise adopt an important function in the novels under discussion in the preceding chapters, *Soul Tourists* differs slightly from them in its presentation of the single categories. Whereas previous texts either display a complete suppression of specific differential categories or set two elements in opposition to each other, *Soul Tourists* pursues yet another strategy in its engagement with the topic, especially as far as the sex/gender dichotomy is concerned: Apparently not aiming at a merger of the two sides, the opposite 'poles' of a binary opposition are kept intact and treated as separable units. Yet, despite the fact that we are dealing with two autonomous spheres, the two elements are nevertheless shown to combine in a perfect union. Throughout the entire (temporarily limited) fusion, the both units are – slightly reminiscent of the yin and yang sign – kept apart but still bound together inasmuch as each element is necessary in

---

[222] Tomlinson, John. „Globalization and Cultural Identity." *The Global Transformations Reader. An Introduction to the Globalization Debate*. Eds. David Held and Anthony McGrew. Cambridge *et al.*: Polity, [2]2003. 269-77. 270-1, orig. emphases.

order to form a complete 'whole'. Instead of blurring margins and fuzzy edges we are therefore confronted with a phenomenon that could, metaphorically speaking, be described as two sides of a coin or as the two hemispheres of a globe. On the level of the protagonists, this fusion is experienced as a moment of ultimate belonging and oneness.

Structurally speaking, this idea of proximity and mutual understanding is mainly conveyed via two means: First, it is created by way of reference to specific topics. This strategy is, for instance, employed in the discussion of 'Europeanness'. Via the novel's introduction of black figures into European history, the seemingly all-white tradition relying on a neat distinction between the (white) West and the (foreign, black) East is destabilised. What is more, European history is shown to consist of more than one cultural formation even though the contribution of the respective non-white traditions have not exerted the same lasting influence with most of its members by now having fallen into oblivion. This alternative perspective on the history of 'Europeanness' allows for a bonding between the 'black Europeans' in the novel. While they are implicitly also reunited with white European culture, the reconciliation with what is at first perceived an incongruent heritage is placed in a more prominent position in the text since both protagonists initially struggle with their self-image and the role ascribed to them in an apparently interrupted lineage. In the end, however, it is only Stanley who truly succeeds in overcoming this rupture by discovering a (hi)story in which to inscribe himself. This move likewise enables him to come to terms with the troubled relationship with his father. The strategy of choosing a specific image, topic, or leitmotiv may also be observed with regard to sex/gender differences. Here, the motive of sexual intercourse – culminating in a blissful union – plays the most important role.

A second strategy to create the impression of belonging and intimacy is located on a textual or stylistic level and results from the use of specific rhetorical devices, linguistic features, and typographic elements. Accordingly, the novel for instance communicates ideas such as proximity and close affiliations by purely visual elements. Amongst other typographic means, paragraphs and indented lines are used to mirror the degree of proximity between the protagonists and to illustrate their gradual estrangement. In the reverse case, i.e. as an expression of belonging, their thoughts flow into each other without any interruption by punctuation marks. The effect of this feature is increased by the recurrent use of specific styles and genres. As becomes clear over the course of the novel, the same rhetorical structures are employed recurrently in order to portray the protagonists' thoughts and feelings.

To conclude, *Soul Tourists* offers a new perspective on the topic of difference inasmuch as it goes beyond established boundaries. Moreover, it considers differential categories such as race/ethnicity from a different angle, thereby transcending traditional dichotomies as, for example, the distinction between black and white. In this context, I would like to stress again that this alternative perspective does not consist in a 'hybrid' view on the topic but rather offers a presentation of various elements that remain separate but are nevertheless shown to be compatible. While the novel refrains from providing a cure-all formula with which to solve the general problem of integrating different heritages and cultural traditions into the larger framework of a 'European' identity or culture, it nevertheless presents one option which constitutes a viable solution for the story's protagonists.

Louise Doughty: *Stone Cradle* – Same- and Otherness in Everyday Culture

By contrast to the focus on the 'black community' in Great Britain or, respectively, the United States discernible in the novels discussed in the previous chapters, Doughty's *Stone Cradle* centres on an aspect of internal difference which is frequently neglected both in sociological studies and in literary renditions of the topic. Other than the previous narratives, Doughty centres on a less visible minority group by drawing attention to the status of gypsies[223] within British society. This thematic focus adds a new perspective to the discussion of Englishness/Britishness as it moves away from the currently dominant debate, which mainly deals with the controversy about the state of integration of black or Asian minority groups, i.e. first or second generation immigrants from the Caribbean, Africa, and the Indian subcontinent. This public discourse undoubtedly also informs the general perception of 'hyphenated' Britons. Seeing that the debate in the overwhelming majority of cases pertains to people from a non-white background, it does not come as a surprise that the term 'ethnic minority' is, in general, applied to either black or Asian citizens whereas the Travellers are not as readily included in this category. In fact, it was only in 1989 that the Romany were finally recognised as an ethnic group in its own right.[224] In order to familiarise the reader with the habits and traditions of this less conspicuous group, Doughty depicts their way of life via an exemplary biographical story. Hereby, her self-proclaimed aim consists in increasing the general awareness of the predicaments faced by a community who have had to endure slander and political maltreatment in the past and who still suffer from discrimination and cases of racism. This fact in itself does not distinguish the Romany from other minority groups in Britain, who are likewise confronted with marginalisation and disadvantaging. A clear difference does, however, show when literary or

---

[223] In the introduction to this section, I have already expounded on the controversy arising from terminological issues. Even though the term may be found in official accounts and in academic publications (especially older ones), use of the expression 'gypsy' will be avoided here as it is, in the majority of cases, regarded as derogatory by the group itself. Instead, I will refer to this people as 'Travellers' – one of their chosen self-descriptions – or Romany. Nevertheless, whenever the term 'gyspy' is used in academic publications which obviously do not intend to present the Travellers in a negative light, it will be retained without further comment. The extensive and highly controversial discussion about 'true' Travellers and so-called New Age Travellers will not be considered here as it bears no relevancy for the discussion of the novel. Moreover, it has already been profoundly studied and described elsewhere. For a detailed account of this issue, see Hawes, Derek and Barbara Perez. *The Gypsy and the State. The Ethnic Cleansing of British Society.* Bristol: SAUS, 1995.

[224] Previous to this acknowledgement, a lengthy debate about the status of the Romany had taken place, provoking heated discussions about whether the Travellers constitute a distinct ethnic group or not. Related to this controversy is the question of whether the Romany, once given the status of an ethnic minority, should be entitled to the same privileges and programmes for integration/advancement as other national minorities (Hawes, 1995, 7).

filmic renditions of the topic are taken into consideration. While the last years have seen a large number of films and comedy programmes such as *East is East*, *Bend It Like Beckham* or *The Kumars at No 42*, which all address the everyday experiences of hyphenated Britons in a humorous fashion, no comparable productions exist for other minority groups. The same holds true for the field of literature, where second generation immigrants such as Monica Ali and Zadie Smith have, with the help of intricate marketing campaigns, been established as the literary stars of the thirty-something generation and been promoted as the spokespersons of this up-and-coming group. The chic or 'coolness' ascribed to a 'black' or 'Asian' background, however, does not extend to cover all 'non-indigenous' citizens. Consequently, the Travellers continue to be perceived as somewhat alien to British culture and integration measures directed at them still remain limited.[225]

In my analysis of *Stone Cradle*, I will focus on the specific narratological structures of the novel as well as on the presentation of everyday culture in the text. Thereby, I want to demonstrate in how far *Stone Cradle*'s treatment of difference differs from the approaches discussed above and in which ways the concept of Sameness is applied here. With respect to the two narrators, special attention will be paid to the question of how internal differences are dealt with and which role exoticism and foreignness play in the portrayal of the Romany way of life.

Generic Features and Narratological Structures – *Stone Cradle*'s Interplay of Two Narrators

At the beginning of the story, the two female protagonists, Rose and Clementina, who alternatingly act as autodiegetic narrators stand in opposition to each other. In the subsequent development of the plot, however, the text employs a number of narratological strategies to create a structural bond between the two women. Besides the switches between these two speakers, the specific arrangement of plot elements with certain periods of time covered twice from two different perspectives as well as meta-narrative comments on the activity of storytelling as such serve to link the narrators on a structural plane. As a result,

---

[225] It is only very recently that attempts are being made to dispel the 'gypsies'' reputation for petty crime, fraud, and a general unwillingness to work. An example of such an attempt may be found in an Irish project where a calendar titled *Beauty Has No Boundaries* (featuring 12 women from the Travellers' community) has been published in order to "[challenge] people's idea of what a Traveller woman looks like" (Sharrock, David. „Glamour shot takes Ireland's travelling women out of the caravan." *Timesonline*. 28.04.2007. 17.12.2008. <http://www.timesonline.co.uk/tol/news/world/europe/article1717062.ece>).

a subtle connection between the two women ensues even though they hail from two entirely different cultural backgrounds. In addition to that, the use of two autodiegetic narrators has also implications for the generic classification of the novel, a feature which will be outlined in greater detail below.

The particular structural arrangement of the single parts of the narrative which are set off from each other by the change of the narrative voice provides a first hint at the general approach in dealing with difference pursued in the novel. With regard to the stance taken towards difference (and, concomitantly, the conveyance of the idea of Sameness), one may basically distinguish between two levels of perception. While the characters, who are located on the level of the diegesis, are blind to certain similarities and potential bonds, the connections emerging between the two women clearly show on the level of the reader as they are allowed insights into the 'minds' of *both* protagonists. Likewise, similarities created via structural means are only recognisable from a heterodiegetic position so to speak. As far as the structural bond between the narrators is concerned, a first indication of a proximity between them consists in the explicit ascription of individual parts of the narrative to either Rose or Clementina. As a whole, the novel is divided into five parts, which are embraced by a prologue and an epilogue. The narrative starts with a table of contents, which lists the periods of time covered in the story. It is already at this early stage before the story even starts that the intricate temporal structure of the novel is disclosed. All in all, *Stone Cradle* comprises several decades covered twice, whereas other stretches of time are only presented from the point of view of one of the main figures. Accordingly, we detect an overlap of Part 1 (1875-1895) and Part 2 (1877-1901) as well as double coverage of the years 1895-1901 because of the time span forming the subject-matter of Part 3 (1895-1914). After this initial sequence, events are told by one of the female protagonists, with the other's perspective being included in this account. This feature may be considered a first structural indication of Rose's and Clementina's slow approachment as they gradually gain the capacity to speak for each other.

The women's narratives are framed by two short sections entitled *Prologue – Peterborough 1949* and *Epilogue – Peterborough 1960*. These passages are both related by an extradiegetic-heterodiegetic narrator. In the *Prologue*, Elijah acts as focalizer whereas in the *Epilogue*, this function is given to his daughter Mehitable. Thereby, two 'outsider figures' are endowed with the authority to 'speak'; they are, however, not attributed the same status as the autodiegetic narrators in the core narrative. While Rose and Clementina tell their story in a first person narrative, Elijah and Mehitable merely serve as focalizers whose feelings and thoughts are communicated to the reader indirectly via the narrator's voice. Prologue and epilogue are furthermore set off from the main section by the use of present tense, which creates the impression of immediacy but, at the same time, increases the contrast to the women's stories narrated in past tense. This general arrangement reflects the changes in the character constellation over the course of the story: While, shortly after their elopement, Rose and Elijah seem to form an impenetrable union, gender differences soon re-emerge and it is finally Rose and Clementina rather than the spouses who hold the family together. Although the women's relationship remains detached during her lifetime, Rose, when facing death, feels Clementina to be the only reliable person: "It came to me that Clementina, my mother-in-law, was the one member of my family I could rely on to tell the truth."[226] For this reason, it seems justified to argue that Rose's faith in Clementina is expressed on a structural level by the fact that Clementina is entitled to 'speak for' Rose. Similarly, Mehitable, the focalizer of the last part of the story, is linked to Elijah by their shared estrangement from Rose. Although Mehitable, like her father, loves her mother dearly, she is unable to show her emotions and withdraws from the family after having been rejected by Rose as a child. Nevertheless, in the last instance, it is actually her, the odd one out, who gains the deepest insights on the true relationships and power structures within the family.

Equally remarkable in this context is the great significance attributed to the activity of storytelling which serves as a means of both preserving memories and of perpetuating (cultural) knowledge otherwise doomed to fall into oblivion. For this reason, one may argue that the act of writing or story-telling as such assumes an 'ethical' quality inasmuch as it provides a possibility to pay respect to previous generations by keeping their memory intact.[227] Via (family) narratives, individual members are enabled to inscribe themselves into the larger framework of a continuous genealogy. Moreover, by fulfilling their duty to previous generations – i.e. by passing their ancestors' life story on – family members may entertain the hope that their memory will likewise be transmitted to their successors and kept alive by them. This knowledge of forming part of a longer line of development that transcends an individual's lifespan represents an

---

[226] Doughty, Louise. *Stone Cradle*. London *et al.*: Simon & Schuster, 2006. 288. Hereafter quoted as Stone Cradle.

[227] This ethical dimension of narratives per se has been discussed in great detail by Ricoeur. In his reflections on the topic, he pays particular attention to the interplay between narrative texts and 'reality': "Wie tragen die von der Fiktion hervorgerufenen Gedankenexperimente, mit allen ethischen Implikationen, die wir später besprechen werden, zur Selbstprüfung im wirklichen Leben bei?" Having expounded on a number of possible objections to the assumption of 'real life' being influenced by fiction, Ricoeur finally concludes: "Alle diese Argumente sind durchaus berechtigt: Die Mehrdeutigkeit des Begriffs des Autors; die „narrative" Ungeschlossenheit des Lebens; die Verstrickung der Lebensgeschichten untereinander; der Einschluss der Lebenserzählung in eine Dialektik von Wiedererinnern und Antizipation. Jedoch scheinen sie mir nicht auszureichen, um den Begriff einer Anwendung der Fiktion auf das Leben ins Abseits zu stellen" (Ricoeur, Paul. *Das Selbst als ein Anderer*. Übers. Jean Greisch. München: Wilhelm Fink Verlag, 1996. 195-7).

important element in the construction of the narrators' personal identities.[228] In the very last passages of the novel this aspect is spelled out and reflected on openly. It is striking to note that, Mehitable, the 'outsider', is, as it were, given the last word. This gesture may be interpreted as a sign that she, despite the tensions between her and her mother, is not excluded from the large family narrative after all:

> As she and Scarlet walk briskly down the path, she thinks, funny how there is this huge wall between the living and the dead – and funny that I should think it funny. [...] When you look at a grave it's about as significant as looking down into a puddle. All you see is yourself, peering back up.
>
> Maybe, one day, someone will come and look at my grave, maybe somebody I don't even know, and all they will see is themselves peering back, but they won't know that. They will think it's me. She finds the idea heartening. I will be thought about. Someone will wonder what it felt like to be me. And that is how we live on, in other people's heads, in their thinking things about us, even if they get it wrong. It's a nice thought, she thinks, that nobody can know us, that we are thought about but safe, secret. (Stone Cradle 351)

As these examples demonstrate, the structure of the novel as a whole mirrors its approach towards the treatment of difference. While, in the beginning, the women's positions seem diametrically opposed, their paths – and storylines – converge later on. In this context, the motive of the family adopts prime significance as a symbol of union and belonging since it knits together two entirely different traditions. On a structural level, those affiliations are underscored by the intricate chronological composition of the text, which assembles the individual components of the plot into a well-rounded narrative. Seeing that the parallels and similarities are not actively sought for by the protagonists themselves and, at times, not even recognised by them, I will not classify this strategy of dealing with difference as a further instance of Sameness. While in *On Beauty* the characters deliberately exploit the potential offered by constructions such as the black family, the protagonists in *Stone Cradle* display no such desire or even awareness. Therefore, in the latter case, we are rather confronted with the *possibility* for bonding and commonality. The full extent of this potential, though, is never exhausted and, in its entirety, only unfolds when scrutinised from the perspective of the reader, who is in a position to compare the experiences and feelings of the respective figures and to draw parallels between them.

---

[228] For a theoretical analysis of different types of memory as well as modes in the preservation of knowledge see Assmann, Jan. *Das kulturelle Gedächtnis. Schrift, Erinnerung und politische Identität in frühen Hochkulturen*. München: C. H. Beck, 1992. esp. 48-56.

For this reason, the usage of the image of the family differs markedly from its employment in *On Beauty*. While, in the latter case, the metaphor of the family is extended to cover, for example, people with the same complexion, the notion of the family in *Stone Cradle* exclusively relates to genealogical kinship and thus lacks the metaphorical component which is very prominent in *On Beauty*. Moreover, family cohesion is seen to arise less from a 'spiritual' bonding than being fixed by birth into a given context. Accordingly, family ties are primarily maintained on pragmatic grounds with much less emphasis being placed on the potential emotional support to be derived from them or their possibilities for community building. In fact, it is only after Rose's death and the subsequent breakdown of the former household structures that the other members realise the family's vital functions. Finally, at the very end of the novel, three of the children begin to approach again and try to re-establish some commonality. This turn of the plot may be read as an implicit confirmation of the need for a modicum of continuity which can, for instance, be achieved by way of active participation in the family narrative. The value of lasting bonds and stable affiliations is therefore recognised *ex negativo* as it were.

Apart from the overall structure of the novel, we discover further stylistic devices which establish a connection between the two autodiegetic narrators. Here, one of the most striking features consists in the rhetorical and stylistic makeup of the respective accounts as well as the different registers used: Both narrators' styles are characterised by an easy-going, conversational tone resulting from the use of simple syntactic structures with short paratactic, at times even elliptic, sentences. As neither of the protagonists has undergone any extensive schooling, the straightforward, simple form of their narrations may be seen as a reflection of their respective levels of education. Yet, the comparatively unelaborated way of expression also allows for a different interpretation and must not necessarily be taken as a sign of a general lack of education or intelligence. To the contrary, against the background of the setting of the novel, it may likewise be read as a marker of 'authenticity' and an indication that the reader is presented with a 'truthful' and accurate account of lower class life in England in the late 19th and early 20th century. Moreover, a feeling of immediacy arises since the formulations mirror features of oral communication. This assumption is backed by linguistic elements such as the spelling of words in tune with their pronunciation rather than in accordance with grammatical rules, for example in "a young 'un" (Stone Cradle 11) or "fella" (Stone Cradle 93). Similarly, 'ungrammatical' syntactic constructions imitate the characteristics of spoken language as in "What was the fella what done it?" and "just so's you knew" (Stone Cradle 95).

With regard to the register used in both the stories, we detect another linguistic aspect which serves to illustrate the interaction between the protagonists and their gradual approach. While, at first, it is only Clementina who blends Romany words such as *vardo, befoedo mush, kushti, Dei,* or *biti chai* into her account, Rose, over the course of her story, likewise begins to adopt some of these expressions and to use an increasing number of Romany terms. Especially at the beginning of the novel, though, the two women do so with different intentions: In Clementina's case, the Romany words can be read as a sign of her pride in her cultural roots. In addition to that, they serve as a means to draw a clear line between Romany and *gorjer* society. Rose, by contrast, mainly uses 'gypsy' language when tensions within the family run high. In these instances, she deliberately inserts Romany terms into her story in order to demonstrate her ability to understand the secret messages passed on between Elijah and his mother. It is only at a comparatively late stage in the story that Rose likewise begins to take a certain pride in her family's mixed ancestry and decides to ignore their being discriminated against because of their 'in-between' status:

> The judging never stops when you're neither one thing nor another – I had learned that by then. In East Cambridge my kids got picked on for being *gipsies* and on the road they got picked on for being *half'n'halfs*. So from now on I wasn't making any allowances for anybody, any more. We was us, and anyone who didn't like it could *ife*" (Stone Cradle 244, orig. emphases).

A further stylistic device which links the two narrators is the use of irony. As various instances reveal, irony, to them, constitutes an important means in coping with difficult situations and painful experiences. Nevertheless, certain events assume a humorous note only in hindsight as is the case with Clementina's encounter with her 'personal madman'. What originally must have been a shocking experience for a young girl is retrospectively turned into a funny anecdote: "You should have seen the look on Dei's face when she saw me walking back towards the camp, my very own lunatic following close behind" (Stone Cradle 28). This self-irony, which at times verges on sarcasm, prevents Clementina from lamenting her fate and from giving in to depression:

> A wave of honesty came over me, and I wanted to cry out, but it's never been right for you, Lijah. What did you have to go off and marry a *gorjer* girl for? [...] Fortunately, I am quite good at ignoring the voices in my head when they talk inconvenient. (Stone Cradle 231)

This sense of (self)irony turns out to be a characteristic feature of both of the women's styles since each report is interspersed with puns and humorous comments such as Rose's explanation of the origins of her name:

> My mother called me Rose because I was born in the Garden of Eden. She might as well have called me Carrot, or Swede, to be perfectly honest, but as a child I liked to tell myself that I was born beautiful and perfect, like a flower in a garden (Stone Cradle 92).

In addition to that, the structural bond between the two protagonists is highlighted by repeated comments on the process of narration as such. Both speakers frequently address the reader directly, and thereby offer additional information, provide comments on past events or even tease the readership as, for example, when Clementina talks about Elijah's father: "I know rightly what you're wondering. It's what everyone wonders in a story like mine. What was the fella what done it? Who was Lijah's father? Well, you might ask..." (Stone Cradle 14). These passages interrupt the continuity of the main narrative and suggest a direct connection between the reader and the narrative instance. By way of conjuring up this impression, the two women stylise themselves into storytellers with immediate contact to their audience.[229] The overall style of the narrative with its informal diction fits the communicative situation evoked by the direct addresses since the tone of the novel is reminiscent of a spontaneous conversation rather than an elaborately structured account intended for written publication.

These features evoke a parallel to the tradition of oral story-telling. In fact, what *Stone Cradle* presents is a creative engagement with this narrative convention, which looks back on a long tradition and which may be found in a great number of different 'cultural' contexts. For a considerable period of time, oral narratives served as the prime means for the transmission of both fictional and 'factual' knowledge to future generations.[230] Nevertheless, until quite recently, only little

---

[229] Obviously, this strategy constitutes a conventional device, which is usually employed to create a feeling of immediacy. Moreover, it has frequently been exploited for a variety of comic effects. Instances of this strategy may already be found in early 'canonical' examples such as Sterne's *Tristram Shandy*.

[230] As Newall points out, orally transmitted stories continue to fulfil an important function in specific cultural contexts. According to her study, oral narratives have not lost their significance in specific non-western communities and are also still being perpetuated by immigrants within western society (see Newall, Venetia. „The significance of Narrative in Modern Immigrant Society: The Indian Community in Britain." *Storytelling in Contemporary Societies*. Eds. Lutz Röhrich and Sabine Wienker-Piepho. Tübingen: Narr, 1990. 165-72). With regard to the Western context, Kvideland observes that oral story telling has suffered a loss of significance due to the advent of modern technologies so that "today we are far less dependent on oral transmission than

critical attention has been paid to this form of literary expression. As to *Stone Cradle*'s citation of this convention, it is worthy of note that the text displays several aspects characteristic of this genre but bends them slightly so as to make them fit the context. These elements consist in direct addresses to the reader/listener, a highly individualised register, comparatively simple syntactic structures, and the technique of slowing the action down so as to create suspense.

In view of the setting of the novel, the reference to this form of presentation does not entirely come as a surprise since, as a cultural technique, oral storytelling is frequently associated with 'gypsy' culture:

> [f]olk narratives are a central expressive form in Traveller culture, a form Travellers use in their interactions to tell each other who they are (cf. Braid 1996a). While not all Travellers consider themselves storytellers, oral narrative forms are highly valued among Traveller communities and virtually everyone tells personal experience narratives. [...]The process of traditionalisation plays an important role in establishing and legitimating the continuity of both individual constructs of worldview and the attunements of worldview formed among individuals who perceive themselves to be members of collectivities. [...] Specific personal experience narratives, family stories, folktales and legends traditionalised in this way can be used to teach or remind individuals who they were and therefore who they are.[231]

Again, differences between the main characters show: While Clementina stems from a background in which the habit of storytelling is firmly rooted, Rose hails from an environment which attaches much less importance to this practice. In her social context, community culture, a shared heritage, and family roots are not valued as highly as by the Travellers and fewer attempts to preserve common lore and to pass it on are made. Nevertheless, both narrators choose the same form, a phenomenon which may be read as a further stylistic indication of proximity or similarity. This impression is furthered by the fact that, at times, it

---

earlier generations. We receive narrative material through radio, TV, dailies, magazines, books and xerox-copies. All these media fit well into the private sphere and its one-way communication patterns. We no longer depend on the fellowship between storyteller and audience. This means that the storytelling-activity becomes more and more professionalized" (Kvideland, Reimund. „Storytelling in Modern Society." Eds. Lutz Röhrich and Sabine Wienker-Piepho. *Storytelling in Contemporary Societies*. Tübingen: Narr, 1990. 15-21. 17).
[231] Braid, Donald. „The Construction of Identity through Narrative: Folklore and the Travelling People of Scotland." *Romani Culture and Gypsy identity*. Ed. Thomas Acton and Gary Mundy. Hatfield, Hertfordshire UP, 1997. 38-66. Even though Braid primarily refers to Romanies living in Scotland, his general findings seem applicable to England as well.

is highly difficult to attribute individual passages to one of the speakers because of the great likeness in terms of tone and forms of expression. In fact, without the information offered by the headings, it would sometimes be all but impossible to identify the actual narrator at a specific moment in the book. This aspect adds to the impression that the women's life stories converge and that they gradually gain the authority to 'speak for each other'.

The Adoption and Subversion of Generic Traditions in *Stone Cradle*

On first sight, *Stone Cradle* displays a variety of characteristics which render the novel close to the genre[232] of the bildungsroman[233]. In tune with the conventions of this genre, the story traces the life of an individual from youth to adulthood. In the process, decisive events leave their mark on the protagonist's character and transform them until they grow into accepted members of society. Up to this point, the plot structure in *Stone Cradle* follows Gutjahr's definition of the bildungsroman with the elements she describes undoubtedly being present in the book:

> Erzählt wird demnach die Entwicklungsgeschichte eines jugendlichen Protagonisten bis ins Erwachsenenalter hinein als Weg der Selbstfindung und zugleich sozialen Integration. Der Bildungsgang gleicht dabei einem Reifungsprozess, bei dem natürliche Anlagen in einem gesellschaftlichen Umfeld über Konflikt- und Krisenerfahrungen zur Ausbildung gelangen. [...] Nach den Kinder- und Jugendjahren unter spezifisch häuslichen Bedingungen und Erziehungsforderungen folgen Jahre der Welterkundung, in denen es durch Wanderschaft oder Reisen zur Begegnung mit bisher unbekannten soziokulturellen Kontexten kommt.[234]

---

[232] On the problematic classification of individual texts into genres, see Suerbaum, Ulrich. „Text, Gattung, Intertextualität." *Ein anglistischer Grundkurs. Einführung in die Literaturwissenschaft.* Hg. Bernhard Fabian. Berlin: Erich Schmidt Verlag, [9]2004. 82-125.

[233] It is certainly open to debate whether the application of the term bildungsroman is still useful since it has been attributed to such a broad range of texts that one may even go so far as to claim that it has lost its sharpness and, as a result, been transformed into an imprecise catch-all category. Yet, despite its lack of definitory clarity, I have chosen to employ the term nevertheless since it is still generally associated with a number of characteristic features likewise to be found in *Stone Cradle*. See Ratz, Norbert. *Der Identitätsroman. Eine Strukturanalyse.* Tübingen: Max Niemeyer Verlag, 1988 for a discussion of the heuristic value of the term bildungsroman and its limitations. Moreover, I am grateful to Prof. Lubkoll for pointing out that even seemingly prototypical bildungsromane such as Goethe's *Wilhelm Meister* do by no means all follow the same patterns and that therefore the existence of a 'bildungsroman-template' constitutes an illusion.

[234] Gutjahr, Ortrud. *Einführung in den Bildungsroman.* Darmstadt: Wissenschaftliche Buchgesellschaft, 2007. 8.

Taking this definition as a benchmark for genre classification, we immediately observe that in *Stone Cradle* significant changes have been carried out. First of all, the story covers the lives of *two* protagonists rather than one and is embedded into a frame narrative which is not the case in a 'regular' bildungsroman. Moreover, the action does not evolve in a strictly chronological sense but leaps back in time whenever a shift between the two narrators occurs.[235] A second deviation may be detected with respect to the characters: While the vast majority of bildungsromane deal with the fate of a male hero[236], *Stone Cradle* focuses on the lives of two women. Remarkably, the main figures are not famous or outstanding in the popular sense but, to the contrary, represent two perfectly 'ordinary' women. Taking a closer look at their individual development, we, however, realise that both of them undergo a comprehensive educational programme (involving, especially in Clementina's case, a great deal of travelling) which exerts a considerable influence on the formation of their personalities. An examination of the precise nature of this programme of formation reveals that the type of 'bildung' the women achieve is diametrically opposed to enlightenment notions of education hailed in the majority of bildungsromane focussing on a male hero. Accordingly, Rose's and Clementina's 'schooling' does not consist in the acquisition of humanistic knowledge but rather in gathering the skills to survive in a hostile environment and to deal with adverse situations. Likewise, neither Clementina nor Rose visit any type of educational institute but are rather forced to adapt to circumstances and to learn how to cope with difficulties. These experiences finally endow them with considerable cultural knowledge and social skills. What is more, especially Clementina's insightful and perspicacious comments hint at her being an intelligent and by no means 'uneducated' person despite her lack of formal qualifications. This modification of the notion of 'bildung' provides one aspect which might be seen to inscribe *Stone Cradle* into the tradition of the female bildungsroman with its concentration on the specificities of a decidedly female form of experience and formation. While it is open to debate at which point the crucial turn towards a specifically female form of experience took place and whether narratives such as *Pamela* and *Moll Flanders* qualify as samples of the 'female bildungsroman' in the present sense, it has been repeatedly argued that this shift constitutes a development subsequent to the consolidation of the male bildungsroman. Accordingly, Kleinbord Labovitz states that "this new genre was made possible only when Bildung became a reality for women, in general, and for the fictional heroine, in

---

[235] Taking Goethe's *Wilhelm Meister* as role model, one might argue that the use of a first person narrative situation as such constitutes a deviation. Most studies, however, do not name this element as a decisive feature of the genre of the bildungsroman.

[236] This phenomenon may already be derived from the great number of theoretical works on the bildungsroman bearing expressions such as "and his brothers" in their titles.

particular"[237]. Moreover, Kleinbord Labovitz offers a definition of 'bildung' better suited to the requirements of the female bildungsroman: "*Bildung*, thereafter, for the female heroine would, of necessity, take place under circumstances radically different from those of the male hero. *Bildung* would function from her life experience rather than from a priori lessons to be learned".[238]

A remarkable aspect in reference to *Stone Cradle*'s engagement with the genre of the bildungsroman pertains to the women's status in society. Whereas many bildungsromane trace the gradual integration of an initially obstinate subject into established society – finally finding his position within firmly hierarchical structures – we observe the reverse process in *Stone Cradle* with the protagonists moving out of established society rather than being integrated into it. Both Clementina and Rose become increasingly isolated from their former communities and, for this reason, are forced to withdraw into the smaller circle of the family. What is more, because of her Romany background, Clementina has, according to establishment standards, never belonged to English/British society at all. Nevertheless, when she gives up her life as a Traveller, she adopts some *gorjer* habits and starts to participate in (English) working class life. This movement away from institutionalised social structures in order to create a personal sphere and to pursue an individual way of life constitutes a further token of *Stone Cradle's* proximity to the genre of the female bildungsroman exemplified by the works of (feminist) writers such as Drabble, Lessing, and Carter.[239]

To summarise, the two most striking features with respect to *Stone Cradle*'s reference to the bildungsroman as a generic template consist in its choice of two 'uneducated' female protagonists and a setting which transcends the realm of established British society. A possible aim of this digression from the patterns of the male bildungsroman might be to demonstrate that other forms of education exist beside the enlightenment ideal which must not be easily dismissed and should be valued in their own right. Likewise, the choice of female protagonists calls for a re-valuation of female experience.

---

[237] Kleinbord Labovitz, Esther. *The Myth of the Heroine: The Female Bildungsroman in the Twentieth Century. Dorothy Richardson. Simone de Beauvoir. Doris Lessing. Christa Wolf.* New York, Berne and Frankfurt: Peter Lang, ²1988. 6-7.

[238] Kleinbord Labovitz, ²1988, 246.

[239] For a discussion of the female bildungsroman and a select bibliography see, for instance, Wojcik-Andrews, Ian. *Margaret Drabbles's Female Bildungsromane. Theory, Genre, and Gender.* New York *et al.*: Lang, 1995.

As a second genre, *Stone Cradle* cites autobiographical or life writing[240]. Here, the parallels are even more obvious than in case of the bildungsroman since we are dealing with two clearly identifiable narrators telling the stories of their lives in the first person. Yet, despite this feature, *Stone Cradle* does not conform to the conventional definition of autobiography as "a self-produced, non-fiction text that tells the story of its writer's life"[241]. I have already outlined the implications of substituting the (traditionally male, white) protagonist with a (liminal) female figure in my discussion of the form of the bildungsroman and its citation in *Stone Cradle*. For this reason, I will only briefly summarise the most significant aspects as far as the genre of life writing is concerned so as to avoid a mere iteration of observations which pertain to both formal conventions.[242]

The most obvious divergence from the formula of conventional autobiography[243] apparently arises from the fact that the novel does not cover only one but two life stories and that the women's accounts are framed by third-person narratives with two further characters acting as focalizers. Moreover, as analysed above, the plot is not related in a strictly chronological sequence. The transcending of generic rules, however, does not pertain to all elements of this genre. Rather, certain conventional features are retained which may be read as an indication that the modifications are performed deliberately and should not exclusively be interpreted as a sign of the characters' ignorance of specific traditions and conventions. Hereby, I would like to draw attention to the different ap-

---

[240] The problems of genre definition with respect to autobiography have been amply discussed elsewhere. For an overview of individual positions see, for instance, Wagner-Egelhaaf, Martina. *Autobiographie*. Stuttgart und Weimar: Metzler, ²2005.

[241] Jolly, Margaretta. „Autobiography: General Survey." *Encyclopedia of Life Writing. Autobiographical and Biographical Forms*. Ed. Margaretta Jolly. London *et al.*: Fitzroy Dearborn, 2001. Undoubtedly, one may object to this definition on the grounds that it does not take into account the long-established form of fictive autobiographies. In view of Doughty's explicit reference to the fact that her novel is based on real-life experiences of members of her own community, I will nevertheless stick to the definition set out above with its emphasis on some non-fictional components.

[242] The specificities of female autobiography as well as the changes in critical attention have been amply demonstrated. Wagner-Egelhaaf, for example, states "Dass die Tradition der Selbstbiographie am männlichen, weißen, westlichen Selbst orientiert ist, lässt sich nicht zuletzt darauf zurück führen, dass die Autobiographie namentlich in einer Zeit Konjunktur hatte, nämlich im 18. Jahrhundert, als sich ein bürgerliches Selbstbewusstsein herausbildete, das natürlich ein männliches war. [...] So ist es nicht weiter erstaunlich, dass sich auch die wissenschaftliche Auseinandersetzung mit der Autobiographie auf die **männliche Tradition** konzentriert hat [...], die mit steter Regelmäßigkeit aufgerufen werden kann, wenn es um die Problematik der Autobiographie geht. Es stellt sich in der Tat die Frage, in welcher Weise das autobiographische Schreiben von Frauen an dieser Tradition partizipiert und ob es so etwas wie eine spezifisch weibliche Tradition der autobiographischen Selbstdarstellung gibt" (Wagner-Egelhaaf, ²2005, 96-7, orig. emphases).

[243] Again, counter-examples abound so that it is undoubtedly open to debate whether one may assume the existence of a conventional or established form of autobiography at all or whether single realisations prove so divergent that they can, ultimately, hardly be grouped under the same label unless we presuppose a very wide definition.

proaches in terms of the beginning and ending of the two accounts. Accordingly, Rose's narrative sets in with an established opening formula providing information about the circumstances of her birth[244] as well as her growing up:

> My name is Rose Smith and I was born on Paradise Street, in East Cambridge. I wasn't a Smith when I was born, of course. I was Rose Blumson. [...] I became a Smith when I married my husband, Elijah Smith, who I met when he came fruit picking at the orchards that belonged to my stepfather. That was later, of course. (Stone Cradle, 91)

Clementina, by contrast, modifies this pattern by beginning her story with her son's birth. Only later on does she offer any information about herself by way of comments and memories interspersed into her story. Thereby, her narrative is differentiated from Rose's relation right from the start with similarities only showing later on. At the same time, however, Clementina likewise uses conventional formulations and phrases, albeit with respect to her son rather than herself. The specific choice of words hints at a deliberate alteration of the usual pattern which starts with the protagonist's own birth:

> Elijah Smith was born in the graveyard of the church at Werrington, a village in the Soke of Peterborough. I can tell you this for certain, *as I am his mother and so was there at the time.* (Stone Cradle 11, my emphasis)

This passage subtly pokes fun at the beginning of those autobiographies which start with the narrator's birth, an event about which he or she in fact cannot have any personal memories but is forced to rely on external sources. Clementina, by contrast, immediately stakes her claim by asserting her authority about the events she describes in her story as she emphasises her presence in the situations in question.

---

[244] Again, one of the core objections to the completeness of any life writing arising from the lack of reliable information on the beginning of one's own life might be brought forward. This point of critique, though, can be dismissed with comparative ease as it is a common strategy – both in fiction and in real life – to use substitute narratives by sources judged reliable. As Neisser claims "[p]eople often begin narratives with their own birth, although they do not remember it; sometimes they even start with the deeds of their ancestors. Later events may also be reported without being actually remembered, if the narrator is sufficiently sure of them" (Neisser, Ulric. „Self-narratives: True and false." *The Remembering Self. Construction and Accuracy in the Self-narrative.* Eds. Ulric Neisser and Robyn Fivush. Cambridge: Cambridge UP, 1994. 1-18. 2).

As far as the endings of the two life-stories are concerned, a further disparity between the two narrators shows. Although both accounts finish with the protagonists' deaths, the last weeks leading up to their passing away are presented in two completely different modes. While, in Rose's case, her gradual decline is dealt with explicitly and the narrative gives a graphic image of the pain she has to endure, Clementina's last weeks are described as a far less painful 'fading away' into the past. In addition to that, there is a striking contrast as to the narrators' awareness of the proximity of death: Despite her corporeal weakness and a temporary inability to speak, Rose's account remains perfectly lucid and structured right until the end. At times, this aloof behaviour evokes the impression that she has all but abandoned her body since corporeal reactions are reported in an almost clinical, detached fashion. Moreover, a tension arises from the fact that Rose's voice is clear and unfaltering while her physical capabilities increasingly fail her and leave her in a condition, which, as one might expect, would actually preclude such an analytical stance:

> My sight began to blur. The shape of her sitting in the chair wavered, became diagonal. [...] I tried to arch my back slightly, as if I could lift myself away from the pain, but I knew it was no use. [...] Scarlet came quickly, with the pills and a glass of tepid water. She sat by me and stroked my hand while the pills did their work, oh so slowly, and made the pain a dull, bearable ache, instead of a fire. Afterwards, she left and I dozed for a while. (Stone Cradle 286-7)

The same holds true for the very moment of her death, which she describes as a gliding over into a state of tranquillity and peace (Stone Cradle 293).[245] By contrast to the calm, observing attitude brandished by Rose and her impressive mental clarity, Clementina grows increasingly confused in her last weeks. This transformation is mirrored by the style of her narrative which begins to lose its structure and becomes more and more disordered. Towards the end, Clementina even entertains doubts about the reliability of some of her own memories, for instance when she reflects on the encounter with her 'very own' madman (Stone Cradle 318). Similarly, she is troubled by the correct sequence of events in her life:

> I get confused sometimes. Sometimes I wonder who I am telling my story to, for it is like I am telling a story over and over in my head. And sometimes it feels like I'm there, right back in it, and I lose myself, and

---

[245] It is striking to note that Rose's narrative voice all but 'lives on' because it informs the reader about her last living moments and even covers the point of her actual death.

then at other times it's just remembering, like any other old fool. Sometimes, it's like there's someone listening. (Stone Cradle 319-20)

Ultimately, Clementina loses herself in the past. Yet, it is only at this point that
her determination to keep her knowledge of Elijah's father to herself fails and
that she reveals her secret. Apparently, the past proves too strong to be suppressed any longer and former events begin to resurge after all. Although a
similar phenomenon may be detected as far as Rose is concerned as she is likewise haunted by troubling memories shortly before her death, only Clementina
loses herself in them.

With respect to genre ascriptions, however, the question of the speaking sub-
ject(s) ultimately proves of even greater interest than these purely structural
aspects. First of all, we need to consider the status of the speakers in terms of
their 'fictionality' or 'authenticity'. While, by now, there is a general consensus
that autobiography – even though depicting the course of a truly existing individual's life – retains some fictional or constructed element, it is nevertheless
generally assumed that the speaker is a 'real' person.[246] In *Stone Cradle*, this is
not the case. Yet, despite the narrators' 'fictionality', their accounts assume a
representative quality, a feature which is suggested by the acknowledgements
preceding the text:

> The characters in the novel are invented but many of the incidents that
> occur are drawn from the memories and recollections of real-life
> sources, some of whom prefer to remain anonymous. My debt to them
> is immeasurable. Paracrow tutis, my Petulengros, all Petulengros and
> jinimengro pals everywhere. (Stone Cradle, n.p.)

It is Doughty's professed aim to preserve the cultural heritage of the Romany
people as well as to keep memories alive or, respectively, to unearth them in
order to make them available to a broader public. Against this background, especially Clementina acquires an 'in-between' status with regard to her truth
value as she is not modelled after one specific living person but rather represents a blend of the experiences of a number of Romany women. Due to this
'semi-fictional' or rather 'semi-real' status, her narrative assumes a specific
significance as it (allegedly) describes authentic events, which have happened in

---

[246] By now, studies on the reliability of autobiographical writing have repeatedly questioned its
truth value and have come to acknowledge its 'fictional' quality (see Jolly, Margaretta. „Criticism
and Theory since the 1950s: Structuralism and Poststructuralism". *Encyclopedia of Life Writing.
Autobiographical and Biographical Forms*. London *et al.*: Fitzroy Dearborn, 2001).

a similar fashion to truly existing persons.[247] At this point, the notion of 'authenticity' comes to play a considerable role. Despite the controversy on the definition of 'authenticity' as such and the question of whether textual representations can ever be 'authentic', the reference to real life sources still tends to endow the text with a certain authority as this gesture implies that the reader is not dealing with merely 'fictional' episodes but rather receives information on 'real' – and therefore 'true' – incidents. Hereby, the knowledge that a real-life referent, i.e. a living person who has undergone the hardship related in the novel, exists, might increase the effect of the events depicted in the text and make them appear more serious and touching.

Against the background of this observation, it is worthwhile to have a closer look at the different communities introduced in the novel. Seeing that Clementina hails from a social sphere that promotes values and follows rules with which the majority of readers are probably not familiar, I deem it useful to draw upon the concept of autoethnography in my further analysis of *Stone Cradle*. According to Jolly, autoethnography denotes a form of life writing which is "practised by subjects who are "unauthorized" in the autobiographical tradition"[248]. As to the presentation of consciousness and the construction of personal identity, the literary form Doughty chooses for the novel differs slightly from the convention described by Jolly who claims that "[a]utoethnographic writers understand identity as collective or transindividual, located at a complex "contact zone" between metropolitan and indigenous sites, and as a métissage that braids together multiple, disparate discourses"[249]. Even though these elements are certainly present in *Stone Cradle*, they are orchestrated in a different way. Collective identity, for instance, is not understood as located in an 'in-between' zone but rather conceptualised as grounded in a clearly defined and strictly limited sphere. Consequently, at the beginning of the novel, the reader is presented with two seemingly distinct collective identities, each of which is unambiguously located within a specific cultural context. As a result, an opposition unfolds between white working class identity and Romany identity. In the initial stages of the text, these two spheres do not merge and points of contact are restricted to inevitable business encounters. It is only later on that boundaries begin to blur and that the dichotomy becomes untenable in this clear-cut form. However, it has to be pointed out that this merger only takes place on an individual level and is confined to the members of the Smith family. We there-

---

[247] At this point, we perceive the effect of a paratext most clearly: While, without the acknowledgements, the novel could have been read as 'merely' another fictional text, the emphasis on its real-life sources accords it a special status which the text might otherwise not have had. At least, the readers' reactions are guided insofar as they are indirectly asked to think of the incidents related in the novel as 'real', which might render them even more moving or shocking.

[248] Jolly, Margaretta. „Autoethnography." *Encyclopedia of Life Writing. Autobiographical and Biographical Forms.* Ed. Margaretta Jolly. London *et al.*: Fitzroy Dearborn, 2001.

[249] Jolly, „Autoethnography".

fore do not witness the emergence of a Romany-English identity but rather a – to some extent forced – adaptation to altered circumstances. This observation is confirmed by the fact that the protagonists constantly have to negotiate between the social contexts within which they move. Moreover, they, by necessity, have to abandon elements from their former cultural circle (and thus their cultural identity) as soon as they adopt practices from the 'opposite' or alien realm.[250] This practice results in a highly individual form of cultural identity as each of the protagonists contrives their own eclectic version of a Romany-English iden-tity – in this case, a cultural identity is consequently not derived from member-ship in a specific group but rather necessitated by having been ostracised from one's former community. This aspect is reflected by various instances in the text in which the protagonists express their feeling of being marginalised. The 'collective' identity arising from membership in the Smiths' 'mixed' family therefore apparently remains deficient and cannot provide the same degree of stability offered by the former versions of collective identity based on class or community affiliations.

This aspect is problematised even further since Clementina has at no time in her life entertained a 'sufficient' feeling of belonging to the Romany community as is highlighted from the beginning of the text. Consequently, a tension between personal and collective identity ensues which is triggered by the clash of exter-nal expectations and individual feelings. The novel hereby seems to suggest that personal identity and collective identity do not necessarily complement each other and that the two can even come into conflict with each other when a col-lective identity is not freely chosen but rather imposed upon an individual by the social network of their community. Furthermore, the development of the plot implies that a satisfying personal identity does not necessarily have to be moored exclusively in one cultural context but can also be located in a contact-zone[251]. Yet, since the protagonists struggle to master their multiple affiliations,

---

[250] Apparently, this process is not always a voluntary decision but rather an enforced one as the protagonists are ousted from their respective communities when they begin to engage with the 'other' side. This description is in tune with Stewart's observation that "the very powerful indi-vidualist current in Gypsy culture appears to pose a threat to the continuity of the community. […] Gypsy community organisation testifies to the success with which they have resisted the attempt by the outside world to lever members out of the groups, but this has not been done with-out a constant struggle. In response to their effective enclosure in a hostile world the Gypsies developed a battery of communal devices to protect themselves, summed up in the term *Romanes* – a term which refers both to Romani, the Gypsy language and to 'the Gypsy way of doing things'" (Stewart, Michael. „The Puzzle of Roma Persistence: Group Identity without a Nation." *Romani Culture and Gypsy Identity*. Ed. Thomas Acton and Gary Mundy. Hatfield, Hertfordshire UP, 1997. 82-96. 87. orig. emphasis).

[251] I have deliberately chosen the expression "contact zone" rather than 'in-between' or 'third-space' so as not to evoke notions from Postcolonial theory. The contrast to Postcolonialism's third spaces results from the fact that the contact zones I am referring to are purely private spheres constructed by a very small number of individuals, in this case the Smith family. Moreover, those

the final achievement of this state remains a potentiality rather than an accomplished fact.[252] The topic of collective identity is discussed once more on a metalevel: In view of the "Acknowledgements" preceding the story, it may be argued that Clementina is introduced as a representative of the Romany women of her time. This move, in turn, implies that her way of life exemplifies 'typical' Romany culture and that she stands for a Romany collective identity.

When positioning this concrete realisation of autobiographical writing performed in *Stone Cradle* within the general framework of theoretical writing on the topic of self-perception and personal identity, we detect a striking feature as, in its presentation of the narrators' consciousness and self-images, the novel contradicts a large body of recent publications. While both narrators are haunted by anxieties and fears about their future and question some of their past decisions, they do not entertain any doubts whatsoever about the truth value of their stories and maintain a homogeneous self-image. Thus, the stability of the concept of personal identity – understood as a definable, lasting quality – is never challenged. In this regard, *Stone Cradle* runs counter to theories which stress the impossibility of a stable identity and hint at the intrinsic fragmentariness of subjectivity. In her study of the position of the biographer in Postmodernism, Wood Middlebrook claims that

> the author cannot assume that "he" speaks from a secure center of culture, from the apex of the intellectual pyramid that provides the most trustworthy view of reality. [...] In this upheaval the biographies I have glanced at here stand as models of de-centered subjectivity. All are marked by what I have labelled the postmodern anxiety about author-

---

realms do not encourage the 'melting' of two cultures, so that the individual elements of each cultural background remain clearly discernible. What is more, they are not truly integrated into a character's personal identity; rather, newly adopted habits remain moored in their original cultural contexts and are resorted to by the protagonists in the knowledge of behaving in an 'uncharacteristic' way.

[252] In its focus on personal identity rather than collective or group identities, Doughty's *Stone Cradle* differs significantly from the majority of autobiographical works written from an 'unprivileged', or formerly neglected, standpoint. This is confirmed by Marcus when she suggests that "[s]tudies of working class life-writings and those written by men and women from ethnic minorities have stressed both the importance of collective identities and the diversity of individual and group affiliations. The ranges of recognised autobiographers and forms of life-writing have expanded in tandem, while 'autobiography' as conventionally defined is often judged to be a limited and inappropriate means of representing these non-hegemonic subjectivities and identities" (Marcus, Laura. *Auto/biographical Discourses. Theory, Criticism, Practise*. Manchester and New York: Manchester UP, 1994. 222-3).

ship: awareness that both author and subject in a biography are hostages to the universes of discourse that inhabit them.[253]

The insecurity of authorship and the subject itself is precisely *not* the impression conveyed in *Stone Cradle*. The novel rather seems to imply that, despite all transformations and changes in attitude provoked by the misery and hardship they have to endure, the protagonists 'essentially' stay the same and thereby, so to speak, remain true to themselves. This gesture creates the impression of an inner 'core', which lends continuity to their actions and their general conduct[254]. This portrayal may be interpreted as a sign of a decisive shift in popular practises of lifewriting in favour of a revaluation of the subject and an acknowledgement of its capacity for agency.[255] What is furthermore worthy of note here is that the notion of a permanent coherency within the life of an individual does not completely rule out the possibility of change. To the contrary, both Clementina and Rose do revise a number of their former positions; nevertheless, this reversal of opinions is not perceived as a break with their former selves but rather seen as a different direction taken after new insights have been gained.

Moreover, as the final passage of the novel on the duty to perpetuate one's own family history indicates, a general willingness to remember is deemed more important than an exact reconstruction of a life-story[256]. Thus, what is primarily

---

[253] Wood Middlebrook, Diane. „Postmodernism and the Biographer." Eds. Susan Groag Bell and Marilyn Yalom. *Revealing Lives. Autobiography, Biography, and Gender*. Albany: State University of New York Press, 1990. 155-165. 164-5.

[254] This continuity is primarily achieved by narratives means. The effect of this type of narrative identities, especially in connection with the perpetuation of memories, has been discussed in great detail by Ricoeur who claims that "to speak of memory is not only to evoke a psychological faculty which has something to do with the preservation and recollection of traces of the past; it is to put forward the 'narrative' function through which this primary capacity of preservation and recollection is exercised at the public level of language. [...] If each of us receives a certain narrative identity from the stories which are told to him or her, or from those that we tell about ourselves, this identity is mingled with that of others in such a way as to engender second order stories which are themselves intersections between numerous stories" (Ricoeur, Paul. „Reflections on a New Ethos for Europe." *Paul Ricoeur. The Hermeneutics of Action*. Ed. Richard Kearney. London *et al.*: SAGE, 1996. 3-14. 6).

[255] Apparently, one may once again argue that the development as such does not constitute a novelty in itself and that similar patterns may be found in earlier literary examples. Nevertheless, I would like to claim that this perception proves significant in view of the strong focus on the fragmentariness and instability often displayed by both fictional and theoretical texts in the last decades.

[256] The impossibility of giving a complete and entirely 'truthful' account of oneself has been discussed repeatedly from various perspectives. For an examination of the shortcomings of human memory with respect to personal past, see Neisser, 1994. A more philosophical discussion of the problem with particular attention to the question of the 'beginning' of the self may be found in Butler, Judith. *Kritik der ethischen Gewalt*. Übers. Reiner Ansén. Frankfurt a. M.: Suhrkamp, 2003. See also Butler, Judith. *Giving an Account of Oneself*. New York: Fordham UP, 2005.

called for is an interest in one's personal past as well as the readiness to actively participate in the preservation of memories. This thematic line suggests that, through the act of narration, a continuous (meta)narrative can be constructed which encompasses all members of a family and moors them into an over-arching structure. Tellingly, this larger structure includes all members of the family[257], even the alleged 'black sheep'. For this reason, it proves significant that Elijah and Mehitable, the alienated spouse and the estranged daughter, act as focalizers in the passages framing the two women's narrative. Moreover, the story starts and ends in a cemetery. This choice of setting endows the novel with a circular structure which can be read as an expression of continuity – despite the somewhat gloomy realisation that in the end, there is nothing but death (an implication alleviated by the fact that a character lives on in the memories of their loved ones).

As briefly mentioned in the discussion of the reliability of the two reports it proves intriguing that apparently neither of the women perceives the project of giving an account of their lives as a problem. Rather, both of them seem to feel assured of their authority to tell their story and thus set out on what Butler terms an inachievable endeavour. As she repeatedly states especially in her more recent publications, complete self-knowledge is impossible. This fact, for her, simultaneously forfeits the possibility of a complete and truthful account of oneself. Moreover, a close connection is assumed between this problem and what Butler calls ethical violence:

> Suspending the demand for self-identity or, more particularly, for complete coherence seems to me to counter a certain ethical violence, which demands that we manifest and maintain self-identity at all times and require that others do the same. For subjects who invariably live within a temporal horizon, this is a difficult, if not impossible, norm to satisfy. The capacity of a subject to recognize and become recognized is occasioned by a normative discourse whose temporality is not the same as a first-person perspective. This temporality of discourse disorients one's own. Thus, it follows that one can give and take recognition only on the condition that one becomes disoriented from oneself by something which is not oneself, that one undergoes a de-centering and "fails" to achieve self-identity.[258]

---

[257] This privilege, though, only applies as long as the characters dwell within the realm of the family. As soon as a figure leaves the family circle (either voluntary or involuntarily), the awareness of their presence likewise wanes and their story finally ceases. This phenomenon may be read as an indication of the power of narration which can both preserve and erase memories by way of in- or excluding them in a 'master-narrative'.

[258] Butler, 2005, 42.

Nonetheless, I would like to argue that – counter to Butler's proposition – the opposite is the case in *Stone Cradle*: Here, the protagonists do actually give an account of their own lives. Even though the life stories are undoubtedly incomplete, the gaps in the narratives are not perceived as a problem. In fact, it appears that the ultimate aim pursued by Rose and Clementina does not consist in a complete rendition of an entire life-story with all details, i.e. perfection in terms of temporal coverage is not what is actually sought.[259] Although there is no denying the validity of Butler's hypothesis that a self-account can never be complete this does not truly seem of any import here as the novel employs strategies by which to circumvent the problem (either by way of substitute narratives or by neglecting certain periods of time, a move which does by no means impinge on the general integrity of the narrative).[260] What is more, Butler's silent assumption of the essential function of self-narratives for the construction of personal identity appears questionable. As Neisser observes, the "claim [that life narratives are the basis of personal identity and self-understanding] goes too far: Self-knowledge depends on perception, conceptualization, and private experience as well as narrative (Neisser, 1988). Self-narratives are *a* basis but not *the* basis of identity"[261].

In *Stone Cradle*, a coherent self-identity is silently taken for granted by the protagonists both with respect to themselves and as far as others are concerned. This conviction must, however, not be understood as an act of ethical violence

---

[259] This is in tune with Freeman's observation brought forward in his analysis of Roth's autobiography. With regard to the starting point he comments that "the project at hand, however much it might aim toward the revelation of the wholly factual, is irrevocably narrational and fictive: what unites beginning and end is the process of writing itself, a fundamentally poetic act in which the twists and turns of what had formerly been present become figured into a story of the past. [...] As I will argue in greater detail later on, the autobiographer – as well as the biographer, the historian, and, last but not least, the scientist – does not simply bind together the available facts, because [...] the very determination of what is to *count* as a fact derives from the questions (and the hypotheses) one brings to the task of inquiring" (Freeman, Mark. *Rewriting the Self. History, Memory, Narrative.* London and New York: Routledge, 1993. 117-8, orig. emphasis). Telling a story about oneself thus first and foremostly comprises a process of selection and a decision on the arrangement of individual *memories* to turn them into a consistent story. This coherency is not achieved by the gapless coverage of a specific timespan but rather results from the way in which single instances are related and tied together so that they convey the illusion of a continuous development.

[260] At this point, it is worthy of consideration whether there might be a split between theoretical writing and the current literary production. Even though Butler's theory is most certainly valid with respect to the impossibility of giving an account of oneself, I believe that a number of literary conventions have already been established, which circumvent this problem by forgoing the project of a *complete* account from the start. In my opinion, this can be read as a sign that individuals, in principle, do strive for a stable, coherent, and lasting identity, irrespective of whether this security could, in the last instance, be dismantled as an illusion.

[261] Neisser, 1994, 1, orig. emphases.

in the Butlerian sense because ruptures within the conduct of a character are certainly not depicted as a failure on this figure's side but rather seen as a temporary misjudgement. The encounter between Rose and her step-brother illustrates this stance:

> Just before I turned back, I looked ahead, up the street, and there he was. […] I didn't want to talk to him. I just wanted to stare, to take him in. He was both changed beyond all recognition and not changed – so smart, so much older, but still the same thin figure, the pale features. It was nearly thirty years since we had last set eyes upon one another. […] I walked back down the High Street, my head full of thoughts. It was only as I reached the market place again that it came to me. Oh William, I thought. You loved me, didn't you? Loved me properly, I mean. I thought back to the time on the farm – it seemed like such an age ago, and it was: another century, before the children, before the War that took so many of our children. […] But William had loved me. I was sure of that. (Stone Cradle 272-5)

Williams's being both changed and un-changed is a first indication of Rose's belief in an enduring element within a person's character. Moreover, certain emotions, such as William's love for Rose, are shown to persist irrespective of the chances of success and may therefore be interpreted as an expression of a figure's 'true' feelings. The sudden change in Rose's perception of William is presented to result from her previous inability to recognise his true feelings and intentions instead of being provoked by a profound change in *his* character.

While the other – as encountered in other characters located on the level of the diegesis – only plays a minor role in the construction of personal identity[262], this selfsame other (in the sense of a counterpart or vis-à-vis) proves of major significance on the metalevel of the (implied) reader. It therefore gains its main import not in the form of a 'real' person but rather as a function already embedded in the text because of its generic features. As has been highlighted before, the narrative strongly relies on the tradition of oral storytelling. Although literature may generally be assumed to be directed at a recipient, the relationship between reader and addressee adopts a particular significance in the convention of oral storytelling as the presence of a listener is explicitly invoked by remarks

---

[262] Here, we are faced with a further problem of Butler's strategy as she seems to imply that the 'other' is – by contrast to its conceptualisation by Lévinas – represented by a concrete other person, a tangible vis-à-vis. The precise nature of this other is, however, never specified in detail. This omission leaves much room for speculation on, for instance, the exact way in which the act of 'being addressed' – according to Butler an inevitable precondition for the self to come into being – is carried out.

uttered solely for the benefit of the audience. Therefore, even though this 'other' as personified by the 'listener' does not actively bring the story into existence, the position of the implied reader is nevertheless embedded in the text itself as a vital function. Seeing the importance ascribed to the preservation of memories after a person's death – coupled with the assumption that this feat can only be achieved by narrative means – the process of reading all but adopts an ethical component since, metaphorically speaking, it is up to the reader whether a character dies or lives on. In view of the 'semi-real' status of figures such as Clementina, this task assumes an even greater gravity. Due to this specific positioning of the reader by getting him or her involved in the creation of another 'grand narrative', the motive of safeguarding memories via narrative means is doubled as it figures, first, on an intratextual level and, secondly, on the metalevel of narrator and reader/listener. In fact, the obligation to narrate as well as the duty to listen constitute one of the major topics of the novel. What is more, the reader is introduced to a 'foreign' cultural circle via Clementina's account. Apart from a survey of the events of her childhood and her adult life with the Travellers, she provides a number of myths and fairy-tales circulated among the Romany which serve to explain certain habits and traditions.

In view of the great importance attached to community life and the community's impact on an individual's development, I would, once again, like to return to the question of genre definitions. In addition to the immediately recognisable genres of the bildungsroman and (female) autobiography, *Stone Cradle* also contains elements of what Zagarell defines as 'narrative of community'[263]. According to her definition, this genre comprises works which

> take as their subject the life of a community (life in "its *everyday* aspects") and portray the minute and quite ordinary processes through which the community maintains itself as an entity. The self exists here as part of the interdependent network of the community rather than as an individualistic unit. Writers of narrative of community give literary expressions to a community they imagine to have characterized the pre-industrial era. Narrative of community thus represents a coherent response to the social, economic, cultural and demographic changes caused by industrialism, urbanization, and the spread of capitalism.[264]

Although *Stone Cradle* does not display all of these elements listed by Zagarell – the action's scope, for instance, is not limited to pre-industrial times – a great

---

[263] For a more extensive definition of this genre, see Zagarell, Sandra. „Narrative of Community: The Identification of a Genre." *Signs* 13,3 (1988): 498-527.
[264] Zagarell, 1988, 499, orig. emphases.

proximity is discernible nevertheless. This holds particularly true with respect to the "interplay between empathy and analysis"[265], which shows most plainly in Clementina's accounts of rituals and cultural practices as well as in the non-linearity of the plot structure. Moreover, Zagarell points out the importance attributed to storytelling in examples of the narrative of community, a phenomenon we likewise observe in *Stone Cradle*. Seeing the general significance ascribed to various types of communities in the novel, the following part of my analysis will deal with their respective depictions and examine the functions each of these communities fulfils in greater detail.

Forms of Bonding – The Family as a Substitute for Community Affiliations

At the beginning of the story, two separate communities – the Romany as opposed to 'English' society[266] – are set off against each other. Before turning to the analysis of these communities, I would like to draw attention to the terminological difficulties associated with the concept of community as such, a problem which has, especially in sociological studies, provoked extensive debate. According to Tönnies's seminal definition, communities arise from the general connectedness of all vegetative life.[267] Unlike the processes of opinion formation taking place in a society, the volitions of individual members within a community are, in Tönnies's eyes, produced by the general will. This assumption is mirrored by the two communities introduced in *Stone Cradle*. What is described here, though, is less the concordance of individual and general will

---

[265] Zagarell, 1988, 516.

[266] Especially in early sociology, the problematic definition of community (as opposed to society at large) constituted one of the major points of interest. For an overview of individual positions, see, for instance, Esser, Hartmut. *Soziologie. Allgemeine Grundlagen*. Frankfurt und New York: Campus, 1993. Consult especially pp. 336 *et passim*.

[267] Tönnies's classical definition describes the origins and functions of community as follows: "Die Theorie der Gemeinschaft geht solchen Bestimmungen gemäß von der vollkommenen Einheit menschlicher Willen als einem ursprünglichen oder natürlichen Zustande aus, welcher trotz der empirischen Trennung und durch dieselbe hindurch, sich erhalte, je nach der notwendigen und gegebenen Beschaffenheit der Verhältnisse zwischen *verschieden bedingten* Individuen mannigfach sich gestalte" (Tönnies, Ferdinand. *Gemeinschaft und Gesellschaft. Grundbegriffe der reinen Soziologie*. Darmstadt: Wissenschaftliche Buchgesellschaft, 1979. 7, orig. emphasis). Community is hereby clearly set off from society: „Die Theorie der Gesellschaft konstruiert einen Kreis von Menschen, welche, wie in Gemeinschaft, auf friedliche Art miteinander leben und wohnen, aber nicht wesentlich verbunden, sondern wesentlich getrennt sind, und während dort verbunden bleibend, trotz aller Trennungen, hier getrennt bleiben trotz aller Verbundenheiten. Folglich finden hier keine Tätigkeiten statt, welche aus einer a priori und notwendigerweise vorhandenen Einheit abgeleitet werden können, welche daher auch insofern, als sie durch das Individuum geschehen, den Willen und Geist dieser Einheit in ihm ausdrücken, mithin so sehr *für* die mit ihm Verbundenen als für es selber erfolgen. Sondern hier ist ein jeder für sich allein, und im Zustand der Spannungen gegen alle übrigen" (ibid., 35, orig. emphasis).

but rather a clash of the protagonists' views with 'majority' opinion. In Clementina's case, the tension between external expectations as well as compulsory forms of behaviour and her own wishes proves particularly pressing. At a comparatively late point in the story does Clementina finally admit that, for her, the enforced collective identity maintained by the community has always constituted a burden rather than a source of security. Yet, it is only when she has achieved the status of a partial outsider that she finds herself in a position to spell out these thoughts openly:

> In truth, it was just like always. I wasn't at all sure where I belonged. It's horrible, that feeling, the knowing-you-are-different. That knowledge – that there is a wrongness or a badness or a not-fitting-in-ness that is inside and around you the whole time. In Paradise Street, it was easy. I was an outsider because I was one of the People, a Romany woman and proud of it. But now I was back among others of my kind and it turned out it was not so simple at all. There was still something not quite right with me – something lost, or taken. (Stone Cradle 205)

Clementina apparently judges her feeling of alienation as a form of personal defect or character flaw. This assumption is suggested by various statements and formulations in the novel such as "a wrongness or a badness or a not-fitting-in-ness that is inside and around you the whole time" and "not quite right with me". The passage quoted above likewise points at the intrinsic heterogeneity within the Travellers' community.[268] This façade of complete homogeneity can therefore only be upheld by the exertion of constant pressure on individual members so as to make them conform to community rules as well as by deliberate efforts to suppress all forms of behaviour which might threaten the coherency and inner stability of the group.

The importance of a general willingness to act in tune with the group's regulations is underscored by the permanent promotion of the value of unity and constant assertions of the superiority of Romany culture as opposed to *gorjer* habits.[269] These ideas are inculcated in children within the community from an

---

[268] In fact, as recent analyses of intercultural structures have shown, this observation applies to any form of community, as all larger groupings of people are beset by tensions resulting from internal differences.

[269] Easthope describes this perception of 'alien' or 'other' elements as a potential threat in his analysis of personal and collective identity: "What is the case for individual identity must hold equally for collective identity, for those groups whose members identify with a common object and so find identification with each other. All collective identity (clan, nation, region, ethnic group) identifies self by denying the other, demarcates inside from outside, stretches a distance between 'us' and 'them'. The condition for collective identification - 'my blood, my family, my kin, my clan, my nation, my race' – is an ever-present and potentially violent expulsion of those

early age on. This education (or, respectively, indoctrination) leaves a strong mark on Clementina, for whom the feeling of being different remains a terrifying experience and who suffers considerably when she is excluded from her former circle (Stone Cradle 205).

The meticulously tended notion of a closed-off community open only to a restricted number of people is comparable to the idea of the black community discussed in the previous chapters. As could likewise be observed in the latter case, permanent efforts are required in order to uphold the illusion of homogeneity and to thereby keep the concept as such intact. By contrast to the discussions of the black community, though, the implicit judgement brought forward in *Stone Cradle* is far more critical. While Zadie Smith's 'metaphorical families' are in the majority of cases considered a source of stability and support by the protagonists, the obligatory group identities in *Stone Cradle* are mainly experienced as a burden and perceived as a restriction of personal freedom. Attitudes towards collective identities in *Stone Cradle* also differ from stances taken towards the black family inasmuch as the collective identities here are not solely intended to provide a framework for individuals seeking succour and stability. Because of the group's precarious social status, a tight cohesion among its members constitutes an existential necessity as the Travellers could not survive without their extensive informal networks and groupings. In order to guarantee the persistence of these networks, it is inevitable that the notion of a strong collective Romany identity is fostered permanently. As a consequence, the ensuing 'us-vs.-them' feeling on the one hand provides security and stability to its members but, on the other hand, also curtails personal freedom and obliges individuals to accept established traditions and rules without questioning their legitimacy or use. With respect to the organisational patterns of the Romany community it is striking to note that it is entirely structured along family lines. Thereby, belonging to a specific family automatically leads to 'membership status' as a Traveller. At the same time, however, this also means that outsiders face grave problems when trying to be accepted into this close circle as is exemplified by Rose's failed introduction to the community.

In fact, Clementina is not the only character forced to break with her 'original' community since Rose likewise experiences the difficulties of life in a strictly regulated circle and finally decides to leave her familiar environment. In her case, though, the situation is slightly different as the pressure to conform to the rules is not exerted by her social environment but rather results from the strict hierarchy within the family. Accordingly, while she still lives alone with her

---

who are *not* 'my blood, my family, my kin, my clan, my nation, my race'" (Easthope, Antony. *Englishness and National Culture*. London and New York: Routledge, 1999. 219-20, orig. emphasis).

mother in Cambridge, the small family is comparatively well integrated despite Rose's being born as an illegitimate child. Seeing that this fact represents "a common enough story" (Stone Cradle 92), it does not provoke ostracism. Yet, on her mother's marriage, Rose is extracted from the town community and forced to live in the hostile atmosphere of her step-father's household. It is here that she first gets in touch with the Travellers. While Rose herself is still unbiased and open towards the 'strangers', her stepfather firmly discourages any contact to the "gipos" (Stone Cradle 103) and slanders them as potential thieves (Stone Cradle 175). Yet, not least because of the cold ambiance on the farm, Rose feels drawn to this 'exotic' cultural sphere which she experiences as tidy, well-organised, and caring so that she chooses to elope with Elijah. As a consequence, a process of estrangement begins. Here, it has to be pointed out, though, that Rose is clearly aware of this risk and deliberately takes it. She even derives a certain satisfaction from the knowledge that her step-father is sure to become the object of village gossip because of her elopement. Only later on, after having settled down in Cambridge, does Rose realise the degree of exclusion from the social sphere she was formerly firmly grounded in. This marginalisation, however, does not primarily arise from Elijah's being a 'gypsy' but rather results from his unreliability and his failure to procure a living for the family, a situation which forces Rose to continuously borrow money and food from her neighbours (Stone Cradle 163). When the family has to fly Cambridge for this reason without prior warning, Elijah and Clementina attempt to integrate Rose into the Travellers' community and to thereby resume their former way of life. This endeavour, however, is doomed to failure as their fellow Travellers refuse to accept Rose as a member into their circle. Surprisingly, despite her initial vexation at the marriage and her rejection of Rose as a daughter-in-law, Clementina now tries to speak up for her and to defend her against her fellows. Moreover, she does not blame Rose for being unable to adapt to a life on the road, which, seeing her otherwise quite tough stance, comes as a surprise:[270]

> We were on Stourbridge Common for the whole of the winter, waiting for springtime when the weather would be good enough for us to take to the highway on our own. It wasn't a bad winter, as winters go, but still not exactly the best time to be getting used to life on a Traveller camp.
>
> It was hard on the children, and harder still on Rose. Morselina Smith took against Rose so bad that I found myself obliged to stick up for her

---

[270] The description of 'mixed' families being excluded from the Romany community is in tune with Okely's observations on the status of 'outsiders' and the chances of their being recognised as a Traveller. Okely states that "[a] person with two gorgio parents cannot claim the right to be called either a Traveller or a Gypsy. Full membership can never be attained, despite marriage with a Gypsy, although he or she might participate more or less fully in the travelling society" (Okely, Judith. „Gypsies Travelling in Southern England." *Gypsies, Tinkers, and Other Travellers*. Ed. Farnham Rehfisch. London: Academic Press, 1975. 55-83. 61).

and put the word around that anyone who had a problem with the *rawnie* had better come and see me. *Well, she was mother to my grand-children, after all.* (Stone Cradle 183, second emphasis mine)

At this point, it becomes increasingly clear that birthright in itself does not guarantee full membership in the Travellers' community. When Clementina temporarily gives up her travelling lifestyle[271], she ceases to be treated as an insider to the group. The same process of ousting may be observed as far as Elijah is concerned. With both of the spouses having lost their position in their former social spheres, they, almost by necessity, withdraw into the much smaller unit of the family which, over the course of time, comes to take on those functions formerly provided by their social environment.

At this point, a parallel to studies on the forms of organisation within Romany communities unfolds. As Greenfields outlines, the 'core' family represents a crucial element among the English Travellers.[272] To uphold this structure, a widespread habit consists in the practice of inter-marriages among families who have known each other for a long period of time. This custom guarantees a modicum of stability and security since long-standing alliances may be consolidated further and the coherency within the group is strengthened simultaneously. Seeing that this 'marriage policy' serves as a mechanism of social control, Elijah's decision to marry outside the prescribed circle constitutes a clear breach of rules. Once again, Doughty thus draws on attitudes to be observed in 'real-life' situations as well. The general aversion towards 'mixed marriages' is, amongst others, discussed by Greenfields in her study on everyday life and common practices among the Romany. Despite a slightly higher degree of tolerance to be witnessed in more recent times,

> marriage between Gypsies and Travellers of different ethnicities may be greeted with caution or disapproval by older travelling people who may believe that a wedding to someone whose background and family are well known and who is a member of the same community offers more stability and cultural continuity. Where the spouse is from a non-Gypsy or Traveller background, [...] the transition to a stable family unit may sometimes be quite slow, as the newcomer will need to learn a different set of skills and values, and may sometimes find that it is difficult for them to be accepted. [...] Despite acceptance by the community, however, it is our experience that (even, for example, when a couple may

---

[271] On the significance of travelling as part of gypsy identity, likewise see Okely, 1975.
[272] Greenfields, Margaret. „Family, Community and Identity." *Here to Stay: The Gypsies and Travellers of Britain*. Eds. Colin Clark and Margaret Greenfields. Hatfield: Hertfordshire UP, 2006. 28-56.

have been married for thirty years), the *gorjer* spouse will usually make clear that they are not an 'ethnic' Traveller, as they can never fully attain the status of a person who has been born and brought up as a member of the community.[273]

Within the Smith family, the first obstacle to be overcome arises from the ethnic differences between the spouses and the ostracism each of them is confronted with on the grounds of having married outside 'their' circle. From this point on, the family unit has to act as a substitute for lost community affiliations. Strikingly, right from the start, it is primarily the women who are anxious to keep the family together. It seems that only they realise its true value and its all but existential function in the current situation.[274] As could be observed before, the female line proves of prime importance. To some extent, this feature reproduces the worn cliché of women being more prone to emotional behaviour and being 'by nature' better equipped for the organisation and maintenance of a successful family life. This impression is backed by plot elements such as Clementina's becoming aware of the true significance of family lines and her position in the succession of generations at the moment of giving birth, an experience which changes her profoundly and which establishes an almost spiritual link with all the mothers in the family preceding her. The same holds true for Rose. Although she does by no means represent the traditional loving and caring mother figure, it is ultimately her who keeps the family together – an achievement only valued after her death when the family begins to disintegrate. In tune with this (intra-familiar) failure to realise Rose's true role, the relationship between her and her mother-in-law remains comparatively cold and distanced up until the end. Surprisingly, Clementina all of a sudden declares her sympathy for Rose briefly after her death:

> 'You and Mum didn't really like each other all that much, did you?' she [Scarlet] said. She said it quite gently, just stating the fact, without any accusation.
>
> I stopped what I was doing and looked at her. 'Your mum and I were close as close can be for thirty years,' I said. 'I don't know what to do now she's not here.' (Stone Cradle 310)

---

[273] Greenfields, 2006, 37.

[274] Similar to the portrayals in previous chapters, we are once again presented with the idea that the family requires permanent efforts and 'emotional' work in order to stay functional. Thus, a certain proximity is discernible to, for instance, the orchestration of Sameness via the family as a value in itself in *On Beauty*.

The impression of a deep connection between the two female protagonists is strengthened by the final image of their being buried in the same grave. Rather than the spouses being 'united in death', it is, strangely enough, mother-in-law and daughter-in-law who are laid to rest side by side, or, to be more precise, on top of each other due to financial considerations. Elijah's decision for this arrangement retains a peculiar note as it is neither in tune with habits in Romany culture nor with the traditions in Rose's former community. Seeing that the tombstone even bears the wrong inscription – listing Rose's name as "ROSIE SMITH" (Stone Cradle 349) and placing Rose "on top of" (ibid.) her mother-in-law – the two women's identities all but blur. As a result, the impression arises that, in a certain respect, the two female figures are merged into one unit in which neither of them is allowed to keep their former identities.

In connection with this observation, it proves fruitful to scrutinise the perception of gender roles by the characters themselves, in particular the relationship between Elijah and the two women in his life, i.e. his wife Rose and his mother Clementina. Being brought up by a single mother, Elijah spends a large period of his life with Clementina, who is, so to speak, directly substituted by his wife. After Rose's death, initial arrangements are re-established by Elijah's moving in with his mother again. Even though this step seems a quite common practice among the Travellers[275], the implication remains that Elijah never truly leaves the mother-son-relationship. Moreover, by choosing his mother as his confidante, he apparently fails to reach the same degree of intimacy with Rose. Whenever existential problems occur, Elijah is portrayed to consult his mother rather than to turn to his wife. Due to the tensions arising from Rose's being left out of those conversations, the two women end up competing for Elijah's attention and both of them try to exert an influence on him. This situation is exacerbated by the fact that each of them defines herself in terms of the relationship with the pater familias. In addition to that, they both derive their authority from their positions as mother or, respectively, wife. Especially at the beginning of the relationship between the young people, Clementina is reluctant to let her son go and feels betrayed by his behaviour; likewise, in later sequences, she continues to demand the respect and obedience due to a mother so that Elijah is torn between the respective expectations of mother and wife – a problem he usually solves by a visit to the pub. Yet, despite this competitiveness, the protagonists come to form a close unit over the years, a development which first and foremostly emerges due to the shared intention to keep the family together and to prevent it from lapsing into absolute poverty and misery. In this respect, the funeral arrangements outlined above may likewise be interpreted as a symbol of a deeper connection between the two women which, as it were, unites *them* in death rather then the two spouses.

---

[275] See Oakly,1975 on the topic of characteristic structures of Romany households.

Furthermore, the text offers frequent references to the various functions fulfilled by the family and provides a number of comments on the necessity to respect a child's duties and obligations towards their parents. These remarks leave the reader in no doubt that, in *Stone Cradle*, the family unit is recognised as the last source of stability and support left to the Smiths. Interestingly enough, a concept which is frequently taken as an intrinsically bourgeois value is thus promoted by both Clementina and Rose despite their entirely different backgrounds in terms of traditions and upbringing.[276] While the potentially oppressive effect of the obligatory homogeneity of a larger group as experienced by Clementina in the Travellers' community is realised and spelled out, the value of the family as such is, by contrast, never challenged. Even though Clementina is aware of Mehitable's being treated unfairly by her mother and although she pities the girl, she remains strict in her rejection of 'disrespectful' behaviour: "It doesn't do to let children speak ill of their parents, even when they're absolutely right" (Stone Cradle 226). Likewise, after Rose's death, Clementina rebukes her grandchildren for not caring sufficiently for their father. What troubles Clementina most is the fact that her grandchildren only come to visit Elijah out of a feeling of duty and obligation. Her reaction reveals that she perceives duties

---

[276] With respect to the general perception of the family as a value rather than a way of life effectively chosen, Garrett observes that "the relatively low proportion of 'normal' British families does not reflect the symbolic or ideological importance of the conventional family unit, which remains strong despite its minority status. The two-parent, patriarchal family continues to be regarded by many as the most important of all social institutions, bearing the brunt of responsibility for producing well-adjusted, law-abiding citizens. […] In short, the overall desirability or legitimacy of the institution itself is rarely questioned, at least within mainstream political debate" (Garrett, Roberta. „Gender, Sex, and the Family." *British Cultural Identities*. Ed. Mike Storry and Peter Childs. London and New York: Routledge, 1997. 129-62. 133-34). On the general perception of the family as an institution as well as on the difficulties arising in the context of studying family structures, see the following: Charles, Nickie. *Gender in Modern Britain*. Oxford: Oxford UP, 2002. Fink, Janet. „Private Lives, Public Issues. Moral Panics and 'the Family' in 20th-Century Britain." *JSBC* 9/2 (2002): 135-48. Silva, Elizabeth B. and Carol Smart. „The 'New' Practices and Politics of Family Life." *The New Family?* Ed. Elizabeth B. Silva and Carol Smart. London *et al*.: Sage, 1999. 1-12. With respect to possible definitions of 'family' as well as the symbolic value attributed to the concept, consult especially Newman, Davic M. and Liz Grauerholz. *Sociology of Families*. Thousand Oaks *et al*.: Pine Forge Press, ²2002. It is striking to note that, implicitly, the novel cites the clichéd ideal of the extended family as a harmonious and caring unit, an image which is still circulating within Western society: Even though the (nostalgic) notion of large families uniting several generations under one roof runs counter to sociological evidence, ideas of the 'lost' family unit are still being perpetuated. Coontz describes this phenomenon as follows: "Extended families have never been the norm in America; the highest figure for extended-family households ever recorded in American history is 20 percent. Contrary to the popular myth that industrialization destroyed "traditional" extended families, this high point occurred between 1850 and 1884, during the most intensive period of industrialization" (Coontz, Stephanie. *The way we never were. American Families and the Nostalgia Trap*. New York: HarperCollins, 1992. 12). Despite the fact that Coontz refers to an American context, her general argument appears applicable to Great Britain as well, at least as far as myth-building with regard to family life in the past is concerned.

and feelings as inextricably intertwined: Although Clementina insists on the observance of certain rules, she does not do so in order to enforce them merely for propriety's sake. By contrast, they, for her, denote a way of paying respect and showing one's love for another person. As a result, the rigid role models and fixed guidelines on individual behaviour are attributed an important function in stabilising family relationship and in strengthening affiliations. In addition to that, inflexible structures regulating both minor aspects such as daily tasks and graver questions such as the interaction between men and women in general preserve established ways of life and pose an obstacle to change. Moreover, they serve to consolidate gender roles and to cement the 'gap' between the sexes.

Besides its function as a 'safe haven' and a last source of support in times of crisis, the family also operates as a repository of traditions and rites. Especially Clementina is intent on passing her knowledge on to her grandchildren and to thereby ensure that her cultural background is not entirely lost. Many of the practices she teaches the children or performs herself qualify as what Hobsbawm defines as 'invented tradition',

> taken to mean a set of practices, normally governed by overtly or tacitly accepted rules and of a ritual or symbolic nature, which seek to inculcate certain values and norms of behaviour by repetition, which automatically implies continuity with the past. [...] 'Tradition' in this sense must be distinguished clearly from 'custom' which dominates so-called 'traditional' societies. The object and characteristic of 'traditions', including invented ones, is invariance. The past, real or invented, to which they refer imposes fixed (normally formalized) practices, such as repetition. 'Custom' in traditional societies has the double function of motor and fly-wheel. [...] What it does is to give any desired change (or resistance to innovation) the sanction of precedent, social continuity and natural law as expressed in history.[277]

Apparently, traditions can come to fulfil a function which is similar to that of oral story-telling. In both cases, the intention is to retain the specific 'cultural' knowledge of a certain group and to establish a continuity which is based on the adherence to specific rites, practices, and beliefs. This line of continuity represents an important aspect in the construction of personal identities as it allows

---

[277] Hobsbawm, Eric. „Introduction: Inventing Traditions." *The Invention of Tradition*. Eds. Eric Hobsbawm and Terence Ranger. Cambridge: Cambridge UP, 1983. 1-14. 1-2.

individual subjects to position themselves within a larger context and to see themselves as part of a longer line of development.[278]

At the same time as being raised according to traditional Romany standards, the Smith children grow up under the influence of working-class society and its customs. Accordingly, the girls are eager to go "Mayladyin'" (Stone Cradle 227) and to thereby take part in the activities and entertainments of their peers in the neighbourhood. As a result, cultural practises within the family begin to mix, an event which marks the starting point of a 'new' tradition exclusively practised by the Smiths themselves. Due to their status as 'semi-members' of both communities, they, in the end, only have got their family to rely on, a situation that Rose comments on as *fait accompli* and which she does not challenge any longer:

> It was right for us – a decent roof over our heads but a little bit separate from the *gorjers* in the rest of the village. I had come to feel our differentness, as a family, and to be happy that we weren't slap bang in the middle of the village with everybody watching and judging us the whole time the way it had been when we lived in East Cambridge. We had been judged on Stourbridge Common, too, mind you. The judging never stops when you're neither one thing nor another – I had learned that by then. In East Cambridge my kids got picked on for being *gipsies* and on the road they got picked on for being *half 'n' halfs*. So from now on I wasn't making any allowances for anybody, any more. We was us, and anyone who didn't like it could *ife*. (Stone Cradle 244)

This passage aptly demonstrates to which extent the frontiers shift over the course of the story. While, initially, Rose considers herself as part of the working-class community, she, later on, gradually becomes aware of her marginalisation due to her marriage to an 'outsider'. Interestingly enough, her self-image likewise undergoes a profound change since she, after some time has passed, constructs her personal identity on the basis of the affiliations to her family, which she perceives as a unit set apart, an opinion which is expressed by the

---

[278] This need for (the illusion of) stability and permanence is frequently challenged by 'postmodern' theories of identity which focus on the fragmentarising elements of personal identity and the alleged lack of a lasting core or essence. Other accounts, by contrast, allow for a general desire for unity and continuity as is, for example, the case in the *New Keywords* entry on identity: "The question of identity centers on the assertion of principles of unity, as opposed to pluralism and diversity, and of continuity, as opposed to change and transformation. In one respect, what is at issue is the cultivation and valuation of self-hood and **personal identity**, with a concern for the sameness and continuity of the individual" („Identity." *New Keywords. A Revised Vocabulary of Culture and Society*. Ed. Tony Bennett. Malden, M.A.: Blackwell, 2005. orig. emphasis).

formulation "we was us". Moreover, Rose begins to draw upon aspects of Romany culture when positioning herself. This fact shows in the deliberate use of 'gypsy' expressions and her reference to other villagers as 'gorjers'. Although there are previous instances in which Rose uses words from the Romany language, the choice of register in the above passage differs markedly from the examples discussed earlier. By contrast to those prior instances, Rose does here not feel excluded from the conversation taking place between Elijah and his mother; at this later stage of the story, she rather draws a line between herself and the members of the social sphere she formerly took as her own.

In Clementina's case, the reverse holds true: Having initially been loath to give up her life on the road and, at times, disappearing for prolonged spells of time in the summer months, she begins to adopt some of the formerly denounced *gorjer* habits and even comes to value the convenience of living in a house. In the end, she even feels that she has finally returned home.

> I still liked my little place. I had to it just how I wanted. I didn't miss being on the road at all, although I never closed my front door unless it was really freezing. [...] And I would think, the strangeness of ending up here. *During all the things that were happening to me in all the years previous. Here was waiting for me, all along.* (Stone Cradle 229, orig. emphasis)

Contrary to all expectations, Clementina's small house provides her with the opportunity of settling down and being entirely 'herself' without being marginalised or made to feel an outsider. This development may be interpreted as the strongest sign of her having moved out of the circle of the Romany community, where travelling is considered a vital part of Romany culture with participation in this practice constituting an important marker of affiliation. Clementina's blending of two ways of life culminates shortly after Rose's death. Feeling it her duty to treat her late daughter-in-law in the same way she would do with a Romany relative, the old woman decides to perform the necessary rites in order to set Rose's soul free. Rose is therefore laid to rest according to both the standards of her former community, in which she lost her status of a full member, and to those of the Travellers' community, in which she had never been accepted. Thus, once again, the family pursues its very own way and thereby implicitly defies both sides.

Everyday Culture and Exoticism in *Stone Cradle*[279]

As highlighted previously, two specific strata of society play a pivotal role in *Stone Cradle* and are portrayed with great acuity. Since both communities form part of the same society, a further point of interest consists in the mutual perception of these two circles. In this context, the construction of auto- and hetero-stereotypes proves highly revealing as it sheds light on strategies to maintain the alleged 'cultural' homogeneity within one group and illustrates how the 'other within' is instrumentalised for this purpose. The focus on the role of minority groups within processes of identity formation on a collective level reflects a current trend in sociology, where the discussion of the function of communities within a nation has recently gained new momentum:

> Neue Modernisierungsperspektiven, in welchen die Suche nach Gemeinschaft keine archaische Kategorie mehr war, entwickelten sich him Zuge der postmodernen Herausforderung schnell. Gemeinschaft wurde unter dem neuen Modewort „Identität" zur Schlüsselfrage, wobei die Gesellschaft immer chaotischer erschien. Die Dichotomie Gemeinschaft-Gesellschaft muß in diesem Entwicklungsrahmen in den Gesellschaftswissenschaften allmählich neu konzipiert werden. Dabei sollte Gemeinschaft eher als ein konstitutiver Teil von Gesellschaft anstatt im Rahmen eines Differenzierungsprozesses von Gemeinschaft in Richtung Gesellschaft betrachtet werden. Gemeinschaft wird immer wieder neu konstruiert, wenn Gesellschaften sich wandeln. [...] Es geht dabei um die kulturelle Konstruktion von Gemeinschaft, um gesellschaftliche Ordnung herzustellen.[280]

---

[279] Merriam-Webster defines exotic, amongst other things, as "strikingly, excitingly, or mysteriously different or unusual <*exotic* flavors>" („Exotic." *Merriam-Webster Online*. 2008. 25.12.2008. <http://www.merriam-webster.com/dictionary/exotic>). The aspect of a thrilling yet safe experience is likewise foregrounded by Ashcroft *et al.* when they trace the etymology of the term: "During the nineteenth century, however, the exotic, the foreign, increasingly gained, throughout the empire, the connotations of a stimulating or exciting difference, something with which the domestic could be (safely) spiced. The key conception here is the introduction of the exotic from abroad into a domestic economy" (Ashcroft, Bill *et al.* „Exotic/Exoticism." *Post-Colonial Studies. The Key Concepts*. London and New York: Routledge, 2000). In view of the long presence of Travellers in England, the process of an 'importation from abroad', does not take place as an actual act. Meanwhile, the opposition between the domestic and the allegedly foreign is still clearly visible in *Stone Cradle* so that the notion of something foreign being injected into a different cultural context applies after all.

[280] Stråth, Bo. „Die kulturelle Konstruktion von Gemeinschaften." *Alltagskultur im Umbruch*. Hg. Wolfgang Kaschuba *et al.* Weimar, Köln und Wien: Böhlau Verlag, 1996. 153-170. 154.

While Stråth concentrates primarily on the construction of communities intended to strengthen the established order of society at large and to provide citizens with a re-newed sense of belonging, *Stone Cradle* describes the conceptualisation of seemingly homogeneous communities. This ostensible homogeneity is exploited to erect firm boundaries between 'us' and 'them'. Accordingly, both groups are anxious to maintain unambiguous dividing lines by which to set themselves off from the allegedly less civilised counter-community. In the process, heterostereotypes – such as the representation of the other as dirty, sluggish, and duplicitous – are developed, which are, in turn, employed as a foil in the production of (positive) autostereotypes. Hereby, all 'bad' or negative habits and character traits are projected onto the realm outside one's own group so that a certain moral or civilisatory superiority may be claimed. In the union between Elijah and Rose, this binary structure breaks down. Via this collapse of seemingly natural patterns and oppositions, two important features of both communities are revealed: On the one hand, the inherent heterogeneity of each circle is disclosed since it becomes obvious that the alleged homogeneity does by no means represent a factual state but rather an illusion that may only be maintained by the constant exertion of pressure on individual members in order to make them conform. On the other hand, we witness an increasing number of similarities between the two spheres which, at the outset of the novel, are perceived as two worlds apart by the characters themselves. Finally, it is worthwhile to consider the implications of this merger for established notions of Englishness/Britishness. Within this context, the novel seems to be intended to increase the general awareness that aspects of national culture have been – and continue to be – suppressed in order to uphold the illusion of national homogeneity. Usually, this happened and happens at the cost of minority cultures with their specificities frequently being erased in order to render them more compatible with majority culture and to prevent the fragmentarisation of national culture.

Seeing that the novel extensively deals with the daily routines of both of the protagonists, the topic of everyday culture seems best suited for a comparative analysis of the two realms and an assessment of how difference is treated in this context. In view of this thematic outlook, I follow the definition of 'culture' as "the texts and practices of everyday life".[281] When we take into account that both communities depicted in *Stone Cradle* belong to lower, less privileged strata of society, it does not come as a surprise that everyday life in these spheres is shaped by duties and hardship. Moreover, a recurrent concern consists in the need to earn a sufficient amount of money so as to provide for the family. This routine of daily chores is only interrupted by fundamental changes

---

[281] Storey, John. *Cultural Studies and the Study of Popular Culture: Theories and Methods.* Edinburgh: Edinburgh UP, 1996. 2.

and decisive events such as childbirth and death. Having both been reared under such similar conditions, Clementina and Rose do from the beginning share specific experiences such as the hardship of raising a child on one's own or, respectively, being raised without a father. The regular recurrence of certain incidents lends a leitmotivic structure to the text as a whole. Besides the problem of 'fatherless' children, the early death of the mother constitutes a further reiterated feature. These shared experiences of hardship, misery, and deprivation, however, are not exploited as the foundation of an emotional bond or considered as a potential link. To the contrary, in a heated row, Rose even uses her knowledge of Elijah's being an illegitimate child against Clementina. Thus, in the women's direct interaction, the differences in terms of age (and the ensuing question of the respective positions in the family hierarchy) prove too strong to be overcome. Nevertheless, when existential threats arise, Rose heavily relies on her mother-in-law. This fact becomes most apparent when her labours suddenly set in and Rose calls out "*Mother!*" (Stone Cradle 154, orig. emphasis). Here, affiliations and proximity arise mainly from pragmatic considerations rather than from emotional closeness or deep-felt sympathy.

A further question which is discussed repeatedly with respect to communal or everyday life is the relationship between the sexes. For most of the time, the differential category of sex/gender is presented as a strong barrier. Correspondingly, several passages which comment on the dealings between men and women suggest that a lack of knowledge (often due to the early loss of a mother figure) leads to profound misunderstandings and prevents the spouses from truly communicating with each other. According to Clementina's own assessment, this ignorance of the interaction between men and women resulted in her being raped by one of the leaders of her community:

> *Oh Dei and Dadus, why did you keep me so protected? Why did I not know what happened if you gave a man any sort of encouragement, and that sometimes it could happen whether you encouraged him or not?* (Stone Cradle 331, orig. emphasis)

The traumatic experience of her violation as well as the ensuing feeling of shame[282] even prevent Clementina from entering a satisfying sexual relationship

---

[282] Once again, Doughty's description of the situation proves highly 'authentic' or 'life-like'. As various studies on the topic suggest, a feeling of shame and the impression of being 'guilty' of or having provoked the crime constitute very common reactions to the experience of being raped. For a more detailed account see Feldmann, Harald. *Vergewaltigung und ihre psychischen Folgen. Ein Beitrag zur posttraumatischen Belastungsreaktion*. Stuttgart: Ferdinand Enke, 1992. Likewise consult Tiber Egle, Ulrich (Hg.) *et al. Sexueller Mißbrauch, Mißhandlung, Vernachlässigung.*

in her adulthood. When she finally accepts Adolphus Lee's proposal, the union is based on the precondition never to have sex, a promise Adolphus faithfully keeps for the entire twelve years of their marriage (Stone Cradle 75). The relationship between Rose and Elijah is likewise beset by misunderstandings and a lack of communication. After the initial bliss of the first weeks spent together, a feeling of alienation quickly sets in. Although passages which report conversations between Elijah and his mother as well as sections in which Rose addresses the reader directly to talk about her feelings prove that, in principle, the spouses still love each other, they fail to communicate their sympathy so that a final reconciliation before Rose's death does not take place. The only functional and satisfying relationship described in the novel is represented by Clementina's parents, who live in a close union based on mutual support and love. Due to her mother's early death, though, this image of harmony and happiness within the frame of the nuclear family does not last for long.

The decision to present differences in terms of gender as comparatively rigid and difficult to overcome may be seen as an attempt to paint an 'authentic' picture of both working-class and Romany life at the time in which the story is set. Scenes such as Clementina's comment on the increasing openness about the topic of sex and Rose's remark on the great number of single mothers (rendering illegitimate childbirth an almost 'normal' state) conveys the impression that the reader is being given an account of things as they 'really' were.

Against the background of whether *Stone Cradle* presents an 'authentic' picture of everyday life/everyday culture, a further aspect worthy to be taken into consideration consists in the function of exoticism.[283] Hereby, we may distinguish between two forms, which result from the alternating perspectives of the two narrators. While Rose comments on the strange nature of her mother-in-law's beliefs and practices, Clementina is incredulous when confronted with some of the 'gorjer' habits. These remarks are likely to provoke different reactions in the reader: Having most probably been socialised in a non-Romany environment and being familiar with certain notions of working-class/farm life, the average reader will follow Rose in her perception of Clementina's stance as, at times, slightly odd, superstitious, and irrational. Moreover, there is a distinct element of gossip in some of Rose's accounts which the reader, due to the chosen form

---

Erkennung und Behandlung psychischer und psychosomatischer Folgen früher Traumatisierung. Stuttgart und New York: Schattauer, 1997.

[283] In this context, I would like to emphasis once again that I by no means wish to imply that an 'authentic' portrayal of 'things as they really were' should be the aim of a novelistic text. To the contrary, my interest consists in how the impression of authenticity is conveyed by way of rhetorical structures and textual features. Moreover, I deem it important to consider signals of 'realness' embedded in the narrative especially as far as the impact on the reading process and the general perception of the book is concerned.

of presentation, is invited to share. Hereby, Rose's choice of words tends to imply that Clementina occasionally acts insanely and cannot be taken entirely seriously. At the same time, Rose seems to indulge in gossiping with her motherly friend Lilly, for which Clementina constitutes a welcome object since it gives her the chance to vent her anger about her overbearing behaviour. In the exchange between Lilly and Rose, one may furthermore detect a fascination with the 'strange' behaviour displayed by Clementina. Rose's accounts of her mother-in-law's antics prove slightly reminiscent of the modes of presentation adopted in freak shows, which likewise relied upon their visitors' fascination with the peculiar, foreign, and, therefore, pleasantly frightening and wondrous:

> If it hadn't been for Lilly, I am not sure how I would have got through those first few weeks. Elijah's mother was the most *peculiar* person I had ever met. Her ways were beyond me. Each afternoon, I would *escape* to Lilly's bedside and tell her of the latest *antic*. 'And yesterday, she served up some potatoes and she had not put any cabbage in gravy on my plate and it took me all my courage to say something to her and do you know what she said?'
>
> 'go on…'
>
> 'She snapped at me, it's bad luck for a woman in your condition to eat anything green. […]'
>
> 'Oh, God knows, Lilly, the woman is completely batty and Elijah never says a word to her and what am I supposed to do?' (Stone Cradle 146-8, emphases mine, last emphasis orig.)

In contrast, the reader is unlikely to share Clementina's horrification at the *gorjers'* habit of using the same basin for different purposes and of watering their plants with the same water they previously used for washing themselves. These passages from Clementina's view therefore fulfil a double function. First, they add to the impression of Romany culture being distinct from traditional 'English' ways of life and may be read as instances of the 'exotic' within one's own nation. At the same time, however, they serve to demonstrate that 'normality' is always a construct depending on the standpoint of the observer. Descriptions from the Travellers' perspective thus gradually reveal that, in many cases, 'adequate' or 'regular' behaviour is defined differently. Simultaneously, Doughty problematises the complex question of 'normality' or 'normal behaviour' by adding another twist to the accounts of 'characteristical' behaviour when she has Clementina comment on the need to meet the *gorjers'* expectations:

> I taught her [Mehitable] how to curtsey so her calliper shoed and she looked brave for trying. I taught her how to hold a lady's palm and trace

the lines on it with the very tip of her finger. [...] 'You must hold the hand firmly, but touch softly. That way, a person feels protected, cared for, coaxed. [...] For a moment, they have been concentrated on – and that's what they are paying you for. They are paying you for being curious about them.' (Stone Cradle 204)

As far as the general representation of Romany culture is concerned, one witnesses a strange tension between perspicacious, critical comments, which take into account the hardships arising from a life on the road,[284] and a nostalgic, idealising view of a way of life outside 'established' society and allegedly free from its constraints. Although the description of Romany habits brought forward in *Stone Cradle*, which clearly defies common stereotypes circulated among established English society, may be interpreted as an attempt to counteract the general negative perception of 'gypsies', it, at the same time, tends to convey the impression that living on the road constitutes an alternative to the drudgery of conventional lifestyles. In tune with this assumption, several sections are imbued with a sort of campfire romance which implies that the Travellers, unlike other strata of society, still retain a closer contact to nature and that they manage to live in tune with their environment from which city-dwellers have long become alienated. In addition to that, several passages which offer explanations on Romany customs and routines suggest that we are dealing with an attitude towards life which is not dominated by Enlightenment ideals such as rationality, scientific explicability, and factual verifiability. Thereby an image of the Travellers is produced which presents them as pragmatic and well-equipped for their daily tasks but, simultaneously, as not inclined to analytical reflection or elaborate thought: "It is not really done to just sit and think when you're a Traveller, especially a *biti chai* like me. Thinking doesn't get a fire built, nor catch a rabbit to stick on top of it" (Stone Cradle 17, orig. emphasis).

The same holds true for the discussion of the Romany system of beliefs as well as for the anecdotes and myths passed on orally in the group. A revealing example of this phenomenon may be found in Clementina's interpretation of the story of the ghost pig:

Looking back now, I think I know what the Ghost Pig was – it wasn't the pig itself, not really. It was evil in the landowner and his friends. It was all the *gorjer* evil in all the *gorjer* world that got together and stamped on Absalom Smith's face when he was beaten and lying on the

---

[284] Notably, *Stone Cradle* quite accurately reports government actions curtailing the Travellers' rights and posing considerable obstacles to their itinerant way of life. For a detailed account of legislative measures and the political treatment of the 'gypsy question' over the last centuries, see Hawes, 1995.

ground. [...] It was sort of like the realness of life that lies in wait for you and jumps out. That is why it was so frightening, for all of us. When you are a Traveller, you are never allowed to forget that whatever you have might be taken away from you at any minute. [...] That's what it's like being one of us. And the Ghost Pig is always out there, to remind you, in the dark or even in the daytime. Everybody has their own Ghost Pig, in my opinion. It follows you, even when you're not thinking about it. It never goes away. (Stone Cradle 218)

This quote is noteworthy in terms of its line of argument which combines 'analytical' remarks, i.e. observations in tune with the standards of Western logic, with 'superstitious' comments. On the surface, this gesture can be read as an indication of Clementina's still being rooted in Romany society and its way of thinking. Contrary to this conjecture, however, the rhetorical structure of the paragraph implicitly demonstrates the constructed nature of 'common sense', 'rationality', and 'logics' by offering new explanations of certain phenomena which transcend a purely scientific, fact-based approach. Clementina's portrayal as an otherwise reasonable, insightful person as well as her awareness of her own inclination to superstition underscore the impression that the reader is not confronted with merely a deluded, outdated worldpicture which can be easily dismissed as irrational. To the contrary, this specific depiction may serve to introduce a different way of thought which diverges from Western or 'enlightened' concepts. In several similar scenes, the novel covertly claims that this alternative perspective on reality, should, irrespective of its incongruity with established notions, be valued in its own right. Yet, despite this concealed appeal for a general openness towards alternative perspectives, passages such as the one quoted above run the risk of contributing to the image of the Travellers as somewhat peculiar and alien to Western culture as their system of beliefs seems to contradict the notions of logic and factuality which is most likely entertained by the gross of readers. This effect is even more prone to arise as it chimes in with and possibly even reactivates a nostalgic and romanticising view of gypsy life, the origins of which can be traced back to the 19th century. By way of example, one might cite Arnold's poem "The Scholar Gipsy", as an illustration of a romanticising depiction of the Romany way of life which is presented as an antidote to the corruptions of modern society:

> The scholar-gipsy is championed in the poem as a seeker of truth who has forsaken rational knowledge for the inspiriting wisdom of nature. [...] For Romantics the gipsy was a symbol of pre-industrial life, an unspoilt noble savage who was untainted by corrupt society.[285]

---

[285] Dougill, John. *Oxford in English Literature. The Making, and Undoing, of 'The English Athens'*. Ann Arbor: Michigan UP, 1998. 148.

In fact, when we analyse the account of the young scholar, who leaves established society in favour of 'gipsy lore' in greater detail, we witness some parallels to the evaluation of Romany customs in *Stone Cradle*. I would like to underpin this hypothesis by quoting an excerpt from the poem:

> And near me on the grass lies Glanvil's book—
>
> Come, let me read the oft-read tale again!
>
> The story of that Oxford scholar poor,
>
> Of pregnant parts and quick inventive brain,
>
> Who, tired of knocking at preferment's door,
>
> One summer-morn forsook
>
> His friends, and went to learn the gipsy-lore,
>
> And roam'd the world with that wild brotherhood,
>
> And came, as most men deemed, to little good,
>
> But came to Oxford and his friends no more.
>
> But once, years after, in the country lanes,
>
> Two scholars, whom at college erst he knew,
>
> Met him, and of his way of life inquired.
>
> Whereat he answer'd; that the Gipsy crew,
>
> His mates, had arts to rule as they desired
>
> The workings of men's brains,
>
> And they can bind them to what thoughts they will.
>
> 'And I,' he said, 'the secret of their art,
>
> When fully learned, will to the world impart;
>
> But it needs heaven-sent moments for this skill!'[286]

This impression of a proximity between this depiction and the presentation in *Stone Cradle* is increased by the fact that Clementina is firmly moored in a culture with a strong tradition of oral story telling and that she actively engages in passing on the Travellers' myths herself. As Braid points out, "[f]olklore is often associated with that which is old, with tradition as conservation of the past. [...] In temporal terms, if Travellers posess folklore they must maintain direct

---

[286] Arnold, Matthew. „The Scholar Gipsy." *The New Oxford Book of English Verse. 1250-1950.* Ed. Helen Garnder. Oxford and New York: Oxford UP, 1972. 690-96. 691.

connections with the past and therefore they must not be living in the same temporal reality as the rest of us."[287] Mayall likewise observes that the figure of the gypsy as a mysterious, impenetrable character has repeatedly been used in poetry and fiction and at times even informed earlier studies of Romany culture:

> Closely associated with the notion that Gypsy life was guided by omens and ritual was the romantic relationship they were said to have with nature. They were seen as a primitive people living a natural life untroubled by the cares of civilisation, able to preserve intact their magical beliefs and practices.[288]

While *Stone Cradle*, in general, does not lapse into mystifying descriptions of specific traditions practiced by the Travellers, there are nevertheless scenes which link Clementina to 'mystical' proceedings, for instance when she considers resorting to the skills of a Romany healer rather than having to rely on a trained medicine to ease Mehitable's fits: "It was like there was a devil in her [Mehitable]. I even started to wonder if I should take her out into the country and find one of our people who could really help" (Stone Cradle 191). Likewise, despite having lived in *gorjer* society for a substantial period of time, Clementina is anxious to observe Romany burial rites after Rose's death as she believes that only those can set her soul free.

Difference and Similarity – A Potential Left Unexploited

To conclude, as the foregoing analysis of the novel has demonstrated, *Stone Cradle* differs markedly from the texts examined in Section I as far as the treatment of differential categories is concerned. In its negotiation of difference, the novel sets two communities within British society off against each other. Hereby, specific narrative structures – especially a leitmotivic series of topics combined with the citation of established literary genres – are employed to create a row of parallels and bonds between two seemingly incongruous realms. Contrary to the approaches displayed by the texts in Section I, these proximities in most cases only show on the level of the reader, whereas the characters themselves remain ignorant of the full extent of potential similarities. This holds particularly true for passages relating a character's thoughts, which are, shortly afterwards, followed by a section which has another character expressing the

---

[287] Braid, 1997, 41.
[288] Mayall, David. *Gypsy-Travellers in Nineteenth-Century Society.* Cambridge: Cambridge UP, 1988. 76.

same notions. Due to a lack of communication, though, no exchange takes place so that parallels in the respective vitae or shared feelings are not recognised by the protagonists themselves. For these reasons, substitute communities such as (metaphorical) families do not assume the same ideological quality as is, for instance, the case in *On Beauty*. This phenomenon results from the fact that differences are usually overcome out of pragmatic considerations and that the functions formerly fulfilled by the community have, by necessity, to be taken over by the family. Therefore, similarities and common features are to a lower degree drawn upon for the construction of personal identities (especially with respect to their 'cultural' component). While the texts discussed previously portray the respective protagonists achieving to surmount the divisive potential of differential categories and show how they succeed in the establishment of moments of Sameness, *Stone Cradle* rather presents the reader with a conceptual play or thought experiment but not an actual state experienced by one of the characters. Even though the text hints at possible ways of negotiating difference, none of them is put fully into practice. What is more, in dealing with the topic of difference *Stone Cradle* performs a slight shift of focus as attention is directed at sex/gender, age, and 'culture' rather than ethnicity.[289]

As to the general representation and treatment of difference, the novel does neither aim at blending differential categories into some sort of 'hybrid' construct nor does it argue for their being upheld as separate, insurmountable entities. Instead, *Stone Cradle* demonstrates the possibility of overcoming potentially divisive elements within the context of a certain group (usually limited to a small number of persons) provided that all its members are willing to participate in this effort. Moreover, by contrast to my previous examples, *Stone Cradle* critically discusses the effects of an enforced similarity which does not leave any room for individuality. The novel may furthermore be categorised as a text which abandons strategies frequently referred to as 'postmodern' since it suggests that stable identities exist – at least in the protagonists' perception. This implication is primarily communicated via the citation and subsequent modification of established rhetorical and generic structures. Another decisive feature of this return to certain pre-postmodern conventions consists in the simultaneous reconsolidation of the subject.[290] While *Stone Cradle* discerningly reflects

---

[289] Undoubtedly, the discussion of 'cultural' differences is closely connected to the question of ethnicity since, at least at the beginning of the novel, the English and the Travellers are opposed to each other as two separate ethnic groups. Nevertheless, differences in terms of ethnicity figure less prominently as the novel progresses.

[290] This gesture seems to be in tune with a re-newed interest in roots, heritage, and biography currently evolving in Western societies. As Deguen states "C'était autrefois une lubie de marquise, un luxe égocentrique réservé à ceux et celles qui avaient eu une grande destinée. Aujourd'hui, c'est encore un cadeau un peu cher, certes… Mais on peut habiter au fin fond du Perche, avoir eu une petite vie pépère, et… en faire un livre. […] La « biographie personelle » s'est dépouissiérée et démocratisée. […] C'est dans l'air du temps: la généalogie, la quête des racines,

on the burdens of a 'binding' or obligatory ethnic identity and points out its drawbacks and risks, there is no doubt about the viability of the concept of personal identity as such. Even though individual characters may experience bouts of insecurity with respect to certain decisions and actions, they, ultimately, do not question the core of their identity and feel authorised to relate their own story. In this context, the problem of the alleged impossibility of giving an account of oneself is circumvented in different ways. As to the problem of relating the beginning of a life as well as its end the novel offers two solutions. In Rose's case, we are presented with the conventional strategy of resorting to a 'substitute' narrative: Speaking about her birth, an event of which she does not have any personal memories, Rose draws upon external sources which she considers reliable to such a degree that she integrates them into her own life-story. This strategy counters Butler's suggestion of the impossibility of giving an account of oneself, in particular as brought forward in *Kritik der ethischen Gewalt*. Even though Butler is certainly right about an individual's inability to retell the moment of his or her birth, it seems doubtable whether this failure really implies an unfillable void. With respect to *Stone Cradle*, one may argue that the lack of knowledge is not *perceived* as a shortcoming since it is compensated by substitute narratives which provide, at least in the protagonists' eyes, a satisfying alternative. Concerning the problematic of an adequate self-narrative, Butler writes further:

> In diesem Sinne wird also eine Geschichte erzählt, aber das >Ich<, das diese Geschichte nicht nur erzählt, sondern in ihr auch als Erzähler in der ersten Person erscheinen kann, stellt einen undurchsichtigen Punkt und insoweit auch eine Unterbrechung der Abfolge dar, einen Bruch in der Erzählung, das Aufbrechen des Nichtnarrativierbaren inmitten der Geschichte. [...] In der Tat werde ich eingeführt als eben jenes, wovon keine Rechenschaft gegeben wird oder gegeben werden kann. Ich lege Rechenschaft von mir selbst ab, aber vom >Ich<, das sein Leben erzählt, kann es keine Rechenschaft von sich selbst geben, weil es nicht zum Schauplatz der Adressierung zurückkehren kann, auf dem es eingeführt wird, und weil es nicht sämtliche rhetorischen Dimensionen der Adressierungsstruktur erzählen kann, innerhalb derer die Rechenschaft selbst erfolgt.[291]

Undoubtedly, this assumption cannot be contested per se. What, in contrast, seems questionable is whether the "I" does in fact perceive the impossibility of

---

la nécessité de s'inscrire dans une lignée et de laisser des traces de sa brève existence sont définitivement devenues la marotte de Monsieur Tout-le-Mond " (Deguen, Florence. „Offrez-vous le livre de votre vie." *Revue de la Presse*. Fév. 2007. 10).
[291] Butler, 2003, 80-1.

giving a full account of oneself as a failure or shortcoming. Moreover, in view of the long tradition of autobiographical or life writing it appears likely that, in particular with respect to literary narratives, the vast majority of readers will not expect a chronologically complete account due to their familiarity with the conventions of these genres.

Seeing the subject-matter dealt with in *Stone Cradle*, the novel additionally inscribes itself into a line of development comprising an increasing body of works which deal with history and the importance to understand the past in order to make sense of the present. According to Gauthier, this

> desire to create narrative is based on more than a need to problematize and subvert; it also derives from a need to assert and establish a story that one can believe. [...] No matter what theorists may assert about the veracity of fictional reconstructions of history, readers will walk away believing they have acquired some knowledge about the way life was lived in the past and how that past connects with the present.[292]

In view of Louise Doughty's extensive knowledge of the Romany way of life as well as her access to 'real-life' sources, this desire for 'authenticity' is certainly catered to in the greatest extent a 'fictional' description may achieve.

---

[292] Gauthier, Tim S. *Narrative Desire and Historical Reparations. A. S. Byatt, Ian McEwan, Salman Rushdie*. New York and London: Routledge, 2006. 12-13. The term 'narrative desire' was initially coined by Brooks in his study *Reading for the Plot*.

Ian McEwan's *Saturday* – A Return to Essentialist Dichotomies or a Farcical Subversion of the Bourgeois System of Values?

Ian McEwan's *Saturday* offers a sixth and final example of yet another approach towards the treatment of difference in literary texts. Contrary to most of the previous novels, which focus primarily on the aspect of ethnic difference, *Saturday* addresses this topic in a more implicit fashion and combines it with reflections on further differential categories within English society. Seeing that the protagonist (and focalizing figure over vast stretches of the text) stems from a white upper-middle class background, questions such as the compatibility of an 'ethnic' identity with established notions of Englishness/Britishness play a less prominent role. The concept of Englishness/Britishness as such, however, constitutes one of the prime concerns of the novel even though it is tackled in a way entirely different from the approaches presented before. Due to the strong concentration on protagonist Henry Perowne, whose perspective dominates the entire novel, the focus is clearly placed on the upper-middle classes. Hereby, the portrayal of English society proves remarkable inasmuch as the narrative seems to resort to essentialising notions and to adopt quite rigid views with respect to social and 'cultural' boundaries. One of the main aspects to guide my reading of *Saturday* will therefore consist in the question of whether McEwan's novel truly performs a return to all but simplistic binary oppositions or whether the text likewise allows for a second reading subverting these clear-cut dichotomies.

Another feature which markedly distinguishes the novel from the other texts in this section is its – apparent (?) – establishment of precisely definable cultural and social circles: Instead of concentrating on the persisting presence of 'foreign' elements in English, or, respectively, European society, *Saturday* draws clear boundaries between a white, bourgeois 'us' and an initially unspecified non-Western 'other'. For this reason, I will place one focus of my reading on the treatment of intercultural differences as well as their being contrasted with intracultural, i.e. mainly class differences. In each case it will be demonstrated which strategies are employed to render the unfamiliar less threatening and therefore manage- and controllable. Another crucial point arises from the specific role attributed to (high) culture and its location in a particular stratum of society which, right from the start, excludes for instance the working classes. Finally, I will scrutinise the system of values which is (allegedly) promoted by the protagonist and, at least according to one possible interpretation of the text, also silently sanctioned by the structure of the novel as such.

As highlighted in the introduction to the second group of analyses, McEwan's *Saturday* constitutes a special case inasmuch as it allows for two different, highly contradictory readings. While the phenomenon that a literary text invites a number of interpretations is unlikely to provoke any surprise (and is in fact one characteristic feature in the definition of 'literariness' per se), the ambiguity of *Saturday* nevertheless represents a striking element since the 'message' allegedly conveyed by the text alters dramatically from one reading to the other. Thus, it is, on the one hand, possible to read the narrative as a conservative endorsement of bourgeois values with a concomitant celebration of the way of life promoted by the middle classes. On the other hand, though, the text may be understood as a highly sarcastic subversion of those self-same values and a caustic comment on the complacent, holier-than-thou attitudes displayed by aspiring upper-middle class professionals such as the novel's protagonist. In the following analysis, I will first present a 'conventional' reading of the text centring on its treatment of differential categories and examine the value judgements potentially implied by the narrative. Subsequently, by reading the text 'against the grain', I will show how this first interpretation may be subverted by a change of 'classification', i.e. by the subsumption under a different generic label. This switch from what may be termed a 'realist' approach to a 'farcical' interpretation of *Saturday* proves to have significant implications for the novel's engagement with the topic of difference and the resulting conclusions.

A 'Conventional' Reading: *Saturday* as the Return to an Essentialising Understanding of Difference

Binary Oppositions as a Principal Structuring Device

One of the main structuring principles in McEwan's *Saturday* consists in the contrasting of binary oppositions. While, as the story develops, some of them prove difficult to maintain and turn out to be far less clear-cut than they appear at the beginning, other oppositional pairs are kept up throughout the novel or re-established later on which, at times, lends the narrative a Manichean quality. Overall, we may identify five pairs of binary oppositions which overlap at certain points as they are embodied by the same figures or turn out to be interconnected. The fields set off against each other are work vs. private life, the sane vs. the mentally disturbed, the West vs. the (Islamic) rest, the well-to-do upper-classes vs. the street scum, and, finally art vs. science.

The first opposition I would like to analyse in greater detail is the juxtaposition of the Western world with the allegedly hostile, threatening, and dangerous Islamic East. These two spheres are evoked in this homogenised way right at the beginning of the story when Perowne watches a plane on fire approaching the British capital. With the memories of 9/11 still vivid, Perowne immediately ponders the possibility of yet another terrorist attack. Although, by contrast to the 9/11 assaults, he would in this case be involved directly and not only participate as a spectator, Perowne's perception remains aloof and appears to be shaped by the structures of a media broadcast. As a result of this reaction, he appears detached and seems to act like a mere bystander or observer witnessing a catastrophic event on TV but not being personally affected by it:

> It's already almost eighteen months since half the planet watched, and watched again the unseen captives driven through the sky to the slaughter, at which time there gathered round the innocent silhouette of any jet plane a novel association. […] The fiery white core and its coloured tail have grown larger – no passengers sitting in that central section of the plane could survive. That is the other familiar element – the horror of what he can't see. Catastrophe observed from a safe distance. Watching death on a large scale, but seeing no one die.[293]

---

[293] McEwan, Ian. *Saturday*. London: Vintage, 2006. 16. Hereafter quoted as Saturday.

Thus, while still watching the burning plane, Perowne identifies familiar 'plot elements' which he immediately associates with a terrorist act.[294] Here, we can likewise detect the influence of the media on the general perception and interpretation of certain events. Accordingly, while the first report of the plane crash retains a neutral tone and largely sticks to verifiable facts, later accounts are tainted by speculations on potential links to terrorist networks which are not grounded on a factual basis but play on the public paranoia of another terrorist attack on the western world. Without having been given the opportunity to present their versions of the events, the two pilots are accused of having planned an assault on the English capital merely on the grounds that they presumably hail from an Islamic country. Further stereotypical assumptions follow suit such as the Metropolitan Police behaving in a racist way discriminating against the crew. Yet, in a later bulletin, all these accusations have to be abandoned. Most strikingly, this is done in an off-handed fashion with the rectification being reduced to the laconic statement that "the correct procedures were followed. Both men insist they've been treated with courtesy by the Metropolitan Police" (Saturday 180). Moreover, the alleged Islamic fundamentalists turn out to stem from Riga, to possess Russian passports, and to be employed by a Dutch company.

This episode allows for two (complementary) strands of interpretations. First of all, it serves to illustrate that, for many people, the experience of crisis and catastrophe has assumed an all but mediatic – and therefore detached and distanced – quality. Due to this lack of personal involvement, catastrophic events risk being transformed into horrific but nevertheless thrilling scenarios to be watched from a safe distance. At the same time, media images are revealed to be exploited as a foil which allows for the streamlining of initially inexplicable experiences into a familiar framework. This phenomenon is exemplified by the plane crash: Since 9/11 any plane on fire approaching a city is almost automatically associated with a wilful and planned attack by the 'other', i.e. the non-Christian, Islamic realm, on the Western world. Moreover, the outcome of the investigations on the plane crash demonstrate that seemingly neat boundaries begin to blur on second sight and that a black-and-white division of the world – even though highly convenient – proves too simplistic. Although this realisation does not figure as an overly innovative or progressive insight, the discussion of the dangers of automatically labelling non-Westerners as terrorists and thereby classifying them unquestioningly as a potential threat to the Western system of

---

[294] It is already at this early stage in the novel that the text's preoccupation with the topic of media coverage and its impact on public opinion shows. Accordingly, all potentially decisive events are related both through the eyes of the focalizer and, subsequently, reduplicated by news broadcasts. In this context, it is interesting to note that the perception of the protagonist himself and his way of structuring certain events has obviously been informed by patterns used by the media.

values is given great space in the novel and constitutes one of its main thematic foci.[295]

The difficulty arising from the attempt to clearly distinguish between 'friend' and 'foe' is extended by a plot sequence which deals with the demonstration against an imminent war on Iraq. Once again, boundaries are shown to become fuzzy when the situation is analysed more profoundly. In this case, the rupture even runs through the protagonist's family as the Perowne children – unlike their father – do by no means perceive the outbreak of a war as inevitable, a conviction they share with thousands of demonstrators protesting against a military invention on Iraq.[296] These reflections on the nature and causes of terrorism are supplemented by further examples of both 'legitimate' and 'illicit' upsurges against oppressive regimes (Saturday 123). Those examples serve to illustrate the subjective quality of any assessment of the 'legitimacy' of anti-governmentalist movements. Moreover, they highlight to which degree judgements depend on the standpoint and cultural context of the evaluator as the value system he or she is immured in will unavoidably inform the stance taken on specific issues. Therefore, the large number of people protesting against a war on Iraq does not come as a surprise in view of their having been socialised within the Western system of values with its high estimation for rights such as freedom, democratic procedures, and free speech. Interestingly enough, the discussion of whether a pre-emptive strike is advisable turns out to be closely connected to the differential category of age: Accordingly, Perowne, largely owing to his personal contact to an Iraqi citizen and his knowledge of the latter's experiences, draws attention to the crimes perpetrated by Saddam:

> The genocide and torture, the mass graves, the security apparatus, the criminal totalitarian state – the iPod generation doesn't want to know.

---

[295] At this point, it also proves worthwhile to consider the topicality of the novel as such since McEwan comments directly on the political situation at the time of his writing of *Saturday*. This focus is further hightlighted by his drawing attention to the role of the media in interviews and articles discussing both the events of 9/11 and the publication of *Saturday* which, as he states, was "written in the shadow of the event" (Caminada, Carlos. „Ian McEwan, Finishing New Novel, Ponders World After Sept.11" *Bloomberg.com*. 15. July 2004. 26.12.2008. <http://www.bloomberg.com/apps/news?pid=10000085&sid=a4L6SJH6SmN0&refer=europe>).

[296] Here, we encounter a brilliant example of how readers' reactions might be guided by the development of events in 'reality', especially when contested political decisions are concerned. In view of the outcome of the military intervention in Iraq, the sympathies and support for the Bush government's attack have decreased considerably. As an article in the *Times* which retrospectively comments on the strike confirms, "President Bush's popularity ratings have now reached an almost record low: two years after a triumphant reelection [...], the Administration is becalmed and the machine that has put seven of the past ten presidents into the White House is creaking" („The Race has Begun." *Timesonline*. 27.08.2008. 24.01.2009. <http://www.timesonline.co.uk/tol/comment/leading_article/article2332573.ece>).

Let nothing come between them and their ecstasy clubbing and cheap flights and reality TV. But it will, if we do nothing. (Saturday 191)

Apparently, Perowne accuses the younger generation of deliberately closing their eyes to aspects which do not fit their line of argument. At the same time, though, Perowne himself begins to shuttle between two positions when entering another context and adopts shifting stances, depending on whom he is talking to. Thus, while he insists on the inevitability of a war on Iraq when in the company of members from his family, Perowne's conduct changes in the presence of his colleague Jay:

He's a man of untroubled certainties, impatient of talk of diplomacy, weapons of mass destruction, inspection teams, proofs of links with Al-Qaeda and so on. Iraq is a rotten state, a natural ally of terrorists, bound to cause mischief at some point and may as well be taken out now while the US military is feeling perky after Afghanistan. [...] Whenever he talks to Jay, Henry finds himself tending towards the anti-war camp. (Saturday 100)

As the outcome and success (or rather lack of success) of the military operation in Iraq have shown, McEwan undoubtedly has a point when he draws attention to the dangers of seeing the world in black and white terms and when he issues a warning not to succumb to media-transmitted images and pre-formed opinions. Still, this message risks to assume an overly didactic hue which sometimes even renders it slightly simplistic. Moreover, in view of the large numbers of both fictional and theoretical accounts which address the same topic and discuss it on a far more abstract level, some of the book's initial thrust seems to have been lost here.[297]

A second binary opposition which is introduced right at the beginning of *Saturday* is the sphere of work as opposed to the realm of private life. Tellingly, the novel, as already indicated by the title, is set on a Saturday, a day which in our present society is in general regarded as a day off from work. In the Perowne family, though, work has come to adopt such an overbearing significance, that it also seems to dominate the couple's spare leisure time. This fact is reflected by Perowne's reconstruction of the previous evening: "Rosalind must have drawn the covers over him when she came in from work. [...] Forty-eight years old, profoundly asleep at nine thirty on a Friday night – this is modern professional

---

[297] The problems arising from writing on highly topical issues have likewise been pointed out by Tait (Tait, Theo. „A rational diagnosis." *Times Online*, Feb. 11, 2005. 06.12.2007. qtd. <http://alcorn.blogspot.com/2005/02/poker-we-play-poker-at-my-house-once.html>).

life" (Saturday 6-7). Even though the protagonist displays a clear awareness that his family life has become increasingly governed by the respective demands of his and his wife's jobs, this insight does not provoke any regret but obviously constitutes an element of pride. In a society which upholds the creed of work as "the ultimate badge of health" (Saturday 24), a 'work for work's sake' ethos has been installed irrespective of its impact on a person's social or family life. Rather than allowing for a well balanced ratio between work and free time, this creed seems to value the activity of working to total exhaustion as such without questioning the efficacy of this behaviour. The impression of work having gained an overwhelming significance within the Perowne family is backed by the protagonist's musings about single medical cases: In his recollection of the individual steps of a performance, clinical details as well as the duration of each stage are permanently commented on, usually in order to stress Perowne's professionalism, his high ability, and his great dexterity. Simultaneously, though, his accounts are interspersed with sarcastic comments on the procedure, which prove revealing with regard to his perception of patients and colleagues as well as his general attitude towards them:

> For an old friend, a specialist in Ear, Nose and Throat, Perowne opened up an acoustic in a seventeen-year-old boy – *it's odd how these ENT people shy away from making their own difficult routes in.* [...] He made a long incision across her abdomen and *wasted valuable time, up to his elbows inside her*, searching for the battery wire. (Saturday 8-9, my emphases)

In combination with the detached tone and the medical terminology used, the impression imposes itself that individual fates have receded into the background. This stance towards patients renders them mere items on the ward's daily agenda. Likewise, unforeseen incidents are treated as unwelcome disturbing factors and are perceived as a nuisance since they prevent the 'machine' from working efficiently. It is from this smooth running of his 'firm' as he calls it as well as from the feeling of being entirely capable and in control that Perowne derives greatest satisfaction:

> Well, in ambitious middle life it sometimes seems there is only work. [...] For certain days, even weeks on end, work can shape every hour; [...]. Henry can't resist the urgency of his cases, or deny the egotistical joy in his own skills, or the pleasure he still takes in the relief of the relatives when he comes down from the operating room like a god, an angel with the glad tidings – life, not death. (Saturday 23)

Strikingly, both Perowne's and his wife Rosalind's professional performances are endowed with an all but erotic quality and seem to offer the deep gratification hardly found in private life anymore. Against this background, the aspect of why Perowne agrees to operate on Baxter assumes a different hue and allows for explanation other than Perowne's feeling of professional obligation towards the hospital, a point I will return to below.

The two oppositional pairs to be discussed next – class and mental health/sanity – display a certain overlap as they are primarily exemplified by the two protagonists Perowne and Baxter. During their first encounter, in the scrape over the car accident, class boundaries come to the fore. Hereby, when getting out of his car to examine the damage, Perowne initially feels superior to his raggedly dressed opponents. What is more, the scene has an unreal, 'mediatic' quality for him as it seems to follow the rules of television drama and popular entertainment:

> He is cast in a role, and there's no way out. […] A century of movies and half a century of television have rendered the matter insincere. It is pure artifice. Here are the cars, and here are the owners. Here are the guys, the strangers, whose self-respect is on the line. Someone is going to have to impose his will and win, and the other is going to give way. Popular culture has worn this matter smooth with reiteration, this ancient genetic patrimony that also oils the machinations of bullfrogs and cockerels and stags. (Saturday 86-7)

However, when the street gang fails to adhere to Perowne's middle-class notions of a hostile encounter on the street, which, due to the lack of any personal experience, is strongly informed by TV series, he temporarily loses control and, for the first time in the day, is confronted with real physical violence. Even more importantly, the danger is now no longer channelled through a media broadcast but affects Perowne directly. This fact is significant inasmuch as the threat of violence has been looming ever since Perowne watched the plane on fire descend on London. Yet, counter to previous expectations, the day's threat does not arise from an only vaguely defined, not clearly identifiable Islamic terrorist network but rather from the 'other/Other within'. Strikingly this other as personified by Baxter does, on first sight, not even stand out as being different but rather represents an (albeit under-privileged) member of Perowne's own national background. This circumstance may be read as a further indication of the novel's aim to convey the message that, in particular after 9/11, there is a danger of the public opinion being influenced by stereotypical notions of non-Western realms so that the unknown is immediately (even though mistakenly) identified as the enemy. With respect to Baxter's function in the novel, it has been argued that

> *Saturday* presents a dramatic ethical confrontation between two charac-
> ters within an essentially comic textual structure that obfuscates the se-
> rious social implications of that encounter. [...] The thug Baxter repre-
> sents the ease with which the threatening other can infiltrate the privi-
> leged world of the predominantly middle class.[298]

Seeing that Perowne's confrontation with Baxter and the latter's subsequent breaking into the Perowne's family home is permanently juxtaposed with reflections on the causes of terrorism and speculations on the dangers arising from Islamist terrorism, I'd like to counter this claim by arguing that a sole focus on Baxter as the 'other' in a Lévinasian sense limits the wide range of topics addressed in the novel to a simplistic opposition and reduces the thrust of the text to the somewhat bathetic message of the need to integrate the under-privileged into our present capitalist society. In my opinion, the crucial point of this encounter consists in the ironic twist that, in the end, the real danger does not emanate from the unknown or the exotic but rather from Perowne's very own cultural (if probably not social) sphere.

The two episodes which involve Baxter and Perowne are at the same time closely connected to the opposition between private life and the sphere of work as well as the discussion of sanity. During the clash, Perowne soon detects signs of a medical condition in Baxter, which he quickly diagnoses as indicators of Huntington's disease. Once again, the register of the passage in question – similar to many of the preceding descriptions – is steeped in medical detail. Remembering the symptoms of the disease, "poor self-control, emotional lability, explosive temper, suggestive of reduced levels of GABA among the appropriate binding sites on striatal neurons" (Saturday 91), Perowne quickly recovers his self-confidence as he seems to be treading familiar ground again. Although, for a brief moment, the street has proved a frightening and less secure space than the secluded area of the operating theatre, Perowne's medical knowledge allows him to escape. Apart from providing a counter-point to the potential terrorist threat laid out at the beginning of the novel, the scene furthermore serves to open up the discussion of what constitutes health or, more specifically, sanity.[299] Unsurprisingly, Perowne draws upon Foucault, one of the classical au-

---

[298] Well, Lynn. „The Ethical Otherworld: Ian McEwan's Fiction." *British Fiction Today*. Eds. Philip Tew and Rod Mengham. London and New York: Continuum, 2006. 117-27. 125-6.
[299] This thematic aspect is extended by the subplot dealing with Perowne's mother. Since this episode does not contribute any new aspects to may line of argument, I have largely omitted it here. As far as biographical speculations about parallels between McEwan and his main character

thorities on the topic of madness, whose theories he, however, rejects as whims:[300] "In her second year at Oxford, dazzled by some handsome fool of a teacher, Daisy tried to convince her father that madness was a social construct, a wheeze by means of which the rich – he may have got this wrong – squeezed the poor" (Saturday 92). This laconic dismissal adds to Perowne's self-proclaimed status as a thoroughly 'scientific' person who does not believe in anything but the 'hard facts of life', i.e. biological processes and anatomic details.

The depiction of Perowne as the ultimate embodiment of scientific thought and 'rational' explanations leads to the last binary pair to be analysed in this chapter, the opposition of art versus the (natural) sciences. Within the Perowne family, roles are clearly distributed: Perowne himself, as a neurosurgeon, unquestionably stands for the achievements of modern technology, whereas his father-in-law, the renowned poet John Grammaticus[301], represents the sphere of fine arts and belles lettres. While Perowne's wife, who works as a lawyer for a newspaper, occupies some sort of middle ground, the children obviously follow their grandfather in choosing music and poetry as their respective careers. Nevertheless, the seemingly clear-cut boundaries embodied by the contrast between Henry Perowne and his father-in-law begin to shift when we consider the way in which Perowne is staged in the text, an aspect I will return to below.

The Arnoldian Ideal of Culture – Poetry as an Antidote to Violence

A rather unexpected turn of the plot takes place at the climax of the narrative when Baxter forces his way into the Perowne's family home and threatens members of the family with sheer physical violence. This event turns out to be one of the decisive moments in the story inasmuch as it constitutes one of the

---

are concerned, though, the passage has attracted great attention since McEwan's mother apparently suffered from a comparable medical condition.

[300] As is the case with the vast majority of 'great' writers, theorists, and scientists mentioned in the novel, the reader is only given a very vague idea of their theses and achievements so that the quoting of these authorities at times verges on pure name-dropping. Seeing the variety of fields the novel grazes, one might also argue that citing the respective canonical authorities of each field is intended to create the impression of a firm grounding in 'high-culture'.

[301] John provides yet another example of a speaking name; while John's (unlikely) surname clearly indicates his profession, the street gang is likewise characterised by their lack of a 'proper' name as in Baxter's case ("'Henry Perowne.' - 'Baxter.' - 'Mr Baxter?' - 'Baxter.'", Saturday 87) or as regards their linguistic association with the world of petty crime as is exemplified by Nark.

nodal points which lead to the extreme ambiguity of the text and open up the possibility of two contradictory readings.[302]

Apart from the tension arising from the direct confrontation between the protagonist and the (admittedly far weaker) antagonist, the passage proves memorable in terms of its solution. Having been humiliated and menaced by Baxter, Daisy, acting on her grandfather's cue, succeeds in temporarily defusing the situation. Reciting one of 'her' poems to Baxter, she provokes a sudden mood swing which transforms the aggressive, hostile street thug into a peaceful, guidable person. Strikingly, this effect is not achieved by one of Daisy's own texts – which, in fact, display a certain provocative, flirtatious tone chiming in with the collection's title "My Saucy Bark" – but rather results from her recitation of Matthew Arnold's Victorian poem "Dover Beach". The choice of this particular poem adopts a symbolic quality since at least those readers familiar with Arnold's other writings will immediately associate his name with a very specific and highly eclectic concept of culture. In fact, Arnold is today mainly received as a cultural critic with less attention being paid to his poetic oeuvre. Therefore, the development of the story immediately after Daisy's recitation may be interpreted as a revival of the Arnoldian notion of culture. In discussions of this element of the novel, similarities between the cultural climates informing both Arnold's and McEwan's writings have been highlighted which, in both cases, can be seen to emerge from a moment of cultural crisis[303]. To my assessment, however, a far more important parallel between McEwan's novel and Arnoldian thought consists in the general conceptualisation of the class system as well as the definition of culture and the role ascribed to it within the social system. When analysing the value judgements about Baxter and his background, one immediately notices that *Saturday* unambiguously mirrors the class system set out by Arnold in *Culture and Anarchy*, and that protagonist Henry Perowne seems to share the basic assumptions of this treatise. In *Culture and Anarchy*, Arnold depicts the working classes as intrinsically lazy and uncivilised and sets them in stark opposition to the upper and middle classes. Thus, a dichotomy

---

[302] Undoubtedly, this ambiguity is increased when we take into account previous novels written by McEwan. Even though it is certainly open to debate whether a writer's earlier texts should be considered, it nevertheless seems highly unlikely that, especially in the case of an almost 'canonical' contemporary writer such as McEwan, the readership at large will be able to divest themselves completely from certain expectations and assumptions towards a new book by a well-established author with a very distinct style. It is probably also for this reason that the readiness to search for alternative readings increases since it might definitely strike some recipients as odd that a writer renowned for 'postmodern' fiction should all of a sudden abandon this mode in favour of a comparatively crude, to some extent even reactionary, realism.

[303] On the cultural climate at the time of Arnold's writing, see Machann, Clinton. *Matthew Arnold. A Literary Life*. Basingstoke and London: Macmillan, 1998. 83-4.

unfolds between what Arnold terms the Philistines and the Populace[304]. In general, Arnold presupposes the existence of a tripartite system. Hereby, he distinguishes between "*Barbarians*, *Philistines*, *Populace*, to denote roughly the three great classes into which our society is divided".[305] In the subsequent sections of the study, each class is characterised and ascribed specific features. Via this procedure, Arnold establishes a clear hierarchy between the three strata of society. Unsurprisingly, the working classes are presented as lowest in rank not only because of their meagre financial means but also as far as their 'moral' or 'civilisational' status is concerned since they are associated with excess, a lack of self-control, and an inclination to anti-social behaviour:

> The graver self of the Barbarians likes honours and consideration; his more relaxed self, field-sports and pleasure. The graver self of one kind of Philistine likes fanaticism, business, and money-making; his more relaxed self, comfort and tea-meetings. Of another kind of Philistine, the graver self likes rattening; the relaxed self, deputations, or hearing Mr. Odger speak. The sterner self of the Populace likes bawling, hustling, and smashing; the lighter self, beer.[306]

Perowne apparently shares these notions of the lower classes, whom he considers a potential threat to his own safety due to their alleged inclination to crime and their general unwillingness to participate in the world of business. Moreover, he associates them with drug abuse, anti-social behaviour, and degeneration. As various comments proffered by the protagonist suggest, he thus clearly perceives the lower classes as inferior whereas he constantly prides himself on his own intellectual superiority. In addition to that, the confrontation between members of the Perowne household and Baxter, the representative of the lower echelons of society, reflects the unbridgeable gap between the upper-middle and the lower classes.

The proximity between Arnold's and Perowne's convictions may even be taken one step further. Accordingly, one could argue that *Saturday* acts out Arnold's theorisation of culture inasmuch as Culture (in its approved, canonical form)

---

[304] In *Culture and Anarchy*, Arnold sets out his theory of the English class system identifying three different classes: "Thus we have got three distinct terms, *Barbarians*, *Philistines*, *Populace*, to denote roughly the three great classes into which our society is divided; and though this humble attempt at a scientific nomenclature falls, no doubt, very far short in precision of what might be required from a writer equipped with a complete and coherent philosophy, yet, from a notoriously unsystematic and unpretending writer, it will, I trust, be accepted as sufficient" (Arnold, Matthew. *Culture and Anarchy*. Ed. R. H. Super. Ann Arbor: Michigan UP, ²1980. 143, orig.emphases).
[305] Arnold, ²1980, 143. On first sight, the term Barbarians might appear misleading as it seems to indicate 'uncivilised' behaviour. See pp.140 *et passim* for Arnold's specific use of the term.
[306] Arnold, ²1980, 145.

constitutes an effective antidote to antisocial behaviour, or, in Arnold's terms anarchy. Hereby, it is striking to note that, despite a temporal gap of more than a century, Perowne seems to share the key features of Arnoldian thought. He, for instance, likewise relies on established, canonically approved figures and does not include elements such as popular culture into his definition of 'culture' per se. This impression is backed by his mentioning various examples of Culture (capital c) throughout the novel.[307] He, for instance, flaunts his knowledge of canonical authorities on a variety of subjects which, in his estimation, sets him off from the uneducated members of the lower classes such as Baxter. Especially this stance renders Perowne's conduct reminiscent of Bourdieu's theory of habitus since he is repeatedly portrayed as being engaged in activities which may be considered characteristically bourgeois. Those activities range from driving a showy car, via shopping for exclusive (and costly) seafood – coupled with a knowledge of how to prepare it – to an elaborate taste in music expressed by a preference for selected recordings of classical concerts. All these habits and tastes distinguish Perowne from the so-called lower classes and may be seen as an indicator of his being a 'cultivated' person.

As a closer look at these cherished activities and items reveals, Perowne in general brandishes a notion of culture which verges on the anachronistic since it includes almost exclusively 'classic' Enlightenment authorities, canonical authors, and composers who are widely held as 'culturally valuable'. The protagonist thus obviously promotes a bourgeois ideal of both Culture (in the sense of high culture) and, closely connected to this field, education (in the sense of bildung). This attitude once again chimes in with the definition of culture and its function as set out by Arnold in *Culture and Anarchy*. In Arnold's view, culture may wield a reforming power and therefore represents a possible antidote to anarchy:

> Through culture seems to lie our way, not only to perfection, but even to safety. [...] Thus, in our eyes, the very framework and exterior order of the State, whoever may administer the State, is sacred; and culture is the most resolute enemy of anarchy, because of the great hopes and designs for the State which culture teaches us to nourish. [...] So that, for

---

[307] The only possible exception to this rule may be found in Daisy's poems. These are, however, frequently criticised as too frivolous and as bearing traces of her life in 'morally loose' Paris. Via these associations, they are implicitly marked as inferior to the other texts alluded to in the narrative. With regard to the 'true' source of Daisy's poems Lawson states: "[T]he quotations from Daisy Perowne's debut volume of poetry are actually published lines by Craig Raine, giving the book an additional subplot in which, beyond the plot's call on various sections of the Metropolitan police, you expect the literary cops to arrive and arrest Daisy for plagiarism" (Lawson, Mark. „Against the flow." *guardian.co.uk*. 22. Jan. 2005. 06.12.2007.
<http://books.guardian.co.uk/reviews/generalfiction/0,,1395825,00.html>).

the sake of the present, but far more for the sake of the future, the lovers of culture are unswervingly and with a good conscience the opposers of anarchy.[308]

It is precisely this potentially reforming effect of culture and its power to deflect violence that is orchestrated in *Saturday*. Having heard Arnold's poem recited by Daisy, Baxter abstains from humiliating her any further and, at least temporarily, behaves in a more 'civilised' way.

To shed more light on the conception of culture promoted by the protagonist, it proves worthwhile to examine in greater detail the poem which provokes the all but miraculous mood swing in Baxter. Conveniently, for those readers less well versed in 19th century verse, the full text of the poem is printed as an appendix at the end of the book so that it becomes possible to retrace the scene again and to experience Arnold's poetry at first hand. The poem can therefore be considered as a link between the intratextual and extra- or rather metatextual level since it, on the one hand, constitutes a 'complete' text on its own but, on the other hand, also fulfils a crucial function within the plot structure of *Saturday*. As far as the poem itself is concerned, several aspects prove remarkable: To begin with, in view of the complex web of allusions[309] in "Dover Beach" as well as its use of archaic forms such as "hath" (l. 33), it does come as a surprise that Baxter, a poorly educated street thug, is apparently able to decipher elaborate metaphors and to comprehend the meaning of the whole text on merely hearing it twice. What is more, a simple recitation of a poetic text is claimed to have the power to quell the antagonist's aggression completely, an important precondition for his final overpowering. Lastly, Culture is, in the final instance, represented as the prerogative of the upper or upper-middle classes since canonical poetry is exploited for their ends.

Returning to the general treatment of differential categories in the narrative, I would like to point out that, at the end of the novel, the two formerly opposed spheres of science and art fuse when Perowne employs his medical knowledge for saving lives (even though it is now the villain's life which is imperilled). Hereby, we witness a striking aspect with regard to the device which safeguards the life of a) the upper-classes and b) the lower classes. While the bourgeois Perowne family escapes from the precarious situation by a combination of high culture and cleverness, the villain is ultimately entirely incapacitated and has to

---

[308] Arnold, ²1980, 222-4.

[309] For a conventional analysis of the images and the mythology referred to in "Dover Beach", see, for instance, Zimmermann, Hans-Joachim. „Matthew Arnold. Dover Beach." *Die Englische Lyrik. Von der Renaissance bis zur Gegenwart*. Bd. II. Hg. Karl Heinz Göller. Düsseldorf: August Bagel Verlag, 1968. 162-179.

be salvaged with the help of purely medical/scientific means. This split is likewise indicated by the spatial arrangements in the two passages dealing with the respective threats and afflictions. While Daisy's performance takes place within the family home, the action subsequently moves to the operating theatre for a last time and thus enters the scene where Perowne has already been shown to excel. Daisy's ('cultural') achievement is thus supplemented by Perowne's scientific contribution. The fusion is completed in the final image of Perowne operating on Baxter with the "'Goldberg' Variations" (Saturday 250) playing in the background to accompany the surgery.[310] Seeing this treatment of the art-science-dichotomy throughout the text, one may argue that *Saturday* inscribes itself into a tradition praising a well-rounded education in the sense of bildung, which neglects neither the natural sciences nor canonical culture. Consequently, what seems to be promoted is the bourgeois ideal of the studium generale, a type of formation which aims at producing 'civilised' individuals with at least a basic knowledge in all 'classical' domains of learning and which renders them perfectly equipped for the demands of a career in high society.

To conclude, according to this mode of reading, *Saturday* appears as an all but reactionary text which is intent on re-establishing bourgeois norms and values and promotes an eclectic, elitist concept of culture which exclusively appreciates renowned authorities. While the validity of the bourgeois system of values as well as competing definitions of culture (and the ensuing differentiation between high culture and low culture) are certainly open to debate, there can be no doubt about the problematic and biased quality of the depiction of the lower classes as criminal, uncivilised and, both literally and metaphorically speaking, diseased. The interpretation presented above, however, is by no means the only possible way of approaching the novel. When categorised as a different genre and read against the background of the conventions of the farce, the text appears in a completely different light. It is probably due to this reason that, on its publication, the narrative has provoked very mixed reactions and has been both fêted as another of McEwan's masterpieces and dismissed on the grounds of its moralising stance.

---

[310] Perowne's taste in music has repeatedly been interpreted as yet another sign of his characteristically bourgeoise taste and aspirations.

Reading 'Against the Grain',[311] Saturday as a Satirical Comment on the State of English Society

Even though – as demonstrated above – McEwan's *Saturday* undoubtedly allows for an interpretation which understands the general outline of the plot as an implicit affirmation of bourgeois values, several features may be considered signs of the farcical as well as melodramatic qualities of the text.[312] This 'reading against the grain' has considerable implications for the general interpretation of the novel, especially as far as its stance towards the promoted system of values is concerned.

The proximity to the genre of the farce arises primarily from structural elements, which, combined with further features such as the exaggerated, at times almost parodied characterisation of the protagonist, serve as pivotal points when we approach the novel from this angle.[313] First of all, I would like to draw attention to some terminological problems provoked by the labels 'farce' or 'farcical'. Both as a genre description and in its usage in everyday discourse, the term 'farce' has undergone considerable changes over the centuries. Still, with respect to 'farce' as a literary genre, certain elements prove constant in the definitions brought forward by the respective critics. Those shared features are, on the

---

[311] Some of the arguments brought forward in the following analysis were initially developed during a discussion with members of the Doktorandenkolloquium at Erlangen University. I am grateful to my colleagues and would like to thank them for their suggestions to sharpen my reading of McEwan's *Saturday*. I am particularly indebted to Prof. Feldmann, who encouraged me to attempt a reading against the grain and to approach the text from a completely different angle.

[312] Apparently, one of the possible objections to this approach consists in the fact that farce constitutes an intrinsically dramatic genre, which is intended for the performance on stage. Nevertheless, I would like to argue that similar structures may be found in narrative texts as well and that certain features of the dramatic genre are also transferable to prose writing. The same holds true for melodrama which, usually, likewise refers to a dramatic form of representation but can also be understood as a specific mode the features of which may be found in non-dramatic texts as well.

[313] Not unlike melodrama, the literary genre of farce has, for a considerable period of time, been deemed 'inferior' and thus not worthy of extended critical analysis. Older studies frequently dismiss farce on the grounds that one of its main purposes consists in the creation of laughter. A telling example of this general scepticism towards laughter may be found in Bentley's *The Life of The Drama*, who, in his chapter on farce, comments: "Actually, there is no ratio between enjoyment and the duration of audible laughter. But too little laughter is better than too much. If no comedy, however great, could make people laugh all the time, there could be a great comedy that never made them laugh at all. How often, incidentally, does one really listen to laughter? It is quite an ugly sound. How often has one looked at people while they do it? It is not a pretty sight. And how little laughter there is on stage in a good theatre! The place for laughter is the auditorium" (Bentley, Eric. *The Life of the Drama*. London: Methuen, 1965. 236). Nusbaum Smith offers a critical discussion of this definition of the farce in Nusbaum Smith, Elizabeth. *The Society of the Incomplete: The Psychology and Structure of Farce*. Ann Arbor: University Microfilms, 1970. For the revaluation of farce from the 1970s onwards, see Quaschnowitz, Dirk. *Die Englische Farce im frühen 20. Jahrhundert*. Studien zur Englischen Literatur. Bd. 4. Münster und Hamburg: Lit, 1991. 3-4.

one hand, a challenge to established values and, on the other hand, a general intention to provoke laughter in the audience. Since *Saturday* does not constitute a dramatic farce, I will stick to the definition of farce as a mode of presentation. I hereby follow Mack who characterises farce as "[eine] Darstellungsintention von literarischen Texten verschiedenster Genres [...], die dann einen mehr oder weniger starken 'Farcenaspekt' annehmen."[314] This tendency is clearly detectable in *Saturday*, especially as far the portrayal of the present state of English society is concerned. With respect to the function of this farcical mode, however, Mack highlights the intention to trigger laughter which is not subject to any restrictions – "[Lachen], das keine Dezenzpflicht noch eine sonstige Begrenzung durch gesellschaftliche Wertsetzungen oder Sinnvorgaben kennt, alles und jeden zum Gegenstand nehmen kann und um seiner selbst willen vollzogen sein will"[315]. In this general formulation, the latter feature does not apply to *Saturday* since the incidents related in the text will to my assessment not have a predominantly humorous effect on the reader. If laughter is provoked at all, it is not the tension-abating laughter – i.e. the classical 'comic relief' – but rather a bitter, sarcastic laughter arising from the ironic turn of events.

Yet, seeing the general subject-matter of McEwan's novel, the genre of the farce still appears suitable as an analytic tool since it allows for a reading which understands the story as a comment on the state of a specific strata of English society, in this case the upper-middle classes, and a critical assessment of their reaction to a possible threat to their way of life or a challenge to their (bourgeois) system of values. This assumption is confirmed by the outcome of the plot, which re-establishes normality and order, another element characteristic of the genre of the farce. In view of the fact that the threat of a potential terrorist attack persists nevertheless, the situation remains tenuous, a phenomenon likewise to be observed in many farcical texts:

> It is true, as a matter of observation, that many, though by no means all, farces end with a return to normality. But is it much more than a token restoration of order, a precarious patched-up truce in the perennial fight against the forces of disorder? Isn't what often remains more vividly in the imagination, the darker or wilder events that have preceded it? I would suggest that the best farce leaves us with the troubling thought – what if disorder is the norm, anarchy and chaos do prevail, and the Lord

---

[314] Mack, Gerhard. *Die Farce. Studien zur Begriffsbestimmung und Gattungsgeschichte in der neueren deutschen Literatur*. München: Wilhelm Fink, 1989. 31.
[315] Mack, 1989, 33.

of Misrule has taken over, not just for a festive two hours of make-believe, but indefinitely?[316]

With respect to the effect these farcical elements exert on the reader, it certainly appears doubtful whether the novel's main aim consists in the provocation of laughter. Rather, cynicism and sarcasm – likewise characteristic traits of the farce – seem to dominate here. As I will demonstrate in the following analysis, cynicism plays a particularly significant role with regard to the conclusion of the narrative. For these reasons, I will primarily focus on two aspects in my interpretation of *Saturday* as a farce: These are the structural features of the novel which approximate it to this genre and the depiction of the protagonist.

Melodrama and Farce – Structural and Generic Features in *Saturday*

To begin with, I would like to scrutinise the structural aspects which suggest a reading of *Saturday* as a farcical text. The following paragraphs will therefore highlight those elements which may be understood as a deviation from the 'realist' mode and thus offer a starting point for an interpretation of the novel as a satirical comment on the peculiarities of the upper-middle classes rather than a 'factual' description of the state of English society.

In structural terms, the genre of the farce is characterised by formalistic patterns which are primarily based on figures such as repetition and reversal.[317] In McEwan's text, especially the former feature – repetition – is applied. Accordingly, the novel starts with the protagonist's waking up early in the morning. This plot sequence, which covers the incident with the plane on fire and Perowne's subsequent attempt to gather information via a news broadcast, is followed by a second awakening mirroring the opening scene of the text. Finally, at the end of the narrative, Perowne finds himself once again next to his wife in bed and the reader is thus offered a third awakening scene. In addition to this repeated motive of the protagonist's getting up from bed, the impression of a circular or at least repetitive structure arises from the fact that Perowne's day follows a firm routine consisting of a number of recurrent activities. Among the most prominent of these occupations are his either waiting for the next news broadcast to come up or his actually watching the news. Since those TV broad-

---

[316] Smith, Leslie. *Modern British Farce. A Selective Study of British Farce from Pinero to the Present Day.* Houndmills, Basingstoke and London: Macmillan, 1989. 9.
[317] Mack, 1989, 35.

casts likewise focus on the same topics again and again, the feeling of an ines-capable routine or loop is increased even further.

The overall structure with its circular patterns lends the text a slightly claustro-phobic quality, as, at the end of an eventful day (or, more precisely, the early morning of the next day), the protagonist finds himself in exactly the same situation as at the beginning of the story. Tellingly, Perowne immediately re-sumes his previous conduct by returning to his position as remote observer high above the square. By contrast to the first scene in the novel, though, no unspeci-fied threat looms over the city now; the only living beings to populate the space are the familiar figures of "[t]hree nurses [...] walking across the square, talking cheerfully, heading in the direction of his hospital to start their morning shift" (*Saturday* 279). This restoration of the usual peace and quiet of the place – strik-ingly embodied by figures from Perowne's own profession – indicates that the danger emanating from an unknown other has been warded off and that the potential threat has, for the moment, been pushed back beyond the margins of English society. What is more, the family, despite the turbulent occurrences of the day, has not lost its integrity and survived the 'assault' as an intact entity. With the elimination of the concrete and immediate danger represented by street thug Baxter, the intra-familiar harmony is restored and daily routines are taken up again at once. Even though a certain anxiety persists since the terrorist threat cannot ultimately be resolved, Perowne still musters a confident stance which may be seen to bespeak his belief in his chosen way of life and his bourgeois creed. Although the protagonist admits to the possibility that London might become the target of a terrorist attack, he apparently locates this potentiality in a remote, still hazy future and does not entertain any fears for his safety at this precise moment:

> London, his small part of it, lies wide open, impossible to defend, wait-ing for its bomb, like a hundred other cities. [...] The authorities agree, an attack's inevitable. He lives in different times – because the newspa-pers say so doesn't mean it isn't true. But from the top of his day, this is a future that's harder to read, a horizon indistinct with possibilities. (*Saturday* 276)

Interestingly enough, this reflection on a future extremist attack is immediately preceded by a reference to the threat posed by the 'other within', i.e. the city's criminal, drug abusing lower classes. At the same time, we discover a certain escapist stance which adds to the impression of a claustrophobic setting: In or-der to safeguard themselves against all possible dangers, the Perowne family withdraws into the secluded sphere of the family home, a realm which is me-ticulously shut off from the outside world. The extreme degree of this fortification against the 'evil from without' is symbolised by the security mechanisms installed to protect the inhabitants (even though, all safety precautions turn out to be futile as Baxter's act of housebreaking demonstrates). Hereby, a clear dichotomy is proclaimed between the safety of the inside and the potential dangers intruding from the outside which have to be fended off:

> They [the double front doors] give straight on to the pavement, on to the street that leads into the square, and in his exhaustion they suddenly loom before him strangely with their accretions – three stout Banham locks, two black iron bolts as old as the house, two tempered steel security chains, a spyhole with a brass cover, the box of electronics that works the Entryphone system, the red panic button, the alarm pad with its softly gleaming digits. Such defences, such mundane embattlement: beware of the city's poor, the drug-addicted, the downright bad. (Saturday 36-7)

It was especially after the 9/11 events that this reproach of withdrawing into the secluded, private sphere of the home was raised against the English upper middle-classes, who were sometimes accused of taking refuge in their own sheltered world instead of tackling the social and political problems at hand. In a certain respect, this reaction is mirrored by *Saturday*'s protagonist Henry Perowne. While he does occupy himself with the question of whether a strike on Iraq is legitimate or not, other matters obviously adopt a much greater significance for him. Accordingly, he perceives the demonstration first and foremostly as an annoying obstacle which prevents him from arriving at his weekly squash match on time. Further instances of this concern with private matters abound in the ensuing description of Perowne's daily routine. Despite the risk of an imminent war, which is repeatedly discussed on the news, Perowne seems equally (if not even more) preoccupied with preparations for the family dinner. Additionally, reflections on political issues and social problems are frequently interspersed with musings about the coming evening and potential altercations between members of the family. This tendency to focus on one's own secluded sphere and one's personal concerns proves most prominent when, at the end of the novel, Perowne begins to outline his plans for the future. Here, the terrorist threat and the danger emanating from the city poor are blended into a scenario which deprives the capital of its previous attraction as a dwelling place:

> [A] time will come when they find they no longer have the strength for the square, the junkies and the traffic din and dust. Perhaps a bomb in the cause of jihad will drive them out with all the other faint-hearts into the suburbs, or deeper into the country, or to the chauteau – their Saturday will become a Sunday. (Saturday 276)

In this dystopian scenario, Perowne even ponders the possibility of a relocation to France and the settlement in the chateau inherited from Rosalind's mother. In view of the chateau's location in the French countryside, this image is clearly reminiscent of the topical motive of a pastoral retreat into a bucolic setting. Interestingly enough, increasing the physical distance to a metropolitan area is considered a practicable means of escaping any sort of danger. Accordingly, an imaginable escape route leads via the suburbs to the countryside and, finally, includes a translocation to the remoteness of a chateau on the continent. Undoubtedly, this plan constitutes an intrinsically upper-class solution since the option of moving to a second home is obviously only open to the privileged few.

With regard to the overarching structures organising the general framework of the novel, melodramatic patterns – next to the farcical elements examined above – exert an important influence on the set-up of the plot. As I have already expounded in greater detail, the genre of the farce aims at the provocation of strong effects in the spectator or, respectively, the reader. For this purpose, farcical texts are usually based on formulaic patterns. We encounter the same phenomenon with regard to melodrama, a literary convention which likewise seeks to trigger a number of emotions in quick succession in the audience. Comparable to the means employed by farce, melodrama moreover relies on the exploitation of spectacular, 'non-realistic' plot elements. Therefore, the integration of melodramatic features seems particularly well suited in a farce-like text since both genres follow similar rules: "The starting point in farce may be normality; but that normality is pushed further and further towards absurdity, anarchy, even nightmare. Once a hostage to fortune is given, accident and mischance multiply."[318]

When we compare the formulaic quality of the two genres, it becomes obvious that melodrama resorts to fixed plotlines to an even greater extent. Consequently, its innovative potential is highly limited by rigid conventions at least as far as the structural make-up is concerned. Therefore, almost all examples of texts usually referred to as 'melodrama' or 'melodramatic' exhibit a similar plot structure, which can be summarised as follows: The first scene establishes an idyllic and harmonic tableau which is soon destroyed by the irruption of evil embodied by the villain. This first intervention of the villain leaves the hero temporarily incapacitated. The resulting defencelessness of the heroine allows the villain to pursue his evil machinations without interference from the male counterpart, who struggles to extricate himself from the situation he got caught

---

[318] Smith, 1989, 11.

in. Meanwhile, bereft of any support, the heroine has to fend for herself and to protect her decency and (both bodily and moral) integrity from the villain's assaults. While she succeeds in doing so for a considerable stretch of time, the final scenes bring about a crisis, which proves too grave for the heroine to cope with on her own. Only at this late moment in the drama does the hero finally re-enter the stage so as to accomplish the ultimate defeat of the villain and to restore the initial tableau of harmony, peace, and order. This pattern – especially with regard to the interaction between male and female characters – may be observed in *Saturday* as well with Daisy, acting as the damsel in distress, Baxter embodying the evil villain, and Perowne adopting the role of the hero saving the imperilled women. I will return to the implications of this aspect below.

The Hero – An Embodiment of the 'Benevolent Doctor' or a Version of the 'Mad Scientist'?

Moving away from purely structural elements, I would like to discuss another integral feature which contributes to the farce-like quality of the novel: the characterisation of the protagonist. While the question of his being a likeable character or not ultimately depends on the subjective perception of single read-ers[319], there cannot be any doubt about his displaying certain neurotic traits. Perowne, for instance, exhibits an all but obsessive preoccupation with his own body and constantly checks himself for possible signs of bodily decay. Hereby, almost any physical reaction is interpreted as a potential harbinger of illness and 'degeneration'. Due to his excessive fear of a loss of his physical prowess, Perowne muses constantly about which hobbies he will have to give up in the future, with running the marathon and playing squash being the prime subjects of reflection. His anxiety, however, is not confined to the fields of sports but covers almost any sort of activity such as walking down the stairs at a quick pace:

> He steps out of the bedroom and then, sideways on, skips down the first run of stairs two at a time, without holding down the banister for safety. It's a trick he learned in adolescence, and he can do it better than ever. But a skidding boot heel, a shattered coccyx, six months on his back in

---

[319] Personally, I am convinced that individual preferences should not impact on the interpretation of a literary text. Nevertheless, the potential for identification with the protagonist seems to constitute an important incentive when reading the story and is apparently also likely to exert an influence on the general perception of the text. At least this is implied by Macnaughton's statement: "I was attracted to the central character as a person, and intrigued, as a doctor myself, in McEwan's portrayal of him as a doctor" (Macnaughton, Jane. „Literature and the "good doctor" in Ian McEwan's *Saturday*." *Medical Humanities* 33 (2007): 70-74. 70).

bed, a year rebuilding his wasted muscles – the premonitory fantasy fills less than half a second, and it works. He takes the next flight in the ordinary way. (Saturday 150)

This precaution is only abandoned at moments of competition and rivalry as, for example, during the regular squash match with his colleague from hospital, Jay. Here, the protagonist displays the same obsessive energy and ambition which is likewise discernible in his attitude towards his job. Despite the potential harm great exhaustion might do to his health, Perowne succumbs to the desire to beat Jay in the match: "There's only the irreducible urge to win, as biological as thirst" (Saturday 113). Tellingly, Perowne's wish to triumph is presented as a natural urge, an inbred instinct which spurs him on. Seeing the setting of this scene – an unwatched one-to-one encounter between two opponents – the passage may be read as an ironic comment on Perowne's notion of masculinity. He, for instance, comments explicitly on this lonely, face-to-face encounter and the implications of the fact that "no one's watching, no one cares, not their friends, their wives, their children" (ibid.). He apparently infers from this situation that all the usual obligations can be neglected for the moment and inwardly reduces the confrontation to an almost anachronistic fight between two male contenders who, being freed from any 'surveillance', are no longer obliged to follow the rules of social decorum. Perowne's exaggerated ambition as well as the high significance he ascribes to winning this 'battle' likewise show in remarks such as "Fight to the death" and "No pasaran" (Saturday 112) when the opponents resume their game after a break.

The passages quoted above hint at another of Perowne's greatest anxieties: Even though this fear is never spelled out openly, various scenes suggest that the protagonist cannot bear losing control. Accordingly, anytime he is confronted with a situation he fails to grasp immediately – as is the case with regard to the intention of the pilots of the plane on fire or Baxter's behaviour after the car crash – he tries to rationalise the danger and to find solutions by embedding the menace into a known framework. Therefore, Perowne quickly starts to treat Baxter as a medical case, a move that enables him to employ strategies familiar to him from the daily routine at work. The same desire for control, though on a slightly lower scale, shows in everyday life, both in terms of the professional realm and as far as the private sphere of the family is concerned. The all but obsessive urge to stay in control manifests itself, for example, in the protagonist's attitude towards work and the pleasure he derives from performing in the operating theatre:

At the very first stroke of sunflower yellow on pale skin, a familiar contentedness settles on Henry; it's the pleasure of knowing precisely what

he's doing, of seeing the instruments arrayed on the trolley, of being
with his firm in the muffled quiet of the theatre. (Saturday 250)

Likewise, he states that "[t]hough things sometimes go wrong, he can control
outcomes here, he has resources, controlled conditions" (Saturday 246). An
almost identical conduct may be witnessed in the context of family life: Temporarily troubled by Daisy's failure to inform her parents about her pregnancy,
Perowne quickly adapts to the new situation and at once starts to redraft his
plans for the future. Hereby, the possibly most remarkable aspect consists in the
fact that the main character – by envisioning Daisy and her family living in the
large London home – mentally bends the situation so as to render it compatible
with his desire to have everything unfold under his aegis.

In order to achieve and to subsequently maintain this high level of control, the
protagonist usually resorts to the natural sciences as an analytic tool and an
instrument to rectify problems. In this context, especially the medical field fulfils a double function: On the one hand, scientific means are drawn upon to
remedy illnesses and to render an individual 'functional' again, i.e. able to meet
the requirements of a capital society and its demand for bodies fit for work. On
the other hand, medicine provides an explanatory structure for various processes
including feelings and moods, which are reduced to chemical processes. Accordingly, emotional states are likewise subjected to scientific analysis and
traced back to physiological reactions, especially as far as Perowne's own
moods and feelings are concerned:

> An habitual observer of his own moods, he wonders about this sus-
> tained, distorting euphoria. Perhaps down at the molecular level there's
> been a chemical accident while he slept – something like a spilled tray
> of drinks, prompting dopamine-like receptors to initiate a kindly cas-
> cade of intracellular events. (Saturday 5)

This recurrent use of medical terminology hints at a further element in the depiction of Perowne's character which allows for the reading of *Saturday* as a
farce. In view of his exaggerated ambitions and the zeal he exhibits with regard
to work, he may be considered an embodiment of the topical figure of the mad
scientist.[320] Although he does not endeavour to achieve the creation of life –

---

[320] Perowne, however, does by no means constitute the only stock character in *Saturday*. By
contrast, his father-in-law, marked by the telling name John Grammaticus, may be seen as the
parodistic embodiment of the aloof, vain, and inapproachable poet leading a secluded life in an
old chateau in France, where he indulges in debauched carnal pleasures such as excessive drinking and sex with a number of different women.

one of the topics particularly popular in Gothic renditions of the motive –
Perowne tries to succeed in a similar feat by (re)constructing or re-shaping
'mental life'. Seeing that neurosurgery may result in a complete change of personality in an individual, Perowne in a certain way acts as a creator figure. As
he himself states at the beginning of the novel, his main aim when performing
surgeries consists in the restoration of a patient's ability to work: "he takes over
three hundred cases a year. Some fail, a handful endure with their lights a little
fogged, but most thrive, and many return to work in some form; work – the
ultimate badge of health" (Saturday 24). The wording of this passage proves
highly revealing. As soon as Perowne enters the operating theatre, individuals
turn into mere cases whose minds have to be 'repaired'. The possibility of the
patient's death or their being disabled after the treatment is dismissively referred to as a 'failed case' – as are those operations which do not succeed entirely but leave the patient with 'his lights a little fogged', a euphemistic way of
describing mental impairment. Perowne's attitude to both work in general and
to his patients in particular bespeaks a certain arrogance. This impression is
confirmed by his reflections on the pleasure he derives from his occupation.
Especially the self-stylisation into a godlike messenger may be read as a sign of
his all but succumbing to delusions of grandeur:

> Henry can't resist the urgency of his cases, or deny the egotistical joy in
> his own skills, or the pleasure he still takes in the relief of the relatives
> when he comes down from the operating room like a god, an angel with
> the glad tidings – life, not death. (Saturday 23)

This passage shows most clearly to what an extent Perowne trusts in his own
abilities and which importance he ascribes to the work he does, likening it implicitly to a divine act as is indicated by his entrance staging him as a messenger
of God.

The scene also proves interesting in narratological terms since it may be taken
to include a somewhat sarcastic or ironic element. This sarcasm results from an
ambivalence with regard to the speaking voice which, as in the quote cited
above, cannot be identified with ultimate certainty. Consequently, a tension
arises which is triggered by the narrative's oscillation between two perspectives,
i.e. the view provided by the protagonist as a focalizer figure and the assessment
offered by an extradiegetic-heterodiegetic narrator.

Narratological Structures – Tensions as a Result of the Juxtaposition of Narrative Voices

The all but imperceptible, sometimes not even clearly definable, change between two perspectives composes one of the characteristic features of the novel in terms of its narrative structure. In fact, there are several instances throughout the story which display a great ambiguity as far as the 'source' of specific comments and estimations is concerned. Since those passages offer breaks in the otherwise homogenous narrative perspective, a closer examination of the narratological set-up bears interesting insights. While, throughout the novel, an extradiegetic-heterodiegetic narrator is employed with large stretches of the text being presented from the main character's perspective, the focalization alters inconspicuously at selected passages when it switches from internal focalization to (a potential) zero focalization.[321] The ensuing ambiguity of the narrative voice in specific scenes arises from the impossibility to ascribe certain remarks to either Perowne or an external instance commenting ironically on Perowne's behaviour. Of course, the interpretation of an episode or a statement depends heavily on the decision of who is actually uttering it since those observations can either be understood as an ironic comment by the extradiegetic narrator or they may be read as yet another instance of the protagonist's self-confident affirmations. In fact, the ironic quality of the text only shows when we assume that certain passages display cases of zero focalization. Those brief sections, however, which allow for a 'subversive' reading by opening up the possibility of an ironic break and thereby undermine the novel's unquestioned and all-encompassing endorsement of bourgeois values are restricted to a very limited number of scenes. Moreover, minute attention to almost imperceptible alterations in the narrative structure is necessary since the changes between the two types of focalization are performed within brief space and can therefore easily be lost on the reader.

The ambivalence outlined above is also to be found in the scene commenting on Perowne's attitude towards the demonstrators lining up for the march. The se-

---

[321] It is only at one single point in the story that a passage may be attributed to a focalizer other than Perowne. Nevertheless, the question of focalization here likewise remains ambivalent as Jay's perception of the demonstration against a war on Iraq can also be interpreted as Perowne's listening to his colleague's report: "But, it turns out, he's [Jay] been waiting only ten minutes. He lives across the river in Wandsworth; the march forced him to abandon his car by the Festival Hall. [...] Too young for the Vietnam war protests, he's never in his life seen so many people in one place. Despite his own views, he was somewhat moved. This, he told himself, is the democratic process, however inconvenient. He watched for five minutes, then jogged up Kingsway, against the flow of bodies. He describes all this while Perowne sits on the bench removing his sweater and tracksuit bottom, and making a heap of his wallet, keys and phone to store at one of the corners by the front wall" (Saturday 99-100).

quence is imbued with a slight irony which may be taken as an indication that we are no longer dealing with the protagonist's view of the events but that it is rather an extradiegetic-heterodiegetic narrator commenting on his behaviour. Nevertheless, those signs are not strong enough to rule out their being read as reflections proffered by the main character. Moreover, Perowne's position as focalizer is firmly restored well before the end of the passage:

> A second can be a long time in introspection. Long enough for Henry to make a start on the negative features, certainly enough time for him to think, or sense, without unwrapping the thought into syntax and words, that it is in fact the state of the world that troubles him most, and the marchers are there to remind him of it. The world probably has changed fundamentally and the matter is being clumsily handled, particularly by the Americans. [...] Is he so frightened that he can't face the fact? The assertions and the questions don't spell themselves out. [...] This is the pre-verbal language that linguists call mentalese. (Saturday 80-1)

As a closer analysis reveals, this passage employs the technique of juxtaposing two perspectives without clearly indicating whether the focalizer is 'speaking' or whether the events are presented from the point of view of an instance other than him. To increase this ambiguity, the moment of transition when the instance 'who sees' switches from the protagonist to an external narrator is not indicated. Although this procedure provokes some uncertainty, the strategy as it is employed here may be considered 'non-postmodern' inasmuch as it does not aim at disclosing the unreliability of narration as such or at dismantling the notion of a homogeneous text. To the contrary, the use of a second narrative voice serves to establish a further level of meaning in the text which implicitly questions the protagonist's assumptions and values by sarcastically commenting on them. Thereby, the possibility arises to interpret the text in a less 'conventional' way than the (seeming) affirmation of bourgeois values and the depiction of the life-style of the main character might suggest at first hand. Seen from this angle, the novel offers a critique of the attitudes upheld by the middle-classes, especially with regard to their attempt to come to grips with a menacing situation by way of retreating into the safety of their own sheltered homes. Even though this behaviour might prove understandable from a psychological point of view, the tendency to withdraw from public life and to focus on the confined universe of the family home has nevertheless been decried in the post-9/11 period. The assumption of Perowne's sharing this inclination to shut himself off from the world outside is – next to the safety devices installed at his house – backed by passages in the novel which emphasise the protagonist's search for privacy and his unwillingness to be confronted by 'external' events which are not directly related to his person:

Isn't it possible to enjoy an hour's recreation without this invasion, this
infection from the public domain? [...] He has a right now and then –
everyone has it – not to be disturbed by world events, or even street
events. Cooling down in the locker room, it seems to Perowne that to
forget, to obliterate a whole universe of public phenomena in order to
concentrate is a fundamental liberty. Freedom of thought. (Saturday
108)

Yet another indication of a possible ironic break – and thus an implicit critique
of Perowne's stance – consists in the protagonist's self-stylisation as a decidedly non-literary person; coupled with this feature are a great number of both
open and covert intertextual references. In his musings on his daughter's literary
education and the reflections on his own failure to realise the alleged 'magic' of
great literature, Perowne repeatedly lapses into listing individual authors and
works, a procedure which usually turns into a name-dropping of canonical writers and oeuvres. Thus, within the space of one paragraph, he mentions Conrad,
Brontë, Kafka, Shakespeare, Milton, the King James Bible, Paradise Lost,
Genesis, Hamlet, Browning, Clough, Chesterton and Masefield (Saturday
134).[322] Moreover, Perowne remarks dismissively with respect to the seemingly
petty concerns of nineteenth-century female writers:

[W]hen he made his dutiful attempts on Daisy's undergraduate course
in the nineteenth century novel, he recognised all his mother's themes.
There was nothing small-minded about her interests. Jane Austen and
George Eliot shared them, too. (Saturday 156)

Ironically, Perowne grudgingly grants his mother some intellectual capacity
only retrospectively after having found out that canonical writers considered
some of her allegedly petty issues worthy of treatment as well.

---

[322] Perowne's notion of 'literature', which comprises only canonical authors, as well as his dismissal of theorists who explain 'scientific' phenomena by way of social theories, as is, for instance, the case with Foucault, may be read as an ironic comment on the educational ideal promoted by the upper-middle classes with its strong emphasis on 'bildung' in the bourgeois sense.
Seeing that Daisy has supposedly studied English Literature at Oxford, her having ventured no
farther than the Magic Realists seems highly unlikely. Nevertheless, this fairly 'tame' literary
convention already proves impenetrable to Perowne because of its lack of conventional realism.
Perowne's essentially bourgeois outlook and tastes likewise register in his preference for classical
music (supplemented by a profound knowledge of the differences between individual recordings),
jazz musicians such as Evans, Davis, and Coltrane (Saturday 68), and his adherence to English
Enlightenment authorities such as Newton, Boyle, Hooke, Wren, and Willis (Saturday 168).

In the discussion of literature and literary value, fun is implicitly poked at Perowne's lack of understanding of poetic licence since he fails to see the funny side of Daisy's poem 'The Ballad of the Brain on my Shoe'. He remarks rather vexedly that the "poem [...] resulted from Daisy's visit to the operating theatre one morning to watch her father at work. [...] His daughter was present for a straightforward MCA aneurysm. No grey or white matter was lost" (Saturday 139). This passage moreover contains a 'double irony' which is exclusively accessible to those readers who are not only interested in the text but also in the concomitant material published, for instance, on McEwan's own homepage. Even though the question of whether material other than the text should be taken into account in a literary analysis remains debatable, I would like to argue that the specific reception situation in McEwan's case must not be entirely left out of consideration. Here, it is certainly important to recognise the potential effect technical advancements – especially the possibility to publish material on the internet[323] – have on the process of reading and the perception of a book. Against this background, Perowne's annoyed reaction to Daisy's alleged mis-representation of his operating skills in her poem undoubtedly adopts a pro-nouncedly comic effect.

An additional trigger to start off an ironic reading of the novel arises from the 'meta-literary' element introduced in the text via the description of Perowne's taking up the position of an omniscient narrator without being aware of it him-self. Although the simile is never spelled out openly, Perowne clearly acts as if he – like the 'Olympic' narrator – is hovering over the scene, firmly in control of the events passing under his auspices. This interpretation is backed by the register of the passages in question as well as by the formulations used in spe-cific situations which deal with the protagonist's self-positioning (both in purely spatial terms and as far as his stance towards other characters is concerned). Accordingly, various scenes present Perowne perched above the square watch-ing the events going on below:

> They [two figures] cross towards the far corner of the square, and with his advantage of height and in his curious mood, he not only watches them, but watches over them, supervising their progress with the remote possessiveness of a god. (Saturday 13)

This comparison of Perowne's position with that of a god unquestionably ren-ders the image redolent of the status of an omniscient narrator who 'floats'

---

[323] Roberts, Ryan. *Ian McEwan Website.* 12 Jul 2008. 21.09.2008.
<http://www.ianmcewan.com>.

above the scenery below and exerts control over the proceedings or (as in Perowne's case) succumbs to the illusion of being entirely in charge.

The approximation to an omniscient narrator is extended by one of the protagonist's further concerns: his anxiety about his writing skills. Although the main character stylises himself as the exclusively technically minded, non-literary scientist, he nevertheless prides himself on his own style of writing and feels enraged when hit by a temporary inability to write or, in more literary terms, when confronted with a writer's block. Here, we likewise observe an ambiguity in terms of focalization. Especially the last two sentences imply that we are at this point dealing with an instance of zero focalization rather than a sequence with internal focalization:

> He composed a sentence in his head, then lost it on the page, or typed himself into a grammatical cul-de-sac and had to sweat his way out. Whether this debility was the cause or the consequence of fatigue he didn't pause to consider. He was stubborn and he pushed himself to the end. (Saturday 12)

This statement may undoubtedly be read as a sarcastic comment on Perowne's anxiety to stay in control of anything he does and to govern himself to such an extent that he even tries to force his mind to 'function' according to plan. The use of the word 'debility' adds to the impression that we are presented with a case of zero focalization as it ridicules Perowne's habit of explaining all occurrences in scientific terms and to trace them back to biological functions or rather malfunctions. The narratological set-up of this passage moreover serves to create an ironic distance to the protagonist.

Yet another distancing mechanism (and therefore a potential trigger for ironic breakage) is located on an extratextual level. Since McEwan openly promotes Perowne as his alter ego and refers to his proximity to the character both in interviews and on his official website – the latter offering, for instance, "Henry Perowne's Fish Stew. From Ian McEwan's novel *Saturday* with revisions by the author"[324] – the contrast in their respective attitudes towards literature becomes

---

[324] Roberts, Ryan. *IanMcEwan Website*. 12 Jul 2008. 30.12.2008.
<http://www.ianmcewan.com/bib/articles/fishstew.html>. Likewise, in an interview with Weich, McEwan declares that "[Saturday] is a departure from me in that its central character lives in my house, in my square. He's a brain surgeon, so I've been going and watching very closely major brain surgery. [...] there's a certain kind of hard-to-describe, selfless elation that comes occasionally with writing, for example, certainly not all the time, but in moments, half hours, two-hour stretches, when you don't even know you exist. [...] I was looking for a kind of work that might have to draw on this kind of resource daily, and I decided that surgery would fit the bill. And it's

even starker. On an intratextual level, McEwan's 'presence' as an author informs the text in the form of a literary 'joke' only to be grasped by those readers who are familiar with his other books and who have a basic knowledge of the development of British fiction over the last decades. Recipients who have followed the proceedings during this timespan will immediately recognise the covert reference to *The Satanic Verses* and *The Child in Time* in the following passage, in which Perowne reviles the non-realistic approaches in books by twentieth-century writers:

> In more than one, heroes and heroines were born with or sprouted wings – a symbol, in Daisy's terms, of their liminality; naturally, learning to fly became a metaphor for bold aspiration. Others were granted a magical sense of smell, or tumbled unharmed out of highflying aircraft. One visionary saw through a pub window his parents as they had been some weeks after his conception, discussing the possibility of aborting him. (Saturday 67)

At this point, an interconnection shows between, on the one hand, the self-presentation of a writer and, on the other hand, strategies employed in the marketing of a book. Seeing the increasing influence of publishing houses who, by now, frequently accompany the publication of a book by an established author with extensive marketing campaigns, the potential effects of these PR efforts on the reader must not be underestimated. I would like to argue that the impact of the (self)presentation of an author may reach such an extent that it can even influence the assessment of specific scenes. Accordingly, having read the information provided on the author's website, a reader might understand the following passage as an ironic comment or covert joke by the author: "This notion of Daisy's, that people can't 'live' without stories, is simply not true. He is living proof" (Saturday 68). On a purely intratextual level, the statement provides yet another of Perowne's self-proclamations as a fully-fledged scientist and non-literary person. Against the background of McEwan's self-stylisation as Perowne's alter ego, however, the passage assumes an ironic quality as writing literature is exactly what McEwan does for to earn his livelihood – which renders him the living proof of the contrary of what is proclaimed in the quotation.[325]

---

turned out to be absolutely correct" (Weich, Dave. „Ian McEwan, Reinventing Himself Still." *Powell's Books*. 30.12.2008. <http://www.powells.com/authors/mcewan.html.>). The parallel is made even more prominent by Fray, who quotes McEwan with respect to his experiences in the Feburary 15 march: """I was Henry Perowne by then," he says. "I looked like I was on it. Mentally I was somewhere else"" (Fray, Peter. „The enduring talent of Ian McEwan." 07.10.2007<http://www.theage.comau/articles/2005/01/28/1106850082840.html>).
[325] In general, I would like to argue against taking into account a writer's comments on his work or speculating on possible effects on the readership. In view of the almost aggressive marketing

The Consolidation of an Arnoldian Notion of Culture as a Cure-all Remedy

As has been demonstrated above, several episodes adopt a different meaning when read against the background of the generic conventions of melodrama and farce. This is also the case with the climactic showdown when Baxter breaks into the family home. It is at this moment that the melodramatic element in *Saturday* shows best since the passage is modelled precisely in tune with the formulaic patterns employed in melodrama. Hereby, the individual stages of progression and the respective turns of the plot are clearly discernible: First, a harmonious, peaceful situation is established with the family gathering in the living room, getting ready for a shared meal. This tableau is destroyed when Baxter forces entry and threatens Perowne and his family. With his sidekick Nige keeping the men at check and thereby preventing the two potential heroes from protecting the heroines, Baxter first menaces Perowne's wife and subsequently forces his daughter Daisy to undress. In doing so, he inadvertently reveals her pregnancy. Conforming to the plot requirements of melodrama, Daisy, acting on her own, manages to defuse the situation by taking up her grandfather's cue and choosing a poem different from the one Baxter actually expects her to read. Reciting Matthew Arnold's "Dover Beach" from memory, she succeeds in provoking a mood swing in Baxter which temporarily renders him less aggressive. This motive of Baxter being assuaged by a canonical 19th century poem renders the novel particularly suitable for a farcical reading since, if considered in terms of 'realism' or 'credibility', the scene as such carries a highly bathetic note with its depiction of a street thug being overwhelmed by the reforming powers of Arnoldian poetry. Seen within the context of melodrama and farce, though, i.e. against the background of two genres which generally display a strong inclination to exaggeration, distortion, and sarcasm, the poem adopts a significant function.

Above, I have already hinted at the improbability of Baxter's grasping the meaning of Arnold's poem after merely having listened to it twice. In this respect, Baxter defies Arnold's description of the working classes, which the latter characterises as a group of people "which, raw and half-developed, has long lain half-hidden amidst its poverty and squalor, and is now issuing from its hiding-place to assert an Englishman's heaven-born privilege of doing as he likes"[326]. In this context, Arnold does allow for certain deviations from this pattern by assuming that a number of aliens exist in each class, i.e. "persons who are mainly led, not by their class spirit, but by a general *humane* spirit, by the love of human perfection; [...] this number is capable of being diminished

---

and the repeated invitations to draw parallels between the author and his character in the case of *Saturday*, however, it seems impossible to completely ignore these layers of meaning which unfold in the interplay between text and 'metatext' or possibly even text and 'reality'.
[326] Arnold, ²1980, 143.

and augmented"[327]; yet, Baxter's general conduct does not single him out as such an exception. In spite of this, Arnold's poetry allegedly still yields a civilising power which proves so pervasive that it is capable of achieving a profound mood swing even in such a comparably uneducated and 'uncivilised' person as Baxter.[328]

Another important aspect I have not covered so far is Perowne's reaction to the poem. Even though less spectacular than Baxter's response to the verse, Perowne's perception likewise proves revealing. While his daughter's previous attempts to provide him with a basic literary education failed, the protagonist finally finds an access to poetry via Matthew Arnold. In view of the fact that Matthew Arnold is today mainly received as the author of theoretical treatises – the most widely known being probably those concerned with the function of culture – this element proves significant inasmuch as it sheds light on Perowne's own conception of culture and illuminates the system of values he endorses. Although he believes to be touched by one of his daugther's writings, it is once again a canonical authority he responds to.

The incident centring on Baxter ends with a further twist. Once the heroine has warded off the immediate danger to her life, the heroes take over again and – in tune with the melodramatic formula – overpower the villain. Ironically, the 'culturally-minded' heroes themselves do no longer rely on the reforming power of Culture but rather resort to sheer physical violence by pushing Baxter down the stairs and (inadvertently) causing severe bodily harm. Thus, even though culture, or, more precisely poetry, serves as an antidote to violence and antiso-

---

[327] Arnold, ²1980, 146, orig. emphasis.

[328] In view of the second thematic line in the novel, i.e. the potential Islamistic threat, Baxter has been interpreted as Saddam's alter ego. Head, for instance, claims that "[i]n pursuing the allegorical dimension, however, readers may inevitably detect a process of demonization conducted from a Western perspective, most especially in the parallel between Baxter and Saddam Hussein. We may wonder if there is an invitation to speculate on the possibility of a common psychological disorder" (Head, Dominic. *Ian McEwan*. Manchester and New York: Manchester UP, 2007. 181). I would like to contradict this interpretation, which, to my estimation, exaggerates the threat posed by Baxter and his gang. Moreover, in Baxter's case, we are dealing with a clearly defined medical condition, whereas assumptions on the mental state of the Iraqi dictator do retain a highly speculative element. Simultaneously, I shy from equating Baxter's offence, a beating on the street and the subsequent breaking-and-entering, with the mass murder committed in Iraq. Furthermore, I would like to argue that the reference to *Culture and Anarchy* is far more visible in this scene than with respect to the mass demonstrations in Hyde Park. In my assessment, the incident with Baxter primarily serves to underscore the reforming function of culture rather than to "emphasize the unpredictability and subjectivity of the aesthetic response, as well as the contingency of life" (Head, 2007, 189). In his review of the novel, Tait, by way of an aside, hints at the problematic use of the poem: "[T]here are thematic resolutions which seem forced, episodes and ethical dilemmas which are not quite believable: a violent stand-off, for instance, in which a reading of Matthew Arnold's poem "Dover Beach" plays a pivotal role..." (Tait, 2005).

cial behaviour, this remedy works only temporarily and proves insufficient to resolve the situation as a whole. In the end, the villain receives his due (physical) punishment, the danger to Perowne's family is eliminated, and order is restored with Perowne being re-established as the head of the family.

On the last pages of the novel, a moral dimension opens up via the question of revenge: Even though Perowne declares that he will refrain from pushing legal charges against his opponent, he is certainly aware of the fact that Baxter's medical condition will, in the long run, constitute a sufficient punishment for him:

> By saving his life in the operating theatre, Henry also committed Baxter to his torture. Revenge enough. And here is one area where Henry can exercise authority and shape events. He knows how the system works – the difference between good and bad care is near-infinite. (Saturday 278)

Against the background of these reflections I suggest that Perowne's decision to operate on Baxter allows for more interpretations than merely a reading which sees it as an attempt to make amends or to finally be reconciled with the 'other' by saving his life. In view of Perowne's strong sense of duty and his all but Puritan work ethos, the decision to return to the hospital and to perform the required procedure may be seen to be motivated by Perowne's inclination to follow firm principles and his desire to contribute to the smooth running of the 'firm'. This assumption is in tune with Perowne's reaction to his wife's anxious speculation that he might be planning some sort of revenge:

> Even as he frames the question, he knows he's going; superficially, it's simple momentum – Jay Strauss and the team will already be in the anaesthetist's room, starting work on his patient. Henry has an image of his own right hand pushing open the swing doors to the scrub room. In a sense, he's already left, though he's still kissing Rosalind. He ought to hurry. He murmurs, 'If I'd handled things better this morning, perhaps none of this would've happened. Now Jay's asked me in, I feel I ought to go. And I want to go.' (Saturday 239-40)

As to the great professional pride which Perowne displays in other situation, it is certainly open to debate whether his motivation results from his obligation to the Hippocratic oath or whether he is rather spurred on by the need to eliminate an impediment which might prevent 'his firm' from running without interruption. It is for this reason that I would like to argue against a reading which understands Perowne's decision to operate on Baxter as an atonement for the harm done to him previously. As far as far as the question of revenge is concerned, though, the ultimate answer to this problem must be left to the individual reader.

A further controversial aspect in the episode involving Baxter consists in the general approach and stance towards alterity flaunted by the middle classes. Unless one chooses to read *Saturday* as a farce – with the concomitant exaggerations pertinent to the genre – the depiction of middle class behaviour proves highly problematic since both the 'ethnically' other and the 'socially' other are treated as potential sources of danger that need to be either kept at bay or to be brought under permanent control. What renders the approach towards difference in terms of social class even more provocative is the representation of the other as either mentally ill or morally depraved.[329] Especially with regard to Baxter, the novel allows for a very caustic reading of the middle classes' attitudes towards alterity as exemplified by the lower classes. To begin with, Perowne immediately associates the lower classes with crime, laziness, and a general lack of self-discipline. With Baxter embodying the lower classes, the contrast between Perowne's realm of the bourgeoisie and the living conditions among the lower echelons of society becomes even more pronounced as the villain is described as mentally incapacitated by his disease.[330] In the confrontation between Perowne and Baxter, a strict hierarchical scheme unfolds. Even though Perowne is temporarily imperilled by Baxter's physical strength and threatened by his aggressiveness, he finally succeeds in overcoming him thanks to his intellectual abilities. Thus, while the power positions are briefly reversed by Baxter's resort to sheer violence, Perowne soon re-gains the upper hand due to his superior intelligence. On this plane, Perowne does not perceive Baxter as a true antagonist from the start. This impression is confirmed by the solution of the novel when Baxter is sent to hospital for brain-surgery. Although the procedure is, by the inherent logics of the plot, necessitated by Baxter's fall down the stairs, the idea that Baxter's brain needs 'setting right' is certainly likewise implied by this turn of the story.

---

[329] Even though it is undeniably true that the respective exponents of the lower classes with whom Perowne comes to interact **are** in fact dangerous, hostile, and criminal, I still deem it a striking feature of *Saturday* that no other representatives of the working classes are included or even mentioned. For this reason, one might draw certain conclusions about the protagonist's general attitude towards the lower classes.

[330] Apparently, this plot element proves reminiscent of the discourse of degeneration which was particularly virulent in late 19th century England, i.e. precisely at the time of Arnold's writing. In literary engagements with the topic, we find numerous examples of villains who are bodily deformed and thus bear an outwardly visible sign of their interior depravation.

'Defusing' Alterity by Rendering the Other Familiar

A closer analysis of the scenes in which the protagonist tries to cope with foreignness or alterity reveals that an identical strategy is applied both with regard to the ethnically other and with respect to the socially other. At the beginning of the novel, the differential category of ethnicity is highlighted via the opposition between East and West opened up by the protagonist's observation of a plane on fire. Set against the background of the 9/11 attacks, the atmosphere in the narrative is, from the very beginning, imbued with the omnipresent fear of an imminent attack on the English capital. For this reason, the protagonist at once associates the burning plane with a terrorist threat and assumes that what everyone had feared has finally become reality.[331] Despite the lack of reliable information on the true causes of the fire, speculations abound in the news coverage of the incident, a feature I have already discussed above.

What proves remarkable with regard to the treatment of alterity in this context are the strategies employed for its 'defusion'. As I have explained previously, alterity per se is repeatedly presented as a source of potential danger to 'Western' society. This air of a looming threat persists even after the immediate danger has been erased. Here, one may once again observe the phenomenon that the cases of alterity cited – Sadam Hussein constituting a prime example – in fact constitute a major menace to (Western) societies and that fear and possibly even hostility towards such regimes may be considered a justified reaction. Nevertheless, I likewise want to point out that the book offers hardly any counter-examples so that the impression of a malevolent and threatening other all but imposes itself.

As far as the initial menace is concerned, it is striking to note that, while still in the process of attempting an emergency landing, the plane is identified as an ostensible instrument of terrorists at once before there has even been a chance to clarify the cause of the fire leading to the near catastrophe. Moreover, the alleged terrorists are, without any real evidence, automatically situated in an Islamistic context. Consequently, a distinct dichotomy between East and West

---

[331] I am grateful to Prof Blaicher for pointing out that in the cultural climate succeeding the 9/11 attacks, the immediate association of a burning plane with a potential terrorist attack must not per se be read as a sign of a general hostility towards or suspicion of the East. While I completely agree with this supposition, I would nevertheless like to emphasise that, within the logics of the diegesis as transmitted via the news broadcasts, the opposition between East and West with the concomitant value judgements and hierarchisations is deliberately maintained; accordingly, hardly any attempts are made to rectify the sensationalist speculations on the incident aired previously. In fact, news coverage reporting on the true background of the alleged terrorist attacked is ultimately relegated to the end of the broadcast, whereas the initial announcement was placed in the prime slot starting the programme.

unfolds whereby the Eastern stance is depicted as potentially scheming and inimical towards the 'Western' way of life. Despite all hypotheses to the contrary, the crew of the plane ultimately turn out not to be connected to any Islamistic terrorist networks whatsoever. What renders them 'other', however, is the fact that they hail from the 'margins' of Western society. As first media broadcasts report: "It's a cargo plane, a Russian Tupolev on a run from Riga to Birmingham" (Saturday 35). Later on in the story, the crew's national and cultural background is defined with greater precision:

> They are not, the pilot explains through a translator, Chechens or Algerians, they are not Muslims, they are Christians, though only in name, for they never attend church and own neither a Koran nor a Bible. Above all, they are Russians and proud of the fact. They are certainly not responsible for the American child pornography found half-destroyed in the burned-out cargo. They work for a good company, registered in Holland, and their only responsibilities are to their plane. And yes, of course, child pornography is an abomination, but it's not part of their duties to inspect every package listed on the manifest. (Saturday 179-80)

Obviously, this passage oozes with national stereotypes: First, the Russian pilot has to rely upon the support of a translator in order to get his statement through. Seeing the status of English as the standard language in aviation (as well as its function as a 'world language'), the pilot is singled out by his apparent lack of fluency in the lingua franca of his profession. Due to his utterance's being merely summarised by a translator, his justifications are reduced to a few sentences which focus on the differential categories the pilot refers to in order to distance himself from the charges brought forward against him. The aspects stressed by the translator mirror a specific ('Western') world picture in which some nationalities and religions are classified as potentially dangerous, whereas others are considered 'safe'. The pilot is apparently aware of this fact since he eagerly underscores that he is neither Chechen, nor Algerian, nor Muslim – collective identities likely to provoke fear in the current political setting. By contrast, he belongs to a Christian denomination, albeit only by name, thus no danger of extremism arises from that front either. Still, this revelation does not automatically turn the pilot into a fully-integrated member of Western society, which he had previously been suspected to attack. Apart from his insufficient command of the English language, his outsider status is indicated by his pride of being Russian, which, already in purely geographical terms, positions him on the fringes of European society. Moreover, even though the responsibility for his cargo does apparently not form part of the requirements in his contract, the pilot's reputation is tainted by his having transported some American child pornography.[332] This impression is strengthened by the automatic dismissal of child pornography as an abomination. In addition to that, the company's merely being *registered* in Amsterdam may be considered another indicator of the crew's potential involvement in non-legal or semi-legal activities. What proves equally interesting in this context is the 'West's' reaction to the supposed threat (as may be derived from the points highlighted in the media broadcasts). As the TV report stresses, the pilots do not entertain any connections to terrorist networks but rather stem from a territory situated on the boarder of Europe. Due to this location, the alterity confronting Western societies is rendered semi-familiar and therefore immediately judged as more manageable since one is not confronted with an entirely foreign cultural context. Hereby, great emphasis is placed on the fact that, thanks to the expert handling of the case by the authorities in charge, no harm has been done to any English citizen, that the danger has been eliminated, and that the case can finally be closed with correct procedures having been followed. Thereby, both the 'West's' security and its moral integrity are restored.

The same strategy of embedding alterity into a familiar context in order to eliminate its menacing aspects may be witnessed with respect to two plot elements already quoted previously: These are the imminent war on Iraq and Perowne's scrape with Baxter. Obviously, the former topic is closely related to the tensions arising from the East-West-dichotomy outlined above. At various points in the novel, official statements on the perceived inevitability of a war on Iraq intersect with both Perowne's personal reflections on the subject and the opinions brought forward by other characters (reported indirectly via Perowne's estimation of them). While Perowne himself takes a comparatively balanced stance on US politics and ponders the possibility that a military intervention might ultimately lead to a liberation of the Iraqi people, all other figures cited in the book – including Perowne's own children – denounce any form of violence. Still, despite these different opinions with regard to the war on Iraq, all of the characters are without doubt firmly integrated in the Western system of values with its emphasis on rights such as free speech, unimpeded self-expression, and a democratic government. Perowne's own unshakeable grounding in Western 'culture' and his firm belief in its applicability as a benchmark by which to judge other realms shows openly in several passages as, for instance, when he rants against Islamic dress codes enforced on women:

> How dismal, that anyone should be obliged to walk around so entirely
> obliterated. At least these ladies don't have the leather beaks. They

---

[332] Undoubtedly, the motive of a Russian pilot (inadvertently?) transporting US-American child pornography leaves ample room for speculation and allows for a variety of readings including a covert blow at America's alleged moral integrity and superiority.

really turn his stomach. And what would the relativists say, the cheerful pessimists from Daisy's college? That it's sacred, traditional, a stand against the fripperies of Western consumerism? But the men, the husbands – Perowne has had dealings with various Saudis in his office – wear suits, or trainers and tracksuits, or baggy shorts and Rolexes, and are entirely charming and worldly and thoroughly educated in both traditions. Would they care to carry the folkloric torch, and stumble about in the dark at midday? (Saturday 124)

At the same time, this scene once again provides an example of Perowne's essentially conservative stance and confirms his belief in 'traditional' values.

A remarkable aspect with regard to Perowne's endeavours to figure out which political measures should adequately be taken to alleviate the situation in Iraq consists in his desire to understand the 'nature of evil'. Interestingly enough, Saddam Hussein comes to serve as the ultimate symbol of evil. As has been diagnosed with respect to the Islamic world in general, we may here detect another attempt to familiarise alterity in order to render it more understandable and, for that matter, less frightening and easier to control. Apparently, Perowne considers a detailed knowledge of the atrocities perpetrated by the regime as a key to understanding the person behind those cruelties:

> Henry became acquainted with the sickly details of genocides in the north and south of the country, the ethnic cleansing, the vast system of informers, the bizarre tortures, and Saddam's taste for getting personally involved, and the strange punishments passed into law – the brandings and amputations. (Saturday 72-3)

The exclusive reference to the dictator by his first name may be seen as a further method in 'familiarising' the threatening other.[333] In the process of coming to terms with the unknown and potentially harmful other, a strong focus is placed on Hussein's face which is employed as a pars pro toto. It is primarily via the dictator's countenance that Perowne tries to understand his true motives. In the following, these attempts to decipher Hussein's features lead to a discussion of the perception of human faces in general and a reflection on the possibility to glean information about a person's character from them:

---

[333] The practice of using their first names when referring to a politician is much more common in English-speaking contexts than is the case in, say, German news coverage. This aspect needs to be taken into consideration in speculations about using first names as a strategy of familiarising or even belittling a public figure.

> For all the difficulties, the instinctive countermeasures, we go on watching closely, trying to read a face, trying to measure intentions. Friend or foe? It's an ancient preoccupation. And even if, down through the generations, we are only right slightly more than half the time, it's still worth doing. More than ever now, on the edge of war, when the country still imagines it can call back this deed before it's too late. (Saturday 141)

This strategy of instrumentalising the face as a symbol is likewise described by Judith Butler in her collection of essays entitled *Precarious Life*. Apart from an analysis of the practice of employing faces as symbols, Butler's essay "Precarious Life" offers an important distinction between, on the one hand, the 'humanising' effects of faces and, on the other hand, their being rendered symbols of ultimate evil and danger:

> But is the face humanizing in each and every instance? [...] Do we encounter those faces in the Levinasian sense, or are these, in various ways, images that, through their frame, produce the paradigmatically human, become the very cultural means through which the paradigmatically human is established? Although it is tempting to think that the images themselves establish the visual norm for the human, one that ought to be emulated and embodied, this would be a mistake, since in the case of bin Laden or Saddam Hussein the paradigmatically human is understood to reside outside the frame: this is the human face in its deformity and extremity, not the one with which you are asked to identify. Indeed, the disidentification is incited through the hyperbolic absorption of evil into the face itself, the eyes.[334]

In Perowne's reflections on the effect of faces and his efforts to understand how Saddam Hussein's mind works, we find both of the elements analysed by Butler: To some extent, the dictator is de-humanised by his being reduced to a symbol of evil. At the same time, however, alterity becomes personified and is thereby given a seizable form. The formerly unspecified, mysterious threat is thus literally given a name and can, from this moment on, be targeted and, possibly, eliminated.

The same strategy is applied in the incident with Baxter. Remarkably, this occurrence is implicitly linked to the potential Islamic danger. Once the question of whether the pilots of the plane had intended to perpetrate an attack on Lon-

---

[334] Butler, Judith. *Precarious Life. The Powers of Mourning and Violence*. London and New York: Verso, 2004. 143.

don is negated, the threat of violence resurges in the person of the street thug. This move constitutes one of the more surprising turns of the plot as the real danger emanates from the 'other within' rather than from the 'more likely' outside source. From now on, the second differential criterion which heavily informs the novel – class – begins to play an increasingly significant role. Even though we are here no longer dealing with 'cultural' differences, I would like to argue that the term 'alterity' may still be applied as basic features such as the construction of autostereotypes as well as the establishment of hierarchical binary structures are undoubtedly present. Once more, roles are distributed fixedly and connected with implicit value judgements. While Perowne – despite his anger about the slight damage done to his car – acts in a reflected, 'civilised' way, Baxter is depicted as the stereotypical underclass thug. In this context, the choice of words in Perowne's account of his opponent's looks proves highly revealing:

> He's a fidgety, small-faced young man with thick eyebrows and dark brown hair razored close to the skull. The mouth is set bulbously, with the smoothly shaved shadow of a strong beard adding to the effect of a muzzle. The *general simian air* is compounded by sloping shoulders, and the built-up trapezoids suggest time in the gym, *compensating for his height perhaps*. [...] Perowne is familiar with some of the current literature on violence. It's not always a pathology; self-interested social organisms find it rational to be violent sometimes. Among the game theorists and radical criminologists, the stock of Thomas Hobbes keeps on rising. *Holding the unruly, the thugs, in check* is the famous 'common power' to keep all men in awe – a governing body, an arm of the state, freely granted a monopoly on the legitimate use of violence. (Saturday 87-8, my emphases)

The first striking aspect of this passage consists in its portrayal of Baxter as simian-like. Obviously, the use of the adjective "simian" locates him on the margins of 'humanness' and approximates him to the animal kingdom. We, therefore, witness the same strategy in coping with alterity as in the case of the potential terrorists. Each time, the threatening other is embedded into a controllable framework and thereby brought under control. Immediately after having classified Baxter and after having ascribed him his (inferior) place, Perowne stops to consider the 'villain' as a real opponent but rather sees him as a medical or sociological case. This transformation of an unestimable menace into a medical problem re-establishes Perowne's superior position as it allows him to apply familiar strategies and to thereby handle the crisis in an expertly way.[335] As

---

[335] Here, the underclasses are obviously perceived as a world apart. This perception is suggested by statements such as "drug dealers and pimps, among others who live beyond the law, are not

mentioned before, this strategy of turning to the natural sciences for solutions proves characteristic of Perowne's approach in dealing with any type of difficulty.

Apparently, the general strategy of integrating the other into a familiar framework and to thereby rein in the more threatening aspects of difference works in a variety of contexts. Irrespective of whether the protagonist is faced with ethnic or class differences, the first step in the process of 'defusing' the dangerous unknown always consists in transforming 'foreignness'[336] into 'alterity'. This move solves the dilemma of having to deal with an entity which cannot be subsumed under one of the naturalised binary oppositions promoted by the protagonist. These binary oppositions in turn play an important role in the formation of communities since they serve as a basis for the definition of members and non-members: "There are friends and enemies. And there are *strangers*. Friends and enemies stand in an opposition to each other. The first are what the second are not, and vice versa."[337] For that matter, in order to fend off any form of 'foreign' intrusion into the community as well as to prevent potential classificatory uncertainties, all 'newcomers' have to be labelled immediately: "Community effectively defended its dense sociability by promptly reclassifying the few stranges coming occasionally into its orbit as either friends or enemies."[338] What should likewise be taken into account here is a point emphasised by Feldmann and Böhm who state that the 'foreign' as such is, by definition, inaccessible:

> Das Fremde definiert sich in Abgrenzung von seinem Komplementär-begriff, dem Eigenen, und ist zu unterscheiden vom Anderen im Sinne eines *alter ego*, das auf ein *ego* bezogen bleibt, während das Fremde für das Eigene als (zunächst) nicht anschlussfähig betrachtet wird.[339]

---

inclined to dial nine-nine-nine for Leviathan, they settle their quarrels in their own way" (Saturday 88). For this reason, the use of the term 'alterity' appears adequate in this context. The sarcastic tone of Perowne's comment furthermore highlights the system of values endorsed by the protagonist and indicates that he is wont to draw a clear line between the educated ('good') upper-middle classes and the violent, incontrollable street scum.

[336] Strikingly, there exists no adequate translation for the German term 'Fremdheit' in the English language. Even though 'foreignness' and 'strangeness' express the quality of 'not-being-familiar', they do not bear the same complex web of connotations as the German term. Moreover, in an institutional context, 'alterity' has been established as a rough equivalent to Fremdheitsstudien despite the fact that, on closer analysis, 'Fremdheit' and 'Alterität' turn out to denote different states.

[337] Bauman, Zygmunt. „Modernity and Ambivalence." *Global Culture. Nationalism, Globalization and Modernity.* Ed. Mike Featherstone. London *et al.*: Sage, 1990. 143-69. 143, orig. emphasis.

[338] Bauman, 1990, 151.

[339] Böhm, Nadine und Doris Feldmann. „Fremdheit." *Lexikon der Bibelhermeneutik.* Hg. Oda Wischmeyer *et al.* Berlin: Walter de Gruyter, 2009 (i.E.).

Accordingly, foreignness may be turned into alterity via two steps. First, the foreign other has to be identified as a person. This state may be achieved by giving it a face and thus turning it into a graspable, or at least nameable entity. Secondly, further characteristic features are supplemented such as nationality, religion, and class, which locate the formerly foreign into a context that functions along well-known logics. With regard to the concept of alterity, I follow Feldmann and Böhm's definition who qualify alterity, as

> den Anderen von zweien, wobei die wahrgenommenen oder unterstellten Differenzen eine relationale Selbstdefinition über Abgrenzung erlauben. Im Gegensatz zum Fremden (*alios* oder *xenos*) gilt *alter* nicht als ein beliebiger Anderer, sondern als ein *alter ego*, als der zweite von zwei einander zugeordneten und prinzipiell gleichartigen Identitäten.[340]

The second decisive step in the elimination of foreignness is the attribution of 'gradable' features which allow for the establishment of binary oppositions. These binaries are structured in a hierarchical way with the 'familiar' side being identified with positive values such as uprightness, civilised behaviour, and health, whereas negative qualities such as an inclination to crime, deceitfulness, and (mental) illness are located on the side of the formerly foreign, a practice well-known from the construction of auto- and heterostereotypes.[341] In *Saturday*, we find this procedure both with respect to the 'external other', i.e. the alleged threat arising from Islamist terrorism, and the 'other within', here represented by the lower classes.

From a moral standpoint, this general practice of attributing negative values to the 'other' and of presenting alterity as inferior is, of course, highly problematic and has been denounced repeatedly from various academic positions, especially in the fields of Gender and Postcolonial Studies.[342] Nevertheless, the inferiorisation – or even pathologisation of the other – seems to constitute a widespread social phenomenon still to be observed in Western societies:

---

[340] Böhm, Nadine und Doris Feldmann. „Alterität." *Lexikon der Bibelhermeneutik*. Hg. Oda Wischmeyer *et al*. Berlin: Walter de Gruyter, 2009 (i.E.).

[341] I do not want to imply that the 'intention' of the text lies in a general denigration of alterity. In the examples discussed here, however, patterns in dealing with otherness invariably follow the same lines which include, among other things, a hierarchisation as well as a valorisation.

[342] For a brief summary of the points of critique brought forward with respect to this treatment of difference/authority, likewise see Feldmann and Böhm, 2009.

At the very bottom of such strategies we find, both in Europe and in the United States, a particular attempt at refashioning social inequality and conflict in terms of culture and ethnicity, quite often by making use of discriminative moral categories, of imaged standards or qualities of a virtual (native) majority, denouncing others (members of the so-called under-classes, delinquents, unemployed, dropouts, drug addicts, and aliens) not only as outcasts but as pathologically sub-cultural, thus irritatingly creating 'A Nation Apart' (Katz) by maladjustment or by a deeply-rooted general incapability of adjustment or assimilation.[343]

Unless read as a farcical text with a highly sarcastic undertone, *Saturday*, via these implicit judgements and hierarchical constructions, implicitly endorses an inherently bourgeois conception of a (morally) 'good' life. On a superficial level, the novel clearly not only upholds values such as the family, caring, and reliability but also places an emphasis on the outward signs of affiliation to the upper- or upper-middle classes, visible features which invariably also bespeak a certain wealth. Among the elements brandished as markers of middle-class affiliations are, for instance, an 'adequate' lifestyle including a reputable family home, a luxury car, and expensive, sophisticated food. Moreover, education in the bourgeois sense of 'bildung' plays an important role and is consciously employed as a marker of distinction in order to erect a firm boundary between the upper and the lower classes. On an intratextual level, this deliberate construction of an *alter* serves to stabilise the protagonist's personal identity and to sanction his bourgeois way of life. It is probably this tension between a seemingly unreflected endorsement of bourgeois values and the possibility of a 'reading against the grain' which renders *Saturday* so difficult to grasp and at times all but disturbing.

---

[343] Kessler, Michael. „Rupturing Heredity. Fluxions of Identity, Postmodern Discourse, and the Meaning of Race." *Adventures of Identity. Adventures of Identity. European Multicultural Experiences and Perspectives.* Eds. John Docker and Gerhard Fischer. Tübingen: Stauffenburg, 2001. 27-44. 28.

Beyond, After, or Aback Postmodernism? Difference, Belonging, and the Return of the Subject in Contemporary British Fiction

As outlined in the introduction to this study, one of my main initial research interests consisted in novel strategies in the engagement with difference. Apart from offering a concise description as well as a detailed characterisation of these newly emergent forms of dealing with difference, the present thesis like-wise provides a classification of the trend as such. In the course of this, one of the potentially most controversial aspects arises from the attempt to position the novels discussed here within the wider framework of major tendencies in con-temporary British fiction. That holds particularly true with regard to deviations from so-called 'postmodern' patterns. While periodisations in general are prone to fuel heated debate, the situation is undoubtedly exacerbated when it comes to sticking labels to more recent currents, an aspect I will briefly return to below. Despite possible objections against seemingly sweeping characterisations and efforts to distinguish specific styles, I chose to include the topic into my discus-sion after all, especially since the discrepancies between characteristically 'postmodern' approaches and the new strategies described in the respective chapters proved particularly blatant.

With regard to appropriate source material for the study, narrative texts, espe-cially samples from 'popular fiction', turned out to be most suited for an as-sessment of recent developments within contemporary British literature. This selection was motivated by a number of observations: First, there can be no denying the fact that the novel, or, to be more precise, the genre of prose writ-ing, has re-gained momentum in the last years. As a result, narrative fiction is now widely acknowledged as a vibrant form of literary expression, at least as far as the British context is concerned. In addition to that, within the framework of popular culture, the novel undoubtedly constitutes the genre which exerts the highest appeal on the general public. While this basic observation on the popu-larity of the novel as a literary form with a broad audience of course also applies to periods prior to the 2000s, one element which has certainly changed is the increasing nexus between the media and the 'literary world'. By now, the 'me-dialisation' of literature has reached such an extent that one may validly speak of literary marketing as a fully-fledged industry in its own right. In view of the financial potential of bestselling fiction, it therefore does not come as a surprise that publishing houses have taken great efforts (and continue to do so) to push the popularity of successful writers so as to render them 'literary celebrities'.[344]

---

[344] Here, we detect a clear overlap with marketing strategies in other fields: Comparable to the images and values promoted in, say, the fashion industry, the qualities highlighted in interviews and reports are invariably assets such as youth, beauty, and a "from-rags-to-riches-story". What is more, newspaper or magazine articles are clearly intended to establish a rapport between writer and reader as it is continuously pointed out that the authors – despite their recent fame – have not

For the purpose of this deliberate creation of literary stardom, promising book publications expected to gain high sales figures are nowadays usually accompanied by huge marketing and PR-campaigns. Strikingly enough, these campaigns in the majority of cases focus less on the book itself but rather place the person of the author in the centre of attention. Thereby, a widespread marketing strategy consists in drawing attention to parallels between the storyline of a book and its writer's biography, an approach which is most often employed in campaigns for novelists with a migratory background.[345] Besides the efforts taken by the publishing houses themselves, TV formats such as the Richard & Judy Book Club likewise exert a substantial influence and have by now reached the status of media 'institutions'. In this capacity, they even possess the power to boost the sales figures of a book merely by discussing it on the show or by including it in one of the lists for recommended reading.[346] Thus, while the author may be considered dead in academia, (s)he is unquestionably alive, well, and saleable in the literary business.

In view of the fact that the respective analyses intend to tease out possible intersections between fictional motives or themes and concerns encountered by people in 'real life', the choice of the novel as a literary form likewise proved fortunate. Even though I do not claim a direct connection between 'fact' and 'fiction', I nevertheless deem it valid to turn to literature as one possible indicator of widespread concerns and current social problems so as to assess the 'cultural climate' of a specific period of time (provided that one subscribes to the notion of a particular zeitgeist informing an era). Seeing that the novel is traditionally considered the most 'mimetic' genre, I would like to suggest that it is here that we detect the most direct engagement with recent issues of public interest. Accordingly, in the samples of contemporary British literature presented in the single chapters, we may observe a strong tendency towards dealing with topics such as the status of the individual and the impact of social (trans)formations on the subject in late modern societies. In addition to that, the texts address controversial points that presently dominate the public discourse as, for instance, the state of the nation and, related to this issue, the lack of a homogeneous national

---

lost their grip on reality and are still firmly grounded in their original (usually comparatively meagre) background.

[345] In this context, it is striking to notice the clash between academic procedures, where the biographical approach is considered dated and tactics in the marketing business, where the figure of the author is instrumentalised as a selling point especially when he or she stems from an indigent background or when one of the protagonists may be construed as the writer's alter ego.

[346] The Richard & Judy Book Club website even offers the possibility to order those books recommended by the two hosts online (*Richard and Judy Book Club*. 2006. 31.10.08. <http://www.richardandjudybookclub.co.uk/>). For an account of the success of the format as such see Appleyard, Bryan. „How the Richard & Judy Book Club has shaken publishing." *The Sunday Times*, June 15, 2008. 31.10.08. <http://entertainment.timesonline.co.uk/tol/arts_and_entertainment/books/article4120189.ece>.

culture. In this context, the question arises of whether categories such as Eng-lishness and Britishness need re-definition in order to render them compatible with the changed make-up of British society with its growing numbers of citi-zens stemming from a hybrid or 'mixed' background. Moreover, transforma-tions and changes on a supra-national level – globalisation hereby constituting one of the prime subjects – play a prominent role and come to inform the story-lines of many of the narratives.

Besides this general thematic outlook, a further focal point of my examination consists in the modes of presentation employed in the single narratives; at that, I am likewise concerned with possibilities of integrating 'life reality', i.e. topical themes of public interest at a specific moment in time, into a text. Furthermore, the interpretations aim to demonstrate how a narrative comes to reflect certain preoccupations of an era and how it targets a specific readership. With regard to theoretical assumptions on the nexus between reality and fiction, I follow Iser's conceptualisation which suggests a triadic structure between the real, the fictive and the imaginary. This theorisation leads Iser to the following conclusion:

> So gewinnt der Akt des Fingierens seine Eigentümlichkeit dadurch, daß er die Wiederkehr lebensweltlicher Realität im Text bewirkt und gerade in solcher Wiederholung das Imaginäre in eine Gestalt zieht, wodurch sich die wiederkehrende Realität zum Zeichen und das Imaginäre zur Vorstellbarkeit des dadurch Bezeichneten aufheben.[347]

Thus, while the 'ontological' status of the medium in which topics are negoti-ated definitely needs to be taken into account, one may validly argue that it is possible to observe a continuity of specific concerns which can be traced across a variety of discursive fields. Although it does not come as a surprise that fun-damental aspects of human existence such as belonging, affiliation, and the search for lasting points of reference and orientation constitute recurrent themes in literary texts, it still seems significant that those aspects appear to gain prominence in times of crisis. While the 9/11 attacks are commonly deemed a watershed for collective (self)images and identities in the US, the impression arises that one may detect similar reactions in other nations as well which also find their expression in literature.[348] It is for this reason that I am convinced of

---

[347] Iser, 1991, 20.

[348] Let me emphasise once again that I do not believe in a direct influence between political or social events and the literary production. At the same time, though, I deem it worthy of note that aspects such as communality and belonging as well as attempts to overcome the divisive quality of difference dominate a specific strand in contemporary British fiction which coincides with a period of anxiety triggered, amongst other factors, by the climate of fear provoked by the threat of terrorism and the financial insecurity arising from processes of globalisation.

the necessity to bear in mind the historical background of a book as one possible factor informing its themes and the assessment of specific events and developments.

As far as a literary evaluation of current developments in the field of contemporary British fiction is concerned, two main foci have informed the study, which recur in the respective analyses. These are, first, the recent re-valuation of the category of the (autonomous) subject as well as, secondly, the general re-assessment of the activity of writing/narration as such, which places an increased emphasis on the role of narration in processes of identity formation and community building. As the single chapters demonstrate, we may at present detect the emergence, possibly even the beginning consolidation, of a new line in contemporary British fiction. This literary strand can be characterised by its specific way of coping with difference, which may be set off from so-called 'postmodern' approaches inasmuch as it highlights the possibility to employ difference in order to generate meaning. This perception apparently runs counter to a 'postmodern' perspective which considers difference as intrinsically fragmentarising and disuniting. While the issue of difference allows for a comparatively neat distinction between a 'postmodern' as opposed to a 'non-postmodern' approach, a classification in terms of literary styles proves harder to achieve. This problem results primarily from the fact that definitions of 'postmodernism' are highly divergent and that literary criticism is far from having reached a consensus about which writers and texts should be classified as 'postmodern'. Moreover, the debate intersects with yet another controversial subject in the field of literary history. As already indicated by the headline to these concluding remarks, we are still confronted with a great insecurity as to the correct designation for the literary period covering the late 1990s and the early 2000s. In this context, one of the most pressing requests pertains to the problem of whether postmodernism can be considered finished or whether it will still continue well into the 21st century. While there can be no denying the fact that 'non-postmodern' texts are still being produced (and have been produced all through the 1980s and 1990s, the alleged heyday of postmodernism), it is, at the current date, almost impossible to ascertain whether the literary vein described here heralds a new period or whether it merely constitutes a brief and transient revival of a form of fiction that has been largely neglected in academic discussions for a substantial period of time. In order to circumvent this difficulty of sticking a definitive label to the era, many publications choose rather tentative formulations which solely indicate the timespan covered such as "after the millennium" or "after 2000". If an evaluative term is applied at all, most studies do not venture further than "post-postmodernism" (and thereby refrain from proclaiming an entirely new epoch).

What is more, the complexity depicted above is further complicated by the fact that the texts selected for this study may be seen to re-connect to 'pre-postmodern' modes since they display certain characteristic features of mod-ern(ist) forms of writing inasmuch as they quote established genres and pat-terns. [349] At the same time, however, these older styles and genres do not serve as mere templates but are subtly modified. Therefore, the strategy may be un-derstood to bespeak a creative engagement with 'traditional' stylistic models rather than a pure adoption of conventional formulas. [350] While the question of an 'aback' can consequently be negated, the importance of this re-connection as well as an evaluation of the impact of modernist patterns is certainly open to debate.

Lastly, one should make sure not to neglect the position of the literary critic/theorist him- or herself since answers to the problem sketched above, i.e. the classification of a text under a specific label, depend to considerable extent on one's personal evaluation of the significance of specific tendencies within British fiction. Moreover, decisions of this kind are sometimes quite heavily informed by a researcher's self-positioning within the academic field. This as-sumption is confirmed by Head's assessment of the state of the British novel after the year 2000. Similar to the realist vs. postmodernist dichotomy, Head discusses the differentiation between realist and experimental fiction, a distinc-tion which proves, at least in this stark form, untenable: "Interesting and signifi-cant novels are rarely 'realist' or 'experimental' in any simple sense"[351]. Never-theless, the distinction has amply been made and has apparently been consid-

---

[349] Remarkably, this phenomenon seems to be discernible in the context of German literature as well. Here, the reference to modernist strategies in certain writings is so pronounced that some critics even claim a return to pre-postmodern times and a concomitant revival of Modernism.

[350] This revaluation of previous modes does by no means constitute a feature exclusively charac-teristic of contemporary literature. To the contrary, as Bentley states, „[m]ost periods of literary history reveal a set of writers who engage with the dominant literary modes and styles of the previous generation. Some of these writers see themselves as continuers of tradition, others as radical innovators, and some as a mixture of both" (Bentley, 2008, 30).

[351] Head, 2002, 225. With regard to any attempts at pigeonholing the current literary production, Bradford takes a conciliatory stance by stating that "[t]he battle between countermodernists and postmodernists is over, the former have become more flexible and the latter more market-oriented and both now face the pitiless spotlight of evaluation" (Bradford, Richard. *The Novel Now. Con-temporary British Fiction*. Malden, MA et al.: Blackwell, 2007. 244). I personally deem it sensi-ble to abandon overly rigid categories for the classification of individual authors and to concen-trate instead on the texts themselves. One might even ponder whether it could prove useful to avoid broad classifications such as 'postmodern literature' in interpretations as far as possible. Bradford raises another interesting issue when stating that in assessments of the pre-1970s novel the opposition between modernism and realism is commonly introduced (Bradford, 2007, 4 *et passim*), whereas the following decades are frequently characterised along the lines of the post-modernism – realism dichotomy. The proximities of these two dualisms demonstrate the low heuristic value of such exclusively terminological discussions and their comparative futility with regard to the classification of individual texts.

ered valid by a number of researchers. Due to all of these reasons, it is most likely that the controversy about the (post)postmodernism issue will persist for quite some time to come (and will probably not be solved in the near future).

Moving beyond rhetorical and generic considerations, I would like to underscore again the subject-matter addressed by the texts since it is here that we encounter the starkest deviation from what may be termed 'postmodern' issues, i.e. one of the dominant literary modes over the last years.[352] The thematic concerns raised in the selected narratives all circulate around the aspect of difference – in the majority of cases exemplified by the established categories sex, race/ethnicity, and class – and the impact of these criteria on the formation of both collective and personal identities. Thereby, one essential point apparently pertains to the interplay between collective and personal identity as well as to possible ways of negotiating between them and to reconcile clashing demands. Yet, while the texts share the presupposition that an important link between both types of identity exists, the quality of this relationship is estimated in highly divergent ways. Accordingly, the pre-formed self-images offered (or, respectively, imposed) by collective identities can, on the one hand, be experienced as a source of empowerment and help; simultaneously, though, those 'identity templates' can likewise be felt to constitute a grave burden which has to be shed before a successful personal identity may be achieved. In general, though, the basic stance taken towards the topic of identity formation in the single novels can adequately be characterised as 'non-postmodern'. This ascription results primarily from two aspects: First, the narratives assume the possibility of a lasting, stable (personal) identity, and, secondly, they silently posit some kind of essence or inner core, a conjecture which clearly runs counter to postmodernist renditions of the topic. This fundamental proximity in the representation of processes of identity formation proves noteworthy inasmuch as the six narratives included in this examination otherwise display highly divergent features especially as far as style, setting, and tone are concerned.

Another striking parallel results from the fact that the protagonists cling to the *notion* of a uniting bond knitting them at least temporarily into an all but impenetrable unit. Surprisingly enough, the 'materiality' of the affiliations in question seems to be of comparatively low significance as most of the constructions of similarity – Sameness hereby constituting a subcategory – do not withstand closer scrutiny in the long run. Accordingly, in case of the idea of the 'black

---

[352] One may undoubtedly argue that 'entertainment fiction' in the sense of non-highbrow literature has never taken postmodern patterns to an extreme and continued to produce 'reader-friendly' texts with straightforward storylines and conventional plot structures. Within the academic realm, though, postmodern writing has occupied an important place over the last decades and gained a strong presence in discussions of literary developments during this period.

family' for example, the image as such could easily be dismantled on the grounds that differences in terms of class and education still exist; likewise, it could be dispelled by a reference to the fact that many of the alleged members of the black family do not even have 'African' roots but merely participate in the discourse of Africa as the ultimate home-country. Yet, as the narratives show, this objection does neither render the constructions empty of meaning nor does it deprive them of their functionality. To the contrary, on the level of the protagonists this 'illusionary' or, to phrase it in more positive terms, 'spiritual' or ideational bonding fulfils an essential function since it provides crucial points of reference for the formation of personal identities.

Besides the fact that the take on difference defined above constitutes a deviation from 'postmodern' approaches, it is intriguing that the attitude exhibited by the literary characters often mirrors a desire to be observed within 'real' society as well. Accordingly, May states with respect to discussions of ethnic and national identities within the multiculturalism debate: "Indeed, it is now almost *de rigueur* in this post-modern age to dismiss *any* articulation of group-based identity as essentialist – a totalizing discourse that excludes and silences as much as it includes and empowers."[353] Moreover, as regards the existence of nonessentialist group identities, he argues that "the possibility of a non-essentialist, critically-reflective conception of ethnic and/or national identity remains, as does the ability to distinguish between various forms of collective action"[354]. As the respective analyses illustrate, this desire is certainly reflected by fictional texts dealing with the issue. This observation likewise bears the potential to provide a possible starting point for the contestation of 'postmodern' theorising on the topic of identity. One might even venture so far as to claim that theoretical explications of processes of identity formation occasionally clash with the assessment of the situation by the majority of people in 'real' life.

Consequently, while it is at the present moment still too early to proclaim the fully-fledged existence of a new period in the history of the British novel, it is at the same time beyond doubt that we are witnessing a revived interest in the category of difference and, in connection with this thematic outlook, a turn to the problem of personal and collective identities. While these themes are not particularly striking in terms of their avant-gardism or their innovatory qualities – in fact, narratives trying to shed light on processes of identity formation can be found throughout the last decades, probably even centuries – the manner in which the complex is addressed suggests a deliberate abandonment of former

---

[353] May, Stephen. „Critical Multiculturalism and Cultural Difference: Avoiding Essentialism." *Critical Multiculturalism: Rethinking Multicultural and Antiracist Education*. Ed. Stephen May. London and Philadelphia PA: Falmer, 1999. 11-41. 13, orig. emphasis.
[354] May, 1999, 24.

approaches towards this subject-matter. In the individuals' search for lasting affiliations and stable identities, the terminology used proves highly revealing: Many of the images drawn upon – the metaphor of the family hereby constituting a prime example – imply qualities such as durability, reliability, and a specific form of bonding which arises from a commonality of both experiences and feelings. Likewise, 'traditional' values as, for instance, the family or loyalty towards one's relatives are invoked and endowed with a re-newed importance. Similarly, we may discern a profound engagement with the idea of common roots as a potential basis for the generation of affiliations. In this context, the concept of cultural heritage plays a pivotal role and is repeatedly referred to in one way or another. Accordingly, many of the protagonists in the novels either voice their satisfaction and praise the feeling of security gained from the knowledge of forming part of a lineage connecting them to the past or they lament the lack of such ties which is seen to deprive them of an important source for the construction of their self-images. At the same time, the notion of a personal heritage per se, i.e. the idea that some elements are passed on over generations which are vital to the formation of an individual, implies that a human being is to a certain extent determined by their issuing from a specific (cultural) background. Moreover, there is the underlying supposition that having been cut-off from this line of tradition may constitute an all but traumatic experience for an individual since the space reserved for family history remains blank and has to be filled with supplements.[355]

In order to chart these discrepancies and changes concisely, one crucial methodological problem of this study resulted from the choice of appropriate terms and categories for an accurate description of current trends and tendencies. Despite the vast number of existing concepts for the conceptualisation of difference, none of them seemed to grasp the development exemplified by the six novels examined here with precision. For this reason, I decided to introduce the notion of Sameness as an analytic tool for an adequate characterisation of this particular literary vein even though that meant adding yet another category to what might appear an already saturated field. Yet, although there are undeniably certain proximities between Sameness and the idea of social bonding, for instance, I believe that certain shades of meanings are not included in these established conceptualisations and that they do not sufficiently underscore the novel aspects in the specific way of coping with difference presented in the narratives. Via the application of the concept in the single chapters I intended to demonstrate its validity and to highlight the slight but decisive divergencies from the notion of social bonding as well as the fundamental categorial discrepancy between Sameness and, say, hybridity or transculturality. With regard to the latter

---

[355] In this context, an intriguing observation consists in the fact that the supplements to fill this void often adopt the same form as 'real' family narratives.

differentiation, I would like to stress once again that Sameness constitutes a tool rather than a portrayal of a factual, lasting state. This status likewise entails the impossibility of phenomena such as 'Same' identities as opposed to 'hybrid' identities, for instance. In the first place, such a notion could justifiably be descried as absurd because of the temporarily restricted quality of Sameness. As far as the longing for lasting, stable identities displayed by the protagonists is concerned, this chronological limitation would even clash with the aspirations voiced elsewhere. Thus, while the idea of Sameness contributes to the depiction of reliable identities, it is the notion of identity itself which remains stable, whereas Sameness merely relates to specific moments in time. One may therefore claim that the lasting identities sought by the protagonists result from a succession of instances of Sameness, which, taken together, merge to form a persistent and homogeneous self-image.

Another possible point of critique of the concept as such arises from the fact that Sameness cannot be conceived without difference which might, on first sight, evoke the impression of a circular argument. As far as this objection is concerned, I would like to counter that the same observation holds true for the category of difference itself which could likewise hardly exist without the idea of sameness – an aspect which has not prevented its becoming one of the central categories in a variety of discourses. Moreover, the single analyses should have sufficiently illustrated how both notions can be combined in order to yield fruitful results.

By way of conclusion, I would like to return to one of my initial considerations, i.e. the question of whether we are currently confronted with a "beyond, after, or aback" of postmodernism. Undoubtedly, each of the formulations is prone to cause controversial arguments about terminological issues. Since, in the last instance, I consider these purely terminological discussions of little heuristic value with respect to recent developments in the field of contemporary British fiction, I will not venture to answer this question with finality. Nevertheless, to summarise my findings, let me state the following: As my analyses demonstrate, approximately the last ten years have seen the emergence of strategies and patterns in dealing with difference which display a certain connection to modern(ist) approaches. Despite visible citations and references, though, we are not presented with a mere copying of previous patterns, which negates the assumption of a simple 'aback'. While the assessment of the engagement of this new vein with postmodern modes proves harder to achieve, it may be registered that there is a patent discrepancy between the strategies characterised here and what is sweepingly referred to as 'characteristically postmodern' stances (and often summed up by keywords and slogans such as "anything goes", fragmentarisation, and anti-essentialism). In addition to that, first signs of a re-valuation of the process of narration as such are clearly discernible whereby the activity of storytelling is re-acknowledged as a means to generate meaning, a further aspect which may be perceived as non-postmodern. In connection to that, the claim may be raised that fiction is seen to carry a certain potential to impact on the life-reality of its readers – and vice versa (a suggestion obviously to be taken with the proverbial grano salis since positing a direct connection between 'fact' and 'fiction' undoubtedly constitutes an overly simplistic move). As regards the concrete realisations of this aspect, one remarkable quality of the novels discussed here results from the fact that they, despite the grave and serious task ascribed to the act of narration, nevertheless succeed in maintaining a light, easygoing, and entertaining tone. As far as a classification of these tendencies is concerned, decisions ultimately have to be left to each single reader, especially when it comes to the notion of a 'beyond'. So suffice it to say here that British fiction in the 2000s may be qualified by a co-existence of various tendencies and approaches which cannot be subsumed under one single catchphrase. While it still remains to be seen whether the trend heralded by the texts presented here will continue and possibly even broaden in the years to come, the present literary output certainly suggests a turn to a 'serious lightness' and indicates a new view of difference in an increasingly substantive strand of contemporary British literature. Therefore, one thing that may be stated with certainty at the present moment is the fact that the novel is far from being dead and that it possibly even displays a greater vigour and vitality than any other literary genre at date.

Bibliography

Bend it Like Beckham. Dir. Gurinder Chadha. Kintop Pictures, 2002.

Bride and Prejudice. Dir. Gurinder Chadha. Pathé Pictures International, 2004.

„Beyond Signification – Nach den Zeichen. Internationale Graduiertenkonferenz." *Institut für Philosophie. Freie Universität Berlin.* 17.02.08. <http://userpage.fu-berlin.de/~jgs/english.html>.

„Call for End to Racist Rap Lyrics." *BBC News.* 24.04.2007. 30.11.2009. <http://news.bbc.co.uk/2/hi/entertainment/6586787.stm>.

„Das Andere der Trans/Differenz?" *Graduiertenkolleg Kulturhermneutik, Friedrich-Alexander-Universität Erlangen-Nürnberg.* 17.02.08. <http://www.kulturhermeneutik.uni-erlangen.de/konferenz2008/Konferenz%20-%20Das%20Andere%20der%20Trans-Differenz.pdf>.

East is East. Dir. Damian O'Donnell. FilmFour, 1999.

„Exotic." *Merriam-Webster Online.* 2008. 25.12.2008. <http://www.merriam-webster.com/dictionary/exotic>.

„Identity." *New Keywords. A Revised Vocabulary of Culture and Society.* Ed.. Tony Bennett. Malden, M.A.: Blackwell, 2005.

The Kumars at No 42. Dir. Lissa Evans and Nick Wood. Hat Trick Productions, 2001-2006.

„The Race has Begun." *Times Online.* 27.08.2008. 24.01.2009. <http://www.timesonline.co.uk/tol/comment/leading_article/article2332573.ece>.

Ackerman, Terrence. *A Casebook of Medical Ethics*. New York *et al.*: Oxford UP, 1989.

Acton, Thomas and Gary Mundy (eds.). *Romani Culture and Gypsy Identity*. Hatfield: Hertfordshire UP, 1997.

Adler, Jonathan. *Belief's Own Ethics*. Cambridge, MA *et al.*: MIT Press, 2002.

Adonis, Andrew and Stephen Pollard. *A Class Act. The Myth of Britain's Classless Society*. London: Hamish Hamilton, 1997.

Airaksinen, Timo. *Ethics of Coercion and Authority*. Pittsburgh, PA: U of Pittsburgh P, 1988.

Alexander, Claire E. *The Art of Being Black. The Creation of Black British Youth Identities*. Oxford and New York: Oxford UP, 1996.

Anderson, Benedict. *Imagined Communities. Reflections on the Origin and Spread of Nationalism*. London *et al.*: Verso, 2006.

Appadurai, Arjun. *Modernity at Large. Cultural Dimensions of Globalization*. Minneapolis MN and London: Minnesota UP, 1996.

Appiah, Kwame Anthony. *The Ethics of Identity*. Princeton and Oxford: Princeton UP, 2005.
---. *Experiments in Ethics*. Cambridge, M.A. and London: Harvard UP, 2008.

Appleyard, Bryan. „How the Richard & Judy Book Club has Shaken Publishing." *The Sunday Times*, June 15, 2008. 31.10.08.
<http://entertainment.timesonline.co.uk/tol/arts_and_entertainment/books/article412018 9.ece>.

Arnold, Matthew. „The Scholar Gipsy." *The New Oxford Book of English Verse. 1250-1950*. Ed. Helen Garnder. Oxford and New York: Oxford UP, 1972. 690-96.
---. *Culture and Anarchy*. Ed. R. H. Super. Ann Arbor: Michigan UP, ²1980.

Ashcroft, Bill *et al*. „Ethnicity." *Post-Colonial Studies. The Key Concepts*. London and New York: Routledge, 2000.
---. „Exotic/exoticism." *Post-Colonial Studies. The Key Concepts*. London and New York: Routledge, 2000.
---. „Race." *Post-Colonial Studies. The Key Concepts*. London and New York: Routledge, 2000.

Aslet, Clive. *Anyone for England? A Search for British Identity*. London: Little, Brown, and Company, 1997.

Assmann, Jan. „Kollektives Gedächtnis und kulturelle Identität." *Kultur und Gedächtnis*. Hg. Jan Assmann und Tonio Hölscher. Frankfurt a. M.: Suhrkamp, 1988. 9-19.
---. *Das kulturelle Gedächtnis. Schrift, Erinnerung und politische Identität in frühen Hochkulturen*. München: C. H. Beck, 1992.

Axthelm, Peter M. *The Modern Confessional Novel*. New Haven and London: Yale UP, 1967.

Badiou, Alain. *Ethics. An Essay on the Understanding of Evil*. Tr. Peter Hallward. London and New York: Verso, 2001.

Bakhurst, David and Christine Sypnowich (eds.). *The Social Self*. London *et al*.: Sage, 1995.

Bal, Mieke. *Narratology. Introduction to the Theory of Narrative*. Tr. Christine van Boheemen. Toronto *et al*.: Toronto UP, 1985.

Barrow, Robin (ed.). *Academic Ethics*. Aldershot *et al*.: Ashgate, 2006.

Basu, Dipa. „What is Real about Keeping it Real?" *Postcolonial Studies* 1,3 (1998): 371-88.

Baudrillard, Jean. *Revenge of the Crystal. Selected Writings on the Modern Object and its Destiny, 1968-1983*. Ed. and tr. Paul Foss and Julian Pefanis. London and Concord, Mass.: Pluto, 1990.

Bauman, Zygmunt. „Modernity and Ambivalence." *Global Culture. Nationalism, Globalization and Modernity*. Ed. Mike Featherstone. London *et al*.: Sage, 1990. 143-69.

Baumann, Gerd. „Collective Identity as a Dual Discursive Construction. Dominant v. Demotic Discourses of Culture and the Negotiation of Historical Memory." *Identities. Time, Difference, and Boundaries*. Ed. Heidrun Friese. New York and Oxford: Berghahn, 2002. 189-200.
---. „The Re-Invention of Bhangra." *The World of Music* 32 (1990): 81-98.

Beck, Ulrich. *Was ist Globalisierung? Irrtümer des Globalismus – Antworten auf Globalisierung*. Frankfurt a. M.: Suhrkamp, 1997.

Bennett, Andy. *Popular Music and Youth Culture. Music, Identity and Place*. Houndmills, Basingstoke and London: Macmillan, 2000.

Bennington, Geoffrey. „Jacques Derrida." *Deconstruction. Critical Concepts in Literary and Cultural Studies.* Vol. I. Ed. Jonathan Culler. London and New York: Routledge, 2003. 41-51.

Bentley, Eric. *The Life of the Drama.* London: Methuen, 1965.

Bentley, Nick. *Contemporary British Fiction.* Edinburgh: Edinburgh UP, 2008.

Bertens, Hans. „The Debate on Postmodernism." *International Postmodernism. Theory and Literary Practice.* Eds. Hans Bertens and Douwe Fokkema. Amsterdam and Philadelphia. Benjamins, 1997.
---. „The Fiction and the Theory: A Personal Retrospective." *Teaching Postmodernism – Postmodern Teaching.* Eds. Klaus Stierstorfer and Laurenz Volkmann. Tübingen: Stauffenburg, 2004. 27-34.

Best, Steven and Douglas Kellner. *Postmodern Theory. Critical Interrogations.* Houndmills, Basingstoke and London: Macmillan, 1991.

Bhasi, Ishara. „I hate it when they talk about me and not the book." *DNA.* 20.05.2006. 28.11.08.<http://www.dnaindia.com/report.asp?NewsID=1030354>.

Böhm, Nadine und Doris Feldmann. „Alterität." *Lexikon der Bibelhermeneutik.* Hg. Oda Wischmeyer *et al.* Berlin: Walter de Gruyter, 2009 (i.E.).
---. „Fremdheit." *Lexikon der Bibelhermeneutik.* Hg. Oda Wischmeyer *et al.* Berlin: Walter de Gruyter, 2009 (i.E.).

Bohrer, Karl Heinz und Kurt Scheel (Hg.). *Merkur. Deutsche Zeitschrift für europäisches Denken.* 9, 10 (2005): n.p.

Bradford, Richard. *The Novel Now. Contemporary British Fiction.* Malden, MA *et al.*: Blackwell, 2007.

Braid, Donald. „The Construction of Identity through Narrative: Folklore and the Travelling People of Scotland." *Romani Culture and Gypsy Identity.* Eds. Thomas Acton and Gary Mundy. Hatfield, Hertfordshire UP, 1997. 38-66.

Brannigan, John. *New Historicism and Cultural Materialism.* Houndmills, Basingstoke and London: Macmillan, 1998.

Brewin, Christopher. „European Identity." *Why Europe? Problems of Culture and Identity.* Eds. Joe Andrew, Malcolm Crook and Michael Waller. Houndmills, Basingstoke and London: Macmillan, 2000. 55-73.

Brooks, Peter. *Reading for the Plot.* Design and Intention in Narrative. Oxford: Clarendon, 1984.
---. *Troubling Confessions.* Chicago and London: Chicago UP, 2000.

Butler, Judith. *Giving an Account of Oneself.* New York: Fordham UP, 2005.
---. *Kritik der ethischen Gewalt.* Übers. Reiner Ansén. Frankfurt a. M.: Suhrkamp, 2003.
---. *Precarious Life. The Powers of Mourning and Violence.* London and New York: Verso, 2004.

Caminada, Carlos. „Ian McEwan, Finishing New Novel, Ponders World After Sept.11" *Bloomberg.com.* 15. July 2004. 26.12.2008. <http://www.bloomberg.com/apps/news?pid=10000085&sid=a4L6SJH6SmN0&refer=europe>.

Carter, Erica *et al.* „Introduction." *Space and Place. Theories of Identity and Location.* Eds. Erica Carter *et al.* London: Lawrence and Wishart, 1993. vii-xv.

Central Council of German Sinti and Roma. „Realising Equal Treatment: EU Directive for the Improvement of the Situation of the Roma and Sinti Minorities in Europe". *Zentralrat Deutscher Sinti und Roma*. Nov. 2006. 11.08.08 <http://zentralrat.sintiundroma.de/content/index.php?navID=25&tID=14&aID=0>.

Charles, Nickie. *Gender in Modern Britain*. Oxford: Oxford UP, 2002.

Clark, Colin. „Conclusion." *Here to Stay. The Gypsies and Travellers of Britain*. Eds. Colin Clark and Margaret Greenfields. Hatfield: Hertfordshire UP, 2006. 281-9.
---. „Europe." *Here to Stay. The Gypsies and Travellers of Britain*. Eds. Colin Clark and Margaret Greenfields. Hatfield: Hertfordshire UP, 2006. 259-80.
---. „Who are the Gypsies and Travellers of Britain?" *Here to Stay. The Gypsies and Travellers of Britain*. Eds. Colin Clark and Margaret Greenfields. Hatfield: Hertfordshire UP, 2006. 10-27.

Claviez, Thomas. *Aesthetics and Ethics*. Heidelberg: Winter, 2008.

Clayton, Moore, S. „Londonstani." *About.com: Contemporary Literature*. 28.11.08. <http://contemporarylit.about.com/od/fiction/fr/londonstani.htm>.

Coontz, Stephanie. T*he Way We Never Were. American Families and the Nostalgia Trap*. New York: HarperCollins, 1992.

Cornell, Stephen and Douglas Hartmann. *Ethnicity and Race. Making Identity in a Changing World*. Thousand Oaks, London and New Delhi: Pine Forge Press, 1998.

Cottom, Daniel. „Love." *Glossalalia – An Alphabet of Critical Keywords*. Ed. Julian Wolfreys. Edinburgh: Edinburgh UP, 2003.

Critchley, Simon. *The Ethics of Deconstruction*. Edinburgh: Edinburgh UP, 1999.

Currie, Mark. *Difference*. London and New York: Routledge, 2004.

Dahya, Badr. „The Nature of Pakistani Ethnicity in Industrial Cities in Britain." *Urban Ethnicity*. Ed. Abner Cohen. London *et al.*: Tavistock, 1974. 77-118.

Davis, Todd. F. and Kenneth Womack. „Preface. Reading Literature and the Ethics of Criticism." *Mapping the Ethical Turn. A Reader in Ethics, Culture, and Literary Theory*. Eds. Todd F. Davis and Kenneth Womack. Charlottesville and London: Virginia UP, 2001. ix-xiv.

Day, Gary. *Class*. London and New York: Routledge, 2001.

Deguen, Florence. „Offrez-vous le livre de votre vie." *Revue de la Presse*. Fév. 2007. 10.

Depenheuer, Otto. „Nationale Identität und europäische Gemeinschaft. Grundbedingungen politischer Gemeinschaftsbildung." *Nationale Identität im vereinten Europa*. Hg. Günter Buchstab und Rudolf Uertz. Freiburg, Basel und Wien: Herder, 2006. 55-74.

Derrida, Jacques. „Letter to a Japanese Friend." *Deconstruction. Critical Concepts in Literary and Cultural Studies*. Vol. I. Ed. Jonathan Culler. London and New York: Routledge, 2003. 23-7.

Dhaliwal, Nirpal Singh. *Tourism*. London *et al.*: Vintage, 2006.

DJ magazine 74, March 1997. qtd. in Banerjea, Koushik. „Sounds of Whose Underground? The Fine Tuning of Diaspora in an Age of Mechanical Reproduction." *Theory, Culture & Society* 17(3), 2000: 64-79.

Donalson, Melvin. *Hip Hop in American Cinema*. New York *et al.*: Peter Lang, 2007.

Doody, Terrence. *Confession and Community in the Novel*. Baton Rouge and London: Louisiana State UP, 1980.

Doughty, Louise. *Stone Cradle*. London *et al*.: Simon & Schuster, 2006.

Dougill, John. *Oxford in English Literature. The Making, and Undoing, of 'The English Athens'*. Ann Arbor: Michigan UP, 1998.

Drechsel, Paul *et al*. *Kultur im Zeitalter der Globalisierung. Von Identität zu Differenzen*. Frankfurt a. M.: IKO, 2000.

Easthope, Antony. *Englishness and National Culture*. London and New York: Routledge, 1999.

Eibach, Joachim und Günther Lottes (Hg.). *Kompass der Geschichtswissenschaft. Ein Handbuch*. Göttingen: Vandenhoeck und Rupprecht, 2002.

Ellis, Don. „A Discourse Theory of Ethnic Identity." *Discursive Constructions of Identity in European Politics*. Ed. Richard C. M. Mole. Houndmills, Basingstoke and New York: Palgrave Macmillan, 2007. 25-44.

English, James F. „Introduction: British Fiction in a Global Frame." *A Concise Companion to Contemporary British Fiction*. Ed. James F. English. Malden, MA *et al*.: Blackwell, 2006. 1-15.

Esser, Hartmut. *Soziologie. Allgemeine Grundlagen*. Frankfurt und New York: Campus, 1993.

European Commission Directorate-General for Employment and Social Affairs. *The Situation of Roma in an Enlarged European Union*. Luxembourg: Office for Official Publications of the European Communities, 2004.

European Parliament. Resolution P6_TA(2005)0151.

Evaristo, Bernardine. *Soul Tourists*. London: Hamish Hamilton, 2005.

Featherstone, Mike. „Localism, Globalism and Cultural Identity." *Identities. Race, Class, Gender, and Nationality*. Eds. Linda Martín Alcoff and Eduardo Mendieata. Malden MA *et al*.: Blackwell, 2003. 342-59.

Feldmann, Doris und Ina Habermann: „Das Graduiertenkolleg "Kulturhermeneutik im Zeichen von Differenz und Transdifferenz" an der Friedrich-Alexander-Universität Erlangen-Nürnberg." *Anglistik* 14:2 (2003): 105-12.

Feldmann, Doris. „Beyond Difference? Recent Developments in Postcolonial and Gender Studies." *English Studies Today. Recent Developments and New Directions*. Eds. Ansgar Nünning and Jürgen Schlaeger. Trier: WVT, 2007. 117-37.

Feldmann, Harald. *Vergewaltigung und ihre psychischen Folgen. Ein Beitrag zur posttraumatischen Belastungsreaktion*. Stuttgart: Ferdinand Enke, 1992.

Fink, Janet. „Private Lives, Public Issues. Moral Panics and 'the Family' in 20th-Century Britain." *JSBC* 9/2 (2002): 135-48.

Fischer, Peter. *Einführung in die Ethik*. München: Fink, 2003.

Fluck, Winfried. „Fiction and Fictionality in American Realism." *American Studies* 31 (1986): 101-12.

Frank, Manfred. „Subjekt, Person, Individuum." *Individualität*. Hg. Manfred Frank und Anselm Haverkamp. München: Fink, 1988. 3-20.

---. *Die Unhintergehbarkeit von Individualität. Reflexionen über Subjekt, Person und Individuum aus Anlaß ihrer >postmodernen< Toterklärung.* Frankfurt a. M.: Suhrkamp, 1986.

Fraser, Angus. *The Gypsies.* Oxford: Blackwell, ²1995.

Fray, Peter. „The Enduring Talent of Ian McEwan." 07.10.2007<http://www.theage.comau/articles/2005/01/28/1106850082840.html>.

Freeman, Mark. „From Substance to Story. Narrative, Identity, and the Reconstruction of the Self." *Narrative and Identity. Studies in Autobiography, Self and Culture.* Eds. Jens Brockmeier and Donal Carbaugh. Amsterdam and Philadelphia: John Benjamins, 2001. 283-98.
---. *Rewriting the Self. History, Memory, Narrative.* London and New York: Routledge, 1993.

Frye, Northrop. *Anatomy of Criticism. Four Essays.* Princeton NJ: Princeton UP, 1971.

Ganti, Tejaswini. *Bollywood. A Guidebook to Popular Hindi Cinema.* New York and London: Routledge, 2004.

Garrett, Roberta. „Gender, Sex, and the Family." *British Cultural Identities.* Ed. Mike Storry and Peter Childs. London and New York: Routledge, 1997. 129-62.

Gauthier, Tim S. *Narrative Desire and Historical Reparations. A. S. Byatt, Ian McEwan, Salman Rushdie.* New York and London: Routledge, 2006.

Geisen, Thomas. „Kultur und Identität – Zum Problem der Thematisierung von Gleichheit und Differenz in modernen Gesellschaften." *Kulturelle Differenzen begreifen. Das Konzept der Transdifferenz aus interdisziplinärer Sicht.* Hg. Britta Kalscheuer und Lars Allolio-Näcke. Frankfurt und New York: Campus, 2008. 167-87.

Gelfert, Hans-Dieter. *Kleine Geschichte der englischen Literatur.* München: Beck, ²2005.

Giddens, Anthony. *Sociology.* Cambridge and Malden, M.A.: Polity, ⁵2006.

Gill, Jo. „Introduction." *Modern Confessional Writing. New Critical Essays.* London and New York: Routledge, 2006. 1-10.

Gilroy, Paul. *After Empire. Melancholia or Convivial Culture?* Abingdon: Routledge, 2006.
---. *Against Race. Imagining Political Culture beyond the Color Line.* Cambridge, MA.: Belknap, 2000.
---. *Small Acts. Thoughts on the Politics of Black Cultures.* London and New York: Serpent's Tail, 1993.

Glomb, Stefan. „Jenseits von Einheit und Vielheit, Autonomie und Heteronomie – Die fiktionale Erkundung 'dritter Wege' der Repräsentation und Reflexion von Modernisierungsprozessen." *Beyond Extremes. Repräsentation und Reflexion von Modernisierungsprozessen im zeitgenössischen britischen Roman.* Hg. Stefan Glomb und Stefan Horlacher. Tübingen: Narr, 2004. 9-52.

Goertz, Hans-Jürgen. „Geschichte – Erfahrung und Wissenschaft. Zugänge zum historischen Erkenntnisprozeß." *Geschichte. Ein Grundkurs.* Hg. Hans-Jürgen Goertz. Reinbek bei Hamburg: Rowohlt, 1998. 15-41.

Goldberg, S. L. *Agents and Lives. Moral Thinking in Literature.* Cambridge: Cambridge UP, 1993.

Gras, Vernon W. „The Recent Ethical Turn in Literary Studies." *Mitteilungen des Verbandes Deutscher Anglisten.* 4: 2 (Sep. 1993): 30-41.

Green, Michael David. *The Europeans. Political Identity in an Emerging Polity*. Boulder CO and
      London: Rienner, 2007.

Greenblatt, Stephen. „Towards a Poetics of Culture." *The New Historicism*. Ed. H. Aram Veeser.
      New York and London: Routledge, 1989. 1-14.

Greenfield, Liah. „Types of European Nationalism." *Nationalism*. Eds. John Hutchinson and
      Anthony D. Smith. Oxford and New York: Oxford UP, 1994. 165-71.

Greenfields, Margaret. „Family, Community and Identity." *Here to Stay. The Gypsies and Travel-
      lers of Britain*. Eds. Colin Clark and Margaret Greenfields. Hatfield: Hertfordshire UP,
      2006. 28-56.
---. „Gypsies, Travellers and Legal Matters." *Here to Stay. The Gypsies and Travellers of Britain*.
      Eds. Colin Clark and Margaret Greenfields. Hatfield: Hertfordshire UP, 2006. 133-81.

Grossberg, Lawrence. "Identity and Cultural Studies: Is That All There Is?" *Questions of Cultural
      Identity*. Eds. Stuart Hall and Paul du Gay. London *et al.*: Sage, 1996. 87-107.

Gutjahr, Ortrud. *Einführung in den Bildungsroman*. Darmstadt: Wissenschaftliche Buchgesell-
      schaft, 2007.

Habermann, Ina. *Englishness as a Symbolic Form - Identity, Myth and Memory in 1930s and
      1940s English Literature and Film* (Manuscript: 2007).

Hall, Stuart. „Introduction: Who Needs 'Identity'?" *Questions of Cultural Identity*. Eds. Stuart
      Hall and Paul du Gay. London *et al.*: Sage, 1996. 1-17.
---. „Old and New Identities, Old and New Ethnicities." *Culture, Globalization and the World-
      System. Contemporary Conditions for the Representation of Identity*. Ed. Anthony D.
      King. London: Macmillan, 1991. 41-68.

Halliwell, Martin and Andy Mousley. *Critical Humanisms. Humanist/Anti-Humanist Dialogues*.
      Edinburgh: Edinburgh UP, 2003.

Hassan, Ihab. „Beyond Postmodernism: Toward an Aesthetic of Trust." *Beyond Postmodernism.
      Reassessments in Literature, Theory, and Culture*. Ed. Klaus Stierstorfer. Berlin and
      New York: de Gruyter, 2003. 199-212.

Hawes, Derek and Barbara Perez. *The Gypsy and the State. The Ethnic Cleansing of British Soci-
      ety*. Bristol: SAUS, 1995.

Head, Dominic. *Ian McEwan*. Manchester and New York: Manchester UP, 2007.
---. *The Cambridge Introduction to Modern British Fiction, 1950-2000*. Cambridge: Cambridge
      UP, 2002.

Hebdige, Dick. *Subculture. The Meaning of Style*. London and New York: Methuen, 1979.

Heidegger, Martin. *Identity and Difference*. Tr. Joan Stammbaugh. New York, Evanston and
      London: Harper & Row, 1969.

Held, David and Anthony McGrew. „The Great Globalization Debate: An Introduction." *The
      Global Transformations Reader. An Introduction to the Globalization Debate*. Eds.
      David Held and Anthony McGrew. Cambridge: Polity, [2]2003. 1-50.

Hobsbawm, Eric. „Introduction: Inventing Traditions." *The Invention of Tradition*. Eds. Eric
      Hobsbawm and Terence Ranger. Cambridge: Cambridge UP, 1983. 1-14.

Howkins, Alun. „Rurality and English Identity." *British Cultural Studies. Geography, Nationality, and Identity*. Eds. David Morley and Kevin Robins. Oxford: Oxford UP, 2001. 145-55.

Hübener, Wolfgang. „Der dreifache Tod des modernen Subjekts." *Die Frage nach dem Subjekt*. Hg. Manfred Frank *et al*. Frankfurt a. M.: Suhrkamp, 1988. 101-27.

Hutnyk, John and Sanjay Sharma. „Music & Politics. An Introduction." *Theory, Culture & Society* 17(3), 2000: 55-63.

Hutnyk, John. *Critique of Exotica: Music, Politics and the Culture Industry*. London: Pluto Press, 2000.

Inou, Simon. „Schwarze Komponisten: Joseph Boulogne Chevalier de Saint George." *afrikanet.info*. 12. Feb. 2006. 05.07.08 <http://www.afrikanet.info/index.php?option=com_content&task=view&id=316&Itemid=105>.

Iser, Wolfgang. „Fictionalising Acts." *American Studies* 31 (1986): 5-15.
---. *Das Fiktive und das Imaginäre. Perspektiven literarischer Anthropologie*. Frankfurt: Suhrkamp, 1991.

Jenks, Chris. *Subculture. The Fragmentation of the Social*. London *et al*.: Sage, 2005.

Jolly, Margaretta. „Autobiography: General Survey." *Encyclopedia of Life Writing. Autobiographical and Biographical Forms*. Ed. Margaretta Jolly. London *et al*.: Fitzroy Dearborn, 2001.
---. „Autoethnography." *Encyclopedia of Life Writing. Autobiographical and Biographical Forms*. Ed. Margaretta Jolly. London *et al*.: Fitzroy Dearborn, 2001.
---. „Criticism and Theory since the 1950s: Structuralism and Poststructuralism". *Encyclopedia of Life Writing. Autobiographical and Biographical Forms*. London *et al*.: Fitzroy Dearborn, 2001.

Jones, Roger. "Postmodernism." 14.06.2009. <http://www.philosopher.org.uk/index.htm>.

Journal for the Study of British Cultures (*JSBC* Vol. 11, No. 1/04).

Kablitz, Andreas. „Realism as a Poetics of Observation. The Function of Narrative Perspective in the Classic French Novel: Flaubert – Stendhal – Balzac." *Reallexikon der deutschen Literaturwissenschaft*. Hg. Harald Fricke *et al*. Berlin: de Gruyter, ²1997. 99-136.

Kamm, Jürgen and Bernd Lenz. „New Britain: Into the Third Millennium." *New Britain. Politics and Culture*. Ed. Bernd Lenz. Passau: Stutz, 2006. 7-23.

Kamm, Jürgen. „New Labour – Old Classes? Recent Trends in Britain's Social Transformation." *New Britain. Politics and Culture*. Ed. Bernd Lenz. Passau: Karl Stutz, 2006. 55-73.

Kessler, Michael. „Rupturing Heredity. Fluxions of Identity, Postmodern Discourse, and the Meaning of Race." *Adventures of Identity. Adventures of Identity. European Multicultural Experiences and Perspectives*. Eds. John Docker and Gerhard Fischer. Tübingen: Stauffenburg, 2001. 27-44.

Kleinbord Labovitz, Esther. *The Myth of the Heroine. The Female Bildungsroman in the Twentieth Century. Dorothy Richardson. Simone de Beauvoir. Doris Lessing. Christa Wolf*. New York, Berne and Frankfurt: Peter Lang, ²1988.

Kocka, Jürgen. „Europäische Identität als Befund, Entwurf und Handlungsgrundlage." *Europäi-sche Identität: Voraussetzungen und Strategien.* Hg. Julian Nida-Rümelin und Werner Weidenfeld. Baden-Baden: Nomos, 2007. 47-59.

Korte, Barbara and Klaus Peter Müller. „Unity in Diversity Revisited: Complex Paradoxes Be-yond Post-/Modernism." *Unity in Diversity Revisited? British Literature and Culture in the 1990s.* Tübingen: Narr, 1998. 9-33.

Kvideland, Reimund. „Storytelling in Modern Society." *Storytelling in Contemporary Societies.* Eds. Lutz Röhrich and Sabine Wienker-Piepho. Tübingen: Narr, 1990. 15-21.

Lachmann, Renate. „Kultursemiotischer Prospekt." *Memoria. Vergessen und Erinnern.* Hg. An-selm Haverkamp und Renate Lachmann. München: Wilhelm Fink, 1993. XVII-XXVII.

Lambert, Peter and Phillip Schofield (eds.). *Making History. An Introduction to the History and Practices of a Discipline.* London and New York: Routledge, 2004.

Lawson, Mark. „Against the Flow." *guardian.co.uk.* 22. Jan. 2005. 06.12.2007. <http://books.guardian.co.uk/reviews/generalfiction/0,,1395825,00.html>.

Leante, Laura. „Shaping Diasporic Sounds: Identity as Meaning in Bhangra." *The World of Music* 46(1), 2004: 109-32.

Liégeois, Jean-Pierre and Nicolae Gheorghe. *Roma/Gypsies. A European Minority.* London: Minority Rights Group, 1995.

Lipsitz, George. *Dangerous Crossroads. Popular Music, Postmodernism and the Poetics of Place.* London and New York: Verso, 1994.

Löffler, Arno *et al. Einführung in das Studium der englischen Literatur.* Tübingen und Basel: Francke, [6]2001.

Lüking, Bernd. *Der amerikanische «New Humanism» Eine Darstellung seiner Theorie und Ge-schichte.* Bern *et al.*: Lang, 1975.

Maalouf, Amin. *In the Name of Identity. Violence and the Need to Belong.* Tr. Barbara Bray. London: Penguin, 2003.

Machann, Clinton. *Matthew Arnold. A Literary Life.* Basingstoke and London: Macmillan, 1998.

Mack, Gerhard. *Die Farce. Studien zur Begriffsbestimmung und Gattungsgeschichte in der neue-ren deutschen Literatur.* München: Wilhelm Fink, 1989.

Macnaughton, Jane. „Literature and the 'good doctor' in Ian McEwan's *Saturday*." *Medical Humanities* 33 (2007): 70-74.

Malkani, Gautam. *Londonstani.* London *et al.*: Harper Perennial, 2007.

Manzoor, Sarfraz. „Why do Asian Writers have to be 'Authentic' to Succeed?" *guardian.co.uk. The Observer.* 30.04.06. 28.11.08. <http://observer.guardian.co.uk/review/story/0,,1764420,00.html>.

Marcus, Laura. *Auto/biographical Discourses. Theory, Criticism, Practise.* Manchester and New York: Manchester UP, 1994.

Martín Alcoff, Linda. „Introduction. Identities: Modern and Postmodern." *Identities. Race, Class, Gender, and Nationality.* Eds. Linda Martín Alcoff and Eduardo Mendieta. Malden, MA *et al.*: Blackwell, 2003. 1-8.

May, Stephen. „Critical Multiculturalism and Cultural Difference: Avoiding Essentialism." *Critical Multiculturalism. Rethinking Multicultural and Antiracist Education*. Ed. Stephen May. London and Philadelphia PA: Falmer, 1999. 11-41.

Mayall, David. *Gypsy-Travellers in Nineteenth-Century Society*. Cambridge: Cambridge UP, 1988.

McCrum, Robert. "Has the Novel lost its Way?" *guardian.co.uk*. *The Observer*. 28.06.06. 28.11.08. <http://observer.guardian.co.uk/review/story/0,,1784465,00.html>.

McEwan, Ian. *Saturday*. London: Vintage, 2006.

McHale, Brian. *Constructing Postmodernism*. London and New York: Routledge, 1992.

Melucci, Alberto. „Identity and Difference in a Globalized World." *Debating Cultural Hybridity. Multi-Cultural Identities and the Politics of Anti-Racism*. Eds. Pnina Werbner and Tariq Modood. London and New Jersey: Zed, 1997. 58-69.

Mercer, Kobena. „Welcome to the Jungle: Identity and Diversity in Postmodern Politics." *Identity. Community, Culture, Difference*. Ed. Jonathan Rutherford. London: Lawrence & Wishart, 1990. 43-71.

Miller, Daniel. „Why some Things Matter." *Material Cultures. Why Some Things Matter*. Ed. Daniel Miller. Chicago: U of Chicago P, 1998. 3-21.

Mole, Richard and Felix Ciută. „Conclusion: Revisiting Discourse, Identity and 'Europe'." *Discursive Constructions of Identity in European Politics*. Ed. Richard C. M. Mole. Houndmills, Basingstoke and New York: 2007. 208-12.

Musschenga, Albert W. „Introduction." *Personal and Moral Identity*. Ed. Albert W. Musschenga *et al*. Dordrecht: Kluwer, 2002. 3-22.

Neate, Patrick. *City of Tiny Lights*. London: Penguin, 2006.

Neisser, Ulric. „Self-Narratives: True and False." *The Remembering Self. Construction and Accuracy in the Self-Narrative*. Eds. Ulric Neisser and Robyn Fivush. Cambridge: Cambridge UP, 1994. 1-18.

Nelson, Elizabeth. *The British Counter-Culture, 1966-73. A Study of the Underground Press*. Houndmills, Basingstoke and London: Macmillan, 1989.

Newall, Venetia. „The Significance of Narrative in Modern Immigrant Society: The Indian Community in Britain." *Storytelling in Contemporary Societies*. Eds. Lutz Röhrich and Sabine Wienker-Piepho. Tübingen: Narr, 1990. 165-72.

Newman, Davic M. and Liz Grauerholz. *Sociology of Families*. Thousand Oaks *et al*.: Pine Forge Press, ²2002.

Newmark, Kevin. „Deconstruction. See elsewhere, *la différence*, *la dissemination*, for example." *Deconstruction. Critical Concepts in Literary and Cultural Studies*. Vol. I. Ed. Jonathan Culler. London and New York: Routledge, 2003. 28-40.

Nowak, Helge. „Black British Literature – Unity or Diversity?" *Unity in Diversity Revisited? British Literature and Culture in the 1990s*. Eds. Barbara Korte and Klaus Peter Müller. Tübingen: Narr, 1998. 71-87.

Nunius, Sabine. „'Sameness' in Contemporary British Fiction: (Metaporical) Families in Zadie Smith's *On Beauty* (2005)." *Multi-Ethnic Britain 2000+. New Perspectives in Literature, Film and the Arts*. Eds. Lars Eckstein *et al.* Amsterdam and New York: Rodopi, 2008. 109-22.

Nünning, Ansgar and Vera. *An Introduction to the Study of English and American Literature*. Tr. Jane Dewhurst. Klett: Stuttgart *et al.:* 2004.

Nünning, Ansgar. „*Unreliable Narration* zur Einführung: Grundzüge einer kognitiv-narratologischen Theorie und Analyse unglaubwürdigen Erzählens." *Unreliable Narration. Studien zur Theorie und Praxis unglaubwürdigen Erzählens in der englischsprachigen Erzählliteratur*. Hg. Ansgar Nünning. Trier: WVT, 1998. 3-39.

Nusbaum Smith, Elizabeth. *The Society of the Incomplete. The Psychology and Structure of Farce*. Ann Arbor: University Microfilms, 1970.

Nussbaum, Martha C. *Love's Knowledge. Essays on Philosophy and Literature*. New York and Oxford: Oxford UP, 1990.

Oexle, Gerhard Otto. „Mittelalterliche Grundlagen des Modernen Europa." *Was ist der Europäer Geschichte? Beiträge zu einer historischen Orientierung im Prozess der europäischen Einigung*. Hg. Jörg Calließ. Rehburg-Loccum: Evangelische Akademie Loccum, 1991. 17-60.

Okely, Judith. „Gypsies Travelling in Southern England." *Gypsies, Tinkers, and Other Travellers*. Ed. Farnham Rehfisch. London: Academic Press, 1975. 55-83.

Paproth, Matthew. „The Flipping Coin: The Modernist and Postmodernist Zadie Smith." *Zadie Smith. Critical Essays*. Ed. Tracey L. Walters. New York: Lang, 2008. 9-29.

Parekh, Bhikhu C. *The Future of Multi-Ethnic Britain. The Report of the Commission on the Future of Multiethnic Britain*. Profile: London, 2000.

Parker, David. „Introduction: The Turn to Ethics in the 1990s." *Renegotiating Ethics in Literature, Philosophy and Theory*. Eds. Jane Adamson *et al.* Cambridge: Cambridge UP, 1998. 1-17.

Perry, Imani. *Prophets of the Hood. Politics and Poetics in Hip Hop*. Durham and London: Duke UP, 2004.

Phillips, Caryl. *A Distant Shore*. New York: Knopf, 2003.

Plotnitsky, Arkady. „Difference." *Glossalalia – An Alphabet of Critical Keywords*. Ed. Julian Wolfreys. Edinburgh: Edinburgh UP, 2003.

Procter, James. „New Ethnicities, the Novel, and the Burdens of Representation." *A Concise Companion to Contemporary British Fiction*. Ed. James F. English. Malden *et al.:* Blackwell, 2006. 101-20.

Puledda, Salvatore. *On Being Human. Interpretations of Humanism from the Renaissance to the Present*. Tr. Andrew Hurley. San Diego: Latitude, 1997.

Quaschnowitz, Dirk. *Die Englische Farce im frühen 20. Jahrhundert*. Studien zur Englischen Literatur. Bd. 4. Münster und Hamburg: Lit, 1991.

Ramazanoglu, Caroline. „Back to Basics: Heterosexuality, Biology and Why Men Stay on Top." *(Hetero)sexual Politics*. Eds. Mary Maynard and June Purvis. Oxon: Taylor & Francis, 1995. 27-41.

Ratz, Norbert. *Der Identitätsroman. Eine Strukturanalyse.* Tübingen: Max Niemeyer Verlag, 1988.

Richard and Judy Book Club. 2006. 31.10.08. <http://www.richardandjudybookclub.co.uk/>.

Ricoeur, Paul. „Reflections on a New Ethos for Europe." *Paul Ricoeur. The Hermeneutics of Action.* Ed. Richard Kearney. London *et al.*: Sage, 1996. 3-14.
---. *Das Selbst als ein Anderer.* Übers. Jean Greisch. München: Wilhelm Fink Verlag, 1996.

Roberts, Ken. *Class in Modern Britain.* Basingstoke: Palgrave, 2001.

Roberts, Ryan. *Ian McEwan Website.* 12 Jul 2008. 21.09.2008. <http://www.ianmcewan.com>.

Rose, Romani. „Europe's largest Minority - Roma and Sinti Demand Equal Rights." *UN Chronicle* No. 4, 2006. 10.08.08. <http://zentralrat.sintiundroma.de/content/index.php?navID=25&tID=14&aID=0>.

Roszak, Theodore. *The Making of a Counter Culture. Reflections on the Technocratic Society and its Youthful Opposition.* Berkeley *et al.*: California UP, 1995.

Roth, Philip. *The Human Stain.* London *et al.*: Vintage, 2001.

Roy, Anjali Gera. „ 'Different, Youthful, Subjectivities': Resisting Bhangra." *ARIEL* 32(4), Oct. 2001: 211-28.

Sayyid, Salman. „Brasians. Postcolonial People, Ironic Citizens." *A Postcolonial People. South Asians in Britain.* Ed. Nasreen Ali *et al.* London: Hurst, 2006. 1-10.

Schabert, Ina. *Englische Literaturgeschichte des 20. Jahrhunderts. Eine neue Darstellung aus Sicht der Geschlechterforschung.* Stuttgart: Kröner, 2006.

Schlesinger, Philip. „Europeanness: A New Cultural Battlefield?" *Nationalism.* Eds. John Hutchinson and Anthony D. Smith. Oxford and New York: Oxford UP, 1994. 316-25.

Sethi, Anita. „The Curse of Being Labelled the 'New Zadie'. *guardian.co.uk.* 14.11.05. 28.11.08. <http://books.guardian.co.uk/comment/story/0,,1642095,00.html>.

Sharrock, David. „Glamour Shot Takes Ireland's Travelling Women out of the Caravan." *Timesonline.* 28.04.2007. 17.12.2008. <http://www.timesonline.co.uk/tol/news/world/europe/article1717062.ece>.

Shaw, Andrea. „The Other Side of the Looking Glass: The Marginalization of Fatness and Blackness in the Construction of Gender Identity." *Social Semiotics* 15 (2005): 143-52.

Silva, Elizabeth B. and Carol Smart. „The 'New' Practices and Politics of Family Life." *The New Family?* Ed. Elizabeth B. Silva and Carol Smart. London *et al.*: Sage, 1999. 1-12.

Smith, Leslie. *Modern British Farce. A Selective Study of British Farce from Pinero to the Present Day.* Houndmills, Basingstoke and London: Macmillan, 1989.

Smith, Zadie. *On Beauty.* London: Penguin. 2005.

Song, Miri. *Choosing Ethnic Identity.* Cambridge: Polity, 2003.

Stein, Mark. „The Black British Bildungsroman and the Transformation of Britain." *Unity in Diversity Revisited? British Literature and Culture in the 1990s.* Tübingen: Narr, 1998. 89-105.

Stewart, Michael. „The Puzzle of Roma Persistence: Group Identity without a Nation." *Romani Culture and Gypsy Identity*. Ed. Thomas Acton and Gary Mundy. Hatfield, Hertfordshire UP, 1997. 82-96.

Storey, John. *Cultural Studies and the Study of Popular Culture. Theories and Methods*. Edinburgh: Edinburgh UP, 1996.

Stråth, Bo. „Die kulturelle Konstruktion von Gemeinschaften." *Alltagskultur im Umbruch*. Hg. Wolfgang Kaschuba *et al*. Weimar, Köln und Wien: Böhlau Verlag, 1996. 153-170.

Stratmann, Gerd. „The Return of Class: A Conference Report." *JSBC* 11, 1 (2004): 89-90.

Suerbaum, Ulrich. „Text, Gattung, Intertextualität." *Ein anglistischer Grundkurs. Einführung in die Literaturwissenschaft*. Hg. Bernhard Fabian. Berlin: Erich Schmidt Verlag, [9]2004. 82-125.

Tait, Theo. „A rational diagnosis." *Times Online*. Feb. 11, 2005. 06.12.2007. qtd. <http://alcorn.blogspot.com/2005/02/poker-we-play-poker-at-my-house-once.html>.

Taylor, Timothy D. *Global Pop. World Music, World Markets*. New York and London: Routledge, 1997.

Tew, Philip and Mark Addis. „Final Report: Survey on Teaching Contemporary British Fiction." *English Subject Centre* (2007). 03.10.08. <http://www.english.heacademy.ac.uk/explore/projects/archive/contemp/contemp1.php>.

Tew, Philip. *The Contemporary British Novel*. London and New York: Continuum, 2004.

The Runnymede Trust. „The Report of the Commission on the Future of Multi-Ethnic Britain. 25.11.08. <http://www.runnymedetrust.org/publications/29/74.html>.

Tiber Egle, Ulrich (Hg.) *et al. Sexueller Mißbrauch, Mißhandlung, Vernachlässigung. Erkennung und Behandlung psychischer und psychosomatischer Folgen früher Traumatisierung*. Stuttgart und New York: Schattauer, 1997.

Todd, Richard. „Literary Fiction and the Book Trade." *A Concise Companion to Contemporary British Fiction*. Ed. James F. English. Malden, MA *et al*.: Blackwell, 2006. 19-38.

Tomlinson, John. „Globalization and Cultural Identity." *The Global Transformations Reader. An Introduction to the Globalization Debate*. Eds. David Held and Anthony McGrew. Cambridge *et al*.: Polity, [2]2003. 269-77.

Tönnies, Ferdinand. *Gemeinschaft und Gesellschaft. Grundbegriffe der reinen Soziologie*. Darmstadt: Wissenschaftliche Buchgesellschaft, 1979.

Tönnies, Merle and Steven Barfield (eds.). *Teaching Contemporary Fiction. Anglistik & Englischunterricht*. Special Issue 69 (2007).

Tynan, Maeve. „Only Connect: Intertextuality and Identity in Zadie Smith's *On Beauty*." *Zadie Smith. Critical Essays*. Ed. Tracey L. Walters. New York: Peter Lang, 2008. 73-89.

Van Zanten Gallagher, Susan. *Truth and Reconciliation. The Confessional Mode in South African Literature*. Portsmouth NH: Heinemann, 2002.

Veen, Hans-Joachim. „Towards a European Identity: Policy or Culture?" *Why Europe? Problems of Culture and Identity*. Eds. Joe Andrew, Malcolm Crook and Michael Waller. Houndmills, Basingstoke and London: Macmillan, 2000. 41-7.

Wagner, Bernd. „Kulturelle Globalisierung: Weltkultur, Glokalität und Hybridisierung. Einleitung" *Kulturelle Globalisierung – Zwischen Weltkultur und kultureller Fragmentierung.* Hg. Bernd Wagner. Essen: Klartext, 2001. 9-38.

Wagner-Egelhaaf, Martina. *Autobiographie.* Stuttgart und Weimar: Metzler, ²2005.

Walder, Dennis (ed.). *The Realist Novel.* London and New York: Routledge, 1995.

Walters, Tracey L. „Still Mammies and Hos: Stereotypical Images of Black Women in Zadie Smith's Novels." *Zadie Smith. Critical Essays.* Ed. Tracey L. Walters. New York: Peter Lang, 2008. 123-39.

Watt, Ian. *The Rise of the Novel. Studies in Defoe, Richardson and Fielding.* Berkely and Los Angeles: California UP, 1960.

Watts, Alan. *The Culture of Counter-Culture. The Edited Transcripts.* Boston *et al.*: Tuttle, 1998.

Weich, Dave. „Ian McEwan, Reinventing Himself Still." *Powell's Books.* 30.12.2008. <http://www.powells.com/authors/mcewan.html.>.

Weinsheimer, Joel. „Skinner and Gadamer: The Hermeneutics of Sameness and Difference." *Mitteilungen des Verbandes Deutscher Anglisten* 4:2 (1993): 42-57.

Well, Lynn. „The Ethical Otherworld. Ian McEwan's Fiction." *British Fiction Today.* Ed. Philip Tew and Rod Mengham. London and New York: Continuum, 2006. 117-27.

Welsch, Wolfgang. *Unsere postmoderne Moderne.* Weinheim: VCH, Acta Humaniora, 1987.

Wende, Waltraud. „Gender/Geschlecht." *Metzler Lexikon Gender Studies. Geschlechterforschung.* Hg. Renate Kroll. Stuttgart und Weimar: Metzler, 2002.

Wetz, Franz Josef. „Wie das Subjekt sein Ende überlebt. Die Rückkehr des Individuums in Foucaults und Rortys Spätwerk." *Geschichte und Vorgeschichte der modernen Subjektivität.* Bd. 2. Hg. Reto Luzius Fetz *et al.* Berlin und New York: de Gruyter, 1998. 1277-90.

Wojcik-Andrews, Ian. *Margaret Drabbles's Female Bildungsromane. Theory, Genre, and Gender.* New York *et al.*: Lang, 1995.

Wood Middlebrook, Diane. „Postmodernism and the Biographer." Eds. Susan Groag Bell and Marilyn Yalom. *Revealing Lives. Autobiography, Biography, and Gender.* Albany: State University of New York Press, 1990. 155-165.

Worsley, Peter. *Introducing Sociology.* Penguin: Harmondsworth, 1970.

Wren, Thomas. „Cultural and Personal Identity. Philosophical Reflections on the Identity Discourse of Social Psychology." *Personal and Moral Identity.* Ed. Albert W. Musschenga *et al.* Dordrecht: Kluwer, 2002. 231-58.

Young, Robert J. C. „Deconstruction and the Postcolonial." *Deconstructions. A User's Guide.* Ed. Nicholas Royle. Houndmills, Basingstoke and New York: Palgrave, 2000. 187-210.
---. *The Idea of English Ethnicity.* Malden MA *et al.*: Blackwell, 2008.

Zagarell, Sandra. „Narrative of Community: The Identification of a Genre." *Signs* 13,3 (1988): 498-527.

Zentralrat Deutscher Sinti und Roma. „Ergebnisse der Repräsentativumfrage des Zentralrats Deutscher Sinti und Roma über den Rassismus gegen Sinti und Roma in Deutschland." *Zentralrat Deutscher Sinti und Roma.* Oct. 06. 07.08.08. <http://zentralrat.sintiundroma.de/content/index.php?navID=25&tID=14&aID=0>.

Zentralrat Deutscher Sinti und Roma. 07.08.08
    <http://zentralrat.sintiundroma.de/content/index.php?navID=25&tID=14&aID=0>.

Zerweck, Bruno. *Die Synthese aus Realismus und Experiment. Der englische Roman der 1980er und 1990er Jahre aus erzähltheoretischer und kulturwissenschaftlicher Sicht.* Trier: WVT, 2001.

Zima, Peter V. „Why the Postmodern Age Will Last." *Beyond Postmodernism. Reassessments in Literature, Theory, and Culture.* Ed. Klaus Stierstorfer. Berlin and New York: de Gruyter, 2003. 13-27.

Zimmermann, Hans-Joachim. „Matthew Arnold. Dover Beach." *Die Englische Lyrik. Von der Renaissance bis zur Gegenwart.* Bd. II. Hg. Karl Heinz Göller. Düsseldorf: August Bagel Verlag, 1968. 162-179.

Zukrigl, Ina. „Kulturelle Vielfalt und Identität in einer globalisierten Welt." *Kulturelle Globalisierung – Zwischen Weltkultur und kultureller Fragmentierung.* Hg. Bernd Wagner. Essen: Klartext Verlag, 2001. 50-61.

Erlanger Studien zur Anglistik und Amerikanistik

hrsg. von Rudolf Freiburg und Heike Paul

Johannes Rüster

All-Macht und Raum-Zeit
Gottesbilder in der englischsprachigen Fantasy und Science Fiction

Erlanger Studien zur Anglistik und Amerikanistik Bd. 8

LIT

Daniela Geberding
"Memory running out of my mouth so easily, a stream of living water"
Erinnern und Erzählen in den Romanen und autobiographischen Erzählungen von Eva Figes
Ob poietische, der Narration verwandte und sinnstiftende Kraft oder unheimliche, das Subjekt heimsuchende Macht: Die jüdische Schriftstellerin Eva Figes entwirft eine heterogene und ambivalente Poetik der Erinnerung. In Anlehnung an Blumenbergs Metaphorologie deutet die Studie zentrale Erinnerungsmetaphern und veranschaulicht deren Funktion, „logische Verlegenheiten" in Figes' Memoria-Konzepten zu überdecken und ihre eigenen Gespenster der Vergangenheit ästhetisch zu bannen.
Bd. 6, 2005, 280 S., 29,90 €, br., ISBN 3-8258-8388-4

Angela Walz
Erzählstimmen verstehen
Narrative Subjektivität im Spannungsfeld von Trans/Differenz am Beispiel zeitgenössischer britischer Schriftstellerinnen
Es gibt Erfahrungen, die narrativer Darstellbarkeit scheinbar trotzen, zum Beispiel Trauma, Depression, Sexualität, Liebe und Tod. Zeitgenössische britische Schriftstellerinnen erzählen von solchen Erfahrungen in ihren Texten. Um den Besonderheiten der feministischen und postkolonialen Romane gerecht zu werden, entwirft die Studie das Konzept der Erzählstimme neu, als Modus der Simulation von Körperlichkeit, Bewusstsein, Emotionen und unbewusstem Begehren. Im Mittelpunkt stehen die erzählerische Vermittlung und das Zusammenspiel von *gender* mit anderen kulturellen Differenzkategorien.
Bd. 7, 2005, 240 S., 24,90 €, br., ISBN 3-8258-8914-9

Johannes Rüster
All-Macht und Raum-Zeit
Gottesbilder in der englischsprachigen Fantasy und Science Fiction
Religion und Literatur stehen seit ihren Anfängen in einem engen, fast symbiotischen Verhältnis zueinander: Glaubensinhalte werden in narrativer Form transportiert, der Formen- und Symbolreichtum religiösen Denkens prägt unser Erzählen. Diese Studie widmet sich diesen Wechselwirkungen auf einem literarischen Gebiet, das bisher eher stiefmütterlich behandelt worden ist, der im weitesten Sinne phantastischen Literatur, die durch ihre Unabhängigkeit vom Mimesis-Prinzip einzigartige Voraussetzungen für die Auseinandersetzung mit dem Transzendenten bietet. Dies wird im vorliegenden Band in der Entfaltung eines breiten Spektrums von Einzeltexten deutlich, von der skizzenhaft pointierten Kurzgeschichte zum mehrbändigen Epos, von der naiven Affirmation oder hochartifiziellen Kritik zum parodistischen Karneval der Texte. In Form einer theologisch vorstrukturierten Entdeckungsreise von der Schöpfung durch die Weltzeit bis zur Apokalypse beleuchtet der Autor ein weites Panorama moderner und postmoderner Texte, die bisher zu Unrecht im Schatten kanonischer Literaturkritik verharren mussten.
Bd. 8, 2007, 328 S., 29,90 €, br., ISBN 978-3-8258-9851-9

LIT Verlag Berlin – Münster – Wien – Zürich – London
Auslieferung Deutschland / Österreich / Schweiz: siehe Impressumsseite

Heike Paul; Alexandra Ganser (Hg.)
Screening Gender
Geschlechterszenarien in der gegenwärtigen US-amerikanischen Populärkultur
Geschlechterrollen und Geschlechterbeziehungen in der gegenwärtigen US-amerikanischen Populärkultur - in Fernsehserien, Filmen, Computerwelten und Literatur - stehen im Mittelpunkt dieses Bandes. Wie haben Dekaden feministischer und gesellschaftspolitischer Debatten das Männer- und Frauenbild in der Populärkultur verändert? Welches Spektrum männlicher und weiblicher Identitätsentwürfe lässt sich in gegenwärtigen populärkulturellen Diskursen ausmachen, und welche Vorstellungen von Partnerschaft, Gemeinschaft und Familie leiten sich davon ab? Sind populärkulturelle Repräsentationen von Geschlecht und Geschlechterdifferenz in ihrer ästhetischen und politischen Dimension als tendenziell subversiv oder affirmativ im Hinblick auf bestehende Strukturen und aktuelle Diskussionen zu bewerten? Anhand einer Vielzahl von Fallbeispielen, die sich von der Fernsehserie *Sex and the City* bis hin zu virtuellen Schönheitswettbewerben erstrecken, gehen die Autoren und Autorinnen des Bandes diesen und ähnlichen Fragestellungen nach.

Bd. 9, 2008, 256 S., 29,90 €, br., ISBN 978-3-8258-0598-2

LIT Verlag Berlin – Münster – Wien – Zürich – London
Auslieferung Deutschland / Österreich / Schweiz: siehe Impressumsseite

Simone Broders

As if a building
was being constructed

Studien zur Rolle der Geschichte
in den Romanen Adam Thorpes

Erlanger Studien zur Anglistik und Amerikanistik Bd. 10

LIT

Simone Broders
As if a building was being constructed
Studien zur Rolle der Geschichte in den Romanen Adam Thorpes
Als ob ein Gebäude konstruiert würde – so beschreibt Adam Thorpe den Prozess der historiographischen
Forschung. Die unterschiedlichen Konzeptionen von Geschichte(n) und Geschichtsschreibung stellen
bereits seit dem Erscheinen von *Ulverton* (1992) zentrale Anliegen des britischen Autors dar. Diese er-
ste Monographie zum Romanwerk Thorpes setzt es sich zum Ziel, Diskontinuitäten und Brüche eines
Begriffs aufzuzeigen, der angesichts der Multiperspektivität und Polyphonie von Thorpes Romanen aus-
schließlich im Plural, in Form von erzählten „Geschichten", denkbar ist.
Bd. 10, 2008, 208 S., 24,90 €, br., ISBN 978-3-8258-0834-1

LIT Verlag Berlin – Münster – Wien – Zürich – London
Auslieferung Deutschland / Österreich / Schweiz: siehe Impressumsseite